BLACK PHOENIX

THIRD WORLD PERSPECTIVE ON CONTEMPORARY ART AND CULTURE

Edited by Rasheed Araeen
and Mahmood Jamal

PRIMARY INFORMATION 2022

BLACK PHOENIX

JOURNAL OF CONTEMPORARY ART & CULTURE IN THE THIRD WORLD NO1 WINTER 1978 60P

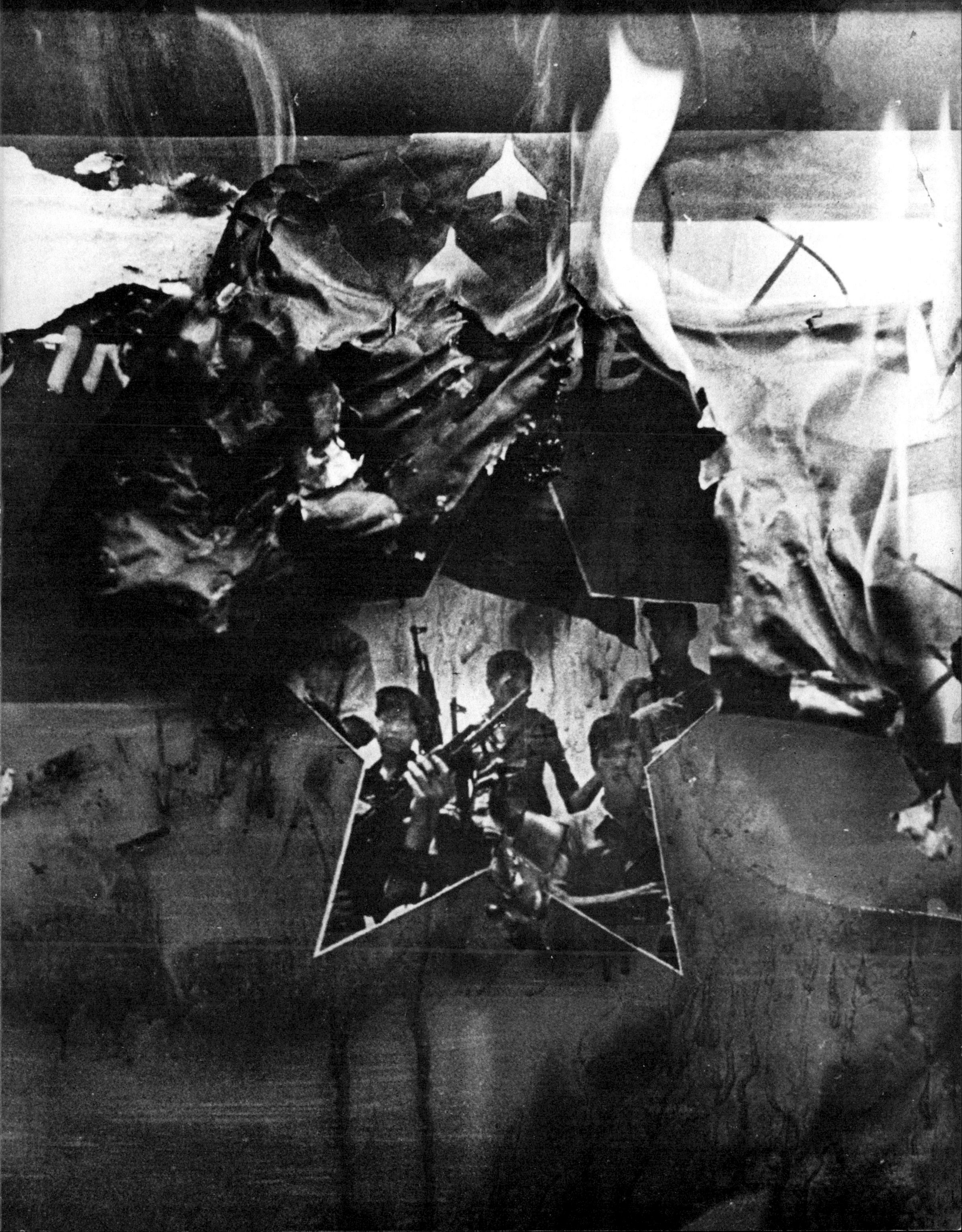

BLACK PHOENIX

Journal of Contemporary Art & Culture in the Third World

NO 1 WINTER 1978 (published January '78)

Editors: Rasheed Araeen, Mahmood Jamal

Black Phoenix **is jointly produced and published quarterly by the Editors.**

BCM BLACKPHOENIX
LONDON WC1V 6XX

Telephones: 01-624 7185, 01-727 6058

Typeset by Bread & Roses (TU) 01-485 4432

Printed by Interlink Longraph Ltd., Mitchell Street, London EC1.

Subscriptions:	**UK**	**Overseas**
1 year (4 issues)	**£3.00**	**£5.00**

All cheques/P.O. payable to ***Black Phoenix***

CONTENTS

ACKNOWLEDGEMENTS

We would like to thank:

Index on Censorship for permission to reprint *In Defence of the word* by Eduardo Galeano.

Studio International for permission to reproduce *The Search for Identity in Contemporary Nigerian Art* by Babatunde Lawal.

Editorial

Black Phoenix is the result of a realisation that we who are concerned with the cultural predicament of the Third World must stand on our own feet and speak with a unified voice, that we must collectively confront, on an international level, those forces which in the name of 'universal freedom of man' are actually causing enslavement of men and women. No matter how inarticulate some of our first attempts may appear, this should not prevent us from speaking up. We can only learn from our own efforts and develop the precision of thought and action.

Black Phoenix is not a journal merely for professional writers or critics (to perpetuate their self-interests) but a platform for discussion, a channel for the exchange of ideas relating to the cultural predicament of mankind in the era of advanced capitalism and imperialism. It represents a commitment to the struggle against cultural domination and hegemony; and all those who are engaged in this struggle—irrespective of their race, colour or creed—are invited to participate in this dialogue.

The Third World is the world of the oppressed. It is the world which was plundered by colonialism and is now being robbed of its remaining resources, natural as well as human. The underlying factor that unifies today all the people of the Third World is that they are subjected, or liable to be subjected, to imperialist domination. While the native bourgeoisie is collaborating unashamedly with international monopoly capital in perpetuating Western domination and in doing so is suppressing the productive and creative potential of its people, there is a growing awareness among the people themselves about their predicament and its causes, and they are in fact struggling for self-determination not only in political and economic fields **but in the creation of their own art and culture as well.**

Needless to say that present-day cultural imperialism has its roots in the Western bourgeois ideology and the concept of white superiority. The cancerous growth of imperialist ideology in the body of the Third World is, on the one hand, progressively destroying the SELF of the Third World, its human identity and dignity, and, on the other, there is a constantly developing antibody to get rid of the foreign matter. The dialectic of this struggle must lead to the emergence of the Third World from neo-colonial wilderness; a black phoenix rising from white ashes. It is not a sentimental proclamation but an identification of/with the force which can and shall transform the world; **it is the recognition of the power of the oppressed to liberate themselves and the oppressor at the same time.**

We reject the widespread and mistaken idea that the technological culture which has been developing in the West is universal and that all people will eventually have to adapt to Western values as part of their modern industrial developments. The emergence of an industrial society in the Third World with its own cultural forms and values is possible only if it develops independently.

It would be naive to think that art or cultural activity alone can change the world or that in our cultural struggle we can ignore socio-economic and political forces. However, the struggle within the domain of art/culture against domination can strengthen the overall struggle. And therefore art must play its own due role in human struggle. No matter how small or marginal its contributions may look, it must not be substituted by anything else. It is imperative to recognize the limitation of art. Beyond or below its inherent social function it becomes a mere propaganda or decoration. However, art must constantly stretch its boundaries beyond the academic/bourgeois limits to reflect upon the changing human condition.

We recognize that cultural struggle is part of class struggle. We do not, however, prescribe to any dogmatic or/and sectarian line. Nor do we accept the primacy of one particular style of art activity over the rest. Our position is clearly expressed by Eduardo Galeano: **"The culture of resistance uses all the media at its disposal and does not allow itself the luxury of wasting any means or opportunity of expression."**

We do not accept the romanticised necessity of material poverty for the artist. To demand for the recognition of one's art activity and to accept money for one's work is not careerism.

Black Phoenix does not constitute a corporate body. The various opinions expressed in the journal are those of the contributors and **we do not necessarily agree with all of them.**

We have started this magazine in very difficult conditions. Everything seemed to be against us: lack of proper expertise, lack of experience of professional writing, lack of material resources and money, etc. It was only the will to survive and struggle that enabled us to take the plunge. We now need your help to continue this struggle. We need your contributions (statements, articles, etc.) and material support (subscriptions, donations, etc.) as soon as possible as to enable us to bring out the next issue in time.

Preliminary Notes for a BLACK MANIFESTO

Rasheed Araeen

Introduction

The problems of contemporary art in the Third World today are part of its socio-economic and political predicaments, resulting from colonialism and its present relationship with the West. We must therefore go beyond formal and aesthetic considerations and look into the historical factors which influenced or suppressed artistic developments in the last few centuries, as well as those forces which are today predominant, in the Third World.

By Third World we mean Asia, Africa, Latin America, and the Caribbean. But we *must* also include in it all those non-European peoples (whom we shall collectively call 'blacks' or 'black people') who now live in various Western countries and find themselves in a similar predicament to that of the actual Third World.

What concerns us here specifically is the situation of contemporary visual art in the Third World. But we cannot meaningfully deal with the problems of visual art alone isolated from the cultural context. What affects culture as a whole is also reflected in art activity.

A cursory glance at the Third World today shows that, even after years of 'independence', its contemporary cultures in general and the visual arts in particular remain what could be described as the stagnant *backwaters* of Western developments or what Paulo Freire[1] calls the 'culture of silence' of the masses.

There does exist, however, an increasing awareness of the situation and efforts are being made to confront the problems. We must therefore look into how this problematic situation is actually being dealt with. **How are Third World people trying to enter the modern era or/and create their own contemporary history? If their voice is muted or not heard at all, what are the underlying causes? And what are the actual alternatives open to them?**

The awareness that the Third World must now find a direction which is different from that imposed on it by the West has been growing; and, in fact, organised attempts pointing towards this goal have recently been made. But these efforts[2] have either remained confined within different regions or lacked a clear (ideological) perspective. They have not therefore made any unifying impact on the overall situation or offered a real challenge to those forces which have been responsible for the present predicament of its art and culture. This is partly due to the lack of *direct* communication of ideas between the Third World countries; and the problem has been further compounded by the extremely oppressive political situation in many Third World countries today—and which is, in most cases, the legacy of colonialism or/and the result of Western imperialist domination.

Although there does exist an opposition to imperialism and questions are being asked about the growing domination of Western culture, the general situation *in practice* remains West-oriented. That is, even when there is a strong tendency among many Afro-Asian countries to maintain the continuity of their own traditions, resulting in the preservation and revival of old forms—particularly their reintroduction in contemporary works, the actual result or its underlying criterion often tends to conform to the standards created in the West. This could be explained by the fact that it is not unusual today for many Afro-Asian countries to seek advice from the so-called Western experts of Oriental/African Art in understanding their own traditional past and to depend on the guidance from the West for contemporary developments.

And therefore Third World artists today are *in general* accepting the 'supremacy' of Western developments in the contemporary field by following whatever styles are developed or produced in the major art centres of the West. This not only uproots them from the reality of their own culture and history, but leads them into an alienated situation which cannot question the domination of foreign values, thereby also denying them any opportunity to develop their art indigenously.

This is not, of course, due to what many Western critics would have us believe. As Edward Lucie-Smith has put it: "In places such as India and Japan, traditional culture between the wars was already in a state of decay; it was natural therefore that artists in those countries should try and rebuild upon the European and American model."[3]

It is typical of many (if not most) Western critics not to see things in the correct historical perspective. Mr Lucie-Smith has very cleverly tried to conceal the actual truth. He might have impressed his own lot, but he cannot fool us. Who does not know that Western colonialism in India—and for that matter in the whole Third World—was directly responsible for what he himself calls 'a state of decay' of traditional culture? And then he has the arrogance to suggest that it should be *natural* for the people, who have been subjected to the traumatic experience of colonialism, to rebuild their future on the model created by those who once were, and still are, their oppressors. This is no more than an attempt to keep the Third World people perpetually under Western domination so that apologists like Lucie-Smith may continue enjoying their international privileges granted by the system they unashamedly serve.

It is essential not to fall into the pitfalls of the Western attitude that tends to disguise the truth. On the one hand, Western interpretation of human history is often extremely biased against non-European peoples and their achievements; and on the other, while ignoring the real dynamics of historical developments, it lays a great emphasis on the *individual* achievements of Western men supposedly struggling against all odds. The fact is that socio-economic and political forces play a fundamental role in moulding, nourishing, supporting, and sustaining all human productive and creative activities, both physically and psychologically.

This brings us face to face with the question of the developments of our own socio-economic and political institutions. The question here really is: what actually happened to these institutions, and why did they fail to play an historical role in providing support to the indigenous developments of arts in the Third World in the colonial period of the last few centuries? The answer to this is, of course, well-known but not widely and fully acknowledged, particularly in the West, for reasons which we hope would become more clear by the end of this manifesto.

Contrary to what we are often told by the West, the colonial era was one of the most exploitative and oppressive periods in human history; and its legacies are still with us today as part of neo-colonialism. This was the period when the West preached **human liberty, equality,** and **fraternity.** But at the same time, it was the very same West which, in brutal and blatant violation of basic human dignity and in contradiction to its own presumed human values, actually enslaved and subjugated the majority of the world's population and plundered its resources for the West's interest alone. The wealth it thus acquired helped the West develop its various institutions. This development was in fact achieved at the expense of ignoring, if not actually suppressing, the historical developments of indigenous institutions. And on top of this, it had the audacity to perpetrate lies about the 'primitiveness' of indigenous Third World peoples whom, as most Western people still believe, the West *only* wanted to 'civilize'.

The truth of the matter is, whether one likes it or not, that the actual aim of colonialism was to merely appropriate other peoples' wealth and resources, by hook or by crook, as a result of which the West was able to become what it is today. As Frantz Fanon has rightly said: **"This European opulence is literally scandalous, for it has been founded on slavery, it has been nourished with the blood of slaves and it comes directly from the soil and from the subsoil of that under-developed world. The well-being and the progress of Europe have been built up with the sweat and the dead bodies of Negroes, Arabs, Indians, and the yellow races.** ***We have decided not to overlook this any longer."***[4] (italics added).

While the West flourished during colonialism, Western art also flourished along with the emergence of its various institutions. The historical developments of Western art of the modern era took place not because of the mental 'superiority' of Western artists (as is commonly believed in the West), but due to the advantage they had by being placed within the complex totality of developing forces of an historical process. And this was made possible to a large extent with the material resources from the Third World. While the historical process in the West provided Western artists with necessary incentives or driving force for their creativity, colonialism suppressed the developments of indigenous art and culture in the Third World by preventing the historical development of the productive forces of its peoples.

For this reason the history of Western art over the last few centuries also becomes an issue here; not only for the fact that its developments took place at the cost of Third World people, but more essentially because of the West's assertion today that its history must be accepted as the mainstream of human developments and that in the light of this all human achievements must be seen. THE ESTABLISHMENT OF EUROPEAN CIVILIZATION AS THE MAINSTREAM IS ONE OF THE MOST CATASTROPHIC DEVELOPMENTS THAT HAVE TAKEN PLACE IN HUMAN HISTORY, DESTROYING OR SUPPRESSING OTHER CULTURES AND CIVILIZATIONS. And today this European MAINSTREAM is used to measure the achievements of the peoples whose very historical developments were suppressed by it. It is therefore not a surprise that the West either ignores other peoples' contributions to human knowledge or history, or it allocates them an inferior status determined by an attitude that sees all non-European phenomena as ahistorical.

This is, of course, a fundamental feature of the dominant ideology that perceives the world in terms of its different parts arranged in a hierarchical order, so that this system serves the interests of those who control it from the top. As such, the West sees the rest of the world as its own appendage and expects all the world resources, natural as well as human, to serve the interests of Western civilization alone. THIS WESTERN PERCEPTION OF THE WORLD HAS REDUCED TODAY THE WHOLE WORLD INTO A 'GLOBAL VILLAGE' WITH A VULGARLY AFFLUENT WEST AT ITS CENTRE SURROUNDED BY STARVING PEOPLE WITH BEGGING BOWLS IN THEIR HANDS.

Moral double standards, arrogance, hypocrisy, and racism are some of the manifestations of the ideology which maintains that Western people alone have a civilized existence and that they should constantly maintain and protect this even at the expense of denying other peoples their humanity. WHILE EUROPEANS ARE HAILED AS PATRIOTS, FREEDOM FIGHTERS AND HEROES, OTHERS ARE DENOUNCED AS BLOODTHIRSTY TERRORISTS. The various attempts of some pseudo-scientists to prove the 'superiority' of the white race, is also part of the same apparatus which deliberately perpetuates lies about non-European peoples. And these attempts to give scientific respectability to racism only reveals the hideous designs of those who are an integral part of the Western imperialist domination of the world today.

The present state of affairs in the Third World is not the result of the 'natural laziness' or 'a lack of imagination' of its peoples, as we are often told by the West, neither is it the legacy of the devastation of some oriental 'barbarian'. It is in fact the direct consequence of the colonial pillage by the 'civilized' West whose pretentious claims to all humanity have now turned out to be no more than a mask to hide its pathologically excessive greed and which has today reached dangerous proportions. The Western obsession for more and more material wealth (mostly in the form of consumer goods), which in the West is euphemistically called 'a higher standard of living', cannot be perpetually fulfilled without further exploitation and appropriation by the West of resources *which are not its own resources.* These resources actually belong to Third World peoples who themselves should now utilize them to fulfil their own needs, by developing their own productive forces and rebuilding their own socio-economic, political, educational, cultural, and artistic institutions *which must be free from foreign domination.*

Against this historical background, therefore, we must place the present predicaments of our art and culture. We must recognise that as long as we allow the West (and for that matter anybody else), willingly or unwillingly, to dominate our lives, we will only be exploited. As long as our physical and mental resources are under its direct or indirect control, our development will either be suppressed or used for the benefit of the West alone, its art and culture, and its civilization. In other words, **we must free ourselves from foreign domination before we can create our own contemporary art and culture.**

But this does not mean that we have no option open to us at present or that we cannot carry on an art activity. Of course, if we continue accepting the general situation today which demands our subservience to the West we are doomed as a people. On the other hand, we can and must stand on our feet and oppose those alien values, as well as our own, which obstruct radical change by preventing the development of internal dynamism of our people; and in the process of confronting these values we can and shall discover new art forms that will authentically reflect our own reality today. However, before we proceed further to look into possible alternatives, we must examine here the various aspects of those forces which are holding us back.

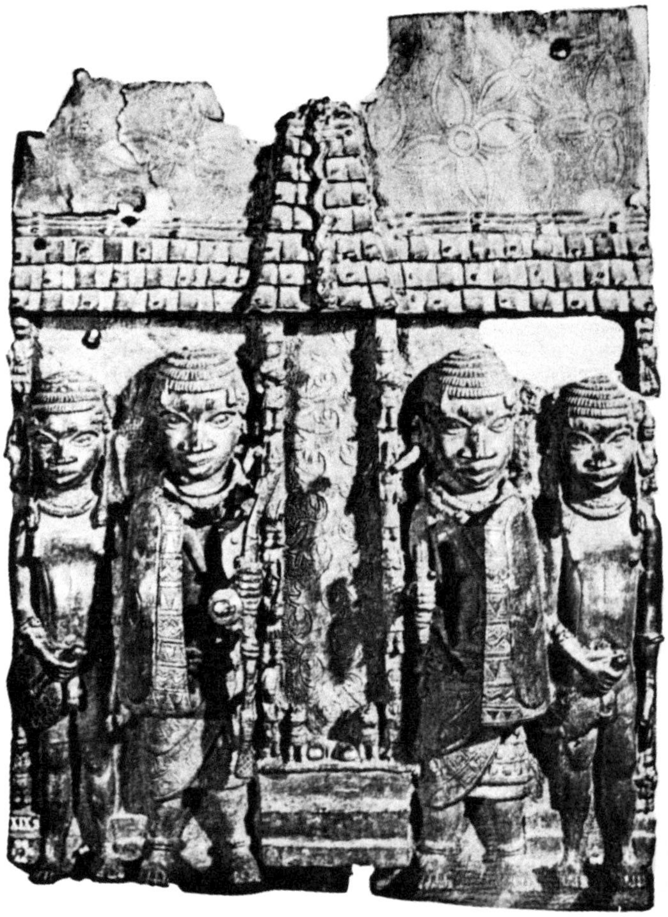

Benin Bronze, The British Museum, London

"The deplorable state of most Benin work is due to the fact that it was eventually plundered by the British when, in 1897, they sacked and burnt the city. In some of the pieces part of the bronze has melted; in others there are gashes caused by their being torn roughly from their places. These, and the burnt ivories, are the mute record of the city's rape."

Boris de Rachewitz, *Introduction to AFRICAN ART*

The Third World Today

One of the important features of colonialism was and is to violently suppress the indigenous culture of the colonized country and then impose its own cultural values on the colonial people. In many instances, colonialism imposed an actual ban on native cultural practices, taking away by force from the people their cultural artifacts. The loot was then transferred to the West. As a result, most of the Third World heritage is today either hidden away stored in the basement lockers of Western museums[5] or insolently displayed in their glass cases as part of the evidence of the West's pride and precious possessions. AFTER EXTERMINATING MILLIONS OF PEOPLE AND THEN LOOTING THEIR BELONGINGS, THE WEST TODAY HAS THE AUDACITY TO CALL ITSELF THE PROTECTOR OF THE ARTISTIC AND CULTURAL HERITAGE OF THE WORLD.

At the same time, colonialism created and creates a native bourgeoisie by giving some of the native population Western colonial education, and by awarding them some socio-economic privileges and a share in political power. In turn, this native class, to quote Amilcar Cabral, "assimilates the colonizer's mentality, considers itself culturally superior to its own people and ignores or looks down upon their cultural values."[6]

With the coming to power of *this* native bourgeoisie, after 'independence'. colonialism is only replaced by neo-colonialism; which in fact is a general phenomenon in the Third World today. One of the most important characteristics of neo-colonialism is the perpetuation of Western imperialist domination in the 'decolonized' countries through Western cultural penetration, against which the native bourgeoisie cannot and does not act as a shield. On the contrary, its own lifestyle facilitates further propagation of Western values, which openly relegate the indigenous cultural life. In effect, it virtually becomes an instrument through which Western culture is projected as civilized and progressive vis-à-vis the 'primitive' and 'backward' native culture.

It is therefore no surprise that, immediately, after the Second World War, Western imperialism under the leadership of its most powerful country, the US, unleashed an unprecedented cultural propaganda in the major cities of the Third World, particularly in Asia and Africa, through its control of mass media (films, TV, glossy publications, etc.). The whole purpose of this propaganda, which constantly assaulted people's senses with alien images of the values of Western life, was to inflict their minds with the illusions of a better life (in the West) and to lure them into believing that they could also possess this life, if only they would abandon their own values; thereby making them develop a sense of their own inferiority. The aim of the cultural aggression, in fact, has always been to make the dominated people totally abandon their own values and accept the projected superiority of imperialist culture, turning them into passive objects of Western domination, since, as Amilcar Cabral has pointed out, "with strong indigenous cultural life, foreign domination cannot be sure of its own perpetuation".[7]

At a time when people were trying to recover from their colonial past and were looking forward to a new future free from foreign domination, this new onslaught from the West not only caused a further loss of national cultural identity among the native bourgeoisie, who thus fell in love with 'Babylon' called AMERIKA; it also disturbed, if not shattered, the sense of direction among the urban 'intelligentsia' who could have otherwise played a positive role in the post-colonial reconstruction of the country. The native bourgeoisie who was supposed to offer a new direction, leading to a better and prosperous life which it had promised to *all* its people during their anti-colonial struggle, instead became an instrument of an accelerated superficial change whose main driving force has been to turn the major native cities into centres of native bourgeois life *based on vulgar imitations of the West.* It set in motion a process whose consequences can be seen today in the Third World cities. A skyscraper rising from/above poverty-stricken shantytowns has become a symbol of 'progress'.

One only has to cast a glance to see the absurdity of present developments in most Third World countries based on the Western prescriptions. Instead of improving the land and waterworks to produce more basic and essential food, either the land is used to produce exportable commodities or the peasants are recruited into the factories where, for example, motor cycles, blue jeans, platform shoes, etc., are assembled/manufactured mainly for the teenage kids of the affluent urban classes. Instead of improving livestock to increase milk production, Coca-Cola factories are set up everywhere. Instead of creating an incentive for the fishermen to catch more fish and providing them with better boats and equipments, the sea-shore is transformed into a holiday resort for the native, as well as international, leisure class and the inhabitants of the surrounding villages are turned into waiters, domestic servants and entertainers. Consequently some Third World cities have become exotic brothels for globe-trotters.

The basic priority, the development of an indigenous economic infrastructure serving the basic needs and interests of all the people, has been virtually ignored. Instead, the country's wealth has been appropriated by the few, through trickery, deceit and bureaucratic corruption, and spent mostly on the importation or production of Western consumer goods and sophisticated military hardware which cannot, of course, fill the hungry bellies of the masses. It simply maintains the Westernized lifestyle of small native elites and their political power.

Any human development which is based on foreign values—unless these values are absorbed through a critical process as part of the indigenous development—disturbs and suppresses the imagination and creativity of people, thereby destroying any incentive for the creation and development of new and original ideas. Instead, it perpetrates/perpetuates imitation, submission and apathy, which in fact characterizes native bourgeois life today. The native bourgeoisie thus ends up trapped in its milieu protecting its selfish interests, incapable of providing any leadership or support for the positive and progressive forces of the people. Instead the people are fed with illusions, vulgar fantasies, religious fatalism, and populist slogans; all this leading to a life pattern which becomes insensitive to its own environment. And if all this is not enough to keep the people contented and/or silent, they are mercilessly put down by the sophisticated oppressive state machinery on which the native ruling classes end up spending most of the country's wealth.

It is therefore clear that the native bourgeoisie, which virtually becomes an agent of imperialist domination, cannot and does not protect the real interests of the people. It gives almost a free hand to the multinational foreign companies which not only exploit the people indiscriminately but cause great damage to indigenous cultural life. The following example, which is typical as well as topical, illustrates how an apparently innocent commercial operation persuades people to abandon their own cultural values and take up Western ways in the hope of improving their life, whereas the actual result is a disaster, economically as well as culturally.

In most parts of the Third World, even today, breast-feeding is not only a common traditional practice, but also an important part of its socio-economic reality. And it cannot be replaced by any other method without a real change, *brought about by the conscious efforts of the people themselves,* in the economic forces, creating a socio-cultural environment in which acts like bottle-feeding and its various implications are fully grasped by the masses. An imposition of bottle-feeding on the other hand, particularly through an aggressive cultural propaganda (euphemistically called 'commercial ads'), would in the present Third World environment naturally create dangerous health hazards and without giving much economic benefit. To say that the Western companies do not understand this simple act, would amount to calling them idiots, which they are not. They couldn't care less as long

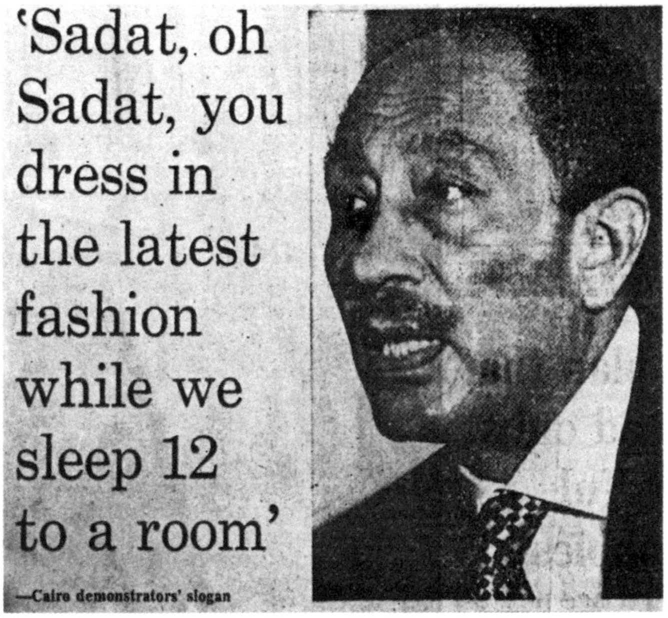

from *The Sunday Times*, 23.1.1977

as they **make money**. If their actions cause malnutrition among children, poverty and starvation, and even deaths, they do not consider it their moral or human responsibility.

It is well known now how Western baby-food producers have been persuading the women in the Third World into giving up their *traditional* breast-feeding in favour of *modern* bottle-feeding, simply to sell their products. In the hope that it would help their children grow better (as suggested by the ads), many poor women switched on to bottle-feeding, even when they did not lack their own milk. It not only deprived them of their hard-earned small income which they had to spend to buy the manufactured baby-milk, it also caused malnutrition and a disease, unknown before, among these children. As a result, many of them died.

The debate here is not about the merits or demerits of breast-feeding or bottle-feeding. Neither is it the question of a 'failure' of the women in the Third World to grasp the new reality of bottle-feeding. It would be very easy, of course, to accuse these women of a 'lack of awareness' of the problems of hygiene in bottle-feeding, but would anybody blame the mothers of the Thalidomide children for their lack of scientific knowledge?

The issue here really is the immorality of the whole money-making operations of the multinational companies in their total disregard of human life. Their aggressive commercial and cultural propaganda deceives people into believing that they can buy a better life by purchasing consumer products (which do not contribute to their welfare but only further their poverty), and undermines people's cultural values which would otherwise protect them from such vicious traps.

The paradoxical situation in which the native bourgeoisie finds itself after 'independence', must also be recognised. On the one hand, its own lifestyle betrays its acceptance of the supremacy of Western cultural values. On the other, it cannot totally ignore the national aspirations of the people and their own culture. A resurgence of interest in indigenous art and cultural activities therefore occurs. But this development, which in most cases is manipulated by the native bourgeoisie to consolidate its political power by making it part of its populist demagogy, often fails to go beyond the level of mere entertainment or a reminder of the past glories.

The exuberant colourful tribal dances at Nairobi Airport, Kenya, welcoming the arrivals of international celebrities, is an interesting example of the manipulation of indigenous culture by a native bourgeoisie *which prides itself on dressing up in European three-piece striped suits even on hot days.*

This is not to say that indigenous national art and culture should not play any role in international affairs. International diplomatic relations alone cannot provide a real dynamic for the historical development of national art and culture in the Third World. In fact, if this becomes the only basis for the preservation or continuation of indigenous art and cultural activities—as is the fact in most cases, the result is their degeneration into an exotic entertainment for those whose actual allegiance lies with foreign culture.

Although the wearing of indigenous dress does not necessarily reflect a genuine commitment to the development of national culture today, in view of the fact that indigenous dress is still an essential part of the masses in the Third World, the European dress of the native ruling classes can only project their separateness from the masses, if not an elevated status whose roots are embedded in European soil.

It is the masses who actually retain and protect the values of their own culture which, in the face of colonial domination, either remains in a state of 'hibernation' or **continues maintaining its dynamism by resisting foreign domination.** Indigenous culture in fact plays an important role in national struggle. But when the native bourgeoisie comes to power and offers foreign prescriptions for the country's post-colonial development, the dynamism of indigenous art and cultural life is either arrested or misdirected. Only the establishment of an indigenous socio-economic and political system, which genuinely serves the needs and interests of *all* the people, can enable the people to develop their own contemporary art and culture as an expression of the new dynamic of a liberated life.

Western Art v. Third World

The people's struggle to move forward in history today cannot be successful until they become, or are made, fully aware of their own role in the historical process, which requires their *full participation on every level.* This also requires their consciousness of their particular historical position from which they want to move forward, and which must be linked to their historical past, their own cultural values and material conditions. The aim of foreign domination, on the other hand, is to take the dominated people out of their history or/and dislodge them from their particular historical position, thereby destroying their *sense of direction.* In other words, the imposition of an alien history on the people demands that they should renounce, if not denounce, their own history, their own cultural values, their right to think and determine their destiny as free people; and that they must instead accept their subservience to foreign values so that they may not be able to lift a finger against their exploiters.

The knowledge of Western art history as part of colonial education must have existed in the countries under colonialism. But the aim of its post-war accelerated propaganda as part of the overall Western cultural onslaught, which pretentiously projected Western art as a higher and universal expression of human life, was to re-establish or perpetuate its pretended supremacy in order to prevent the emergence of indigenous forces in the 'decolonized' countries. And, to a large extent, the West has been successful in re-imposing its history on Third World peoples when they were desperately looking for a new direction to move forward into the future and assert their independent existence as part of all humanity.

When young artists in Asia, Africa and the Caribbean were trying to emerge from the fog of colonialism, they found themselves in something of a dilemma. On the one hand, there was an awareness that their own traditional forms should play a fundamental role in contemporary developments, reflecting not only the spirit of the independent country but their time as well. On the other, they found themselves surrounded by Western forms which were becoming more and more instrusive in the post-independence period. And since most of them were alienated from the people and were actually aspiring to become part of the newly developing urban socio-cultural milieu in which Western values started to play a predominant role, the Western models not only offered them a more attractive alternative but also promised lucrative careers. It is therefore no wonder that so many Third World artists should fall for Western art so easily and without understanding its historical developments.

What we see today in general is either the third-rate imitation of various Western styles (from Cubism to Pop Art), or a hotchpotch of Western techniques and native imagery; the aim being the creation of modern works of art which also *look* ethnically original. The content of these 'experiments' (which can be termed *neo-colonial art*) reflects the confusion and divided loyalties of the native bourgeoisie on which the artists are dependent for their survival, economically as well as socially. The prevalence of *neo-colonial art* today also depends on the fact that it is largely recognised and encouraged by Western Embassies' staff and Western tourists who flock to the capitals of the Third World looking for exotic entertainment and souvenirs.

There also exist considerable forces that defy the above situation, but they are not yet fully recognized. On the one hand there is a strong tendency now to renounce Western art altogether and return to what many Third World artists consider their own heritage. (It is too early to pronounce any critical judgement on the outcome of nationalist tendencies in the Third World. But, since it is part of the overall process which *tends* to create its own independent identity, it is an important step towards the realization of an indigenous development.) On the other, the isolation of Third World artists is a big danger; and is in fact being created by the aggressive role which Western art/propaganda plays on an international level. As such, many Third World artists have been forced to retreat behind their national frontiers. This not only deprives them of an opportunity to expand beyond their ethnic boundaries, it also makes them look exclusively and nostalgically to their old traditions.

Other Third World artists have taken an entirely different direction, by accepting the challenge of this modern age. While conscious of their own indigenous cultural backgrounds (which they sometimes reflect in their work), they recognize the technological nature of various developments in the West. They consider it their legitimate right to make use of contemporary knowledge in their own work (and without feeling any indebtedness to the West), just as Western artists were able to benefit, and are still benefitting, from their knowledge of Afro-Asian traditions (African Sculpture, Islamic Art, etc.). What is singular about these artists is that they are innovators. Thus they contribute to contemporary developments in their own right, by their own original ideas, concepts and synthesis/antithesis; and more importantly they offer a challenge to Western domination by defying the hegemony of art styles perpetrated and promoted internationally by the *transatlantic* gallery circuit of the Western world. But since these artists also defy the expectations of their native bourgeoisie, who would instead like them to be part of its *mediocre* and *vulgar* life, many of them are not recognised in their countries of origin or in the West, where they often end up living as self-exiled residents or 'citizens' of Western countries. (This phenomenon is not only limited to the artists, of course. Many Third World scientists, engineers, doctors, architects, teachers, etc., also end up living in the West.)

Some Latin American artists are recognised for their pioneering works in the post-war development of art in the West, particularly in Kinetic Art. But since their contributions have been widely acknowledged in the West and subsequently in their own countries of origin (perhaps because of their European descent they did not find their identification with the Western mainstream, as well as their own acceptability by the West, problematic), they are outside the scope of this work.

Under consideration here are in fact the underlying causes of the general and predominant phenomenon of *mediocrity* in the Third World today, as well as the general non-recognition of the activities which avoid this mediocrity in defiance of cultural imperialism.

But before we go further, the term *mediocrity* should perhaps be clarified. We do recognize the different levels of developments in different parts of the world at a particular time in history. But it is not an issue here, because there are peoples who are not free to develop their capabilities. They are in fact deliberately deprived of the opportunity of their historical developments, thereby condemning them to a pattern of life in which *mediocrity* takes up a *predominant* position that eliminates all the forces which would/could give the life a new dynamic for its radical change. However, the phenomenon of mediocrity is not exclusively confined to the Third World, as one might think. It is actually international, varying in form and degree in different places. In case of the Third World, its causes are primarily external, while in the West they are internal as well. In the Third World today, it is comprised of forms created by the imposition of alien values which create stagnation in the indigenous process of development. In the West, it becomes a formalist transformation (formal innovations, frequent stylistic changes, fashion, trendiness, gimmicks, etc.), whose real content, in effect, mostly remains the same, sustaining the system that gives it its driving force and which is produced by the system's capacity to dominate and exploit people nationally as well as internationally.

This brings us to the crucial question of the dominance of Western art in the world today. Is Western art really international (in its spirit and expression) or only an instrument of a propaganda? Is internationalism of Western art (and culture) at this juncture in history beneficial to all mankind? If the purpose of internationalism is to bring different peoples nearer to each other and create a better understanding between them, why should it be monopolized by the West? Why aren't the people in/of the Third World playing any significant role in the development of so-called international art?

The question here is not really "of the lack of thought given to the position of the Third World artist in *western* discussions of art" (italics added), as Caroline Tisdall has put it (*The Guardian*, 26 April 1975), but of the exclusion of Third World people from the contemporary developments, controlled and dominated by the West. **The Third World artist is not seeking a position in Western art but his rightful place in the contemporary world which is being denied to him.** If Western art was confined to its own national boundaries or within the Western World and it made no claims to the supremacy in the world, it would have not bothered us at all. Since Western art is pretending to be international, spreading its vicious tentacles all over the world, it is extremely necessary to question its real content and the motives behind its international expansion.

Now let us take the example of American Pop Art. What international significance is there in the images of Coca-Cola, Marilyn Monroe, Pin-ups, the American Flag, Hamburgers, etc? These images are, of course, the *ethnic* images of American culture and there is no reason why they should not play a role in the development of her art. But when these very images are *universalized* through an international projection, their function changes. They are no longer the 'harmless' images of the popular culture or the innocent ambassadors of American art and culture abroad. Their international function is to propagate American consumer culture, through its glorified celebration by Pop Art, in the 'underdeveloped' world, and thus to undermine the indigenous values and their contemporary developments in the Third World.

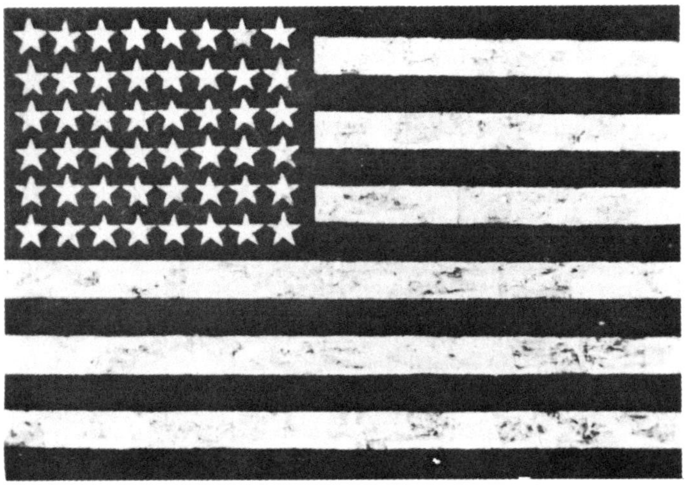

Jasper Johns *Flag* 1954

No wonder that the *ethnic* art of modern 'icon-makers' of American 'high religion' (Pop/Consumer Culture) is considered international art and is reverently placed in the so-called historical mainstream, while the work of the Mexican artist, Diego Rivera, for example, is either ignored by the 'international' art pundits or relegated to 'non-history'. The only 'crime' he seems to have committed was that he defied Western cultural/art imperialism by rejecting the hegemony of art styles created in the art centres of Europe alone. Instead of merely serving the interests of Western civilization and history, he returned to his own people and committed himself to their reality. His work is a reflection of the socio-cultural, economic, and political environment in which he lived. Instead of understanding him in the context of his own socio-historical forces, his work has been dismissed by the Western art pundits as mere propaganda.[8] We do not necessarily agree *fully* with the populist and propagandist philosophy in art, but **is Pop Art not propaganda?** If the West is only concerned with narrow boundaries of stylistic evolution within its own history and considers only the developments taking place in its metropolises, at the expense of other contemporary developments, **what right has it to champion the cause of internationalism in art and culture?**

The myth of the internationalism of Western art must be now exploded. The fact is that there does not yet exist an art which truly reflects international spirit of Man and Woman today. Western art only reflects the particularity of the West and has little to do with the actual reality of the world. It can therefore be said that WESTERN ART IS NOT INTERNATIONAL; IT IS MERELY TRANSATLANTIC ART. IT ONLY REFLECTS TRANSATLANTIC CULTURE OF EUROPE AND NORTH AMERICA. The present 'internationalism' of Western art is no more than a function of Western politico-economic power and its imposition of its values on other people. Therefore, in an international context, it would be more appropriate to call it IMPERIALIST ART.

We are not plyaing here with semantics. If by internationalism is *only* meant an expression of a phenomenon taking place in more than one country, an art movement emerging simultaneously at more than one place across national boundaries as a reflection of their cultural interrelationship, we would have no hesitation at all in accepting the 'internationalism' of Western art. A style of wood carving is still being practised in many places across *national* boundaries of most African countries, but would anybody call this an international style? In the present world context, the word *international* implies *more than just a few Western countries,* unless we accept that these few Western countries (which constitute about 25 percent of mankind) 'represent the whole world'.

Internationalism is now an expression of a global phenomenon, and we are sure Western artists/critics do not disagree with us here. What they may still point out (which many often do, and not without arrogance, to justify their claim of internationalism) is what they consider a *natural* influence of Western art in the world today, which in fact must be placed in the context of cultural imperialism.

However, even when a particular artistic development influences or accelerates developments elsewhere, the former does not by virtue of its influence become a reflection of internationalism. African art, for example, influenced many European artists (some of them even imitated it) at the beginning of this century, giving rise to one of the most important movements in the West, Cubism. But African art did not, as Europeans would themselves say, become international art, nor did the European artists become *Africanized.*

The fact is that the Western mainstream draws material from all sources, sucking knowledge from other traditions and cultures into its own continuing development, often for *change for the sake of change.* Western 'avant-gardists' can now even appropriate the forms which were created hundreds/thousands of years ago by the peoples whom the West would call primitives (they were in fact more aware of the social function of these forms), and with the magic stick of ART HISTORY turn the 'demonism' of ancient tribes into their own 'avant-garde' art.

On the other hand, if Third World artists make use of modern methodology, creating original works that reflect their own contemporary reality, they would often be reminded of their indebtedness to the West, if not looked down upon as if they have actually stolen 'Western' property. It is not uncommon for the Third World artists who use contemporary techniques in their innovations to be seen *on the margin* or as followers of Western art. Instead of accepting them in their own right or as part of what is considered to be an international movement, they are often *Westernized* through a weird logic that can only be a reflection of imperialist mentality.

Nevertheless, the actual influence of Western art in the world today cannot be considered constructive. The nature and pace of the movement of Western art as part of Western cultural penetration in the Third World (facilitated, of course, by the native bourgeoisie) cannot offer an opportunity to the people in general to examine it critically. This is not to say that Western developments do not have positive and progressive aspects which, once analyzed and grasped, may benefit other peoples. But the aggressive propagation of Western values in the countries which are economically/technologically underdeveloped, and particularly when as a result of this the indigenous productive forces are suppressed, it is very difficult, if not impossible, for the people to

Ceremonial Ground Painting/Sculpture by Australian Aborigines

Photograph: The Museum of Mankind, London

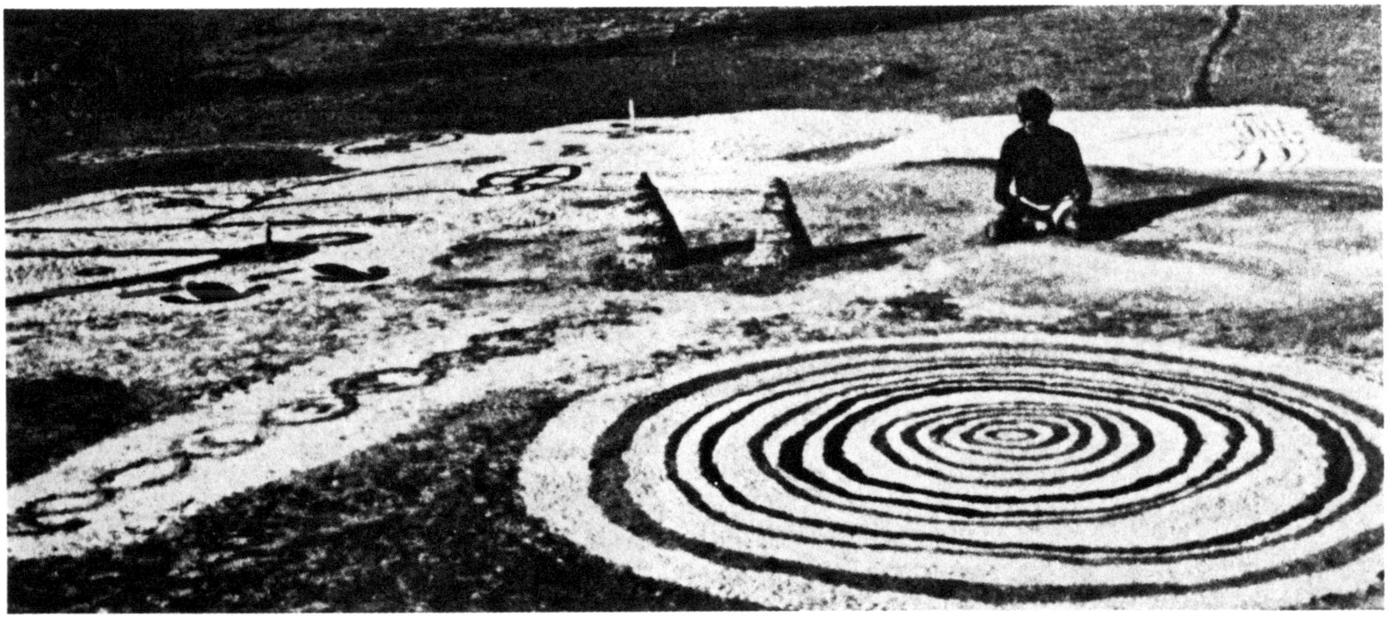

benefit positively from Western developments. It is no surprise that those countries which have understood the real motives behind Western cultural propaganda, have rightly closed their national borders to Western ideas, so they could generate their own developments without foreign interference.

The international expansion of Western art is not incidental, nor is it due to its natural attractiveness. It is in fact part of the West's missionary zeal to 'civilize' the 'primitives' of the Third World. The history of the last few centuries makes us see that behind this mask of civilizing other people, there actually exist insidious intentions whose only purpose could be, and is, to keep the Third World people as an appendage of the West, so that their physical and mental resources are used for the perpetual development of Western civilization alone, creating a vicious circle in which the West continues THINKING, CREATING and PRODUCING, while the Third World remains in a state of APATHY and its people turn into mere IMITATORS and CONSUMERS.

Of course, Western art propaganda *alone* cannot produce these results. But it functions as part of the West's economic, political and cultural operations on an international level: the aggressiveness of Western art/propaganda is actually that of the dominant system. Specifically, the function of Western art *domination* is to deny the Third World peoples of the indigenous developments of their contemporary art, and also to prevent the emergence of a unifying contemporary art movement other than in the West, in order to perpetrate/perpetuate the pretended supremacy of its own art and culture.

It is therefore no coincidence that America was suddenly awoken, after the War, to a realization that she also had her own 'geniuses'. It was a time when America, in order to establish her leadership as the most powerful of imperialist countries, launched a massive world-wide propaganda, projecting herself as the most civilized country of the world. Clinging to her cultural tentacles were her artists, among other things, particularly *action painters* (later followed by *Pop artists*), who thus reached as far as her propaganda could penetrate. As a result, these artists in no time became internationally known, turning many of the newly emerging Third World artists into third-rate Abstract Expressionists (it was also a time when donkeys and monkeys also became 'abstract artists'). It would be an exaggeration, of course, to say that everybody turned to paint-throwing. But it certainly has an enormous impact (since it was so easy to splash the paint around) on the development of what has already been described as neo-colonial art.

The close relationship between Western concept of *international art* and international monopoly capital is obvious. As such, Western art is *mainly* developed and produced in the capitals of the most powerful of Western capitalist countries and by (white) Western artists (for they are the ones acceptable to Western art establishments), and then sold, through the *transatlantic* gallery circuit, at highly inflated prices that turn it into a precious product. Market price thus becomes signifier, content and criterion, which entitles a work of art to a place in 'history' books (propaganda books would be though a more accurate description) that are sent around the whole world for people to read about Western 'geniuses'. Once art is elevated to the position of a precious object through speculation and international publicity, it produces capital for its further propagation as a 'unique object of universal significance', and in turn this adds further to its preciousness, and so on. And since all this takes place exclusively within Western historical and cultural contexts, it enhances Western civilization and contributes to its dominating power.

The whole process of the acceptance (or rejection), evaulation, elevation, propagation and signification of art, is maintained by an economically powerful art market which operates like a stock exchange in the capitals of the Western World—capital, publicity and speculation being its basic and essential tools. It also creates a privileged class of artists who in turn serve this market and its function in the system. Having been elevated to the 'pedestal of genius', these artists not only become trapped in a privileged socio-economic milieu believing in their 'semi-god' status and their 'superhuman' power (like Midas turning *everything* into gold—Picasso comes to mind here), but more importantly they contribute to Western cultural domination by thus becoming instruments of its international propaganda. Their 'superhuman' and international status is in fact no more than an illusion created by all that money which flows into their bank accounts and their elevations as superstars on the world stage.

The numerous and frequent claims of internationalism by the Western artists who are internationally known (the so-called radicals are not exceptions here) are as ludicrous as the very concept of an international art based exclusively on Western values and developments. The fact is that this facade of internationalism is essential for many of these artists to maintain their self-esteem, by being elevated to a position from where they can look down upon the rest of the world. Their neo-colonial mental attitude is nurtured by the politico-economic power of the imperialist West, which provides them with all the material incentives for futile and self-indulgent activities.

If we appear so condemning in our attitude towards the West, it is not because we are against Western people (they are, in fact, also the victims of the same dominant ideology) or that we are envious of their progress/affluence. Neither are we turning our backs on *everything* Western. But, in the present context of our relationship with the West, it is difficult for us to be more charitable towards those who are always endeavouring to accuse us of laziness, lack of imagination/incentives, and so on, thereby obscuring their own misdeeds against humanity by perpetual reiterations of their pretentious claims to all human progress and civilization through their massive international propaganda.

Those apologists of the system who cynically reproach us for not yet creating our own contemporary art with our own values (and of so-called international standards), must now get off our backs. AND STOP TELLING US WHAT WE MUST OR MUSTN'T DO, OR HOW WE SHOULD DEVELOP OUR ART. Instead they ought to examine their own roles in the process and context of cultural imperialism and get rid of their own deliberate ignorance and patronizing attitude (is it asking too much?), so that they may also see the world in its true perspective.

It is to make it clear here that by 'West' we do not mean a monolithic West—or for that matter Third World. We recognize that there are both reactionary and progressive forces on both sides of the dividing line. But although the fundamental relationship between the West and the Third World remains as that of between the dominant and the dominated respectively, **our criticism is not meant to be directed at the progressive forces in the West.**

Blacks in Britain

Imperialist domination does not end with exploitation of Third World people in their own countries. It forces ordinary workers and peasants to leave their homes and search for a livelihood in the alien environment of its socially hostile metropolises. In addition, imperialist cultural propaganda, as well as specific recruitment, effectively lure many educated and trained young men and women into believing that they can find a better and more happy life if they leave their own countries and live in the West. The actual situation in which people from 'underdeveloped' countries thus find themselves living in the advanced industrial societies of the West, does not differ much from one Western country to another. We shall,, however, confine ourselves here to our own predicament *in Britain*, but we do recognize that a similar pattern of racism and exploitation exists in other Western countries employing foreign labour,[9] not forgetting, of course, the US and those Afro-Asian peoples who are still living under the yoke of racist colonial/imperialist rule.

Black people in Britain today cannot be treated in the same way as 25 years ago when we, after being uprooted from our native soils, were rail-roaded into menial jobs. The aspirations of the younger generation of blacks, particularly those born in Britain, are very different. We cannot, and will not, accept only shitwork. If society cannot fulfil our expectations just because it does not wish to see us rising above our present existence at the bottom of the heap, we shall continue fighting ourselves for our rights. If some black kids are in the street, and a few have become what the establishment calls 'muggers', the fault does not *totally* lie with them but with this society.

HOWEVER, TWO MILLION BLACKS AREN'T GOING BACK

RASHEED ARAEEN *Oluwale* (3rd of 4 collage-panels) 1971-73

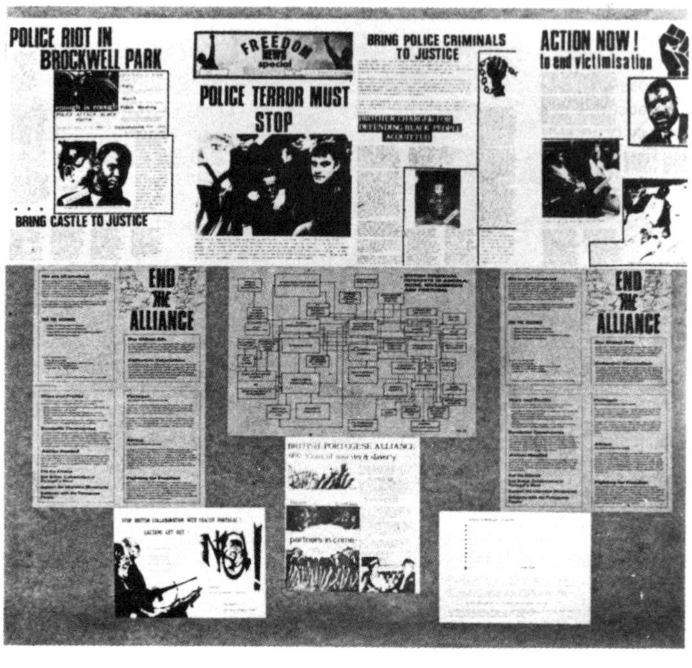

HOME. BRITAIN IS OUR HOME AND WE WILL NOT ACCEPT OUR SECONDARY AND INFERIOR ROLES IN THIS SOCIETY. WE SHALL CONTINUE FIGHTING FOR OUR EQUAL HUMAN STATUS. THROUGH THIS WE ARE IN FACT CONTRIBUTING TOWARDS THE DEVELOPMENT OF THIS SOCIETY INTO A BETTER ONE FOR ALL TO LIVE IN.

What must concern us is not only the blatant manifestation of racism by right-wing fascists who are now demanding our return to the countries of our origin after we have been milked for 25 years as cheap labour, but also the subtle racist attitude that prevails in every field and at every level of British life.

". . . and I certainly wouldn't like to see a Negro minority taking over this country. A lot of nice bus conductors running the government isn't my idea of a sensible way out . . ." John Osborne's above comments *(The Observer* 7 July 1968) on black people are, in essence, not very different from the hysterical outbursts of Enoch Powell. Besides the subtle racism and paternalism of his remarks, his contempt for working people, both black and white, is clear. The absurd notion that blacks are 'taking over this country' reflects the paranoia of his privileged lot. How could half a million 'Negroes' take over a country of about 55 million people, which is still considered to be one of the most powerful in the world? Only racists can indulge in such absurd fantasies!

That Mr Powell is a racist is not even doubted by many white people. What one can't *perhaps* do is to accuse him of hypocrisy. What Powell has so far said, and we are sure he will say it again, is that he is not 'against' black people but only our *number*. He would in fact accept a small number of *us* amongst *his white society* (to do the menial jobs). In other words, he would welcome a considerably reduced number of blacks who, because of their numerical disadvantage, would remain docile and not overstep their roles defined by *him*, and thus would find themselves unable to confront this society with its racist philosophy. But how does Powell's attitude differ from that of Osborne who doesn't appear to like black people demanding more than the crumbs offered by his society?

We have quoted John Osborne *only* because his remarks even today typify a liberal attitude, and that of the establishment, characterized by hypocrisy and paternalism. We are often told that this society is not really racist and that is does offer FREEDOM OF CHOICE, SAME INCENTIVES and EQUAL OPPORTUNITIES to ALL its people. NICE WORDS! BUT ARE THEY ALSO MEANT FOR US? Of course, NOT. We must stick to bus conducting and let THEM write plays or produce works of art. It is no coincidence that black people are often portrayed in the media as waiters, objects-of-fun, exotic/ethnic dancers and entertainers, muggers, smugglers, gangsters, etc., perpetuating the racist myths of *intrinsic* inferiority and criminality of black people.

We have made this country our home. We cannot be pushed around or persuaded to leave. The above attitudes can only perpetuate antagonistic black-white relations. The positive alternative to this would be to accept the legitimacy of black-white conflicts and make concerted efforts to create a process in which these conflicts are constructively resolved for the betterment of the *whole* society. This could only be achieved through openly questioning the historical background and the present roots of racism, and at the same time exposing and confronting the system's manipulation of people's fears and insecurity under capitalism.

We cannot, however, go into all the details of our problems here. What we intend to show specifically is how we are prevented from participating in the cultural life of the country which we have now made our home. If our argument is confined only to black artists, whose presence in the country has been deliberately ignored, it is not because the problems concerning black artists are more important than those of black people at large. The problematic situation of black artists, in fact, reflects a social attitude which affects all of us black people. We cannot therefore separate black artists from the total context of blacks in this country. THE DOOR WHICH IS SHUT ON OUR FACES BY A WHITE LANDLADY IS ALSO THE DOOR WHICH OPENS TO THE ART ESTABLISHMENT.

Now, how does the attitude of the British art establishment towards blacks differ from the general one? This would be better understood if we recognize that the art establishment in general, and its official/public bodies in particular, act as a mechanism to regulate art and cultural activities and thereby assert control over them. Therefore, the function of the art establishment cannot be separated from the ideology of the system. In other words, if racism is part and parcel of the system, it cannot be absent from the components that regulate its art and cultural activities.

Kenneth Coutts-Smith, writing in the catalogue intoduction to 'Second Commonwealth Biennial of Abstract Act', Commonwealth Institute, London, 1965, said: ". . . Some years ago commonwealth artists were arriving in London to work and establish a name, and found themselves in somewhat of a difficult position. Except in very rare instances they were receiving little or no support from the Art authorities in their home countries. At the same time the official bodies in this country, *by the very structure of their charters*, were invariably unable to do much beyond offering encouragement." (Emphasis added)

This structure, we believe, still exists and it cannot be other than *the support structure* for the promotion and the development of art in Britain. In other words, it is the main function of the British art establishment, particularly its official bodies, to encourage, support and thus promote the art activity of its people. The question now is: whom does it actually consider *its* people? The answer to this would be, of course, the British people. But this does not answer everything, because the crucial part of the whole question is: what are the various components that make up British society? Are we black people considered part of this society or merely looked down upon as immigrant workers? Enoch Powell provides us with the answer when he says: "They don't belong to this society. Do they?" (ITV, 5 January 1976). We believe the art establishment does not really disagree with Powell. This becomes evident when we look into its indifference towards black artists, denying them due recognition for their art activities in Britain for the last 20 or so years. This was confirmed at the Third Regional MAAS Conference on Ethnic Arts, London 19 June 1976. In answer to a complaint from a black person, one of the Arts Council's representatives, Ruth Marks, bluntly remarked that the Arts Council was a traditional British institution whose function was to support its own professional artists. The implication here is very clear. Black artists are considered neither British nor professional by the Arts Council—and that must go for the whole art establishment.

When we speak of the British art establishment, we mean the whole art establishment—art galleries, museums, art magazines and books, art schools, and what have you, official and private. But we are more concerned here with the Arts Council of Great Britain and the British Council, which are the main official bodies that support and promote art and cultural activity at home and abroad respectively. These bodies are financed by public money which must surely include the tax money from black people in British society. This means WE BLACK PEOPLE ARE ACTUALLY CONTRIBUTING TOWARDS THE COST OF RUNNING THE OFFICIAL ART BODIES AND THUS TOWARDS THE SUPPORT AND PROMOTION OF ART/CULTURE IN BRITAIN. But what do we get OURSELVES in return? NOTHING, or maybe SOME CRUMBS sometimes.

The official bodies would say that they do not discriminate on racial grounds. Of course, they don't have to hang a 'NO BLACKS PLEASE' board outside their doors. But how many black artists have ever managed to get through? If no door was ever shut on them, IT WAS ONLY BECAUSE NO DOOR WAS EVER OPENED TO THEM. The facts speak for themselves: no black artist has ever been included in any official exhibition or survey representing the various developments of visual arts in Britain since the time we have been here, not to mention any individual show or representation abroad.

If the *absence* of black artists from *what is recognised* is any indication of the real situation in Britain, then it would either mean that there are no black artists—which would again mean that we black people are not interested in art activity—or that black artists are not good enough for any consideration of the art establishment. The truth is that the official bodies, as well as the art establishment at large, have turned a blind eye to the very presence of black artists in Britain and to their actual contributions. Furthermore, the fact that we black people also need, and must have as *our right*, official support for the development of our art and cultural activities, has been *deliberately* ignored. Any suggestion here that the work of black artists might have not been, or may not be, of high standard or any significance, would be nonsensical. There is enough evidence that the work of black artists can be compared with that of their white contemporaries who are recognized both nationally and internationally, *in spite of the fact that black artists have to work under conditions (physical as well as mental) which few white artists would be able to bear for long.*

The art establishment does not have to have an open and declared policy which discriminates between black and white artists. But that does not necessarily mean that a mechanism of control, or an attitude, which denies black artists their access to art establishment and their rightful recognition does not exist. We must not forget that the institutional structure of official bodies was considerably developed and nourished at the time when Britain had a colonial Empire. And since its old structure has not been changed to come to terms with the fact that blacks in Britain are no longer colonial subjects but British citizens, those controlling the official bodies (and the private ones as well) still act, consciously or unconsciously, with a colonial attitude towards black people.

We can understand this better when we appreciate that Britain is still an imperialist power (in neo-colonial sense) whose values are promoted abroad as part of its international cultural propaganda. Its promotional pattern is still based on cultural purism and exclusiveness. Its products are promoted abroad in such a way that it does not contradict the traditional British (English, to be more precise) image. The British image abroad, even today, consists of a white society in which there is a small black immigrant population 'serving its white masters'; and its creative activity must therefore be an activity which embodies white values created and defenced by white artists. One only has to look into the common pattern of British art criticism which seldom fails to point out the Englishness of British art. And since Englishness is only identifiable with white people (ask Powell why!), the English chauvinistic art promotion pattern ignores the art activity of black people in the country, or it relegates it to ethnic pigeon-holes. The merits or demerits of the work of black artists do not even enter into the criterion of selection and recognition. The very mechanism of selection and recognition, based on the idea that white artists are the *only* representatives of British art, disqualifies black artists from being even considered before the merits or demerits of their work become evident. It is not surprising that a black artist who has lived in Britain for the last twenty years or so should strike such a pessimistic note: "They can make all these noises about racism, but when it comes to the crunch they will only push their own boys."

The recent exhibition in Milan 'Arte Inglese Oggi, 1960-76', which was supposed to represent the various developments of art in Britain during that period, is not only an example of Engish art chauvinism but also a deliberate misrepresentation of the actual picture, by perpetrating the lie that contemporary art in Britain is the privilege of whites only. The very title of the exhibition excludes black participation. One wonders, in this respect, if there has been a single protest from Welsh, Irish and Scottish artists who have all been thus lumped together as English, unless none of them was included in the exhibition. Or is it a part of their careerism not to question English domination?

There is no doubt that the official attitude has contributed largely to the perpetration of a white monopoly of British art scene, and in this respect the public bodies have proved themselves incompetent in discharging their duties. They have in fact misused all those funds which should have actually been utilized for the development and promotion of the activities of black people in this country. In view of the fact that we black people live, work and pay our taxes in Britain and thereby contribute not only towards the running of the country but also to its art and cultural institutions, WE MUST DEMAND, NOT AS CHARITY OR SPECIAL FAVOUR BUT AS OUR RIGHT AND SHARE, FULL RECOGNITION OF ALL OUR ACTIVITIES. We must have the right to be shown in all official exhibitions and galleries, without any delay and excuse. We must be paid full remuneration for our work and efforts.

The Arts Council's sponsored report 'The Arts Britain Ignores', by Naseem Khan, which has been published recently, does not present a true and full picture. It has not only *divided* black people into black and Asian groups (as if Asians are not blacks) but pigeon-holed their activities into various ethnic categories, thus relegating them to a subcultural level. It seems to have concluded that black artists have not yet done anything worthwhile outside the narrow boundaries of their ethnic traditions. This must be partly due to the lack of information about the activities of black artists and/or the result of the author's own presumptions. It also appears to be an attempt now, in the face of our growing demands for equal opportunities, to pigeonhole us in such a way as to leave the white population free from the fear of black competition, particularly in the field which most white artists consider their exclusive monopoly—the British mainstream.

The issue here is not, *and should not be*, the ethnicity of black activity: one *could* also say that English art is ethnic. The question here really is why black activity is being relegated to a subcultural level. We must not accept our separate categorization, in order to receive some crumbs. WE MUST DEMAND FULL RECOGNITION OF OUR EQUAL STATUS. IT IS THE CONCEPT OF MAINSTREAM WHICH MUST BE CHANGED TO MEET THE NEW DEMANDS OF THE SOCIETY, AND NOT THE OTHER WAY ROUND, IF WE WANT TO AVOID THE PITFALLS OF CULTURAL BANTUSTANS IN BRITAIN.

Towards Third World Art Movements

The prerequisite for the indigenous developments of contemporary art in the Third World is a *confrontation* with those forces which have, in the first place, caused its underdevelopment and are today actively obstructing its post-colonial regeneration. We cannot expect the indigenous art to flourish under the imposing shadow of an alien culture; and this shadow is not going to disappear until the tree of imperialism is uprooted from our soil. But foreign domination cannot be effectively got rid of as long as there exists a *system* in the Third World (and for that matter in the West as well) that demands its continual presence, physical as well as mental.

Although our commitments lie mainly within the domain of art, this cannot be isolated from life at large and the struggle for its constant transformation. Particularly when the present problems of our art and culture are essentially part of the predicaments of the people violently subjected to foreign domination and their struggle against it, our art activity cannot be removed from this reality.

Our art must therefore be oriented towards anti-imperialist struggle. It does not necessarily mean that art should become a mechanistic instrument of ideological and political struggle. It should be part of the historical process in its own right, making its own contributions. That is, art must *also* wage struggle against domination and reactionary forces/ideas within its own sphere, without being discarded for political activity and without being separated from it. It is not a question of *political art* but an art which embraces the radical consciousness of its time. Those political activists, or ultra-leftists, who see art only as an instrument of political reality and its propaganda and keep on reminding us about the 'uselessness' of art activity (as opposed to political activity), are only revealing their own philistinism, if not actually betraying a lack of understanding of the true function of art, as well as its limitations.

The real function of art, of course, is neither a mere expression of beauty/self, decoration or entertainment(as is commonly understood), nor political propaganda. But this does not mean that art can be *apolitical* or *neutral*. In other words, art cannot but *reflect* an ideology, no matter how implicit it is—unless art can be emptied of all ideas and meanings, which is impossible. The so-called neutrality of art can only mask its sterility or an attitude that actually serves the interests of an ideology or a class.

Art cannot be, moreover, autonomous of culture. The myth of universal art, perpetrated by various art movements in the West in this century, must now be debunked. Behind this facade of universality lay the desire to impose Western values on the rest of the world. The fact is that the conditions under which Western art has been developing and flourishing are very different from those of the Third World. The art of the society whose material foundation is laid on the exploitation of other people, cannot be at the same time an expression of exploited people. While the development of art of a dominant society derives its energies, its dynamism, from its power to expand beyond its own boundaries and impose its values on the people whom it thus dominates and exploits, the art of the dominated people cannot but reflect their own predicament—including their resistance to foreign culture.

The question of how to resist and confront domination, and the values/forms which perpetrate it, becomes central here. This would naturally require, on the one hand, a thorough and critical examination of the various aspects of Western civilization, its art and culture, and, on the other, developing our own methods and forms of art/cultural activity which not only expose the insidious aims of Western cultural penetration in the Third World but also confront it effectively.

This cannot be achieved, however, by ignoring 20th century developments (in the West) and looking exclusively to our own past traditions for the solutions to contemporary problems. Nostalgic return to our past forms would be tantamount to an avoidance of the situation, which demands action against what is dominant and what is dominating us today. We must stay in the contemporary battlefield and fight for our liberation with all means available, the traditional as well as the modern technological. Cultural imperialism makes use of the most sophisticated technological means to dominate us. To confront this we would require not necessarily the same sophisticated technology but a similar *methodology* incorporating our own forms as well as those of others, resulting into antithesis.

The rejection of modern knowledge, and its various forms, in favour of indigenous *traditions* is based on an ignorance or a misconception that attributes modern developments exclusively to Western history. It is important to remember that Afro-Asian peoples had actually developed considerable knowledge before it was taken over by the West at the beginning of this modern era about five/six centuries ago. Even during the colonial period when the Third World people were deliberately prevented from any *direct* participation in modern developments, they did contribute significantly to the historical process.

Modern knowledge now belongs to all humanity. But it does not mean that we, in the name of progress or modernism, must accept THE IMPOSITION OF WESTERN VALUES ON US or that we must concede to Western cultural hegemony in contemporary life. IT IS UP TO US, AND US ALONE, TO MAKE USE OF ALL AVAILABLE KNOWLEDGE IN OUR OWN CONTEMPORARY DEVELOPMENTS.

The knowledge gained from the period when our own developments were suppressed, and when the developments in the West assimilated our art and cultural traditions, could be very useful. It does not necessarily mean that we shall go through a process of learning how to paint or sculpt in Western styles, nor that our contemporary developments should be dependent on Western models. But it is important to be aware of the history of the culture which surrounds us today; and only then, by being in a position to separate its positive and negative aspects, can we accept or reject it.

Our own traditions are, indeed, our assets, and to ignore them would be tantamount to a rejection of our own history and our own identity as a people. But to go back now to our ethnic past, and paint or sculpt like our ancestors used to do, would be a backward step. Mere reminders of our past glories can disregard contemporary reality, denying us the driving force of moving forward. The essence of the past must of course be fully grasped, by looking into how and why certain forms developed in certain periods and what were their relations with socio-economic forces. And if the traditional forms have survived as part of our present life, they must be given a new dimension to play a role in our developments today. However, this can only happen as part of an historical development of our own productive forces, giving birth to new ideas, concepts, values, forms and symbols that reflect the new and changing reality.

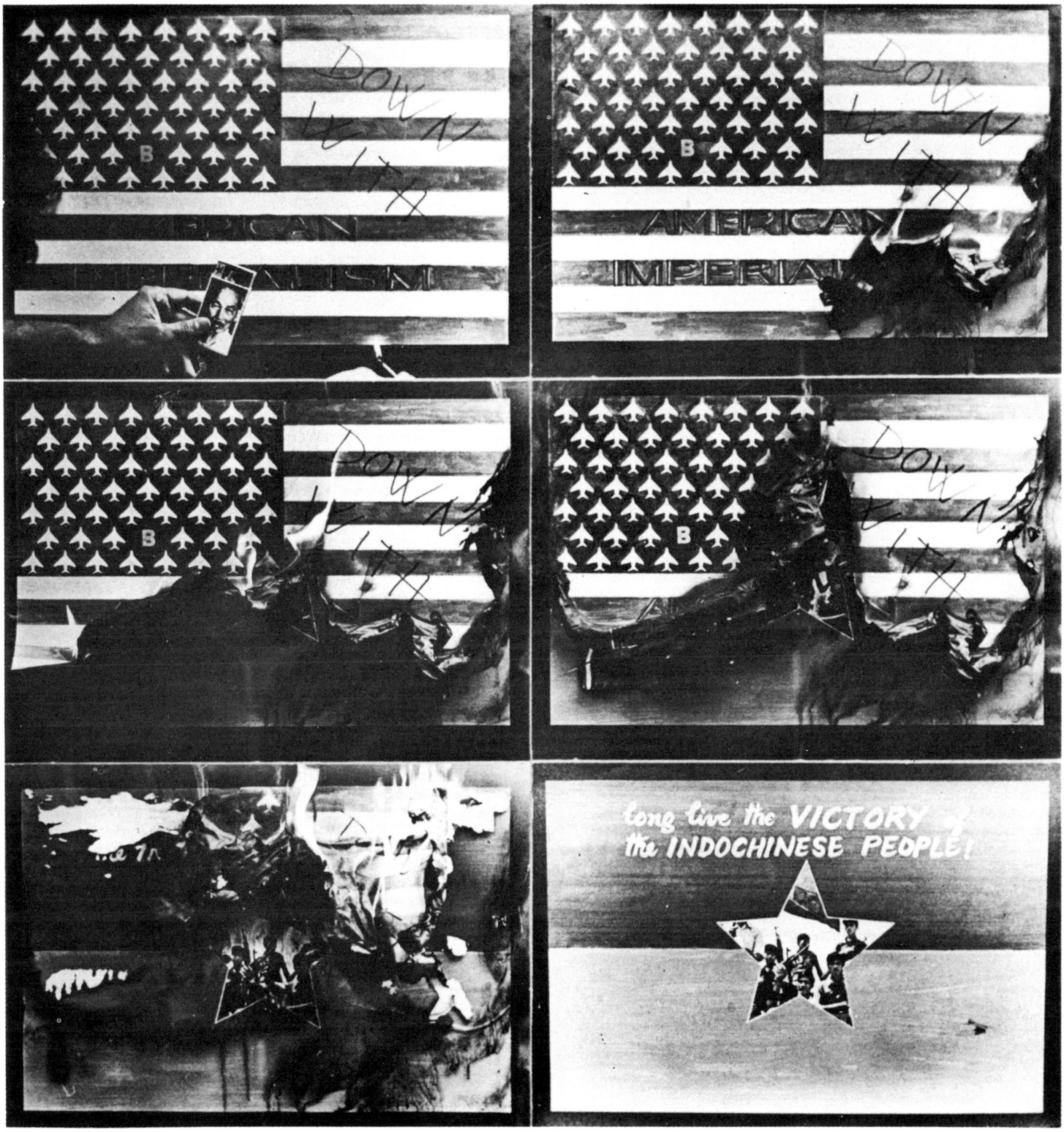

RASHEED ARAEEN *Fire* (6 of 30 or so photo-amal'aags) 1975

What is important now is not WHAT WE WERE IN THE PAST, but WHAT WE ARE TODAY. Whether we live in our own countries of origin or in the West, neither a mechanistic revival of our traditional forms nor a trailing behind on the paths formed by the so-called historical styles of Western art can offer us a positive direction. While rejecting both these options, but still finding ourselves surrounded and dominated by the forces which either demand our return to ethnic traditions or make us accept the hegemony of Western developments, WE HAVE NO CHOICE BUT TO OPPOSE THEM BOTH; AND OUT OF THIS CONFRONTATION WILL EMERGE NEW FORMS THAT TRULY REFLECT OUR PARTICULARITY IN THE WORLD TODAY.

We are no longer *national* entities, in the literal sense of the word. The problems facing us today are not necessarily of national dimensions or characteristics. They are in fact the consequences of the dominating forces *internationally* unleashed by the West. Our efforts, while containing individual/national elements, must therefore transcend both individual and national boundaries to reflect upon the international aspect of our predicaments and to come to terms with a situation that demands solidarity amongst all the peoples who are struggling against the same enemy.

The Third World must evolve its own independent identity, which cannot be, of course, homogeneous. But in its formal diversities, it must embody and express its underlying unity based onthe common historical past and the present reality of 'underdevelopment', also reflecting its *unified* opposition to Western domination. From the problematic situation of the Third World MUST EMERGE AN INTERNATIONAL MOVEMENT, WHICH IS DIFFERENT FROM AND IN OPPOSITION TO WESTERN ART. This would, of course, require the development of our own *international* platform, or communication/gallery network through which we could exchange our ideas directly without Western intermediaries/interference, creating historic links between the peoples whose emergence can offer a new hope to all mankind.

While coming to terms with the modern technological age and our own contemporary reality, which must involve A SEARCH FOR NEW METHODS AND FORMS beyond the narrow/obsolete concept of art based on the Western tradition of purity of painting/sculpture or craftsmanship—and the content of which must be oriented towards our own cultural situation, we must avoid the pitfalls of the stylistic sectarianism which has been one of the hallmarks of the Western avant-garde.

The struggle between different styles for so-called historical primacy is one of the characteristics, if not *the* dynamic, of contemporary art in the West, perpetrating aggressive competition between individuals for recognition. No wonder that the dominant ideology lays so much emphasis on the identity of the individual through one's work; which is actually realized by turning a particular style/form into a precious pedestal on which its innovator, the artist, must stand, maintaining the consistent position for the identification to be established. The recognition thus achieved not only gives a tremendous boost to the artist's inflated ego—a result of alienation, it also provides one with especial material benefits and social privileges. A formal style which must be the function of a content thus becomes content itself, thereby leading the artist into a formalist cocoon in which he/she is perpetually trapped, isolated from the grasp of an actual and changing reality outside.

The Western avant garde is, however, nearly reaching the end of its bourgeois cul-de-sac. On the one hand there is a wild talk about *the end of art*—as if art cannot exist or flourish outside bourgeois art history! On the other, the new 'radicals', in their last and desperate attempts to keep clinging to Art History by perpetuating the so-called evolution of historical styles, are even grabbing whatever material or forms they can get hold of from their flirtation with Marxism, class struggle, the predicament of dominated people, etc., manipulating them only to perpetrate a new formalism. The radical polemics/rhetoric of most Western artists, however, is not applicable to Third World conditions.

We ourselves do not need to look for any material outside our own existential reality, which is in fact part of our peoples' predicaments. We do not have any art-historical axe to grind. We have no art-historical pedestal to stand on and defend bourgeois values or preach sermons about beauty and aesthetics, nor shall we indulge in the futile activity of *art for art's sake.* Our history is in fact the history of the pillage and plundering by colonialism. We must grasp *this* truth and turn it into a weapon of our cultural struggle. FROM CENTURIES OF OPPRESSED EXISTENCE, FROM THE WILDERNESS OF COLONIALISM, THE THIRD WORLD MUST NOW EMERGE, LIKE A BLACK PHOENIX RISING FROM WHITE ASHES.

"... it is necessary to totally destroy, to break, to reduce to ash all aspects of colonial state in our country in order to make everything possible for our people."
- AMILCAR CABRAL

It does not follow from this that we must cut off ourselves from the activities of our Western contemporaries, particularly those who are also aware of their role in society and are aiming at the radical change. Since many of us live in the West, we must avoid isolation and separatism which is no recipe for the positive development of a society in which all people, irrespective of race and colour, must interrelate. But in the present situation it is very difficult. *So long as* Western people speak from their privileged positions and with their usual paternalistic attitude and arrogance, there is no possibility whatsoever for the development of a real dialogue between THEM and US.

The development of a true international platform/movement, from/ to which all cultures could make their unique contributions, is not only possible but desirable in the long run. But if this is to serve the true interests of all peoples rather than become another instrument of selfish Western interests, it must be based on the clear rejection of Western art history as *the* mainstream. The subjective conditions of the affluent Western society—particularly when these conditions have been ahcieved at the expense of the majority of the people in the world, cannot offer a truly international perspective.

The concept of individual geniuses as *the* creators, looking down on the rest of the people as being incapable of an art or a creative activity, is another aspect of the dominant ideology. The present relationship between an individual as a *creator* and the people as mere *consumers* must therefore be questioned. What we could instead do as art/cultural workers in the present transition, before a new society emerges in which art and culture shall be collectively developed and created, is to *initiate* activity which is then taken up *critically* by people; and the eventual development or completion of the work must depend on their actual participation/contribution.

It ought to be made clear that this work is not meant to be an objective analysis. It is *mainly* a personal statement by A THIRD WORLD MAN who, as a result of being uprooted by cultural imperialism from his Asian environment, was sucked into the Western World where he has spent a considerable part of his life in pursuit of freedom of artistic expression in what he has now come to realize is A WHITE MAN'S WORLD. The experience of living in the West has led him to *black consciousness* and to the awareness that HIS REAL PLACE IS IN THE THIRD WORLD. This is an attempt now on his part to re-examine his relationship with the West, and redefine his artistic role in the cultural context of his people, whether they live in their own countries or in the West.

A Third World Praxis

No recipes or prescriptions are being offered here. We must not believe in ready-made solutions. Art cannot be developed by a set of rules but only through an evolving life-process that generates new ideas at every stage of its transformation. Therefore the suggestions here are not meant to be taken as canons to be followed, or guidelines for the production of art. They may in fact trap us, if followed mechanistically, into a dogmatic/formalistic situation stifling our imagination and energies.

Nevertheless, it is hoped these notes will initiate a discussion from which may emerge a clearer picture, providing us with a starting-point in a direction towards a new dynamism which helps us liberate our energies and awaken us from our present lethargic generality. The success of this will, of course, depend on the imaginative and creative response from the Third World people, particularly black people, who may also be thinking in the same way but have not yet come forward or did not have an opportunity to express their ideas.

Cultural imperialism cannot be dealt with by making appeals to its liberal conscience or pretended humanity. So long as we look to others for the solutions of our own problems—and no matter how much noise we make—we will only be ignored or pushed around. We must *ourselves* take a concrete step. These notes are therefore being offered as A PRELUDE to A WORK whose realization and completion depends on *all of us together*, including our Western comrades.

The conceptual structure of *THE PROPOSED WORK* can therefore be laid down in the following order: INITIATIVE/writing of this prelude; CONTACT WITH PEOPLE through its publication; PARTICIPATION by people in the form of their critical intervention; UNIFICATION of all the material thus created by being published together as a completed work (ARTBOOK). RE-CONTACT; return of the completed work to the participants; PROPAGATION/general distribution of the work; and so on . . . .

Would you therefore send your contributions, in the form of WORDS and IMAGES relating to the cultural problems of the Third World. Keeping in mind that the aim of the work is the DENUNCIATION OF AND CONFRONTATION WITH IMPERIALIST CULTURE and THE SYSTEM that perpetuates international domination. Your contributions may also include constructive criticism of the work. The visual IMAGES may be produced, for example, by collective actions (events etc.) against the cultural strongholds of the system, and by documenting them photographically. The decision how to act or what to contribute, however, entirely lies with you.

The material thus received, comprising of statements/criticism/ photographic documentation, will, it is hoped, be published (depending on the availability of publisher or money) as a completed BLACK MANIFESTO, and the copies sent to the participants, who must also send their names and addresses: c/o *Black Phoenix*

(London, 1975-76)

1. For Paulo Freire's works see *Pedagogy of the Oppressed* and *Cultural Action for Freedom*, both published by Penguin, London.
2. Although the activities of *CAYC, Buenos Aires, Argentina*, have been confined to Latin American situation and those of *Artists for Democracy, London,* tend to centre around particular political issues, they both are worth mentioning here. *FESTAC '77* was in fact the most important and spectacular event of 'Black Arts' which took place in Lagos, Nigeria, in January/February 1977.
3. Edward Lucie-Smith, *Movements in Art Since 1945*, Thames & Hudson, London; paperback p.17.
4. Frantz Fanon, *The Wretched of the Earth*, Penguin, London; p.76.
5. A short film *You Hide Me* by Ghanaian film-maker Kwate Nee Owoo (Ifriqiyah Films, London), has thrown some light on the storage of thousands of artifacts in the basement lockers of the British Museum. In addition, there are about two million artifacts, looted mostly from the Third World, being stored in a warehouse, Shoreditch, London, and to which the public in general has no access.
6. Amilcar Cabral, *Return to Source*, Modern Reader, New York/ London; p.45.
7. Ibid.; p.39.
8. Herbert Read, *A Concise History of Modern Painting*, Thames & Hudson, London. Revised edition; paperback p.8.
9. For the predicament of migrant workers in Europe, see *A Seventh Man* by John Berger/Jean Mohr, Penguin Books, London.

Eduardo Galeano
In defence of the word

During long sleepless nights and days of depression, a fly buzzes and buzzes around the head: 'Writing, is it worth it?'

In the midst of the farewells and the crimes, will words survive?

Does this profession, which one has chosen or which has been chosen for one, make any sense?

I am South American. In Montevideo, where I was born, I edited some newspapers and journals; one after the other they were closed down, by the government or by the creditors. I wrote several books: they are all banned. At the beginning of '73, my exile began. In Buenos Aires, we founded Crisis. *It was a cultural journal with the biggest circulation in the history of the Spanish language. In August of last year its last number appeared. It could not continue. When words can be no worthier than silence, it is better to say nothing. And to hope.*

Where are the writers and journalists who produced the journal? Almost all have left Argentina. Some are dead. Others, imprisoned or disappeared.

The novelist Haroldo Conti, or what remained of him, was seen for the last time in the middle of May 1976. Broken by torture. Nothing more has been heard of him. Officially, he was not detained. The government washes its hands. The poet Miguel Angel Bustos was taken from his home and has disappeared. The poet Paco Urondo was killed in Mendoza. The writers Paoletti and Di Benedetto are in prison. As is Luis Sabini, the journal's head of production: he is accused of possessing arms because he had a bullet to make himself a key ring. Our editor, Carlos Villar Arauja, was the first to go. In July 1975 he had to leave the country. He had published a courageous work, with documentary evidence, on oil in Argentina. That edition of Crisis *was put on sale in the kiosks and, six evenings later, Carlos did not come home to sleep. They interrogated him with his eyes covered. The police denied holding him. Two days later he was flung, by a miracle still alive, into the woods of Ezeiza. The police said they had arrested him by mistake. They circulated lists of those condemned to death. The poet, Juan Gelman, editor in chief, had to take a plane. Some time later, they came looking for him in his home in Buenos Aires. As he was not there, they took his children away. The daughter turned up alive. Of the son and daughter-in-law, seven months pregnant, nothing is known. Unofficial government information indicated that they had been in prison and had been set free. The earth has swallowed them up.*

In such stormy times, the profession of writing is dangerous. In such circumstances, one recovers pride and joy in words, or loses respect for them for ever.

1 One writes out of a need for communication and communion with others, to denounce pain and share joy. One writes against one's own solitude and that of others. One assumes that literature transmits knowledge and acts upon the language and conduct of those who receive it, that it helps us to know ourselves better so as to achieve a collective salvation. But 'others' is too vague a term, and in time of crisis and of definition, the ambiguity can come too close to a lie. One writes in fact for the people whose situation one feels identified with, the undernourished, those who cannot sleep, the rebels and the oppressed of this world; and the majority of them cannot read. And of the minority who can, how many can afford to buy books? Is this contradiction resolved by proclaiming that one writes for that convenient abstraction called 'the masses'?

*

2 We weren't born on the moon, we don't live in the seventh heaven. We have the fortune and misfortune to belong to a tormented part of the globe, Latin America, and to be living during a historical period which hits us hard. The contradictions of class society are fiercer here than in the rich countries. Mass poverty is the price paid by the poor countries so that six per cent of the world's population can consume unmolested half of the world's wealth. The abysmal gap between the wellbeing of the few and the misery of the majority is much greater in Latin America, and the methods necessary for safeguarding that gap are more brutal.

The development of a restricted and dependent type of industry on top of outdated agrarian and mining structures did not change their essential distortions and has sharpened social antagonism instead of alleviating it. The skills of the traditional politicians, experts in the arts of seduction and swindling, is now inadequate, antiquated and useless; the populist game of making concessions so as to manipulate is no longer possible, or else reveals its dangerous double edge. The dominant classes and countries resort to the machinery of repression. How else could survival without change be assured for a social system which every day grows more like a concentration camp? How, without barbed wire, to keep the growing legion of the wretched in their places? The more the system is threatened by the incessant growth of unemployment and poverty and consequent social and political tensions, the more reduced the space left for pretence and good manners: in the suburbs of the world the system reveals its true face.

Why not recognise a certain degree of frankness in the dictatorships which today oppress the majority of our countries? Freedom for business implies, in times of crisis, imprisoning people.

Latin American scientists emigrate, laboratories and universities have no resources, industrial know-how is always foreign and very expensive, but why not recognise a certain degree of creativity in the development of a technology of terror? Latin America is making inspired contributions to the world-wide development of methods of torture, techniques for destroying people and ideas, the cultivation of silence, the multiplication of impotence, the dissemination of fear.

For those of us who want to work for a literature which will help to manifest the voice of those who have no voice, the question becomes, how can we act within this reality? Can we make ourselves heard in a deaf and dumb culture? Our countries are republics of silence. Is not the small freedom of the writer sometimes the proof of his failure? How far can we reach and who can we reach?

It is an admirable task to proclaim the world of the just and the free and a worthy role to deny the system of hunger and cages – visible or invisible. But how far away is the frontier? How far do the owners of power give permission?

3 Much has been said about the forms of direct censorship used by various regimes, such as the prohibition of inconvenient or dangerous books or periodicals and the destiny of exile, prison or death dealt out to some writers and journalists.

But indirect censorship operates more subtly. That it is less obvious does not make it less real. Little is said about it. Nevertheless it is what defines most profoundly the oppressive and prohibitory nature of the system from which the majority of our countries suffer. What does it consist in, this censorship which dares not tell its name? It means that the ship doesn't sail because there's no water in the sea: if five per cent of the population of Latin America can buy refrigerators, what percentage can buy books? And what percentage can read them, feel the need for them, receive their influence?

Latin American writers, in the pay of a cultural industry which serves the consumption of an educated elite, belong to a minority which they also write for. This is the objective situation of writers whose work confirms social inequality and the ruling ideology; it is also that of those of us who seek to break with these things. We are blocked by the rules of the reality within which we act.

The present social order perverts or destroys the creative capacity of the vast majority of men and limits the possibility of creation – ancient response to human pain and the certainty of death – to the professional efforts of a handful of specialists. How many of these 'specialists' are there in Latin America? Who do we write for, who do we reach? What is our real public?

Let us be wary of applause. Sometimes congratulation comes from those who think us harmless.

4 One writes to put death off the scent and to strangle the ghosts that pursue one within; but what one writes can be historically useful only when it coincides in some way with a collective need for the conquest of identity. What one would like to happen is I think this, that in saying 'This is what I am' and offering himself, the writer could help many other people to become conscious of what they are. As a means of revealing collective identity, art should be considered a prime necessity and not a luxury. But in Latin America access to the products of art and culture is forbidden to the vast majority.

For people whose identity has been destroyed by successive conquering cultures, and whose ruthless exploitation is part of the machinery of world capitalism, the system creates a 'mass culture'. Culture *for* the masses would be a more adequate definition of this degraded art with a massive circulation, which manipulates consciousness, masks reality and tramples on the creative imagination. Useless for revealing identity, it is a way to wipe it out and deform it, to impose ways of life and patterns of consumption which receive massive diffusion through the media. What is called 'National culture' is the culture of the ruling class, which lives an imported life and limits itself to copying, abortively and in bad taste, so-called 'world culture', or what that is understood to be by those who confuse it with the culture of the dominant countries. In our period, the era of multiple markets and multinational corporations, internationalism applies not just to economics but to culture, 'mass culture', thanks to the accelerated development and massive diffusion of the media. The centres of power export to us not just machines and patents but also ideology. If in Latin America the enjoyment of the good things of the earth is reserved for the few, the majority has to be resigned to consuming fantasies. Illusions of riches are sold to the poor, and of freedom to the oppressed, dreams of triumph for the defeated and of power for the weak. There is no need to be able to read in order to consume the symbolic justifications for the unequal organisation of the world disseminated by television, radio and the cinema.

To ensure the perpetuation of the current state of affairs in lands where every minute a child dies of disease or hunger, we have to be taught to see ourselves through the eyes of the oppressor. People are trained to accept 'this' order as the 'natural' order and therefore as an eternal one; and they identify the system with patriotism, so that an opponent of the regime is a traitor or a foreign agent. The law of the jungle, which is the law of the system, is sanctified, so that defeated peoples should accept their situation as their destiny. The falsification of the past pushes out of sight the true causes of the historical failure of Latin America, where poverty has always fed the prosperity of others: on the small screen or on the big one, the best man wins, and the best is the strongest. Wastefulness, exhibitionism and lack of scruple produce not disgust but admiration; everything can be bought, sold, rented, consumed – not excluding the soul. Magical properties are given to a cigarette, a car, a bottle of whisky or a watch: they provide personality, make you succeed in life, give you happiness. The proliferation of foreign models and heroes goes with the fetishism surrounding products and fashions from the rich countries. Our home-produced photo-romances and TV serials take place in a limbo of cheap illusion, on the margin of the real social and political problems of each country, and the serials we import sell Western Christian Democracy together with violence and tomato sauce.

5 In these lands full of youth, where young people incessantly multiply and cannot find employment, the ticking of the time bomb forces those in power to sleep with one eye open. Multiple methods of cultural alienation, machines for doping and castrating become more important every day. Methods for sterilising consciousness are carried out more successfully than plans for birth control.

The best way to colonise a consciousness is to eradicate it. Operating to this end, whether consciously or not, is the importation of a false counter-culture which is finding increasing adherents among the younger generations in Latin American countries. Those countries which, because of their ossified structures or asphyxiating mechanisms of repression, exclude youth from political participation offer the most fertile ground for the proliferation of a supposed 'protest culture', which comes from outside as a byproduct of the society of idleness and waste, and which, originating in the pseudo anti-conventionalism of the parasitic classes, is directed towards all social classes.

The habits and symbols of the rebellion of youth in the sixties in the USA and Europe came from a reaction against the uniformity of consumerism, but now they are themselves the objects of mass production. Clothes with psychedellic designs are sold in the name of 'liberation'; music, posters, haircuts and dresses which reproduce the aesthetic models of drug hallucination are part of a large-scale industry which throws them at the Third World. Together with the attractive-coloured symbols, youth who want to escape from hell are offered tickets to limbo. The new generations are invited to abandon the pain of history for Nirvana. Certain sections of Latin American youth, when they incorporate themselves into this drug culture, achieve the illusion of reproducing the way of life of their metropolitan counterparts.

Originating in the nonconformism of marginal groups in alienated industrial society, this false counter-culture has nothing to do with our real needs for identity and destiny: it offers adventures for paralytics; it generates resignation, egoism, non-communication; it leaves reality intact but changes its image; it promises love without pain and peace without war. Furthermore, in turning sensations into articles for consumption, it fits perfectly into the 'supermarket ideology' which the mass media disseminate. If the fetishism of cars and refrigerators is insufficient to eliminate anguish and pacify anxiety, you can buy peace, excitement and happiness in the clandestine supermarket.

6 To arouse consciousness and reveal the true reality: can literature lay claim to a better role in these times and in these countries of ours? The culture of the system, culture of surrogates for life, masks reality and anaesthetises consciousness. But what can a writer do, however much his own fire burns, against the ideological machinery of lies and conformism?

If society tends to organise itself in such a way that no-one ever meets anyone else, and reduces human relations to the sinister operation of competition and consumption – lone men using each other and smashing up against each other – what can be achieved by a literature rooted in fraternal bonds and participatory solidarity?

We have reached a point where to name things is to denounce them: Before whom? For whom?

7 Our destiny as Latin American writers is bound up with the necessity for profound social change. To tell is to give oneself: it seems obvious that literature, as the striving for full communication, will continue to be thwarted at the outset so long as there is misery and illiteracy and those in power carry on with impunity, fostering collective imbecility through the mass media.

I do not share the view of those who claim for the writer a privileged freedom unconnected with the freedom of other workers. Major changes of structure must occur in our countries for writers to reach beyond the closed citadels of the elites and express themselves without being gagged, visibly or invisibly. Within an imprisoned society, literature can only exist as denunciation or hope.

In the same sense, I believe it would be a dream to suppose that there is an exclusively cultural way of liberating the creative capacity of people when it has been kept oblivious by harsh material conditions and the struggle for survival. How much talent gets extinguished in Latin America before it manages to manifest itself? How many writers and artists do not even get as far as discovering what they are?

8 Furthermore, can a national culture really be achieved in countries where the material foundations of power are not national, or depend on foreign centres?

If independence is not possible, what meaning is there in writing?

There is no 'degree zero' of culture, just as there is none in history. If we recognise an inevitable continuity between the stage of domination and the stage of liberation in any process of social development, why deny the importance of literature and its possible revolutionary function in exploring, revealing and disseminating our true identity or its projection? The oppressor wants the mirror to give to the oppressed no more than its blank silver. What process of change can urge forward a people which doesn't know who it is nor where it comes from? If it doesn't know who it is, how can it know what it deserves to be? Cannot literature directly or indirectly aid this revelation?

I believe the possibility of such a contribution depends to a great extent on the intensity of the writer's communion with the roots, the vicissitudes and the destiny of his people. And on the capacity of his sensibility to perceive the pulse and rhythms of the authentic counter-culture as it comes into being. Often what is considered as 'lack of culture' contains the seeds or fruit of the 'other' culture, the one which opposes the dominant culture and shares neither its values nor its rhetoric. It is often mistakenly despised for being a mere degraded repetition of the 'cultured' products of the elite or of cultural models mass-produced by the system, but often a popular narrative can be more revealing and valuable than a 'professional' novel, and the pulse of real life is felt more strongly in certain anonymous songs that belong to local tradition than in many books of poetry written in the code of the initiated. The testimony of people expressing their sufferings and hopes in a multiplicity of ways is often more eloquent and beautiful than works written 'in the name of the people'.

Our genuine collective identity comes from the past and is nourished by it – footprints which our own feet follow, steps which foreshadow our paths in the present – but does not crystallise into nostalgia. Certainly, we are not going to find our hidden face in the artificial perpetuation of ethnic dress, customs and objects which tourists demand from conquered nations. *We are what we do, and above all what we do to change what we are*: our identity lies in action and struggle. That is why the revelation of what we are implies denunciation of what prevents us being what we can be. We define ourselves through defiance and through opposing obstacles.

A literature born of crisis and change and deeply immersed in the risk and adventure of its time, can certainly help to create the symbols of the new reality and perhaps illuminate – if talent and courage are not lacking – the signs that show the way.

It is not useless to sing the pain and beauty of having been born in America.

9 The number of copies published or the amount of sales do not always give a true measure of a book's effect. Sometimes a written work gains an influence which is much wider than its apparent diffusion; sometimes it provides answers years in advance to collective problems and necessities, if the artist has actually lived them as doubts and tensions inside himself. The work springs from the wounded consciousness of the writer and is projected into the world: the act of creation is an act of solidarity which does not always fulfil its destiny during the life of the person who accomplishes it.

10 I do not share the view of writers who ascribe to themselves divine privileges not granted to ordinary mortals, nor that of those who beat their breast and tear their clothing asking for public dispensation to live in the service of a useless vocation.

Neither gods nor insects. Consciousness of our limitations is not consciousness of impotence: literature, a form of action, has no supernatural powers, but the writer can achieve his measure of magic when he secures the survival, through his work, of people and experiences that have a real value.

If what he writes is not read with impunity but changes or stimulates the reader in some way, then the writer can lay claim to his part in the process of change: without pride or false humility and knowing himself to be part of something much vaster.

It seems logical to me that language is belittled by those who cultivate a monologue with their own shadows and endless labyrinths. But words have a meaning for those of us who want to celebrate and share the certainty that the human condition is not a sewer. We look for people to communicate with, not admirers, we offer dialogue, not spectacle. We write from a striving for true meeting, so that the reader may be in communion with words that come to us from him and return to him as inspiration and prophecy.

11 To claim that literature on its own will change reality would be an act of arrogance or madness. It seems to me no less stupid to deny that in some degree it can help to bring about change.

Consciousness of our limitations is fundamentally consciousness of our reality. In the fog of hopelessness and doubt it is possible to confront things face to face and fight them out body to body: starting out from our limitations but in opposition to them.

In this sense, it is as much a desertion to write 'revolutionary' literature for the convinced as it would be to write conservative literature dedicated to the ecstasy of contemplating one's own navel. There are people who cultivate an 'ultra-left' literature, apocalyptic in tone, directed at a small public which already agrees with what is being said: what is the risk taken by these writers, however revolutionary they may claim to be, if they write for the minority who think and feel like them and give them what they expect to find? In that case there is no possibility of failure; but there can be no success either. What is the use of writing if not to defy the blockade which the system places round the dissident message?

Our effectiveness depends on our capacity to be audacious and astute, clear and attractive. Let us hope we can create a language with more energy and beauty than that which conformist writers use to salute the twilight.

12 But it is not just a problem of language. There is also the question of media. The culture of resistance uses all the media at its disposal and does not allow itself the luxury of wasting any means or opportunity of expression. Time is short, the challenge crucial and the task enormous: for the Latin American writer committed to the cause of social change, the production of books forms part of a struggle on a multiple front. We do not subscribe to the sacralisation of literature as a congealed institution of bourgeois culture. Documentaries and reports for mass circulation, scripts for radio, cinema and television, and the popular songs are not always 'minor' genres, belonging to a subordinate category, as is believed by some marquises of specialised literary discourse who look askance at them. The cracks that the journalism of rebellion in Latin America has opened in the alienating machinery of the mass media have often been the result of a creative effort and sacrifice in no way inferior in aesthetic accomplishment and effectiveness to good fiction.

13 I believe in my craft; I believe in my instrument. I can never understand how writers could write while cheerfully declaring that writing has no meaning in a world where people are dying of hunger. Nor can I ever understand those who turn words into a target for fury or an object of fetishism. Words are a weapon and can be used for good or evil: the responsibility for the crime never lies with the knife.

I believe that the primordial function of contemporary Latin American literature is to rescue words from that frequent and impure degradation which has served to prevent or betray communication. 'Freedom' is, in my country, the name of a prison for political prisoners and 'democracy' the name for various regimes of terror; 'love' defines the relation of a man with his car and 'revolution' is understood as what a new detergent can do in your kitchen; 'glory' is what a particular toilet soap achieves and 'happiness' the sensation you get from eating sausages. 'Peaceful country' means, in many places in Latin America, 'ordered cemetery', and where it says 'sane man' one may have to read 'impotent man'.

By writing it is possible to offer, despite persecution and censorship, the testimony of our time and our people – for now and for posterity. One may write in order to say, in a sense: 'This is where we are, this is where we were; we are like this, this is what we were like.' Slowly gaining strength and form, there is in Latin America a literature which does not set out to bury our own dead, but to perpetuate them; which refuses to clear up the ashes and tries on the contrary to light the fire. That literature continues and enriches a powerful tradition of fighting words. If, as I believe, hope is better than nostalgia, perhaps this nascent literature may be worthy of the beauty of the social forces which will sooner or later, cost what it may, radically change the course of our history. And perhaps it may help to preserve for the youth to come, as the poet put it, 'the true name of each thing'. □

Translated by William Rowe

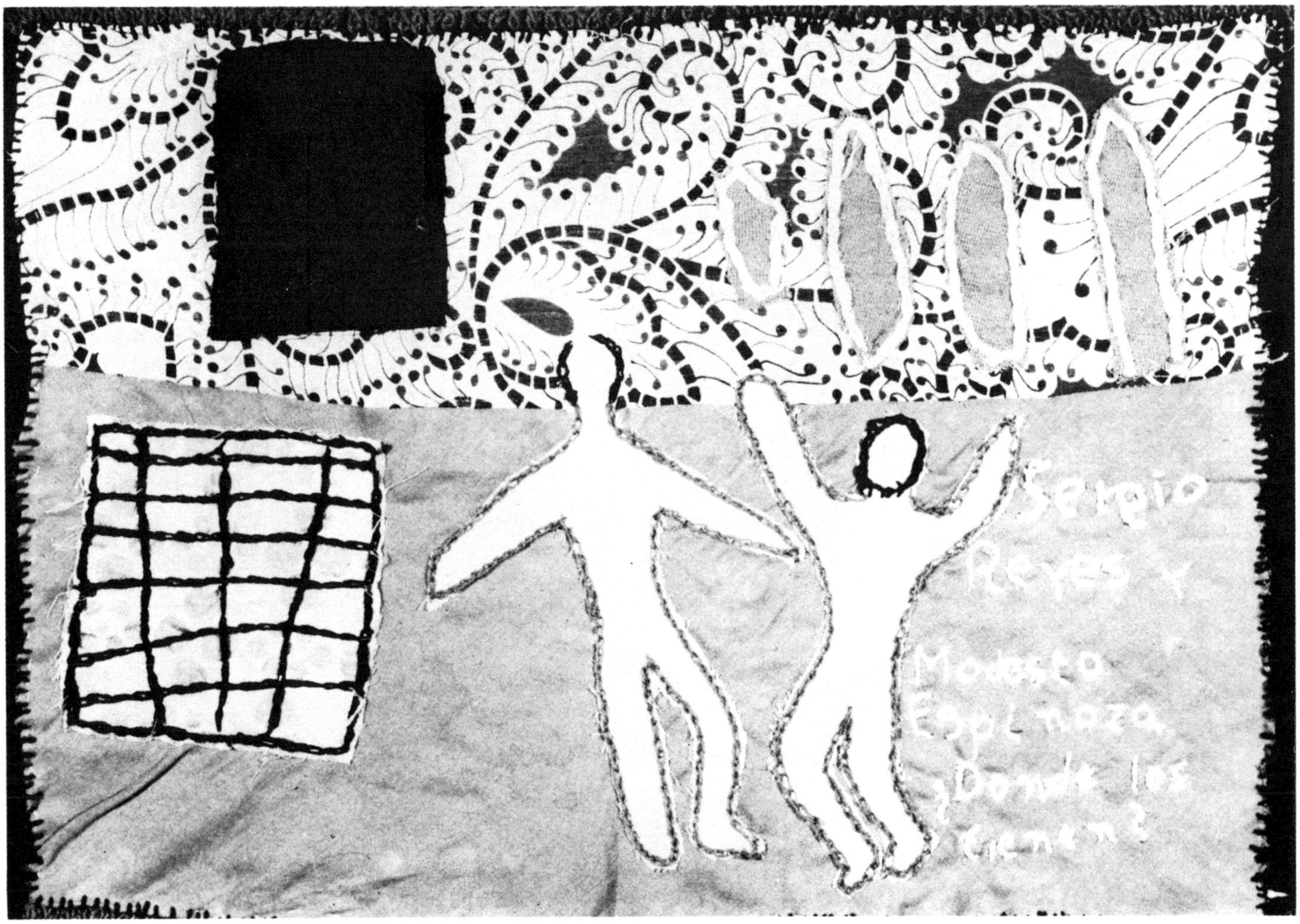

"We want people to know the truth."

PATCHWORK PICTURES FROM CHILE

Report by Guy Brett

On June 14th 1977, 28 Chileans—26 women and two men—entered the offices of the United Nations Economic Commission for Latin America in the capital of Santiago. They were relatives of some of the 'disappeared' political prisoners in Chile; they declared a hunger strike and they refused to leave until they were told the fate of these two thousand people arrested by the military junta and then listed merely as 'missing'.

Because of international scrutiny and domestic resistance, the Chilean junta prefers not to openly arrest people any longer and put them in recognized prisons and camps, but to seize and torture them secretly, without naming them, without charging them. Any attempt by their families to try to trace them is met with harassment, especially by the secret police.

The demonstrators sent an impassioned message to Kurt Waldheim, Secretary General of the United Nations, and he responded by invoking extraterritorial privilege for the mission in Santiago (ie. that legally it was not part of Chilean territory), so the strikers could not be molested by the Chilean security forces. International response to the occupation was so great that Pinochet (the leader of the junta) was forced to agree, at least ostensibly, with two of the strikers' demands—to look into the cases of their disappeared relatives, and not to take reprisals for the demonstration.

Up to now, neither of these promises has been kept. There has been no indication from the Chilean government that the cases have been investigated, and some of the strikers have been interrogated and had their houses ransacked. Nevertheless the strike has shown the courage of these people, who with no powers or security have formed a group to challenge the military regime.

Many of the patchwork pictures—patchworks sewn of scraps of clothing fabric and wool—were made by the families of 'disappeared' prisoners. For example, the above picture was made by the mother of one of the people shown in it, who were arrested together. The four

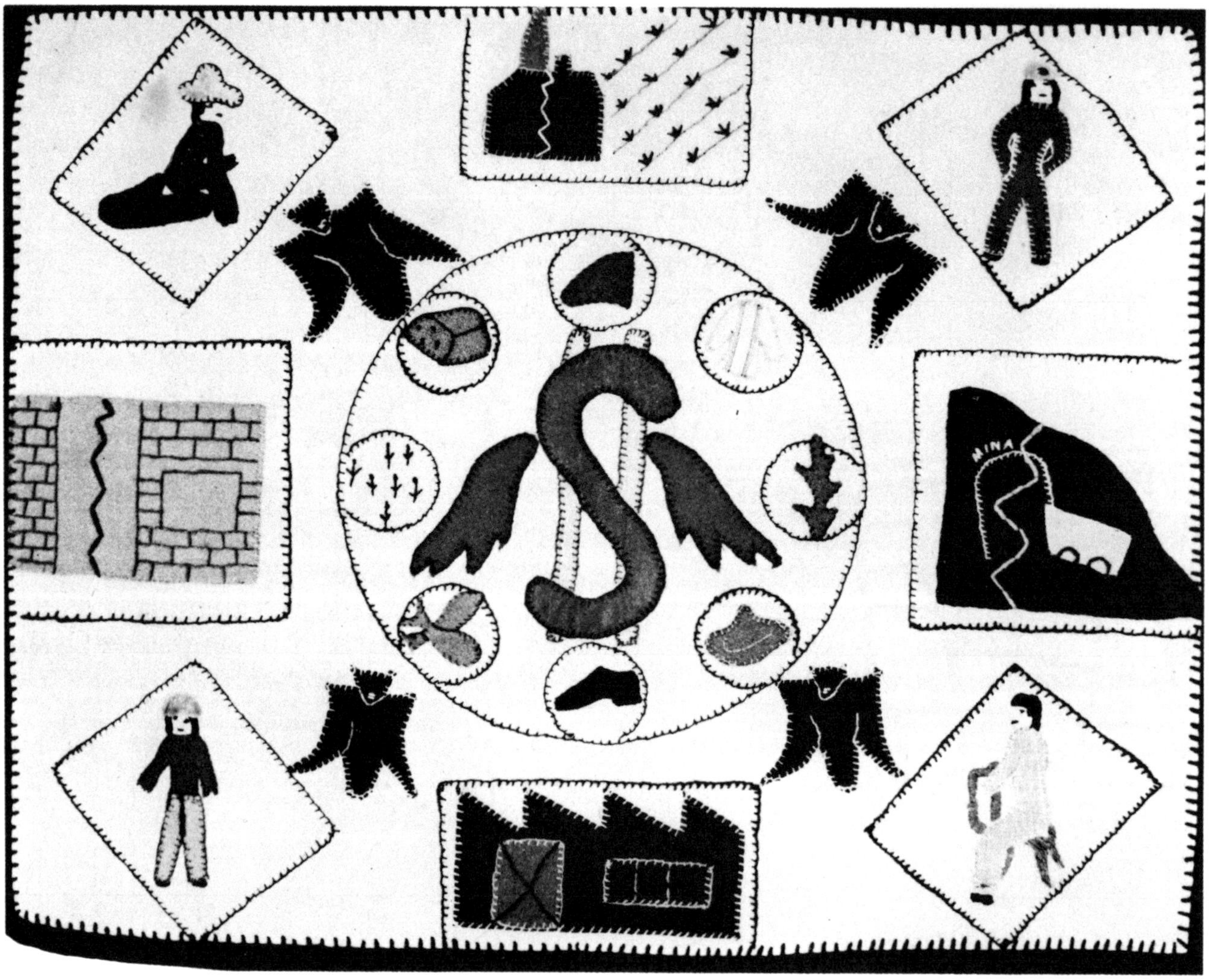

vertical strokes at the top right stand for *Cuatro Alamos* (alamos = poplar tree), the isolation wing of *Tres Alamos*, one of the junta's prison camps.* The dark square to the left stands for . . . some unknown place, the anguish of knowing nothing. "Sergio Reyes and Modesto Espinosa—where are they?"

Several hundred of patchwork pictures like this one have been made in Chile in the last two years, despite the atmosphere of terror. It is a popular art of resistance invented by the people themselves because of an overpowering need to express the bitter experiences they are going through and to find a channel of communication to the world outside. Some of the first of these patchworks were made in the prisons, but now they are nearly all made by women (both by the families of political prisoners and by the families of the unemployed) living in the shanty-towns, the poorest areas around Santiago.

They are not professional artists or artisans, and in general they have worked up and adapted a popular form of embroidery traditionally used to decorate bags and baskets. But their message can be understood anywhere in the world.

These rag pictures come out of poverty. They depict the brutalities and suffering the ordinary people have had to endure from reactionary rulers. They show them in detail. But in doing so they take none of the inhumanity, rigidity and coldness of their oppressors. They can express serious sorrow and at the same time be full of imagination and spirit. In the patchworks this comes out in the brilliant colours, and also in the witty and poetic way the scraps of patterned, mass-produced fabric have been used. Not only the subject, but the whole way they are made is like a message saying that the people will not be crushed and reduced to silence.

How did this movement begin?

The appearance of these patchwork pictures cannot really be separated from a very broad wave of cultural activity in Chile over more than ten years. It began before Allende came to power and continues today despite the intense efforts of the present government to crush it. It has always had a popular character. It has been linked with a movement of masses of people against the conditions, physical and mental, of 'underdevelopment'. Many art forms sprang up in Chile during the Popular Unity period, although they had little time to develop: the New Song movement, street and field theatre, mural painting, publishing of popular educational books and magazines which reached enormous readership for a Third World country, new style comics, the revitalization of crafts which were languishing, and so on.

Among these crafts was one of making pictures from different coloured wools, which was specially admired and encouraged by the poet Pablo Neruda and by the folk-singer and painter Violet a Parra. This peasant art is the nearest antecedent to the present-day patchworks. But there is no direct connection. The patchworks are something new. Their makers have no formal tradition to draw on and express themselves in a direct and childlike way.

The strength of the cultural movement is clear from the way, under the extreme persecution of the right-wing junta, it has adapted itself and survived in new forms. People in Britain will have noticed how Chileans in exile have got together to form new music and theatre groups. Poems, plays, pieces of wood and metal carving have found their way here even from inside Chilean prisons.

The first patchworks after the coup were made to denounce the junta and expose their crimes. It is hard to be sure exactly how it began but probably in a small way among women who saw first the possibility of using an apparently innocuous form like the patchwork—so homely and 'innocent'—as a means of protest. The movement quickly spread wider and wider. Patchwork-making became one of the forms of work organized in the shanty-towns to combat the massive unemployment produced by the junta's economic policies.

* In December 1976 the junta announced the closure of Tres Alamos prison camp, and the release of the prisoners held there. As a result of pressure both inside and outside the country, and after so many have been killed or exiled, the junta are removing some of the more obvious signs of repression. But it would be wrong to assume from this that the character of the regime or the interests it serves have changed in any way. Political prisoners are taken to secret places of detention rather than known ones. The patchworks also refer to less visible kinds of oppression, for example economic measures like the all-out drive to divert food production to export, which is causing literally starvation among the people.

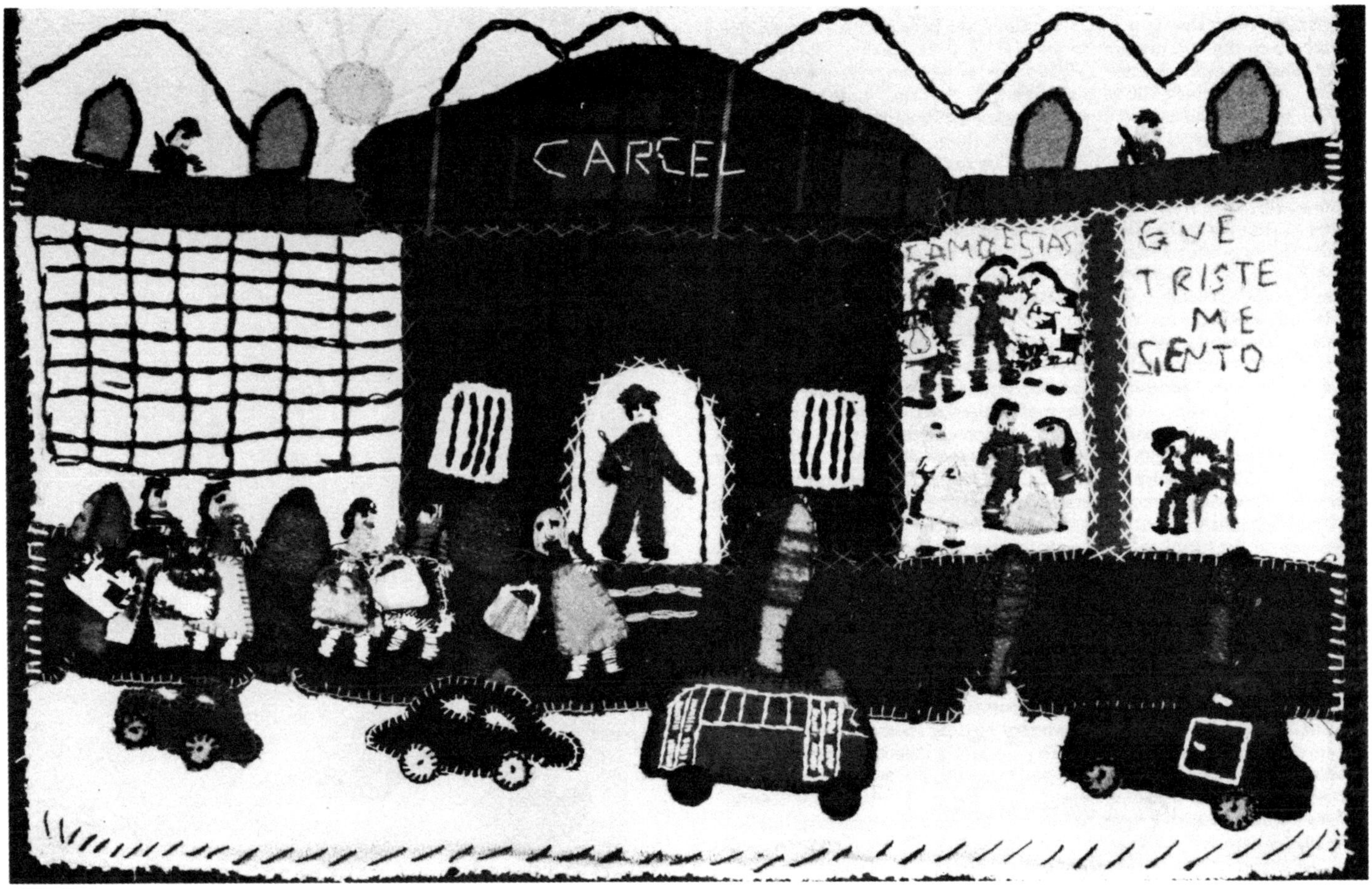

"We have lived through much and we must explain it....We must find some way to say it...... Often one keeps silent through pride, but I'm going to tell these things; I'm not ashamed to do so because everything that has happened to me is true...I can't keep silent because I have lived it."

"In every one there are human figures, especially children, because what you see more than anything in the shanty-towns are children. What we show always has to do with people."

"The colours are always chosen for contrast. Often they are not exactly as we want because we lack materials, but we always try to do it that way. I use darker colours when it's winter or I'm showing something sad...then everything is grey and cloudy. When the weather is good we put the sun and more lively colours. If the subject is happy, we make the colours of the people very beautiful."

"We don't have money or anything else. We have to go out and collect the scraps of material around the factories. That's how we make them and afterwards people buy them... Each time we make them better. It has to be like that because we live from them, it's the only way we have to survive, otherwise nothing at all would come to the house."

The workshops are organized by the people themselves, often with assistance from the Churches, which in Chile have become increasingly opposed to the military government. Patchwork-making, like laundering and sewing, produces a minimal income for women to buy some sort of food, and medicines, for their children. At first they were sold inside Chile, now abroad as well at solidarity meetings and events.

Because people's survival depends on them, these workshops are carefully organized. Production has to be rationalised. They usually consist of not more than twenty women. A treasurer distributes the money obtained from sales. A certain amount is put into a fund to be used for buying materials and for emergencies. The number of patchworks produced has to be controlled. Usually one person makes one a week. At a weekly meeting the new patchworks are looked at and discussed by six women in the group and generally judged against the following criteria:

—that they should be well finished;
—that the forms should be well-composed
—that the subject should be truthful, and really 'say something'.

In fact in the details of these pictures—sometimes disguised and 'coded' because of censorship—is contained a whole chronicle of the lives of Chilean workers today, their problems, all the things that affect them most. You see the day of the Coup, the troops running in the streets; you see the prisons, especially from the point of view of women visiting their men, or trying to find out where they have been taken. You see all the problems of the shanty-towns: the *comedores* (collective kitchens organized to feed the children); a woman going from house to house asking neighbours to look after her child while she searches for work; children selling sweets along the main roads in order to survive; searching the dustbins at night for scraps of food; the cemetery crowded with family names. Sometimes the artist tries to synthesize or to sum up the situation, and then two tendencies appear. One is the religious explanation. Suffering is shown as a modern Way of the Cross; or, for example, a flock of sheep is shown attacked by an eagle. This is the style of lamentation. The other is the analysis of society and of class, the militant style. An example of this kind is the diagram-patchwork showing the dollar hovering over the Chilean economy. On the whole, there are few pictures which do not contain, in some segment, in some detail, an element of hope.

I mentioned before the 'childlike' style of these pictures. The development of modern art has made people in Western countries receptive to the appeal of naivity in art. We have followed painters like Picasso and Klee as they adopted in their own work the spontaneous styles of untrained people, or of artists outside European traditions. This in turn has stimulated a market in which naive art has become a commodity, a fixed category which cannot be allowed to change. To look at the Chilean pictures from that point of view would be patronising and wrong. Their technique is what it is because of circumstances. To get to grips with reality, to go into it deeper, they have every reason to develop their expression.

And this can be felt in many patchworks. The artists are searching for a visual means to express links between events in life, to clarify their own comprehension of society, and therefore to help others and to aid in an effective resistance. Also, naivity has certain advantages. Already certain details which migh appear merely charming and naive (for example, the 'farmyard' scene in the patchwork of the circus) are deliberate disguises for references to real people and places in Chile which cannot be openly shown.

We tend to idolise a conception of 'free expression' in art, perhaps without realising what a great part necessity has played in the evolution of cultural expression in history. Many distinctive styles in all art forms have evolved through the ingenuity of people in evading prejudices, taboos and censorship. One of the characteristics of popular art is this resourcefulness, making use of whatever is to hand (as in the case of these patchworks), without the inhibition which can come from believing in the 'property' of particular materials.

As well as this, the pictures contain many elements which are not dependent on a 'primitive' mode of expression, indications of a popular, democratic art and attitude to life which can be found in any nation and can be expressed in any number of ways.

Even in the most elementary composition there are still details which are given great exactness: for example, how manual work is done; 'machines' which make life easier (eg. the gas-burners under the cauldrons of soup in the *comedores*); the playfulness of children; and always as a background, in any number of colours, the Andes, the magnificent mountains which surround the city of Santiago and stretch like a backbone through the whole of Chile.

The mountains are a continuous reference point above the events in each picture. It is easy to understand their meaning: we will one day become free in our own land. The miserable material conditions which cramp our lives will one day be over and our lives will have the scale of our mountains. This is an expression of feeling that no 'censorship' can succeed in hiding.

Similarly with the artistic aspects, it could be called a matter of dignity, of one's conception of oneself as a human being, which leads the people making these patchworks, however bitter the subject, to use all the art they know, to bring out the hidden qualities and beauty in the thrown-away scraps of material:

"Apart from all this, it's a great joy that people consider that we are making art, that we are artists in this. For us, as housewives, we have never been, or dreamt of being artists or working in that sort of thing. In this there's some compensation for all that's happened. It gives us more strength to go on, to go on struggling to live. God willing, we'll be able to make them better every day."

The shanty-town itself has a double character. The poverty of the houses is not glossed over, the single crude lavatory for the whole settlement is shown, even that it's full of flies. But other details are included with pride: a table and chairs inside each house, flowers, the electric street-lamps and their cables. And there are always people. The way the shanty-town is depicted carries the message that the people must advance step by step from the real situation they are in, and that their advance must be a common one that all benefit from.

There is no rhetoric in these pictures, and very rarely is an expression isolated and carried to extremes. All the undertones and incidentals in the patchworks give an impression of tremendous reserves of strength, of a kind of balance and resilience in the people, in the face of the worst the authorities can do.

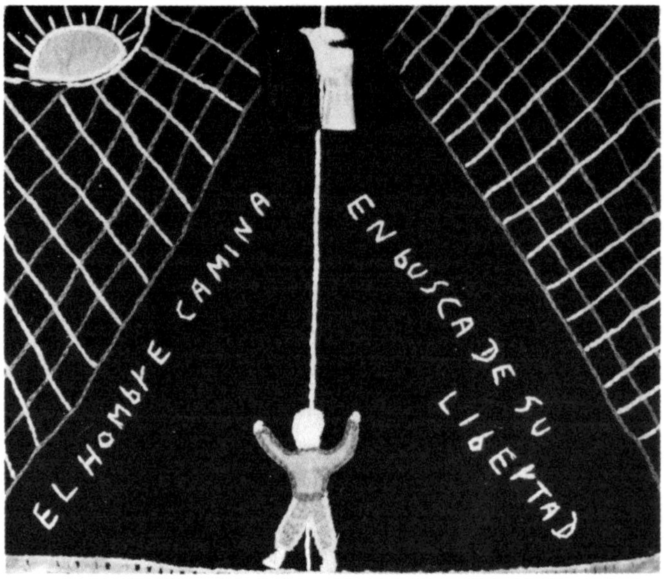

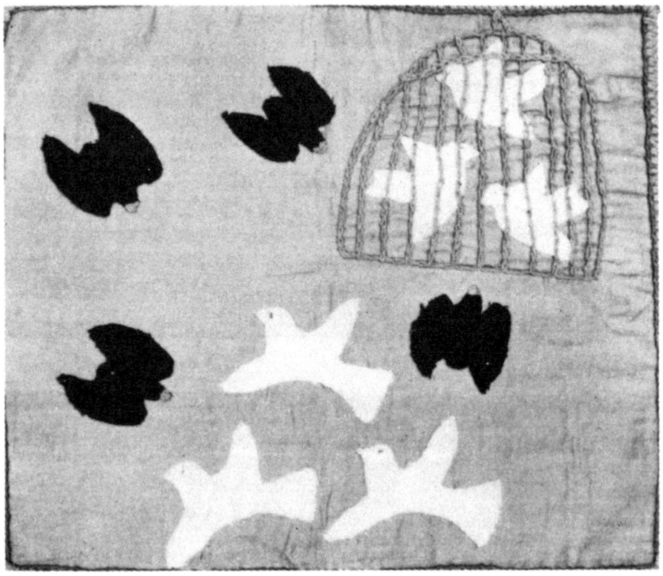

The patchworks will be on display at the AIR GALLERY, 125 Shaftesbury Avenue, London WC2, from the middle to the end of March 1978.

Full colour postcards of the patchworks are available from Chile Committee for Human Rights, 1 Cambridge Terrace, London NW1.
Price 10p each or £1.10 for 12, enclose sae.

The search for identity in CONTEMPORARY NIGERIAN ART[1]

Babatunde Lawal

Contemporary Nigerian art is a reflection of a society in the throes of change. Modern technology is transforming the old order, precipitating a socio-cultural metamorphosis of unprecedented proportions, and art in Nigeria today is a concoction of the old and the new: there is a frantic bid to forge a national identity out of the multi-ethnic images of the past. Unlike his traditional counterpart, the contemporary artist is not restricted to the formal repertoire of his own ethnic group. Ther very fact of his being a Nigerian has legitimized his heirship to the artistic heritage of all the various ethnic groups that now constitute Nigeria. Besides, new religious and economic forces, coupled with rapid industrialization and urbanization, are compounding his experience. Then there is the modern art school, which exposes him to new materials and techniques as well as to the potential influence of other world cultures.

In the era preceding independence, contemporary Nigerian art was for the most part a provincial extension of European modes—a good majority of the artists having been trained in European-type art schools. But in spite of the ebullient appreciation of traditional African art in Europe and America and the crucial role it played in the birth of modern Euro-American art, the teaching of traditional art was largely ignored in Nigerian schools, most of which were owned by missionaries who associated traditional art with paganism.

In the 1960s, following Nigeria's attainment of political independence and the resultant outbursts of nationalism and the call for the revival of her cultural heritage, the need to project a 'Nigerian personality' in art became more imperative than before. Artists not only incorporated traditional forms and motifs into their works but also drew inspiration from folklore and myths. The Society of Nigerian Artists was formed in 1964 to protect the interest of its members as well as to educate the public in matters of art through exhibitions, public lectures and symposia.

However, since the production of art, like any other commodity, largely depends on the 'law of supply and demand', contemporary Nigerian art was to be greatly handicapped by a lack of patronage from the new Nigerian elites who were being attracted by more ostentatious ways of showing off their newly-acquired status. Besides, the depreciation of traditional art by the missionaries, coupled with the neglect of art in schools, had created a 'communication gap' between the artist and the elites. In short, contemporary Nigerian art had to rely for a long time on foreign patronage.

Meanwhile a revival of academic and ethnographic interest in traditional African art was gaining momentum in Europe and America, with the result that many scholars and tourists visited Africa, combing the rural areas for remnants of traditional art. Contemporary African art was largely ignored, being regarded as a watered-down version of European art. Thus William Fagg and Margaret Plass could write in 1964: 'African contemporary art is in large part merely a demonstration that Africans—who are no less well-endowed with artistic genius and intelligence than people of other races—are quite capable of working in the international style of art . . . Rarely in human history can a people have been confronted with an overt and conscious choice between having an art of their own—their greatest contribution to the richness of human culture—and adopting one from abroad, from a supposedly higher civilisation.'[2]

Nevertheless, many of the few foreign patrons who ventured into collecting contemporary Nigerian art were considerably influenced either by their own Euro-American tradition or by the type of image they wished to see of Africa in art; while the artist himself, having studied the market closely, pandered to the tastes of his patrons. Nigerians interested in good quality art were usually put off by the high price which the artist was accustomed to charging his foreign patrons but which only a few Nigerians could afford.[3] As a result, many Nigerians had to content themselves with the cheapest work, or cheap reproductions of works of European artists. In any case, partly because of the different tastes of the patrons and partly because of the different educational background of the artists, contemporary Nigerian art was to develop along four major directions, ie. Neo-traditional art, Signwriter's art, Osogbo art and Avant-Garde art.

Neo-Traditional Art

This has been encouraged partly by the souvenir-hungry tourist and partly by the desire to save traditional art from extinction by finding a new context for it in modern living rooms, public buildings, churches and the like. In the Nigerian context, the term neo-traditional refers to a contemporary artist who has either been trained to work in the traditional style but who now works largely for the tourist market, or has been trained in the modern art school but now works in the traditional style. Although neo-traditional artists such as Lamidi Fakeye, Ben Aye, Festus Idehen, Paul Osifo and Felix Idubor (especially his early works) sometimes succeed in capturing some of the plastic integrity of traditional sculpture, a good majority of neo-traditional art is simply inferior to its traditional models. Yet the carved ebony figure, especially, with its blank, rigid and smoothly polished appearance, sells like hot cakes at airports and hotels. One tourist is reported to have bought an ebony figure because it reminded him of 'Old Africa' in the stupefying glare of modern technology! Such was the demand for this type of art that some academically trained artists were on occasions tempted to 'throw in' a few pieces to the same market.

On the other hand, there was the attempt by the Catholic Church to adapt traditional art to Christian usage. A workshop was set up at Oye-Ekiti in the 1940s where traditional artists and craftsmen worked for the Church, 'manufacturing' madonnas, crucifixes, crib-sets for Christmas, doors, altar-pieces, and so on.[4] Although the workshop produced some admirable pieces initially, it soon ran out of fuel. Traditional art had been severed from its umbilical sustenance, that is, traditional culture and religion: many of the workshop products turned out to be still-born—rigid and wanting in inspiration and expression. For they are now destined for a purely decorative-cum-illustrative context.

Another reason for the dullness of neo-traditional art might be found in the fact that it is frequently produced under factory conditions to meet the heavy demand of the tourist market. As a result, the neo-traditional artist has developed a mechanical attitude to his work, quantity rather than quality being his primary objective. The traditional artist by contrast, worked only to commissions, producing at a slower rate and executing each commission to the best of his ability, although the status of a patron and/or the price to be paid often determined the quality of the work produced.

In any case, a revival of the past for its own sake has deprived neo-traditional art of a soul, which no art can have without being firmly rooted in the socio-cultural dynamics of its own era. What is needed

FELIX IDUBOR *The White Stool* (or *Seated Goddess*) 1960

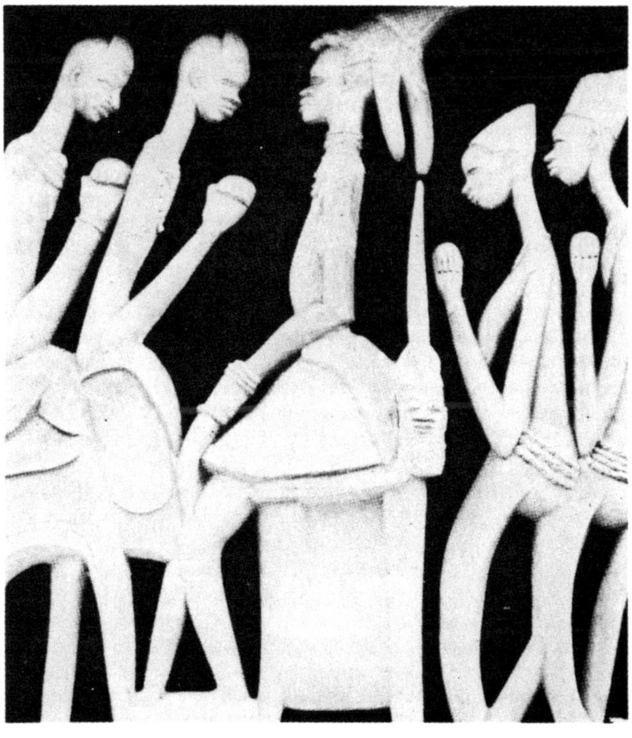

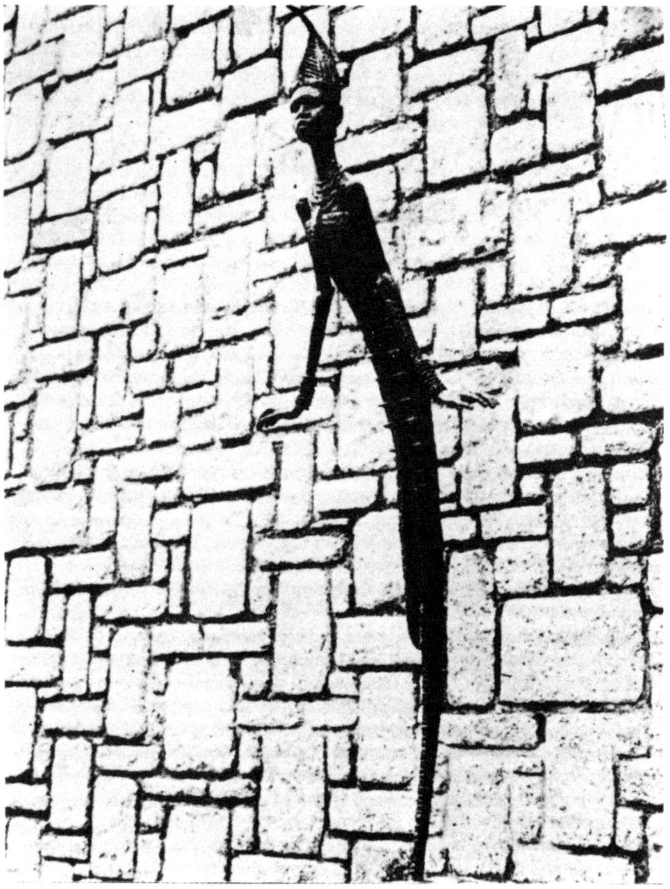

BEN ENWONWU *Anyanwu* (The Rising Sun) 1960

FESTUS IDEHEN *Standing Figure* 1960s

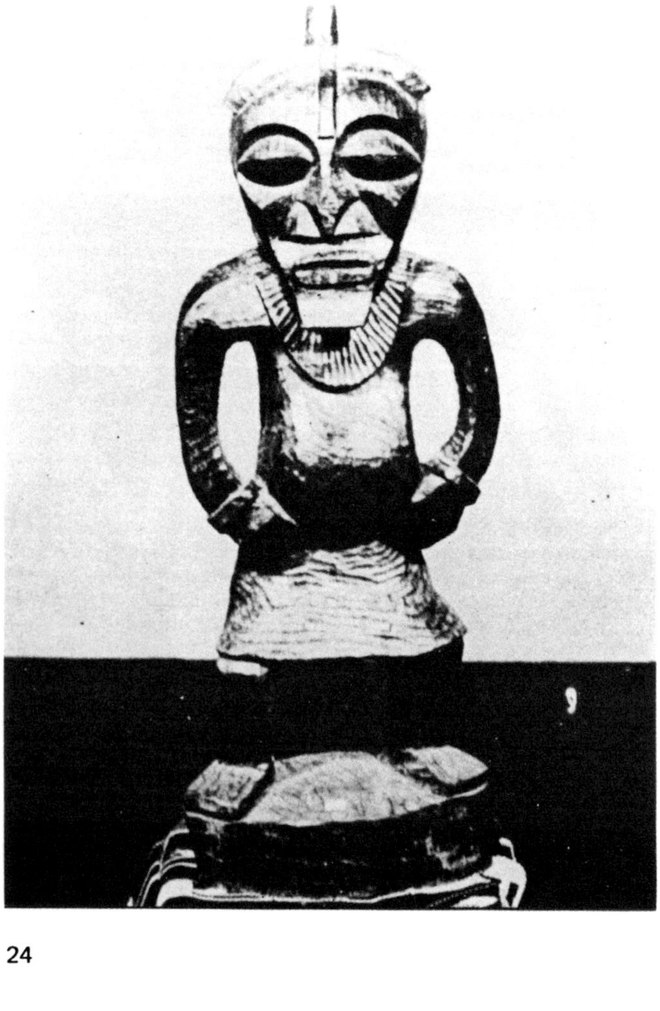

now is a new art that will reflect the cultural realities of the present, while at the same time retaining a link with the past.

Fortunately, artists like Felix Idubor, Festus Idehen and Anthony Efionayi have since realized the limitations of imitating traditional forms and have begun to break new ground. As far back as the 1960s, both Idubor and Idehen distorted their forms to create a 'modern effect', while still retaining some of the characteristics of traditional sculpture.[5] But in recent years, Idubor has been producing more realistic works, though these are not as interesting as his stylized ones. Both Anthony Efionayi and Geoffrey Nwogu have turned their attention to illustrating myths and folklore, creating intricate sculptural forms of great appeal and showing clearly that the neo-traditional artist is no less talented than his traditional counterpart—if only he would pay more attention to quality rather than commercial quantity. By and large, the new directions of Efionayi and Nwogu give us every reason to hope that the neo-traditional artist may not be doomed to becoming a living fossil after all. His salvation lies in how well he can use his imagination to adapt his traditional skills to contemporary realities. In the process, he would have created a new identity for himself instead of masquerading, as he does at the moment, in the robes of his ancestors.

Signwriter's Art

This is the product of the artist who, strictly speaking, has had no formal education in art, be it traditional or modern. He is usually self-taught, having acquired a certain degree of proficiency from copying illustrations and photographs from newspapers and magazines. Sometimes, he may have been introduced to art in the primary school; but unable to go to the secondary school either because of money or otherwise, he ends up taking art as a profession. More often, he begins his career as an apprentice in a signwriter's studio where he is trained in free-hand lettering, spray-painting and other skills. On completing his apprenticeship (which may last between three and five years) he sets up his own signwriting studio, producing signboards for all classes of traders. In addition, he decorates lorries, buses and taxi-cabs, as well as painting murals for night-clubs. In his spare time, he produces small land- and sea-scapes (often copied from beach photographs), using glossy enamel colours. Characterized by a simplistic design and representation, these paintings often betray his limited knowledge of perspective and human anatomy.[6]

Nevertheless, being very cheap and brightly coloured, these paintings have continued to attract the attention of some members of the Nigerian middle class, who like to hang paintings in their living rooms but cannot afford the high price being demanded by the avant-garde artists whose paintings, on the other hand, are not as 'down to earth'. Suffice to say that, since he caters mainly for a local public whose interest in painting lies more in its 'furniture' value than in its intrinsic aesthetic quality, the signwriter hardly bothers himself with the question of a Nigerian identity so long as there is a market for whatever he produces. However, since his land- and sea-scapes are usually ignored by the tourist, to whom they have no specifically Nigerian character, the signwriter has recently been turning out paintings of traditional masks, masquerades and dancers in a desperate attempt to break the monopoly hitherto enjoyed by neo-traditional art.

Osogbo Art

If it took the art of the signwriter such a long time to attract the attention of the tourist, it is partly because of a lack of adequate publicity and partly because it did not involve itself, until relatively recently, in the 'politics' of identity. For these are the factors which helped a more recent phenomenon known as Osogbo art to hit the headlines, both at home and abroad, almost overnight. Osogbo art was initiated at Osogbo in the Western part of Nigeria between 1961 and 1962 by a German national called Ulli Beier. All he did was to sponsor a series of workshops where paint, brush and paper were provided for anybody, especially the jobless, to give free rein to their sub-conscious artistic impulses. The result was a psychodramatic outpouring of images that sometimes invites comparison with psychotic art.[7] In the words of Ulli Beier himself: 'Once a kind of enthusiasm was created, the images began to pour out. The time allowed for the course was not even enough to bother much about techniques. The crudest and cheapest medium was used: emulsion paint on hardboard. The delicate job of the teacher was to move the student in the right direction by a careful selection process . . . It was interesting to see that even though Yoruba folklore often supplied the theme of the painting, the work owed nothing to Yoruba tradition, showed no influence of more recent forms of Yoruba folk art and was not derived from European advertising or illustrations with which the students had been in contact.'[8]

Being essentially an exercise in colour doodling and simplistic representation, Osogbo art no doubt belongs in that category of modern European art which glorifies the primitivism of a naive or 'surrealistic' vision. To quote Ulli Beier again: 'Each student produced three or four paintings a day from which the best were selected every evening and hung till the next evening. By selecting the stronger images, the more honest pictures, and discarding the ones that were derivative or borrowed, the teacher could give direction to the work.'[9]

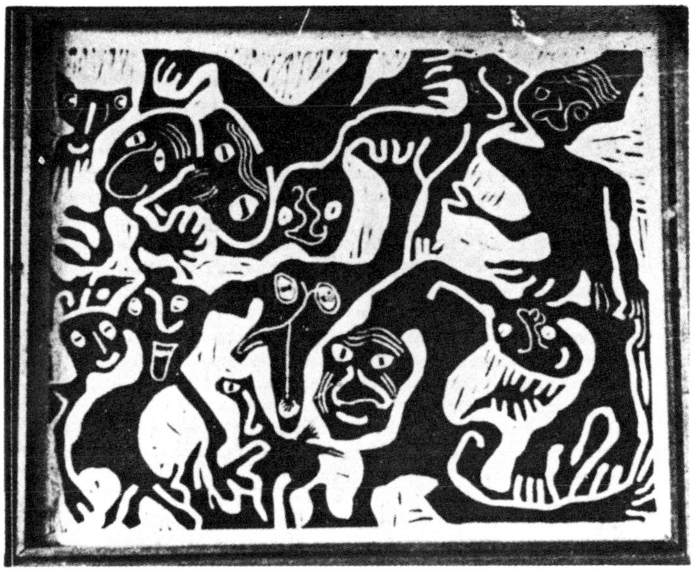

JACOB AFOLABI, Untitled Lino-cut, 1964

Evidently. in the process of 'selecting the stronger images, the more honest pictures', the directors of the Osogbo workshop were indirectly influencing the student to produce a certain species of work which eventually became stereotyped. One can liken this situation to a kind of artificial insemination, since much of Osogbo art has more European than African features. Commenting on Adebisi Fabunmi's lino-cuts, Ulli Beier writes: 'The boldness of the cutting, the symbolism, and the strain and stress pattern of the design give a strong expressionist feeling to these lino-cuts, not unlike some of the woodcuts of the *Brucke* painters early this century.'[10]

There can be no gainsaying that Ulli Beier had been genuinely worried by the Europeanizing tendencies of much contemporary Nigerian art of the 1940s and 1950s, and was eager to pioneer the search for a Nigerian identity. Unfortunately all he achieved, either by accident or by design, is a vicarious projection of his own artistic vision. As Demas Nwoko has pointed out: 'The result of Ulli's school is the existence of half-baked young artists who are completely ignorant of what they are doing, but continue to produce suggested results because they find a ready market in Europe and America.'[11]

At home, Osogbo art was viewed with curiosity, being regarded as a kind of fodder for the tourist, who is usually enchanted by its naivity as well as by the claim that it is a visual projection of Yoruba myths and folklore. But my own experience with some of the artists has revealed that many of the mythological titles are afterthoughts: on one or two occasions, I have been asked by one of the artists to help suggest titles. This is hinted at by Ulli Beier himself in his comment on the paintings of Taiwo Olaniyi (alias Twin Seven-Seven): 'Many of his literary ideas seem afterthoughts of design. Even accidental ink blots immediately suggest shapes to him, and shapes suggest stories.'[12]

In the case of Adebisi Fabunmi's series of lino-cuts of cities, Ulli Beier writes: 'Whether they represent West African towns like *Lagos* and *Takoradi*, or European cities like *Berlin* and *Russian Town,* or whether they are purely imaginary themes like *Ghost Town* or *The Hanging Gardens of Babylon*, the towns all show a certain family likeness.'[13] As a matter of fact, much of Osogbo art is characterized by 'a certain family likeness'—as it were, the vision of a fairyland—so much so that its group exhibition sometimes looks like a one-man show in which even paintings by Georgina Beier are hardly distinguishable.

Depending largely as ti did on Ulli Beier's sustenance and promotion, Osogbo art was to wane rapidly on his departure from Nigeria in 1967.[14] And since they were mostly illiterates who lacked the residual skill as well as the moral conviction to sustain such an art of pure form, a good number of the Osogbo artists now loiter about like army deserters, looking for new employment. What started out as, and promised to be, a short-cut to 'Picasso's Paradise' has suddenly ended up in a labyrinth. Many of the treasure-hunters are now at their wits' end.

Incidentally, Ulli Beier, on leaving Nigeria, has since introduced the Osogbo experiment to New Guinea; and, as expected, the results are the same. Michele Gilbert has aptly summed up the situation: 'The modern New Guinea art which is being introduced under his tutelage, . . . while exhibiting some indigenous iconographic motifs, is in style and media . . . practically identical to that which he formerly helped to develop in Nigeria . . . What is unfortunate, However, when one compares these two groups in New Guinea and Nigeria, is the striking extent to which the style and taste of the Beiers seem to be reflected in the work of artists which they have chosen to promote from these two areas. This has led to a certain "sameness". Does this mean that the Beiers have suppressed indigenous aesthetic values in both these places? If this art is being done for a European market, then surely the demand in our own culture for "individuality" and "originality" in art may destroy the European market for both these schools. On the other hand, if this art is being independently produced for an indigenous but non-traditional market, then it is remarkable how art with such great stylistic similarities has been produced in two very disparate cultures with only one thing in common, the presence of the Beiers.'[15]

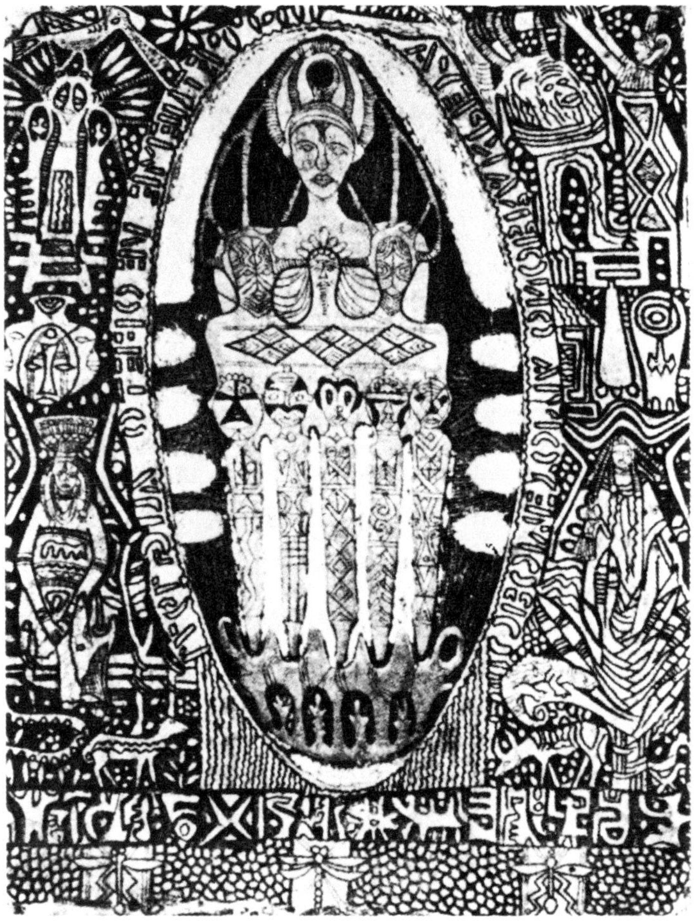

BRUCE ONOBRAKPEYA *Ufete* (The Comb) 1971

Nonetheless, a few of the Osogbo artists, like Taiwo Olaniyi (Twin Seven-Seven), Muraino Oyelami and Jimo Buraimo, have produced some farily accomplished works which, as modern art, will hold their own anywhere in the world. Notwithstanding the shortcomings of the Osogbo experiment, Ulli Beier must be praised for his contributions to the course of artistic development in Nigeria, as well as for providing gainful employment for people who would otherwise have been jobless, thereby becoming a potential menace to society. And even if many Nigerian intellectuals are against the type of identity he has tried to give Nigeria abroad, he has at least succeeded in forcing the academic artists to search for an alternative identity, rather than be content with merely imitating European modes. If only the remaining Osogbo artists would now shake off the apparitions of the workshop and use the experience gained so far to develop an independent vision as well as an 'artistic conscience' of their own, they are likely to produce better and more recognisably Nigerian works in the future.

Avant-Garde Art

This is essentially the product of Nigerians who have been trained in the modern art school. The first generation of Nigeria's avant-garde artists were either trained abroad or at the Nigerian College of Arts, Science and Technology (now Ahmadu Bello University) Zaria, whose staff was predominantly expatriate. So it was that the avant-garde artists of the 1940s and the 1950s were more European than African. However, the nationalistic climate of the post-independence era not only caused those artists to begin to 'Nigerianize' their forms; there was also a gradual Nigerianization of the teaching staff in the art schools, as well as the syllabus. Today, the art departments of Ahmadu Bello University, Zaria, the University of Nigeria, Nsukka, and the University of Ife, Ile-Ife, are headed by Nigerians who also constitute the majority of the teaching staff. Predictably, the new generation of avant-garde artists are more Nigerian in outlook.

The problem facing the avant-garde artist, however, is how to use his newly-acquired materials and techniques to produce a truly Nigerian form while still retaining his individuality. So far, most of the

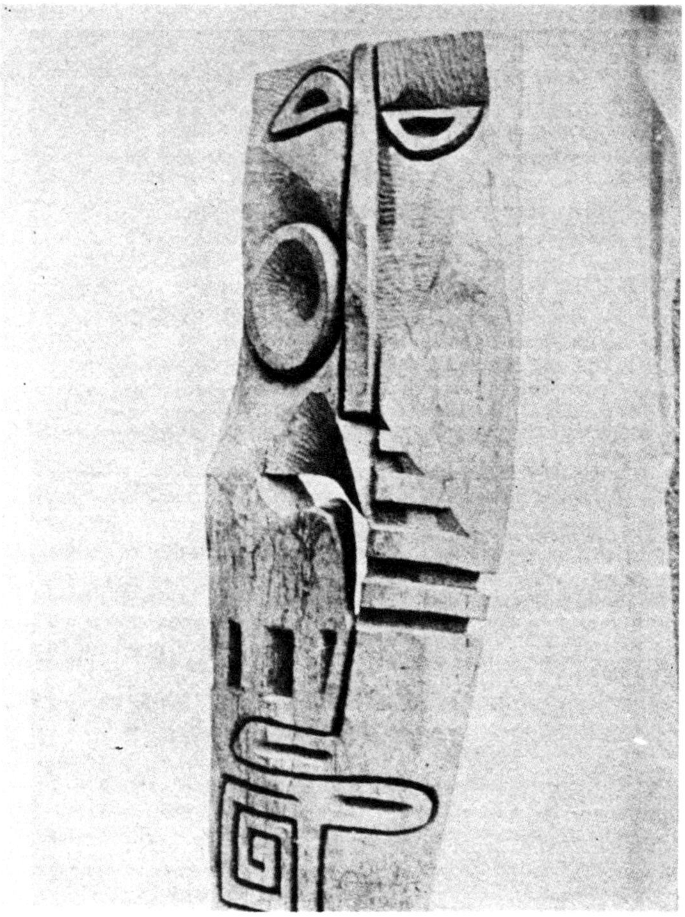

BEN OSAWE *Mask 1* 1970

Judiciary.[19] The uniqueness of this synthesis lies in the expressiveness of the *whole*, rather than in the individualities of the 'ethnic' parts. In his recent series of lithographs on 'African Dances', Ben Enwonwu has succeeded not only in capturing the rhythmical movement of the African dance but also the 'soul' of the dancers.

Demas Nwoko is blazing a new trail in the field of architecture. His New Culture Studio and the church he recently built for the Dominican Order at Ibadan are a successful blend of the spatial orientation of indigenous Nigerian architecture, and the plastic as well as the decorative qualities of traditional sculpture, into contemporary architecture. How blind most modern Nigerian architects have been to these qualities! How long shall they continue to imitate European architectural modes which are more often unsuited to our environmental conditions? It may be true that indigenous architectural technology simply cannot cope with the needs of our era, yet this should not obscure the qualities of traditional architectural forms. The problem probably lies in the fact that Nigeria still depends mostly on Euro-America for the training of her architects. Not until this situation is drastically revised will there evolve a modern architectural form that she can proudly call her own, apart from the economic advantages that will accrue from such a development.

Limitations of space will not allow me to discuss the other artists who are extending the frontiers of contemporary art in Nigeria. Notwithstanding the faltering steps—which are inevitable in any developmental process—much of Nigerian avant-garde art of the 1970s reveals a genuine search for authenticity. The Europeanizing tendencies of the 1950s and early 1960s are beginning to disappear. A new Nigerian breed is in the making.

However, if these expectations are not to become a mere illusion, the current 'communication gap' between the artist and the Nigerian public must be bridged. A lot of art education needs to be done to create a favourable local climate for artistic development and its appreciation. The Society of Nigerian Artists has an important role to play in this regard. For instance, the high price currently being charged by the avant-garde artists especially, even for canvases that are no more than a few splashes of paint, must be reconsidered if many Nigerians are to be encouraged to patronize the arts and influence their direction.

artists in this category have contented themselves with the Nigerianization of only the subject-matter—which then makes their work hardly distinguishable from that of a Maurice Fievet or any other European artist interested in a similar phenomenon. Another group of artists simply see art, especially in its modern form, as an international language, and hardly bother themselves with the question of a Nigerian identity, so long as there is a ready market for whatever is produced. The outcome of this attitude is the 'European imitation' hinted at by William Fagg and Margaret Plass. The paradox is that while contemporary Western art is trying to 'Africanize', this brand of Nigerian avant-garde art is trying to 'Westernize'! Only a few avant-garde artists have seriously addressed themselves to the question of creating a new plastic idiom that will not only forge a link with the past but will also relate to the present, while at the same time sowing new seeds for the future.

On the face of it, a very simple solution may seem to lie in the mere inclusion or transplantation of traditional forms into contemporary painting and sculpture. But then, this might end up an an archaism, especially if done in a slavish manner. A more profitable approach might perhaps be found in an *analytic* study of traditional forms and symbols to be followed by a *synthetic* adaptation to contemporary painting, sculpture, architecture, etc.[16]

Quite a number of the avant-garde artists, like Ben Enwonwu, Bruce Onobrakpeya, Ben Osawe, Ayo Ajayi, Uche Okeke and Demas Nwoko, are already working in this direction. Admittedly, the problem posed by the new materials and techniques is yet to be fully resolved, but the indigenization of form (as distinct from subject-matter) is at a very advanced stage.

Most especially, the forms of Bruce Onobrakpeya are beginning to look more Nigerian than before, radiating a rich indigenous African light that is unique. In his *Ufeto* for instance, Hausa/Fulani, Ibo, Ibibio, Yoruba and Urhobo motifs combine to reflect the cultural diversity of Nigeria.[17] It is an artistic statement of 'unity in diversity'—a popular political slogan in Nigeria. Meaning the comb in the Urhobo language, although the overall design has been inspired by Yoruba adire textile,[18] *Ufeto* focuses on the question of the relationship between the comb and the hair. The central figure, an anthropomorphic comb identifiable with Mother-Nigeria, unites all the ethnic elements in the composition, just as the ordinary comb 'organises' and 'shapes' the hair. The capitation of the teeth of the comb and their rendering as masks recall the role of the latter as the functionaries of the traditional gods and hence agents of social control—a function that has since been taken over by new institutions such as the Press, the Police and the

1 Revised version of a paper first presented at a symposium on Contemporary Nigerian Art, Department of Fine and Applied Arts, University of Nigeria, Nsukka, 22-25 March 1976. I wish to thank the West African Aggrey Society and the Edward W. Hazen Foundation of USA for supporting my research into Contemporary Nigerian Art.
2 W. Fagg and M. Plass, *African Sculpture*, London, 1964, p7.
3 See for instance, C. Ekwensi, 'High Price of Nigerian Art', *Nigeria Magazine*, 88, (March 1966), pp36-41; and Yusufu Zaki, 'Towards an Art Revolution (Reader's Letters)', *Nigeria Magazine*, 87, (December 1965), pp235; 305.
4 For details, see K. Carroll, *Yoruba Religious Carving, Pagan and Christian Sculpture in Nigeria and Dahomey*, London, 1967.
5 See Idubor's relief sculpture on Nigeria's Independence Building at the Tafawa Balewa's Square, Lagos, and Idehen's 'cubist' sculpture illustrated in U. Beier, 'Contemporary Nigerian Art', *Nigeria Magazine*, 68, (March 1961), pp40-41.
6 See U. Beier, 'Signwriters Art in Nigeria', *African Arts*, IV 3 (Spring 1971), pp22-27.
7 For details of the Osogbo experiment, see U. Beier, *Contemporary Art in Africa*, Praeger, 1968.
8 Ibid., pp107-8.
9 Ibid., p107.
10 Ibid., p122.
11 D. Nwoko, 'The Search for a New African Theatre', *Presence Africaine*, no. 75, 3 (1970), p67.
12 Beier, *Contemporary Art in Africa*, p116.
13 Ibid., p121.
14 Ulli Beier returned to Nigeria in 1972 but left again in 1974. Between 1968 and 1972, the University of Ife established the Ori Olokun Centre where a workshop was established which operated like that of Osogbo. Unfortunately, since the pioneers of the Osogbo workshop had already created a tourist market with a particular style, the Ori Olokun artists continued the same style. But when Ulli Beier assumed the Directorship of the Institute of African Studies of the University of Ife, he disbanded the Ori Olokun artists, regarding them as copy-cats.
15 M.V. Gilbert, in a letter to the editor of *African Arts*, published in volume IX, no 2 (January 1976), pp2-3.
16 See also B. Lawal, 'The Artist as a Creative Force in Education and Society', *Presence Africaine*, 86, 2 (1972)
17 See B. Lawal, 'The Mythical Realism of Bruce Onobrakpeya', *Nigeria Magazine*, 120, (June 1976), pp53-56.
18 Compare the format of *Ufeto* with the *adire oloba* illustrated in J. Babour and D. Simmonds (eds), *Adire Cloth in Nigeria*, Ibadan University Press, 1971, figs.1-7.
19 Lawal, 'The Mythical Realism of Bruce Onobrakpeya', op.cit., p55.

A GLANCE AT THE MODERN URBAN DEVELOPMENTS IN THE MIDDLE EAST*

Ayyub Malik

All through history cities have withstood many pressures and undergone changes. Small cities grew larger and became centres of culture or government. Owing to natural disasters or invasions they fell out of favour or disappeared. Most cities, however, managed to adjust to change and absorb new populations and technologies without greatly altering their essential character. New people came in and settled in separate districts and in time evolved a lifestyle and skills that enhanced and enriched the city. Bust mostly the changes were small in scale and effect and the city generally continued to maintain its social momentum and its predominant character.

The unprecedented scale and speed of changes and the movements of populations brought about by the Industrial Revolution in the West created new problems the city had not encountered before. Owing to the internal dynamism of this change the city in the process of its development acquired an administrative structure and many specialists to deal with its many problems. With time, the administration grew in size and became more centralised and sophisticated and the specialists more isolated in their individual disciplines and institutions. The complicated legislation and regulations on the one hand and the professional mystification of simpler human needs on the other, deprived the residents from the full understanding, participation and involvement in the shaping and working of their city. Frequently the administration has been accused of being cumbersome, expensive, inefficient and politically motivated, and the experts of being involved more in their abstract polemics, design theories and maximising the profits of their clients than in the human and social needs of the residents.

It is difficult to explain in detail the roles and responsibilities of the administrative, planning and professional bodies in making the cities as they are. It may, however, be useful to briefly look at them through the eyes of the city's aggrieved residents and social thinkers.

To the administration, the city is a place full of problems to be solved for which progressively more money must be raised by taxes, rates and borrowing. This makes the city increasingly expensive to live in, forcing people to move out, reducing the city's income and making it even more expensive for the remaining residents. More money is somehow raised to subsidise the remaining population, to support the city's service industries and thus maintain its essential amenities. The accusation that the city's administration looks at the residents as mere numbers to be retained, housed and commuted, and that it understands little or pays no attention to their social and community needs, may not be altogether without foundation.

The traffic and transport engineers, in their aim to increase mass mobility, forget the simple needs of people to move around themselves in their city and instead concentrate on the number of cars and trend statistics to plan the size and routes of urban roads. The fact that the urban motorways rip apart long established human communities and

* In 1976 I was invited by KING ABDUL AZIZ UNIVERSITY, Jeddah, to visit Saudi Arabia, and as a result I produced a paper for the Islamic Conference held in London, 21 May 1977. This article is the summarized version of that paper.

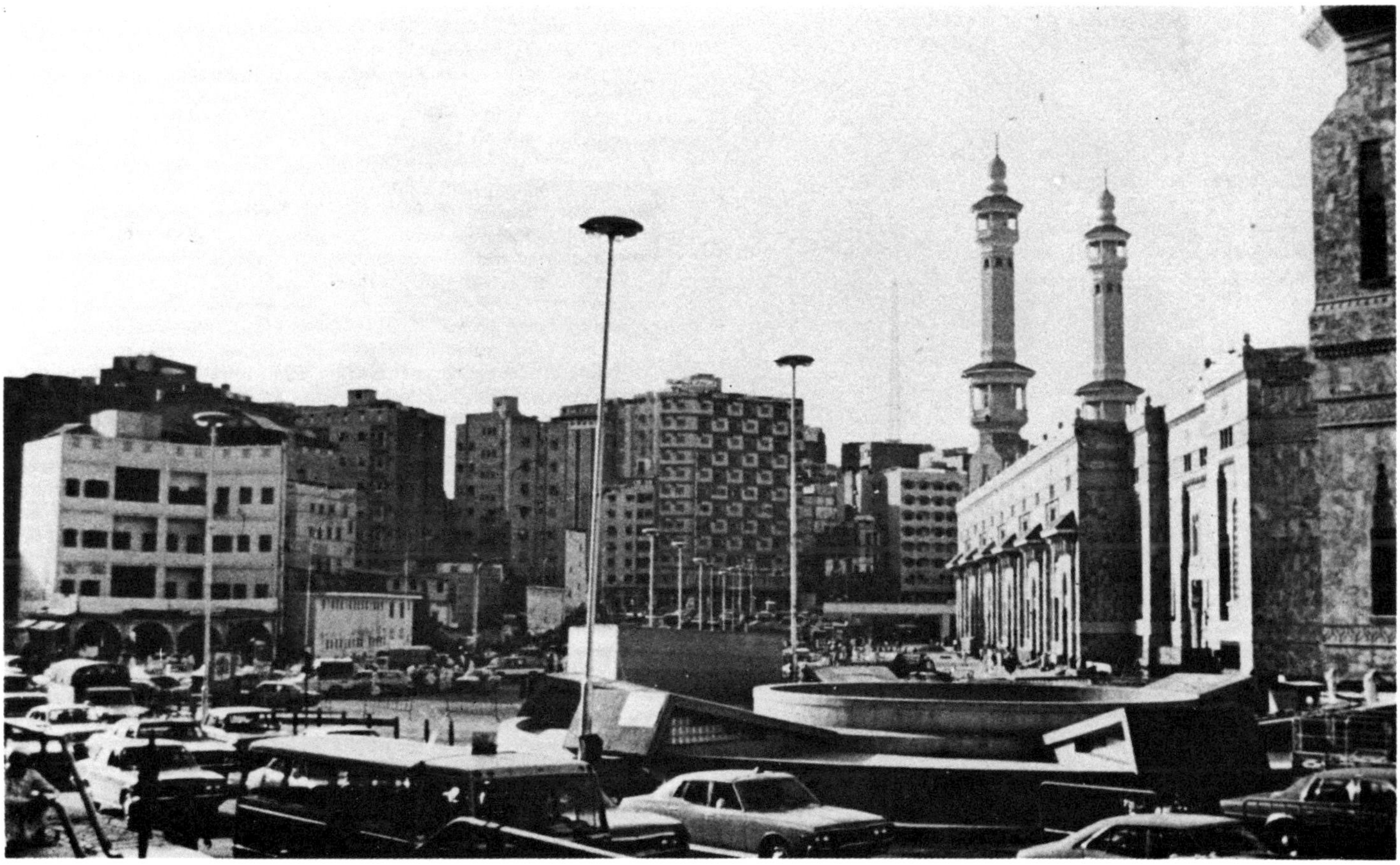

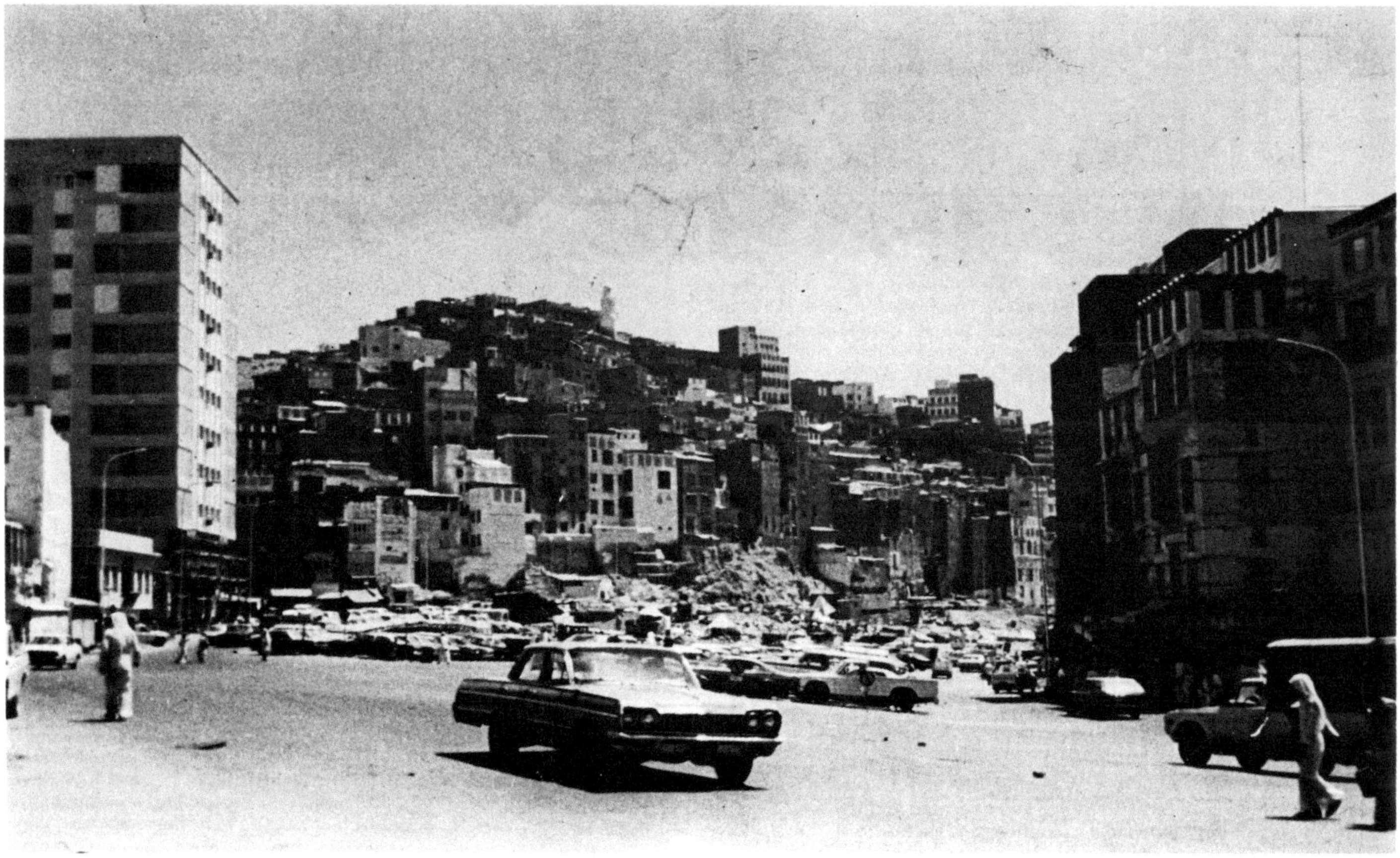

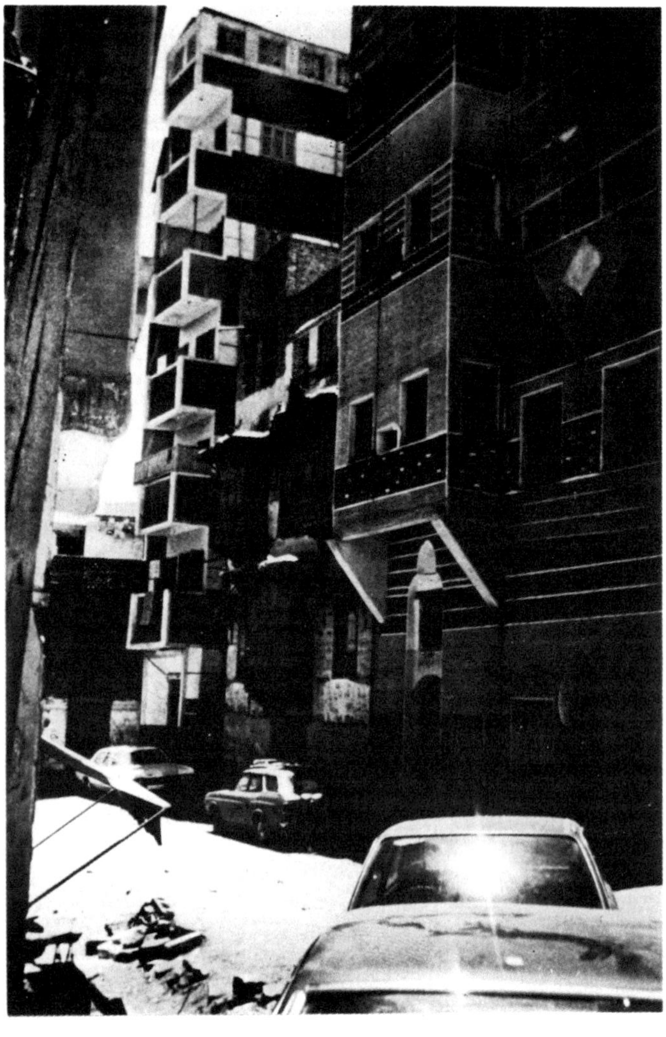

areas of outstanding historical views is of secondary importance.

The planner looks at the city as well-defined isolated districts for living, business, administration, and small and heavy industries, separated by major traffic routes. The diverse, organic and active human nature of the city does not quite lend itself to his 'scientific' analysis and statistics.

The architect, in his desire to participate in creating a technological lifestyle and environment, concentrates on expressing in his buildings the nature of materials and their manufacture. The many diverse requirements and elements of his buildings are neatly packaged in a geometrical box of repetitive elements to produce startling photographic compositions. The fact that this approach degrades the existing visual and historical quality of the city and ignores human scale is not much considered.

The developer sees the city as a place for the exercise of minimum investment for maximum profit. The constant innovatory capacity of the modern technology to increasingly produce cheaper, untried and ill-fitting components help him and his consultants to achieve their aim. Today's developers are the multi-corporate financial institutions, manufacturing and trade corporations and large government bodies. The corporate nature of their investment policies and decision-making, motivated only by maximum profits, develop vast new areas of the city where all the roads, streets and buildings look alike. This destroys the city's historic uniqueness, lifestyle, individuality and sense of place.

Being the first to witness and experience the consequences of the indiscriminate industrial developments, people in the West have demanded for quite some time, and are being increasingly successful in affecting, fundamental changes in official policies towards their towns and cities. There is a progressive awareness and realisation that the present structure of city administrators and experts has grown to the point where there is no overall control or comprehension of the city as an intricate social balance or a human and cultural organism. And this, together with the exclusion of the residents in decision-making processes, has resulted in the inhuman scale and nature of the changes in the cities, which are now constantly in the headlines for being in trouble and unworkable. The people now realise that as long as they delegate their responsibilities to others to decide what is best for them, their cities will always be in trouble.

The positive result of this realisation is that efforts are being made to reduce remote bureaucratic decision-making and to provide increasing opportunities for public participation to affect the development and running of the cities. In time, this will create more social involvement and civic responsibility, a style of life less exploitative and profitable, but more diverse, creative and conducive to human satisfaction and social ideals. In many European and American cities, a start in this direction has already been made. Large decaying old

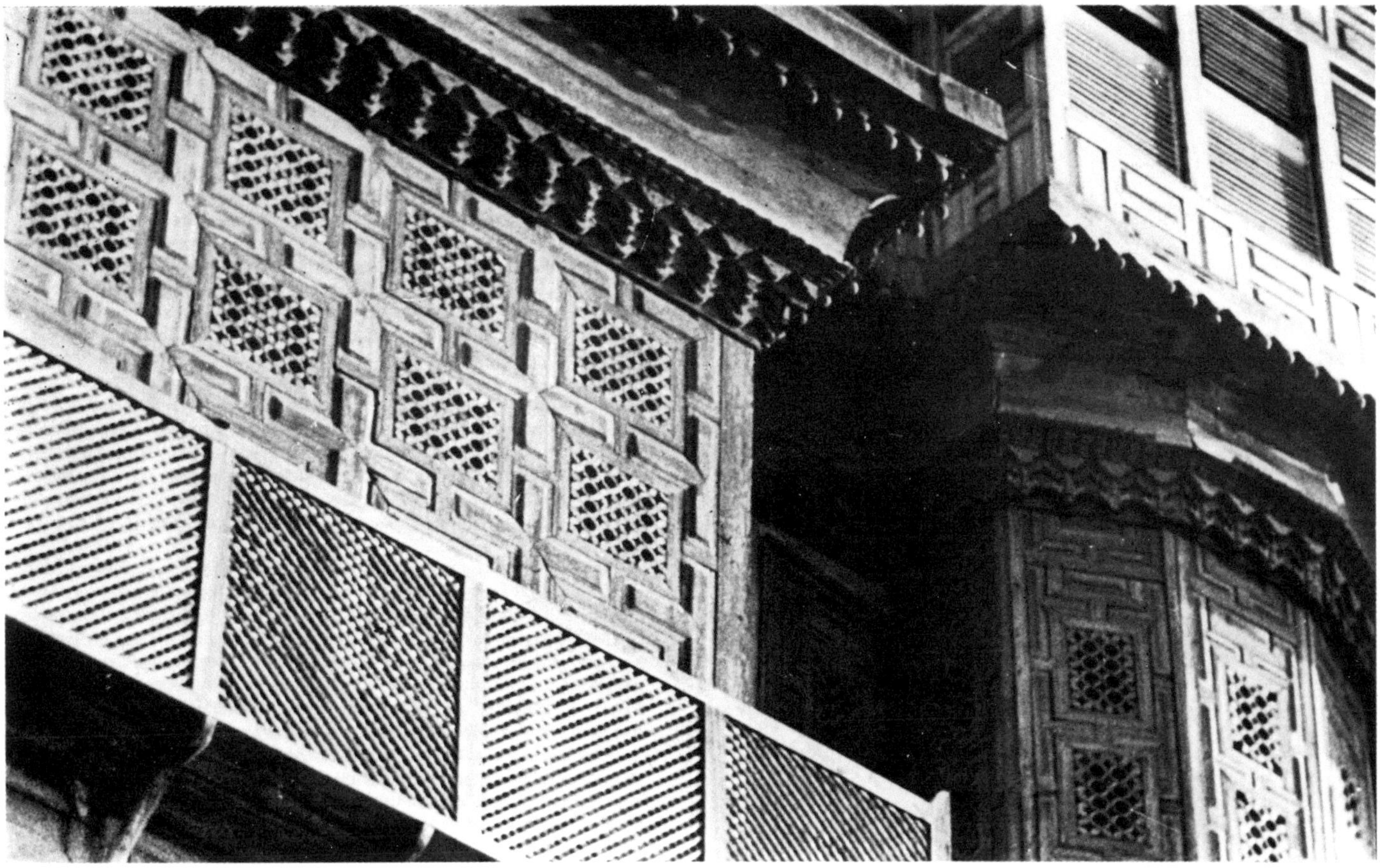

areas and districts of many cities are being sensitively restored, rehabilitated, modernized and grafted without relocating the existing population. The unfashionable areas of the cities are back in fashion and are being occupied by many diverse professional groups and small-scale traders.

Against this background let us evaluate the modern urban developments in the Middle East where the familiar out-dated and well-criticized pattern of the modern western city is being indiscriminately copied. New commercial centres are ringed by the decaying historical districts of the city. These are increasingly being demolished to make way for new urban roads to provide access to the prosperous new suburbs. The old districts, becoming increasingly unhabitable (owing to the lack of services), are vacated by the old residents and are in turn occupied by the new and poor arrivals from the country.

The city's transport problems are similarly being solved by the outmoded concepts of traffic engineering for mass mobility. New developments are in the form of the universal residential and commercial tower blocks, constructed of standardised repetitive building components, producing the same visual image and physical environment of the city as in its western counterpart.

The wholesale destruction of the cities of Mecca, Medina and Jeddah is being carried out with total disregard to their historical character and importance. The cities which took centuries to evolve and develop are being hurriedly bulldozed to make way for the 'ultra-modern' constructions which have no relationship with the cultural or social needs of the people. Neither do they show any sympathy with the climatic and environmental conditions of the area.

Knowing that no scheme of such wholesale destruction and devastation can now be proposed or considered for any western city of whatever historical and cultural merit, and that the masterplans and developments of the historical cities of Saudi Arabia are being proposed and carried out by the well-known international organizations of repute, the obvious question must be asked as to why such a state of professional disregard and irresponsibility has come about? Is it that the international firms working in countries other than their own do not apply the same degree of professional integrity and skill? Is it that in their greed to obtain maximum work (and profit), they have utterly abrogated their professional conscience and human responsibility? Or is it that they are not quite clear as to what is wanted of them, or perhaps that they are not the right people to have been asked in the first place? Are they being asked to do too much too quickly in an unfamiliar cultural, social and physical environment?

From the brief opportunity that I had to see things for myself and from what I have heard discussed and seen illustrated, I think that the reasons are a combination of most, if not all, of these factors; and some of these could be briefly described as follows:

1. Within the framework of western cities, planners and architects work within legal constraints, planning legislations and controls, pressures from various local bodies and the informed opinion of the media and press. They naturally take all this into account in making their proposals. None of these controls, which provide essential guidelines and direction, yet exist in any coherent form in many countries in the Middle East.
2. The architects and planners working within the existing historical cities need special skills, understanding and sensitive attitudes. In the West, any work related to historical cities would only be entrusted to those smaller-sized architectural practices which not only possess special skills but show sympathetic approach to the preservation of the historical and cultural aspect of the city. In the Middle East, most of the new development is being carried out by the multi-national organizations, which specialize in large-scale infrastructure projects—such as airports, hospitals, ports and large industrial and manufacturing complexes—but cannot sympathetically undertake the work in the historical cities.
3. And therefore the developments within the historical and cultural cities of Saudi Arabia in particular, influenced and proposed by the western attitudes and consultants, do not show much evidence of any positive thinking and generally incorporate most of the outdated negative aspects of the western towns and cities.

However, before we proceed further, the essential point to keep in mind is that western people have been part of the Industrial Revolution and evolution of modern technological values, and thus through their participation in the creation of these values they were able to assimilate them. While adapting to the continually changing technological society or lifestyle they were able to evolve social defences and institutional aids to counteract the resulting social, cultural and psychological stresses. What is important is that the values were not imposed on them from abroad. The modern western city is the expression of their own continuous past and present conditions.

And today there exists, in the West, the process of re-assessment and re-evaluation which is not restricted to the many aspects of the city but extends into many areas of human involvement in the present technological society. In fact, social thinkers, philosophers, writers and members of the younger generation are increasingly questioning the inhuman norms and exploitation of the present day western consumer society and are in search of alternatives more sympathetic to human social and creative needs. In their opinion, the prevailing values have reduced man to a unit of absolute labour and efficient production. The aims and ideals of constantly producing increasingly efficient machines of exploitation and extractive technology have caused irreparable environmental damage, exhaustion of resources and pollution. The wasteful planned obsolescence of the consumer society has deprived man

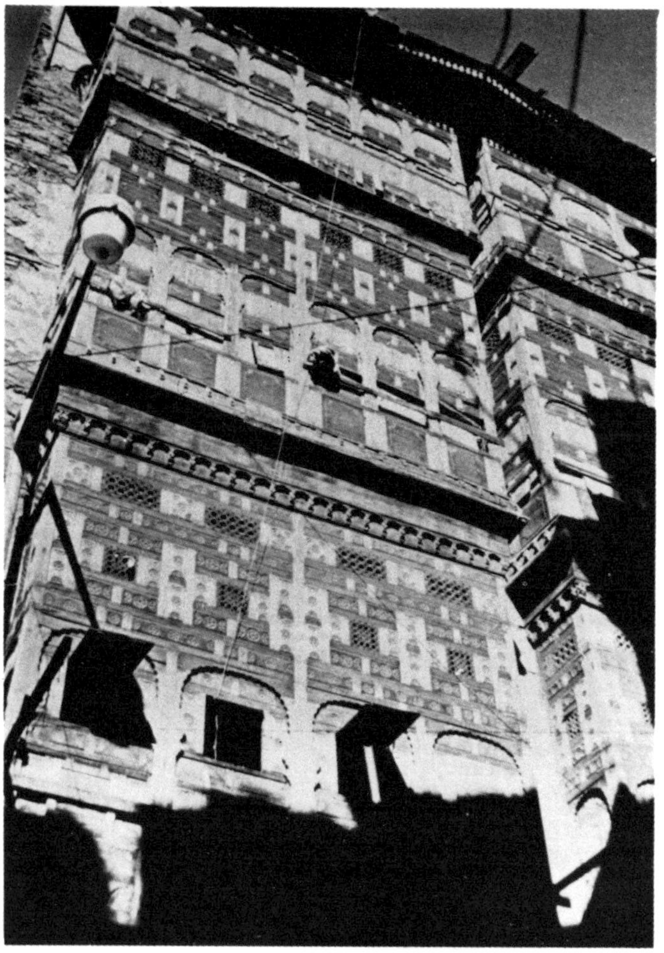

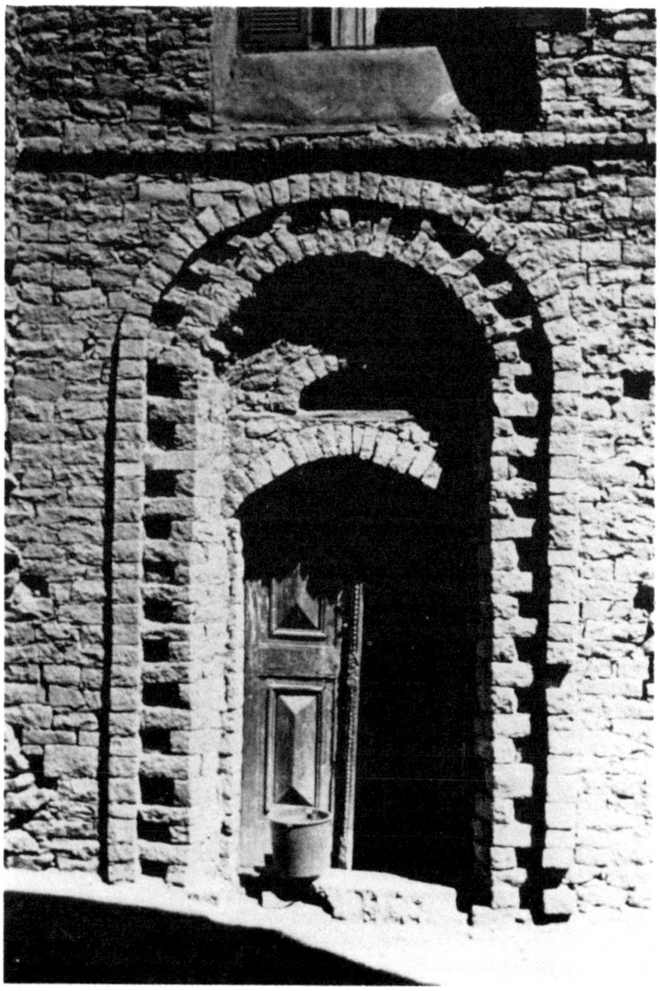

of his creative participation and has in turn created an increasing state of unhappiness and neurosis. There are great hopes that the present re-thinking may be the dawn of a second industrial age in which the relationship between man, machine and product will be based on more understanding and consideration for the environment and man's central position as a friend of the earth rather than a ruthless exploiter.

In the urgent aim and accelerated pace of developments in many Middle East countries, we do not see much evidence of any assessment and selection of viable technologies or the process of assimilation. The results are all too evident in the disintegration of social and cultural values, family and indigenous socio-economic structures. The regional and national arts and crafts, developed, refined and assimilated over the centuries, complete with their balanced, intricate and interdependent social organism, are rapidly becoming extinct. The crafts of pottery, weaving, carpet-making, metalwork, brick-making and stone-carving are all disappearing, destroying skills and the integrated communities of craftsmen. The techniques and symbols of indigenous arts, design and architecture are being overpowered and degraded by western aggressive advertising and manipulation. The out-of-work artists and craftsmen rush to the slums of the cities, without pride or dignity, to become factory workers producing cheap and fake versions of their original artifacts in plastic or/and aluminium, and assemblers of western-manufactured components to produce the goods they often cannot afford for themselves.

The genius of Islam, which produced the beautiful cities of Damascus, Baghdad, Fez, Isphahan, Fateh Pur Sikri and the serene monuments of Iran, Istanbul and the Taj Mahal, has no confidence left in its values, history, culture, and people. It has no real respect left for its historical and cultural heritage. Together we pay rhetorical lip service to our past achievements, while in our museums we store dust-collecting and ill-displayed objects from which we learn nothing. We can take pride in our past architectural glories, but what are we *ourselves* creating today?

The beautiful cities of Fez and S'ana communicate the uniqueness of the cultural achievements of their people. They did not owe much to western knowledge or technology but to the place, to the people who created them. In their totality they express their history, beliefs, skills, and cultural way of life. Fez and S'ana are now the cultural symbols, capital and the heritage of the people. If they choose today the western patterns of development and technology, without sensitive discrimination and cultural filtration, they will never have a choice. Their cities may acquire skyscrapers, motorways and supermarkets, and with this produce the same, or perhaps worse, social consequences than in their western counterparts. In this 'modern' transformation all the long history, social structures and cultural values will be lost. It would become the symbol of nothing, but a visual and human eyesore of the outmoded western values of indiscriminate production and consumption, and machine's inhumanity to man. Alternately, they can learn from their own history, as well as from the west, and evolve sympathetic changes which improve their lives and enhance the existing beauty of their cities.

We still have opportunity of choice. On the one hand we have the western industrial values and aims, which in their short duration have destroyed indigenous human institutions and shown little respect for other cultures and civilizations. On the other hand, with the present economic resources and opportunities in the Middle East, there is an unprecedented scope and possibility to re-establish the productive and creative potential of the people. And thus creating a new self-confidence that has been absent for some time in the Middle East, perhaps also showing possibilities and directions to other countries. Still at our disposal is considerable knowledge of our past achievements and cultural heritage and substantial resources of men and skills not yet contaminated by the dehumanizing consumer and industrial values or on the rebound from its first direct experience of them. This will need constant vigilance and monitoring in the selection and modification of existing technologies to start with, to accept only those which allow a meaningful and creative relationship between men and machines and which do not destroy the indigenous socio-cultural structures. The new criteria will not be whether a particular industry or production system is technically feasible and economically viable, but that it does not degrade the human creative potentials. And it must enhance the quality of life and human relationships in all its many-faceted aspects.

We will need to reconsider and adjust our present beliefs in the innate powers of industrial developments. We will need to modify or do away with machines that make man a mere productive unit of exploitation by other men. New machines will have to be invented that will allow man and woman to fulfil their full human, social and cultural aspirations, infusing their spirituality in the objects they produce. Work will not be separate from other human activities, individual or collective, and an integral part of the total life and living culture. With new positive attitudes and infusion of old social and cultural values, without seeking constant novelty, mere innovation or amusement, we will have the potential of development of a human, equitable and creative civilization, producing new authentic forms of architecture, art, design and crafts, which are organically part of life and symbolically reflect the continuing human aspirations and endeavour.

At this juncture, we might well ask what the aims and nature of industrial and technological development have to do with city, architecture and buildings. But this, indeed, is the essential point. We are well aware of the aims of many countries in the Middle East, particularly of Saudi Arabia, to retain their own essential character and create a dynamic civilization based on their own indigenous values, and that which also fulfil the contemporary needs and aspirations. The city, with all the physical and visual organizations of its various parts, expresses on the one hand all the human activities that take place in it and all the forces that give it its physical form and content, and on the other, provides the natural backdrop against which all the economic, social and cultural activities are meaningfully performed. This essential and organic relationship between what a man creates and what he does with it or in it, is what brings the city into being.

Arab family life has been taking place in the introverted privacy of a courtyard house. If the courtyard space was instead put around the house and rooms arranged either side of a corridor with windows looking out to the street, the lifestyle would inevitably change. The Arab social and economic life takes place in Arab cafes and the narrow streets of a bazaar. The narrow streets which are protected from the unbearable heat of the desert sun, allow one to walk, stop and say salam to a friend and shake hands, and perhaps stay a while for coffee or tea. If the streets become major traffic routes with blocks of offices or flats, the social life will disappear. Moreover, the western way of life, based on indiscriminate production and consumption, does not offer any possibility for man to develop his full potential.

It seems to me, therefore, that if our aim is the creation of a dynamic society and an authentic way of life, then our own basic values together with various ethnic, regional and national social patterns and modes of behaviour, dress, food and family structures should dictate the framework within which new social and urban patterns shall evolve.

It is naive to think that a city is only to do with the width of roads, mass mobility and sizes or heights of buildings. The absurd and misunderstood application of islamic arches and design motifs to totally alien forms cannot create an authentic architecture reflecting our own values. The fact that an office or factory building has arches on its facades does not necessarily express the quality of work or life inside the building or its cultural authenticity.

We do have our own values to create a new society which is modern as well as humane. Some of these values will inevitably need research, examination and re-interpretatation in the context of our life and problems today, in order to discover and re-establish their relevant active principles. This will require time, patience, understanding of the problems. But meanwhile, we must develop and build new infrastructures, hospitals, transport and education facilities, housing and institutions of social welfare. How are we to do all this? We must fundamentally recognise that all through history, the city has, with all her visual and tangible qualities, represented man's cultural capital and savings and continuously expressed his changing material and spiritual condition. Our aim is not only to continue the above tradition of the city but also to make our own contributions to it.

The architectural forms, as seen in their totality in the urban settlements, are an expression of social and cultural ideals and their underlying concepts of human institutions. Although at present, and for some time to come, we perhaps will have to make do with borrowed western forms, our long-term aims must essentially be to clearly restate our own values and ideals to enable us to eventually produce our own architectural and design forms, and in this our surviving heritage will play a fundamentally important role.

We have talked about the need for our cultural defences and the creation of new cultural confidence to rebut many of the superficial glamorous and aggressive values of alien cultures. This is not to prevent or protect the people from coming in contact with the values of other cultures, but an attempt to increase their awareness and understanding of the importance of their own cultural values so that they may be able to make intelligent choices. The cultural filters can act as organs of evaluation and assessment in selecting, adopting and modifying available processes and technologies, so that what they choose are not only economically viable, but compatible with their own cultural values. This will obviously involve the re-interpretation of the values and their assimilations in the new educational systems.

My main concern, therefore, has been to stress the need and importance of retaining and protecting what the future generation will not be able to mend, repair or restore. There are ways of building new cities or expanding existing ones and transport systems without demolishing and destroying the cultural and historical inheritance. In our desire to drive and go somewhere, let us not destroy that which is worth driving for and going to. There are scores of examples of western cities where both the worst and the best have been achieved. Let us learn from their best achievements as well as worst ones so as not to repeat their errors. Our cultural heritage with all its institutions is in our trust from our forefathers—and in this, it is our cultural capital and savings. It is not for us to squander, mutilate or destroy and impoverish the coming generations. On our shoulders rests the heavy burden of responsibility, and we must fulfil it if in history we do not wish to be accused of having participated in the gravest cultural destruction that any generation of human beings has, by its own deeds, brought on itself.

Contributors

Rasheed Araeen is a Pakistani-British artist living in London.

Eduardo Galeano, a leading Uruguayan writer and journalist, was chief editor of the weekly *Marcha* (1961-64) and founded the magazine *Crisis* in Buenos Aires. He is now living in exile in Barcelona.

Guy Brett, former art critic of *The Times*, is a writer and exhibition organiser. He now regularly contributes to *Macula*, Paris.

Dr Babatunde Lawal is Senior Lecturer in the Department of Fine Arts at the University of Ife, Nigeria.

Ayyub Malik, ARIBA, is an architect living in London.

BLACK PHOENIX : NUMBER ONE : WINTER 1978 : CONTENTS

"The myth of universal art, perpetrated by various art movements in the West in this century, must now be debunked. Behind this facade of universality lay the desire to impose Western values on rest of the world. The fact is that the conditions under which Western art has been developing and flourishing are very different from those of the Third World. The art of the society whose material foundation is laid on the exploitation of other people, cannot be at the same time an expression of exploited people."

– RASHEED ARAEEN

"Within an imprisoned society, literature can only exist as denunciation or hope..... The testimony of people expressing their sufferings and hopes in a multiplicity of ways is often more eloquent and beautiful than works written 'in the name of the people'." – EDUARDO GALEANO

"We don't have money or anything else. We have to go out and collect the scraps of material around the factories. That's how we make them and afterwards people buy them...Each time we make them better. It has to be like that because we live from them, it's the only way we have to survive, otherwise nothing at all would come to the house." – WOMEN ARTISTS OF PATCHWORKS FROM THE SHANTYTOWNS OF SANTIAGO, CHILE.

"...a revival of the past for its own sake has deprived neo-traditional art of a soul, which no art can have without being firmly rooted in the socio-cultural dynamics of its own era. What is needed now is a new art that will reflect the cultural realities of the present, while at the same time retaining a link with the past." – BABATUNDE LAWAL

"On our shoulders rests the heavy burden of responsibility, and we must fulfil it if in history we do not wish to be accused of having participated in the gravest cultural destruction that any generation of human beings has, by its own deeds, brought on itself." – AYYUB MALIK

BLACK PHOENIX

THIRD WORLD PERSPECTIVE ON CONTEMPORARY ART AND CULTURE No 2 SUMMER 1978 60p

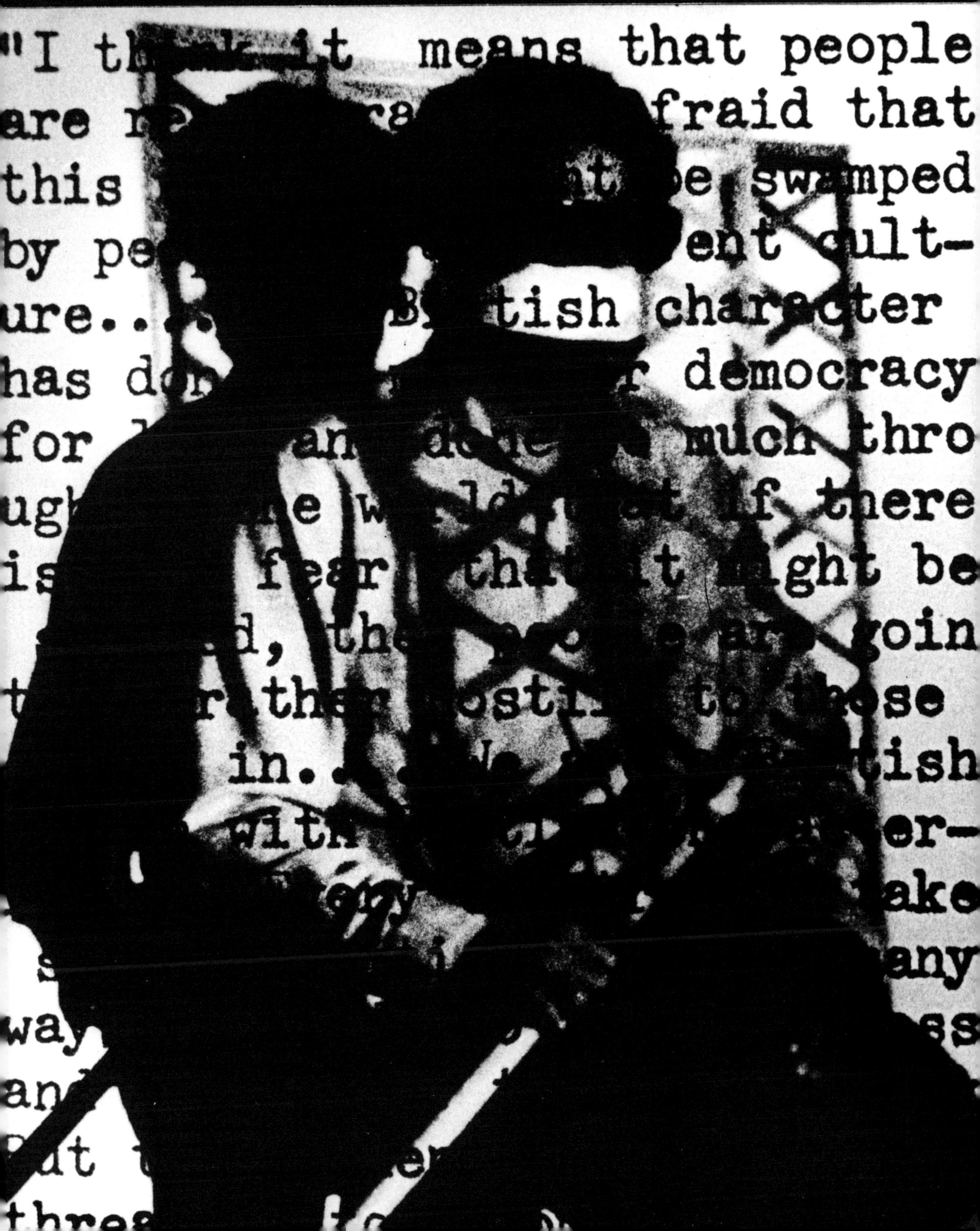

BLACK PHOENIX
Third World Perspective on Contemporary Art & Culture

No 2 SUMMER 1978

Edited and published by:
Rasheed Araeen, Mahmood Jamal

BCM BLACKPHOENIX
LONDON WC1V 6XX

Tel: 01-624 7185

Subscriptions: 4 issues p&p included.
UK £3 EUROPE £4 OTHERS £5
Make cheques payable to *Black Phoenix*

Typeset: Bread 'n Roses (TU) 01-485 4432.
Printing: Interlink Longraph Ltd., London.
Distribution: Publications Distribution Co-operative, 27 Clerkenwell Close, London.

CONTENTS

We apologise to our subscribers and readers for the delay in publication of this issue. The difficulties are enormous, but we shall endeavour to continue this task. And although under the present difficult circumstances we may not be able to publish the magazine quarterly according to our original schedule, we shall fulfil our commitment to our subscribers and provide them with full four issues.

However, we cannot fulfil this task without your help. Send your contributions, subscriptions and donations, as soon as possible. If you wish to discuss with us about your contribution or if you want to help us in any way, do not hesitate to contact us.

The opinions expressed in the journal are those of the contributors and we do not necessarily agree with all of them.

CONTRIBUTORS

Rasheed Araeen was born in Karachi (Pakistan) but since 1964 has lived in London. Although a civil-engineering graduate, he has devoted himself to art and cultural activity. His main concern has been with the dialectical aspect of transformational processes. His first 'sculpture' comprised of *burning of bicycle tyres* in Karachi in 1959. Since early 1970s he has been involved in activities, both artistic & political, which are related to the predicament of the Third World. In 1975-6 he wrote his major work, **Preliminary Notes for a BLACK MANIFESTO**, which questions the pretended universality of Western Art and its international role in the world today, published in our issue No 1.

Kenneth Coutts-Smith is a British art critic/historian now residing in Canada. He is the author of many articles/reviews, as well as two books: *Dada* (Dutton-Studio Vista, 1970) and *The Dream of Icarus, Art and Society in the 20th Century* (Hutchinson, 1970). At present he is holder of a Senior Arts Award from the Canada Council, in order to write two books: one on *Art & Politics*, and the other a study of *Cultural Colonialism*.

Ariel Dorfman is a Chilean writer. Before the fascist coup he was Professor of Spanish-American literature, and at present living in exile in Europe. He has extensively written on literature and ideology, particularly children's literature, in the context of cultural imperialism. His best known work, written in collaboration with Armand Mattelart, is *How to Read Donald Duck, Imperialist Ideology in the Disney Comic.*

Mahmood Jamal is a poet. He was born in Lucknow, India, but now lives in London. Presently he is writing a book on radical Urdu Poetry.

N. Kilele is a Tanzanian student in London.

Chris Wanjala teaches in Literature Department, University of Nairobi, Kenya.

We are being given a guarantee of £250 by the Arts Council of Great Britain in respect of the cost of illustrations in this issue.

SWAMPED?

AN ART STATEMENT/EDITORIAL

SWAMPED! SWAMPED! SWAMPED! IS THE OUTCRY. IT IS THE LIE. IT IS THE TRUTH. "SWAMPED" is the word that reveals the racist face of the British ruling class, behind the facade of humanity a vicious being. SWAMPED is the word that defines today the predicament of the world. SWAMPED IS THE WORLD; swamped by European values, by consumer culture and technology, by guns, tanks and bombers, by poisonous gases and toxic matters, . . . and above all by an ideology that denies humanity to all peoples.

SWAMPED! Or perhaps the word is 'swarmed'. That brings to mind LOCUSTS: the Earth being swarmed by white locusts. The metaphor is not an exaggeration when one looks at the World, the world since the Renaissance. Its destruction and plundering under 'civilisation'.

TEN THOUSAND MEN, WOMEN AND CHILDREN DIE OF STARVATION EVERY DAY.

How could one forget what happened to the American continents, to Australasia, and the innumerable places where the White Man had set his foot? What happened to the Red Man? What happened to so many Amerindian tribes? Where are the Incas, the Mayas . . . ? Where are the Tasmanians? — the "British character" has done the job well!

Everywhere they were welcomed — the Pilgrim Fathers, the conquistadors, the explorers and adventurers, and even the convicted criminals, . . . What did the indigenous peoples get in return for their hospitality and innocence? Murders, genocide, rape and plundering. Those who managed to survive had their means of living taken away, their culture destroyed, their artefacts plundered and stolen.

And now those that "ruled the sea" are frightened of 2 million "numbers" at the bottom of the heap. Could anybody in one's right mind believe that Britain could be swamped, swamped by a few million "people of a different culture" in the next decade? Even if there are going to be 5 million blacks in Britain at the end of this century, so what? Why should anybody be frightened?

There are about 500 million Europeans outside Europe. Should people be afraid of them? And how about the European culture which is alien to the rest of the world?

Our presence in this country is the direct result of what happened, and is happening, to our countries due to the greed and violence perpetrated by the West; the greed and violence that have now been universalised through the imposition of bourgeois ideology in the world. Moreover, YOU asked us to come. Why shouldn't our women (or men) and children join us now?

We came here when you were passing through a difficult period. You needed us to run the factories, the hospitals, the transport system, . . . We worked hard, 12 to 16 hours a day, and helped rebuild the economy which was shattered by the War. But what did we get in return? Racist myths and propaganda about our inferiority! You have the nerve now to tell us that we should go home. Is it your "character" to threaten the people, who had helped you in difficult times, with "rivers of blood"?

FEAR! FEAR! FEAR! "FEAR EATS THE SOUL" — Fassbinder, and destroys the body!

About 1½ million unemployed and more to go. THAT IS THE REAL FEAR. The bourgeois ruling class, which is bankrupt and can no longer deliver the goods, must instead CREATE a fear that has nothing to do with reality, a fear of the unknown. It must utter blatant lies to cover its own misdeeds and incompetence. It must therefore perpetuate chauvinism and racial superiority among the white population to maintain its power.

RACISM HAS NO BIOLOGICAL ROOTS. IT IS A SOCIO-ECONOMIC CATEGORY.

The black community in Britain today is under a constant threat of violence. THAT IS A REAL FEAR. The fear of being attacked in the street by racist thugs, of beng maimed or killed. Two men killed in a month, and we should not worry. "You are being unnecessarily paranoiac", we are often told, "our police is there to help you."

Wednesday 5 July 1978: a gang of some 30 white youths ambushes a group of Bangladeshis who have just come out of the factory after finishing their day's work, in East London. 13 of the Bangladeshis are injured. "I feel like a hunted animal", said Mirjan Ali. "I don't know what will happen tomorrow or after. There doesn't seem to be any reason, but they keep attacking us and shouting abusive language." (Reported by Sasthi Brata in the Observer, 9 July 1978.) A week has passed and as usual no arrests. (The black community has no choice but to get up and fight back; which is already happening.)

EUROCENTRICITY ⇌ HIERARCHY ⇌ DOMINATION ⇌ RACISM

The present-day racism is one of the manifestation of the domination of bourgeois ideology: the black man's predicament is not to be equated with that of the white man. Look at Rhodesia! Everybody is worried about the 'plight' of white man. Every time a white man is killed there is a big outcry in the British press.

Now look at these images from TV, of Rhodesia.

One image: a row of beautiful coffins with flowers waiting for the church service and funeral. The white man has died defending "Christian civilisation"!

Another image: soldiers piling up dead black bodies (look almost mutilated) or throwing them in a ditch, as if they were dead animals. NO COFFINS, NO FLOWERS, NO FUNERAL. . . THE BLACK MAN IS NOT SUPPOSED TO HAVE A SOUL!

More than 600 men, women and children are slaughtered by the South African troops in a raid (in which tanks and fighter bombers, supplied of course by the Western powers, are used) on an Angolan village on 4th May 1978: NOT A SINGLE HEADLINE IN THE BRITISH PRESS.

HOW COULD ONE SHUT ONE'S EYES & MIND TO SUCH BRUTALITY AND BE AN 'ARTIST'? HOW COULD ONE THINK ONLY OF 'ART' WHEN ONE IS SURROUNDED BY SO MUCH RACIST FILTH AND VIOLENCE?

WHAT CREDIBILITY THE WESTERN BOURGEOISIE (perhaps the adjective 'Western' here is unnecessary) HAS WHEN IT TALKS ABOUT ALL HUMANITY (REMEMBER VIETNAM!)? HOW COULD IT TALK ABOUT 'HUMAN RIGHTS'? IMPERIALISM HAS NO LIMITS IN ITS PRACTICE OF MORAL DOUBLE STANDARDS AND HYPOCRISY.

Now let us see if we have really swamped this country. How many black (or non-white) prime ministers we have had in Britain? (You are expecting TOO MUCH.) How many black MPs are there in the Parliament? (How could a black man REPRESENT whites!) Which sector of the British economy is being controlled by blacks? (GRUNWICK. Oh no!) Which are the NATIONAL art/cultural

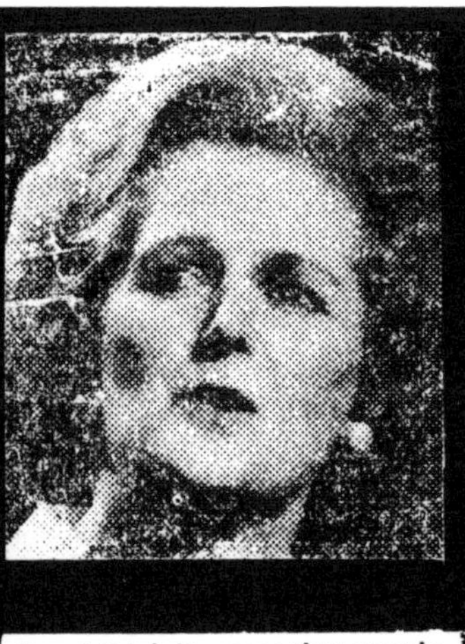

"... I think it means that people are really rather afraid that this country might be swamped by people of a different culture. . . . The British character has done so much for democracy, for law, and done so much throughout the world that if there is any fear that it might be swamped, then people are going to rather hostile to those coming in. . . . We are a British nation with British characteristics. Every country can take some minorities, and in many ways they add to the richness and variety of this country. But the moment the minority threatens to become a big one, people get frightened."

Mrs. Thatcher

KEEP BRITAIN FOR THE BRITISH

Only 200m to absorb

NGATA TE KOROU

Maori teacher in New Zealand

MY PEOPLE are showing great interest in reports from England of the immigration debate at present taking place. Many of them react sympathetically to the determination of Mrs Thatcher not to let her own tribe lose its cultural values in a tidal wave of immigrants, although they seem surprised that the British should feel that less than 5 per cent of the population is a cause for concern.

Perhaps it would comfort the British to know that we Maoris have managed to keep our language and some of our traditions alive in spite of being overwhelmed 10 to one by British immigrants over the last 150 years—and that in spite of a determined attack upon our culture by the immigrant majority which lasted for over a century.

We also notice that elements of British political life wish to send back the immigrants from Asia and the Caribbean. This has given great heart to our own radical young. They claim that, thanks to the British passion for fair play, we can now expect concern for the cultural threat posed by immigrants to Britain to be matched by an equal concern for the threat posed by British immigrants to other cultures, such as our own.

Should any future Conservative, Powellite, or National Front government succeed in repatriating immigrants, we will hope to return your emigrants to take up the vacancies. It so happens that we have almost exactly the same number of "cultural aliens" as Britain has "coloured immigrants"—about 2½ million whites of predominantly British extraction. There seems to be no reason why the indigenous populations of other old Commonwealth countries should not expect likewise.

This would mean that for every West Indian or Indian deported, we could send you, on a fair statistical basis, as replacements, one "pakeha" New Zealander, four Australians, four Canadians, half a South African white, part of a white Rhodesian, and no fewer than 50 American WASPs. It would take some time for you to absorb the extra 200 million people involved, but there is no reason why, if phased over a decent period (say a century) and with sensible birth control measures being taken, England should not be the exclusive home of those who speak English and live in the English manner.

Others among us would prefer more moderate solutions to our immigrant problem—which is the problem of your emigrants. Such people would wish us to absorb what is good in other cultures, while preserving the good in our own. They say that the world is now too small for anyone to claim rights of ethnic homelands, as Hitler did. This, you must agree, shows great tolerance from those whose parents and grandparents were tricked by treaties, robbed by land grabs, ravaged by wars fought for even more land then evicted from what was left as a punishment for resisting the attacks, their children forced into schools in which their own language and cultural values were proscribed. In spite of that our moderates still dream of a world where any man can live wherever he likes.

Our radicals on the other hand say that this is ridiculous and sentimental, and that we should accept that racism exists everywhere, and that everyone should go back to his own ancestral homeland as soon as possible.

They too have a dream, a dream of the forest returning to cover the land which has been almost ruined by intensive and destructive methods of pastoral farming, a dream of the return to a proper balance with nature. Perhaps the day may come again when we can dig kumara, and harvest the fruits of forests, rivers, and the sea. They dream of the warm comradeship of family group and sub-tribe; of telling of ancient stories around the cooking fires, as the long Pacific waves thunder up on empty beaches. And never a single greedy, grasping, calculating, tricky white face to be seen anywhere.

They are depending upon the success of Britain's ultra Right wing.

The Sunday Times, March 19 1978

institutions under the domination of black people? Which black artist is recognised in Britain, or which art-history book, art journal or institution, recognises the presence of black artists in Britain and their contributions to its contemporary art? (Why don't you stick to your ethnic traditions?) How many black artists have been sent abroad to represent Britain? (You must be joking: a black artist representing Britain! Art is not football or boxing.)

Are people really so frightened in Britain that they have stopped travelling by the public transport (since it is run by blacks)? Are people so scared, lest they be poisoned, that they have stopped going to the Indian/Chinese restaurants? Are people so fearful, lest the 'demoniac' spirits of our ancient tribes cast a deadly spell, that they are no longer visiting the British Museum?

Yes, we have swamped your little island with millions of our cultural artefacts; so much so that three million artefacts have to be kept wrapped in the safe-boxes in a Shoreditch warehouse, away from the ordinary people lest their Britian values are threatened. We are very sorry!

Yes, we are grateful that you have given us 'civilisation'. You have given us Rolls-Royces, Mercedeses, colour TVs, pin-striped suits with matching shirts and ties, . . . aeroplanes, guns, tanks, bombers, . . . WE EAT THEM TO FILL OUR HUNGRY STOMACHS!

Thank you for "democracy, for law, and (doing) so much throughout the world. . ." Look at Rhodesia, Southern Africa, Cyprus, Palestine, Northern Ireland . . . !

"OVER 100 DEVELOPING COUNTRIES, WITH 50% OF THE WORLD'S POPULATION, ACCOUNT FOR ONLY 14% OF THE GLOBAL PRODUCT. IN CONTRAST, SOME 25 DEVELOPED COUNTRIES, WITH ONLY 18% OF THE WORLD'S POPULATION, ACCOUNT FOR 66 PER CENT."

The present predicament of mankind is the direct result of bourgeois ideology and its economic system which has now become international monopoly capital. It can only exist and survive by virtue of its exploitation of not only the people in its metropolises but more brutally by super-exploitation of the Third World. It has nothing to offer to the world except starvation and human misery. The capitalist system must now give way (it won't do it by itself, of course) to a system that totally rejects greed and competition as natural and which recognises and fulfills the equal needs of all peoples throughout the world. The resources of the world cannot be left in the hands of a few lunatics of multinational corporate states, who could bring life on Earth to an end by the turn of this century.

How could then one continue creating an art that fails to denounce the inhumanity of the bourgeois ideology? How could one shut one's eyes to the predicament of mankind and continue making an art that ignores the reality of its time; and yet continue making claims about its universality? How could one continue clinging to bourgeois illusions which have in fact led so many artists recently to intellectual masturbation and farting, masochism and self-destruction, pessimism, depression, nihilism, voyeurism, exhibitionism, etc, etc, . . ? The bourgeoisie, of course, loves all this because there is nothing in these states and their resulting activities that would threaten it. It actually pays ANYTHING for that is useless and meaningless, and for that which causes self-emasculation of the artist, thus destroying a potential critic of its ideology or revolutionary.

TO SAY THAT "THIS COUNTRY MIGHT BE SWAMPED BY PEOPLE OF A DIFFERENT CULTURE", AT A TIME WHEN THE WHOLE WORLD IS BEING VICIOUSLY DOMINATED BY THE WEST, IS TO PERPETUATE IMPERIALIST LIES; LIES WHICH MUST BE EXPOSED AND DENOUNCED.

A Message to Margaret

Travelling these roads
That lead to nowhere
These dreams that have no meaning
Have finally come to light
The system Yes the system
Has shown it's colours at last

Lady in Blue Lady in Blue
Now we know your game

Repatriation is the cry
Repatriation is your aim

Sick and tired
Of this merry-go-round

This pain inside
We can't take it no more
We can't take it no more

Vote Vote Vote
We'll not be on any plane or boat

Our fore parents' sweat and blood
Is buried in this land

Our generation
Know no other land

Here we are. . .
Here we'll make our final stand

On this soil we were born
On this soil we will die.

from GRASSROOTS 13

INNOCENCE & NEO-COLONIALISM

A CASE OF IDEOLOGICAL DOMINATION IN CHILDREN'S LITERATURE

Ariel Dorfman

This essay is from a collection of writings completed by the author before the fascist coup in Chile and which were, along with hundreds of literary works, burnt or pulped shortly after Allende's overthrow. The collection was later published as Ensayos Quemados (Burnt Essays) by Ediciones de la Flor, Buenos Aires, 1974. The English translation, by John Lyons, is being published for the first time here.

"Not so very long ago, the earth numbered two thousand million inhabitants: five hundred million men, and one thousand five hundred million natives. The former had the Word; the others had the use of it. Between the two there were hired kinglets, overlords, and a bourgeoisie, sham from beginning to end, which served as go-betweens. In the colonies the truth stood naked, but the citizens of the mother country preferred it with clothes on: the natives had to love them, something in the way mothers are loved. The European *elite* undertook to manufacture a native *elite*. They picked out promising adolescents; they branded them, as with a red-hot iron, with the principles of western culture; they stuffed their mouths full with high sounding phrases, grand glutinous words that stuck to the teeth. After a short stay in the mother country they were sent home, white-washed. These walking lies had nothing left to say to their brothers; they only echoed. From Paris, from London, from Amsterdam we would utter the words 'Parthenon! Brotherhood!' and somewhere in Africa and Asia lips would open '. . . thenon! . . . therhood!' It was the golden age."

—Jean-Paul Sartre
Preface to *The Wretched of the Earth* by Frantz Fanon.

* *

That child you have beside you—close in any case, there is always a child close—is potentially the revolutionary of tomorrow. Just as he may also be the most resolute of defenders of the established order. The process of the socialization of that little human being constitutes one of the neuralgic points in any history: there the attitudes must be generated, the pre-rational assumptions conditioned, which permit that child to grow integrating himself, comfortable, functioning, an enthusiastic cog, in the *status quo*.

The function of mass consumption children's literature in the capitalist society (developed or under-developed) is to collaborate so that the child may pre-interpret the contradictions of reality (for example, authoritarianism, poverty, inequality, etc.) as natural, as he comes across them, as perfectly clear facts, understandable and even inevitable: the child must have in advance within his grasp, the ideological responses which his parents have internalised, forms of thinking, feeling, living, which overcome and unify in the mind the tensions which growing up will make each day more evident. The mechanism in that literature of substituting, compensating, distorting, while secretly justifying or rationalising, while defining a problem falsely so as to solve it triumphantly; re-affirming constantly a complete, invariable system of psychological and moral preferences from which all will be ordered, comes to reinforce the pedagogic process which the dominant class, and the family which is its agent, wishes to impose on the child so that he will carry out a determined function now and especially when older, a process which can be traced in all the products of capitalist societies (books, magazines, ABCs, toys, beds and cots, favourite colours, TV programmes, clothes, decorative objects, etc.). The privileged centre of that education will be the son of the bourgeoisie who is receiving on top the benefits of the system itself, but the children of the proletariat will also be bombarded with these images so that they may consolidate them inwardly, even if their very condition of being exploited will constantly tend to make manifest the falsity of the pattern which is established as norm.

If in this essay we are only going to examine a narrow sector within this immense zone of ideological domination, it is with the intention that it may at the same time make patent the need to analyse the other regions, and with the certainty that in fact the structural models which are revealed will be found duplicated, with significant variations, adapted to the particular *medium* in which is inserted the subjugation in the rest of the sectors.

Furthermore, I would like the present analysis to contribute to a more precise re-cognition of the techniques and methods which are used in children's literature to achieve the submission of the child and his acceptance of the current bourgeois values, calling attention to the danger involved in the persistence of those forms in any society which is transforming its economic and social structures. Even if a new culture could not emerge except when the changes in the ownership of the means of production make more manifest the distance between the bourgeois ideology and the reality which it pretends to embrance, it is no less certain that vigilance with regard to official lingustic forms of the dominators in relation to *those problems*, specific and current, may accelerate the process of de-mythification.

Finally, perhaps a contribution may be made to a theory of the ideology, and of its ambiguous relation with reality, since the manner in which capitalism colonizes its young (the specific modes of concealment, reduction, mystification, inversion, partial or complete lies, and which are bound to relate to the weakest and most problematic links in society, symptomize also the fears and aspirations which derive from the falsification, from the ideal history which seeks to supplant the reality) serves to understand the true history. The mask which man chooses in order to confront his dilemmas, in order to smile in the worrying and questioning presence of the others, in order to simulate a unified and coherent consciousness which enables mental survival with the contradictions, which otherwise would lead to the abysses of madness, of revolution, or to the simple admission of an irrevocable immorality which pursues petty interests without justification, ethical or sublime (impossible, impossible), that mask which the system generates automatically so as to be able to function,[1] is absolutely no different from the face (does it exist?) which pulsates deeper down.

We are going to analyse the books that tell the story of Babar the elephant, which in recent years have begun to penetrate our society, after a success without precedent in the last thirty years in France (and also in other parts of the western world).[2] The reason for choosing this character and not another more popular, rests in the fact that in Babar there is expressed representatively a series of model characteristics which it would be difficult to find assembled with such clarity around another entity of children's literature: it is an almost archetypal model. In any case, when the need arises, parallels will be established with similar methods used in other current forms, especially with the world of Walt Disney.

Basically, Babar's story is that of an ordinary pachyderm who, owing to his strange upbringing and link with the world of men, became the king of the elephants, saving and transforming his country. More recently, on his having a family, the author and reader prefer to concentrate on the little children of Babar.

Babar is born like any old elephant: he grows up and plays in an idyllic reality, among other little animals. However, this adam-like setting is soon to alter, as a 'wicked hunter' kills his mother and forces him to escape from the forest and turn towards the bewildering city. Thus the first contact with civilization turns out negative: it intervenes to kill and to destroy. But the city repays Babar for what it took from him. The female figure of the 'old lady' substitutes for the mother, adopting the elephant. The first thing which Babar wants is 'to dress well': she proffers all the money needed. During the first drawings he walks on four legs: hardly does he lose his nakedness and confront himself clothed in a mirror, he becomes conscious of his skin and of that second skin which is the clothes. Babar begins to model himself on man, to use his two-legged movements. He gets up on two legs. Immediately there follows an educative process: Babar is going to be transformed—without losing his animal appearance—into a human being: he uses a serviette, goes to bed, does gymnastics, bathes in a bathtub and with a sponge, drives his own car, dresses in fashion. "She gives him everything that he wants." A wise teacher instructs him, and thus he learns to write, to add up, etc. He can also glimpse a globe where Africa and America stand out very clearly.

Babar 'progresses': in place of instincts, ignorance, he acquires the knowledge and rules of the world which shelters him, he learns to behave in the face of reality in a certain normative way. Evidently, on a first superficial level, it would appear to be urging the young readers to conduct themselves in a similar way (to be obedient, intelligent, to have good manners, etc.). The child sets out, like Babar without social elements, is also wild, ignorant, walks on all fours, etc. The correspondence between these two innocents, the animal and the child, shapes—as we shall see in greater detail later on—the basis of ideological domination, the mechanism and bridge which will permit the distortion of reality. But it is enough for now to note that Babar is not merely a child: he has, besides, a country of his own, which remains primitive, tribal, naked, a country which has not evolved alongside him. From that reality—strictly from those sectors of his personality still not subjugated and which can never be erased, from his constantly emergent animality—emissaries come to look for him ("two little elephants completely *naked*") [my italics].

This first contact between Babar now civilized, almost adult one could say, and the other elephants, who are like a reflection of what he once was, defines the future of the land of the elephants: his cousins are immediately incorporated into the world of the old lady, she dresses them, and then—as a reward for having babbled the first step—she takes them to eat cakes (the sweet which domesticates, the sweet which calms the tears, which makes lies acceptable, the honey which facilitates the fluid transition towards *status quo*, the sweet-child, the sweet-adult). Having demonstrated the superiority and the infectiousness of his education, counting on allies, on a girlfriend (later he will marry Celeste, his cousin), he can now return to jungle.

"But he will never forget the old lady."

They set off driving, clothed, with suitcases, hooting and making a din. Running behind, on four legs, are the cousins' mothers who had come to look for them: it is the first visible consequence of the lack of civilization. Whoever does not accept those models will be excluded from the pleasures (of driving a car); they will be a bunch of failures.

Meanwhile, the king of the elephants having died accidentally, the arrival of Babar has become providential. "The oldest elephants" get together to elect a new king, "most worried": it is "a fateful day", "what a misfortune". The coming of a Messiah is looked to, a saviour to resolve the problem. In fact the king of the elephants differed from the rest only in the crown he wore; but on eating a "poisonous mushroom" he shows that he is a stupid, ineffectual individual, who performs actions which the child readers would be very careful to avoid. If the king (the best) of the elephants behaves in such a childish and dangerous way, what can be expected of the rest of them? The new government will have to come from outside: it will not be a native but someone educated in the land of men, a civilized being. While they deliberate in despair, Babar leaves the land of men (houses, a square, aeroplanes, a church, cars, in the distance neatly sown fields, monuments) with all the prominent signs of his links with this world. "What fine clothes you are wearing! What a charming car!" Before the great undifferentiated grey mass who welcome them, they appear with defined personality: colour, movement, technique, single them out and are converted into an erect, exterior sign of their personality, their assimilation into the values, objects, and conceptions of the fascinating and unknown world of men. Babar is assigned the investiture of predominance in a barbaric world where all are defenceless and ingenuous. His closeness to the western world (to the world of the adults), to the prestigious centre, will be now and in each future episode, the foundation of his authority, the fountain of his rule. Old Cornelius understands it this way, ("he returns from the city, where he has learnt many things while mixing with men") and he suggests they crown Babar. "Without hesitation", the elephants accept. "Cornelius has spoken *like a book*", that is, like an authoritarian, cultural object, loaded with wisdom, like the book which the elephants don't have but which men do. Cornelius speaks two languages, mediating between alternative worlds.

The reward does not delay. "You have some splendid ideas", Babar tells him (although the only one he has had is that Babar be proclaimed king), "well then, I nominate you general and when I have my crown I'll give you my cap". The one who helped to obtain power is rewarded with rank and with the symbol of civilization: he draws closer to power and its differentiating features. Babar imitates men, Cornelius imitates Babar; subsequently, all will imitate Cornelius and the whole country will turn 'civilised'. Therefore, the first thing Babar does ("he sends the dromedary to the city to buy him some costly ceremonial robes") is to reaffirm his dominance, by communicating once more with the metropolis to accentuate his status externally. In the celebration which follows, the invited animals (all of them, mouse, lizard, hippopotamus, leopard, lion, rhinoceros, giraffe, and, naturally, the elephants) get up for the first time on two legs and dance. Although they are still naked, already they are being transfigured, already they begin to raise themselves, to *better* their condition. They will continue to lose their condition of animals, they will humanize themselves.

But it is not only a question of pedagogic theory, the integration of children (the elephants) into a benevolent adult world (the land of men), rather, that here, more than anything, there is a *theory of history*, the learning of an interpretative system which permits "illumination" of the origins of the contemporary world. Two countries are being related, two antagonistic dimensions, city and jungle, and one of the poles will end up absorbing and subordinating the other. The child will discover as he grows up, the palpable reality that there are developed countries and underdeveloped countries, a situation due to imperialism and to the place occupied by the underdeveloped countries within the international capitalist system. He will also meet with a rational explanation, which justifies and conceals this phenomenon and a series of theoretical and practical answers which are proposed as solutions, so that those 'backward' places may progress. The child's first contact with history will occur through books like those of Babar which—as we shall see—anticipate at another level, and with different means, exactly the same politics which will be propounded to him when he is older.

It tells the history of the incorporation of the non-western continents (America, Asia, but especially Africa) into the contemporary world. But the history has been de-realized, has been disguised. Instead of Europe, there is a city; instead of Africa, a jungle; instead of a negro or an Indian, an elephant; instead of the church or a monopolistic empire, the old lady; instead of a dependent bourgeoisie, Babar. The land of the elephants *equals* Africa without openly personifying it, without attaching the *name* which would have forced a too real and painful identification. It surreptitiously suppresses the linguistic link (the word Africa), which being shot full of contradictions, denunciations, concretions, immediacies, which on demanding a suspicious examination parallel to effective reality, past and contemporary, would invalidate the creation of an ideal history which could later replace that which effectively happened.[3] The history which the child receives as true will do for the other, and will teach to consider it and to put it into perspective, and it succeeds because it doesn't attempt to teach absolutely anything, because it presents itself as ingenuous, fictitious, removed from daily problems, without compromises, neutral, beyond.

But this history is none other than the realization of the dream of the bourgeoisie with regard to their dominated countries. Since the 16th century onwards, capitalism justifies through literature its intervention in other realities, in the utopian hope of being able to construct there a mythical perfect space where the contradictions which afflicted Europe at that time (going through the transition from feudalism to capitalism) will not impinge. The myth of the noble savage, the longing for a beneficent and providential nature (God's steward), the necessity of a Golden Age in which the crisis might be resolved rationally and harmoniously, constituted a means of secularizing the medieval religious myth of Eden and Heaven, the two paradisaical dimensions between which the finite history of men unfolds. The educative ideal for indigenous native populations: there would be united in them the light of their natural reason (logos) and the law of civilized progress (the renascent humanity after a supposedly barbarous Middle Ages). A nation was to be recreated in which nature and civilization could live together, where technological advance did not corrupt but rather bring well-being: a place which would unite feudal qualities and bourgeois qualities and synthesize them without antagonisms. The outcome, as we know, was disastrous. However, Babar, four centuries later, will achieve that which the conquistadors could not do: he will inject progress into that jungle without disturbing the balance of nature. The story will be told of the relation of those two world making no mention of plundering, racialism, underdevelopment and misery, the dream of the bourgeoisie will be narrated, what the bourgeoisie would have wished the non-European world to be. It is a substitutive fantasy with which the author *corrects* (while Babar rules) the defects, difficulties, imperfections of the true historical development, a radiograph of the aspirations of European civilization, and which were never completely lost: the possibility of finding some island, some shore of the universe, which was not contaminated yet, where one could rebuild all the positive aspects of 'progress', sliding out of its dilemmas. This parallel pseudo-history which overcomes the everyday despairs, returning with nostalgia to a heroic, unshakeable project, continues to inspire in the 19th century, when Africa is colonized, and is used in the 20th century in order to intervene in Asia and in other places: it is necessary to save those countries for civilization, and it can't be done, moreover, without impeding its autochthonous being. In the land of the elephants the great contradictions in the history of the development of capitalism are resolved: the form in which Europe approached the natives comes out justified. The present day policy will also come out purified, the policy proposed today as a solution.

But here there is something more than an ideal projection, a deceitful construction. Although only later will it be appropriate to examine in detail in what way the development suffered by the land of the elephants reinforces and con-firms the current neo-colonialist theory, it is important to understand that in the Babar books history is not *ignored*, it is not eliminated. It is sweetened, its sign is changed, it is boiled down, it is inverted, but *the real history is there*, it can be uncovered and traced. The author has abstracted from the history of Africa those undeniable characteristics which, stripped of their immediate concretion and their problem-making connection, will serve to establish a subconscious system of equivalences. Each stage in the life of Babar corresponds formally (or will correspond, as the child continues to locate and recognize them) to a real stage which was produced in the true history. Those aspects have been selected and isolated to function in another context, so that, losing their category of accusation, litigation and denunciation, they remain enclosed within the all-inclusive borders of the dominating ideology. And if it were not so, this literature would not be dangerous, since the child would be shut up in a dream, in an imagination without points of contact with reality, in the anachronistic head of Thomas More or Father Las Casas. If the truth were not in Babar the elephant, hidden, bastardized, distorted, but if it were not as a concealed, correlative parallel, it would be impossible that the equivalences could be revealed to the child, he could not compare the fictitious process in his mind with the real process which will cry out to be interpreted and understood. the possibility of a future subconscious comparison, of a subduing of the contradictions of the dialectic in an obsessively reiterated emotional scheme, can only operate if the same structural stages are maintained, varying the appearance beneath which they are introduced and substantially modifying the consequences of their intervention. The false system becomes representative of the entire reality, because it includes, veiled, the problems which this world is going to continue presenting to the child as he grows up.[4]

We shall try to elaborate proof of this thesis while performing the analysis and obtaining a more complete vision of the effects that civilization has had on the land of the elephants, but it is necessary in any case to examine a concrete example here.

There are elements in the relationships between Europe and the other continents which cannot be denied: the plundering, the violence, the slavery. If these were omitted in Babar, the result would be a lie, and a reading of Babar would not help to interpret anything ideologically. The children would say: You told us that there was no violence in the conquest of Africa. That's a lie; now we know that there was a lot of destruction. If you lied in this, surely you falsify other things as well.

Consequently, violence has been included in Babar. Nobody has tried to deny it. The wicked hunter represents precisely those 'evil' forces, which intervened in the past. Later, when Babar and Celeste are shipwrecked, they are picked up by a captain who 'gives' them (notice, they are not sold) to a circus owner. They suffer slavery, are caged up, lose their *freedom*.

European civilization thus contains conspicuous negative elements. But each time the representatives of the city appear doing wrong to the elephants, up towers the majestic, generous, charitable counter-figure of the positive element of the western Christian world. The old lady wipes out those characteristics, all roads lead to her guardianship and furthermore, it is the cruel, exploitative work of the others which presses the elephants to depend on her. Opposite the threat of extermination and servitude from one sector of the European world, there is an educative ideal, missionary and 'progressive', which wants to enclose Babar and his herd in the great western family. The natives must not be killed or put in chains: it is necessary to *Europeanize* them. It is noteworthy, also, that each time Europe shows itself negatively, the *animals are not clothed* (either because their state is primitive, or because they were shipwrecked—"since they lost their crowns in the storm, nobody has believed that they are the king and queen of the elephants, and the captain has had them locked up in the hold"). It is sufficient to progress so that never again are these interferences repeated, sufficient to match up to Europe, to bear the epiphanic signs of inclusion in the civilized world for the executioner to disappear and by this token the victim: one must be assimilated. And furthermore: the violent moments are established like links in a chain, they are the indispensable nexus between nakedness and clothing, between backwardness and development, between the jungle and the old lady. The stages of conquest and slavery have not been ignored: but the manner of their incorporation allows their meaning to change, the truth to be inverted. While the fact can be withheld, it will be done; but when the pressure of the exploited and neglected sectors renders impossible the simple forgetting of that which contradicts the official version of the facts, ideology splits up this phenomenon and reabsorbs it within the general system, which remains immutable. Certainly, we cannot lie: violence there was. But look how happy the elephants are now.

The procedure of admitting negative features, expelling them towards a remote past, is used constantly in children's literature. Opposite those beings will alwasy appear the authentic heroes, who will wipe out the depravity of yesterday and consecrate the splendour of tomorrow.

Let us see some examples taken from Disney.

Donald Duck, the nephews and Grandma Duck have set off (due to their boredom, a typical situation) in search of adventure in the Far West. "Spectacular scenery, isn't it boys?" "Like television, but in three dimensions". But they are attacked by Indians, who are not *playing*, but hate all ducks. Fifty years ago Buck Duck tricked them twice over, stealing their lands from them and then selling them back when they were no longer valuable. The Indians have to be convinced therefore, that not all ducks (white men) are bad and that the plundering in the past can be corrected. To rise above earlier exploitation and fraud is to abate mistrust: everything has changed, the peoples can reach an understanding, there is room for the marginalized in the present order and civilization, old differences can be forgotten. But behold! Two swindlers appear who want to buy the lands for "a thousand cents". The ducks, however, save the situation: "That is a swindle; they know how valuable the natural gas is which is seeping out in the mine!" The result is that the Indians make peace with the ducks. And how are the natives integrated into the world, once suspicions are allayed? In two ways: a) "A big gas company will do all the work and pay the tribe well". Opposite the swindlers, past and present is the (big) company which will resolve the problems with *justice*. The outsider (Scrooge McDuck?) is not necessarily bad; badness exists where the exact price is not paid (an imposed price, according to what conditions and what market), and b) *tourism*. This solution, which we will see repeated in Babar, means that the Indians sell their 'autochthonous' being and that the adventurers enjoy peace and a holiday. (In which their static ideal is realized, all senseless movement which dominates adventure achieves its resolution. Besides, they can rest without having worked, but meriting it through the misfortunes they have suffered: leisure without previous sweat, deconcretized leisure.)

Another example: the ducks search for a treasure in Aztecland.[5] In the past, the bad conquistadors wanted to snatch the gold from the poor Indians (shown with figures of ducks). And now the 'bad boys' want to repeat exactly the same process. Besides emphasizing thus that history is essentially repetition of an identical contingency in which the bad want to take from the good their property (to which the whole capitalist system clings, without questioning the origin of the money), it allows the Indians' descendents to surmount the past, leave aside an anachronistic attitude and integrate themselves in the contemporary and technical world. The ducks rescue a shepherd's lamb. "I don't know how to repay that kind action." But the shepherd turns out to be the keeper of the treasure: "I maintained the tradition of hiding the loot from attackers". Donald replies: "This is absurd! The conquistadors don't exist any more." There is no reason to isolate riches. The faithful punchline: "Visit Aztecland, admission: one dollar". The natives eliminate the memory of a first bad experience; they open their doors to foreigners, who *are not conquistadors*. Those who come from outside educate the Indian ("This is absurd!") and they explain to him how to exploit his resources. And once again all the agitation is canalized in the holidays. ("Our adventure ends in the forms of a tropical holiday.") Between the routine (with which the story opens) and the leisure at the end, lies the adventure: the ducks are rewarded for having thus helped the helpless. But more than anything the adventure is the means to obtaining riches and reward. Just as gold is the abstraction of work (value) incorporated in the object, so adventure is the abstraction of the effort which is needed (which is suffered) to produce it: adventure is work inverted, negativized, deconcretized. Sweat made fetish.

It is handled in the same way in Babar. Violence is accepted as existent, but its meaning is altered radically.

The ideology contains, therefore, within itself the dream, the aspiration, the ideal scheme, perfect, abstract, but it also imitates reality, while masking it. Thus, for example, the bourgeois dream assured that natives would be found disposed to 'become civilized' and there are Babar and Cornelius to prove it. The first contact between Europe and a 'barbaric' country was by means of the indigenous interpreter: he is the linguistic connector of the two spheres. "Cornelius talks like a book." Examples are manifold, but it is preferable to return to the chronological analysis.

We had left Babar at the happy moment of his coronation. At the same time he weds Celeste; simultaneously the monarchy and family, the kingdom and the possibility of heirs are established. The two springs of the future.

They leave on a honeymoon. To this effect they have a balloon (a loud yellow colour, the same as Babar's crown), in which the two will *rise* above the other elephants. This is a recurrent motif: to *climb*. The first thing Babar rushed to do arriving in the city was to play in the lifts, to seek vertical mobility. Undoubtedly this idea (remember Dumbo the flying elephant) contains the desire to deny the heaviness of the body, of that concrete element which always keeps us so anchored to necessity and circumstances.[6] In other books he climbs mountains to ski (twice), is invited to the land of the birds, acquires a disguise which enables him to fly. There is here an obsession to ascend: the protagonist needs to be accepted in 'society', in the 'high' circles. Having abandoned the vertical position, now on two legs, the elephant only thinks of continuing to rise. The image consolidates the urgency of divesting oneself of the lower condition, of moving up, of being someone greater. Clambering up the ladder which society offers.

But more than this it is important to underline the journey itself. The land of the elephants has lost its exotic quality: it is reserved to be the backyard of Europe. One of the fundamental themes of contemporary story books is 'adventure', the search for new sensations which break the routine and habit, the meeting with dangers (disorders) which could place in doubt the interior and exterior order of the characters, but which they always manage to overcome. In the world of Disney, for example, the remote geographical settings facilitate the search for treasures, since there, evidently, no one is owner of the riches and no one has worked to obtain them. But in Babar this journey fulfils various other specific functions. Already in the bizantine-baroque novels and their contemporary derivatives, the kings (and at times lesser heroes) found themselves scourged by misfortune (shipwreck, captivity, etc.) and, as a result, brought closer to the reader, 'deflated'; but by means of *fortitude* and *magnanimita*[7] they showed themselves worthy of the riches with which providence eventually showered them. They return exalted and triumphant to their country, which meantime has great need of them. Their estrangement serves to show they are indispensable.

However, if we look closely at the story, the ultimate meaning of accidentality is to put them *to the test*. Just like Robinson Crusoe, they arrive on an island, and like him, they don't lose contact with civilization[8] either: they wash their clothes, cook and season their food exquisitely, etc. The two elephants could well have reverted to primitivism, have slid back into bestiality (as occurs in several European novels of the fifties, for example in *Lord of the Flies*, by William Golding). They carry Europe like an internal dimension, have proved their exemplary capacity to govern. And precisely they confront "fierce and wild cannibals", creatures who have not attained civilization. It reproduces an experience much treated in European literature: the contrast of two types of natural creature, one of the positive sign, the other of negative sign.[9] Being civilized, paradoxically, the animals will defeat the men. Opposite the nakedness of the cannibals, the clothes of the elephants; opposite the cannibalism (taboo), the fire which domesticates, the rice and fish. The distance between Babar and the savages implies that there is no possible return to the primitive state. But even more important, it is going to prepare us for the struggle, within the land of the elephants, against those animals (the rhinoceroses) which also have not been civilized, and which is paralleled in the next episode.

In fact there is a war in the land of the elephants. While the old lady is rescuing her friends from the circus (naturally the first thing she does is to *clothe* her proteges and let them rest in separate beds, subdued by a portrait on the wall of their protectress), Arthur (Babar's young cousin) has played a "nasty prank" on a sleeping rhinoceros (a rocket tied to its tail). Cornelius apologizes in a polite tone, promising to punish the child, etc. The rhinoceros is not placated and turns threatening. The war which follows, and in which Babar assures his leadership and, definitively, the superiority of civilization over barbarism, appears to originate thus in a marginal issue, in the eccentric personality of the rulers and, in fact, in their lack of civility.[10] To explain the struggles between the animals (between the Americans, Africans, Asians), there is recourse to their primitive state. These 'lunatics' magnify the facts beyond their reality: "They wanted to catch Arthur to make a meat pie". To avoid further pitfalls, it will be sufficient for the rest of the animals similarly to become sensible, 'westerners'. It does not deny—as can be seen—the struggles in that continent where European ways of life arrive: only that they are not provoked by the Europeans, but rather, on the contrary, the acceptance of civilized patterns is what will allow the 'barbaric' state of war to be left behind. Babar will use his ingenuity, his capacity as strategist, to take on brute force and cruelty: an ingredient of civilization (paint) will serve to disguise his soldiers and frighten his adversaries. "The rhinoceroses, believing they are monsters, flee in disarray, terrified." The economic backwardness, and the natives' superstition, have been decisive: technical ability has tamed those who wished to continue practices at variance with reason. The elephants, being armed (they have technical knowledge which separates them qualitatively from their enemies) will win. The closeness to western interests and all they represent, signifies strengthening the country and defeating the rest. In the drawing, Babar climbs up on one of his own subjects, one of the elephants, lifts his hands in sign of victory, while the rhinoceroses (who are remarkably alike to the elephants themselves in size and colour), are put in chains. Later peace will be signed. The immediate, military effect, has shown the goodness of the system, and augurs the way for the next step: to put this knowledge into elaborating a new, civilized order. The time has arrived to build the first city of the elephants. After the war, a peaceful civilization identical to the European one. The steps to colonization.

The dromedaries "brought Babar his heavy luggage and all the things he had bought when on his honeymoon in the land of men". Magically, the whole of civilization is contained in these boxes. Babar gives a speech: "My friends, in these trunks and bales and cases I have presents for you all and all the tools necessary for the building of our city". For the first time, then, the elephants set to work. It is the crucial moment: the natives build a city which follows European lines. Imperialism penetrates Africa. But the elephants "are happy". "They hammer, pull, push, dig, toss, carry and open their great ears to listen to the old lady's records". In the drawing each one is seen working on his own, a harmonious division of labour. Babar in the middle directing operations.

The end result is cloying docility: each one of them has his own bungalow. At the edges, higher up (climbing, climbing), there is a two storeyed house for Babar, and another identical one for the old lady.

In fact, the old lady has decided to remain with them. But now her character is finally made clear to us: during the war, (with Celeste) she founds a hospital (with a huge Red Cross), where she works "unselfishly". The charitable aspect of her intervention is accentuated. Later she is decorated ("she has done so much for them and the wounded"). In the picture she appears in a white monastic gown and now we can be certain: she is the missionary spirit in Africa (and in other places). Her frail, stretched form, her motherhood without children, her charitable gestures, her spirituality, outline militant Catholicism. But there is no overt reference to religion: she represents Christian values without mentioning them. The war over, she reverts to her original role: education. "She often tells stories to the elephants", who form a circle around her on the ground. Although it is still not the moment to analyse in depth the paternalism in these works, it is necessary to point out that the aboriginals, negroes, natives in general, are treated as 'children' and the exploiting country as the motherland, source and womb of the riches. It is emphasized semantically that it is the metropolis which gives life (light) and gives birth to that poor orphan (the satellite); subsequently it nurses it and hands on the instruments so that it may grow and be educated. The old lady summarizes in one, therefore, the characteristics of the distant mother (grandma, governess, aunt, schoolteacher, and what have you). This is related, besides, to the basic idea that nations constitute one big family. We will see later that this brings as a consequence the idea that underdevelopment is a lack of (biological) growth, an earlier, inferior stage towards maturity, and that therefore it is enough to 'take off', to progress, in order to reach the next stage. When Babar is older he is going to be exactly like the old lady. The ties of emotional and intellectual dependence are also legitimized. It is evident, then, that the bourgeois ideology prefers to avoid—see the case of the ducks, their family of uncles, nephews, cousins, girl friends, but without mothers, children, fathers—the very image of the *father* in this literature. Preferable is a more distant relative, a more ambiguous figure, who rather than dominating grants certain benefits. In effect, then, the paternalistic relationship is consolidated, which tends to create in the 'child' a psychological dependence, a constant waiting for orientations, values, routes, advice and handouts[11] and to cap it all it creates a situation such that when the 'offspring' uses (if he can) the education they have given him, to free himself from the parental yoke or to examine his own situation critically, the relationship is always defended through 'gratitude', through 'loyalty', through 'respect for your elders', through the perennial fairy godmothers.

Babar (son) is going to repeat with his subjects (and with his children) what he has learned in his motherland, the secret, magic, almost Oedipal source of his power: he will treat them as children. "Babar now kept his promise: to each elephant he gave a present, together with good working clothes and lovely holiday costumes." It is an economy—at present—without money, but already there is a form of debt and payment. The elephants "went home dancing". But the drawing is striking: through one door dozens of elephants enter, an amorphous crowd, all on four legs, queuing up to receive their present; from the other door they leave on *two legs*, half-clothed, gifts in hand. A stage in ideal history has come to an end: without snags, a city has been created in the margins of time, without exploitation or money. The dancing will never end.[12]

But their day now appears divided in two, emphasized by two types of outfit: leisure and work. The presents they have received serve to increase their dependence, to remove them from their 'barbaric' state, but with their enthusiastic agreement. The result will be a Garden Party on Sunday: but they will have to work now for the whole week to prepare the occasion.

With clothes comes the division of the elephants. The youngsters go to school, the older ones "have chosen a job". It is something voluntary, implicitly involves great delight: the division of labour appears as necessary, something which benefits everyone equally in a society of exchanges of services. "When Capalousse had holes in his shoes he took them to Tapitor, and when Tapitor was ill Capalousse attended him. If Barbacol wanted to put a statuette in his mantelpiece he told Podular, and when Podular's jacket was worn out Barbacol measured him for a new one. Justinien painted Pilophage's portrait and Pilophage defended him against his enemies. Hatchibombotar kept the streets tidy, Olur repaired motor cars, and, when they were tired, Doulamor played to them."[13]

The model proposed by Babar has had satisfactory effects: the well-being and happiness of his people are evident. The arcadian myth has become reality: the hallowed and natural life of the savage, obtaining all the utilities of technical progress, combines morality and civilization. This privileged space condenses Europe and its nostalgia, it eliminates frictions between developed and underdeveloped countries, between exploited and exploiters. Urban values have not destroyed nature, they have perfected it; the savages have incorporated themselves painlessly into the bourgeois world, just as imperialist mythology had always proclaimed. The European intervention has been a *total success*. The shot which killed Babar's mother, even the cages in which they were locked up afterwards (not to mention those perverse and primitive rhinoceroses who made war for trifles), are things of the past: they have had a rather excellent, miraculous consequence: the development and harmony of the elephants. Thus the basic idea behind Babar is that no such underdevelopment exists, colonialism no longer exists: there are only backward countries which, on imitating the more 'advanced' ('grown up') countries, on importing technicians and setting to work as they should, on bringing in foreign teachers, they will manage to put themselves on a level. It is a model to be followed, a triumphant experiment. And fundamentally it has been so because the *elephants themselves* have achieved it. There is no need to occupy militarily those countries (which would signify, besides, tremendous expense), there is no need to have direct political domination. It is enough to maintain an economic, technical dominance, a dependent bourgeoisie is enough. This is the neo-colonial thesis.

This theory has been described by Basil Davidson:[14] a middle class has to be created which facilitates the step from the primitive to the civilized state, but whose function consists, in effect, in guaranteeing that the economic system of the ex-colonies will continue being a fragment within the world capitalist system. "Almost always", writes Davidson, "the great colonial powers achieved their objective. In so many colonies they assured that the power would be handed to the traditional chiefs (caciques), members of the small educated elites, which were allied to the groups of national businessmen, graduated in the universities, who had ambitions for personal careers in which the superiority of Oxford or Paris, or others similarly styled, would be emulated. The colonial governors naturally did not regard with closed eyes the deficiencies of 'their Africans'; they argued simply, but speaking carefully, that 'these are the best we can find'. Having found those 'best', they did everything they could to insure that this 'government by an elite' should be prolonged. The native political institutions were twisted or were wrapped in simulacra of parliamentary systems copied from the London or Parisian models, and simultaneously a tremendous programme was developed tending to convince the Africans that the essence and the object of political mental hygiene were found in these forms of democracy, and that any other forms were inferior, impossible or conducive to 'communism'."[15]

The growth of Babar follows very closely the development of a dependent bourgeoisie. For this reason it takes on great importance for us, in a dependent country, to analyse and decodify its ideology. To imitate Babar, in Chile, means internalizing the appropriate emulatory methods in order to continue to progress, to arrive at being 'king', it is to accept a particular theory of development and underdevelopment: the need for foreign models, disdain for the backward reality, the desire to educate oneself in accord with those models (modernizing and ultimately technocratic), to understand that the closer one gets to the centre the more one is bound to power and truth, and that there is no way of advancing other than being transformed into the USA or Europe,

....Without being simplistic we may observe that the children who read Babar in France were the same ones who fought in Algeria; that those who read Babar in England support the Labour and Conservative line on South Africa & Rhodesia; as for the North Americans, we know very well where they have been, are, and will be. — A. Dorfman

that it is necessary to adopt a charitable, sentimental, paternalistic stance, towards the dispossessed and the 'weakest', and that in a hierarchical world everything functions well.

But above all, the fundamental instruction is to not see underdevelopment as a product of the development of other nations, to not see poverty and wealth as two sides of the same coin, the two results of the same phenomenon. Underdevelopment, its problems, its difficulties, its miseries, would resemble the turbulence which Europe suffered in the transition from feudalism to capitalism: it is a 'normal' stage within the 'normal growing up' of a nation. According to W W Rostow, it will suffice that those countries mature, that they be more integrated (that they carry on buying capital goods) into the western system, that they 'start off', that they 'take off', for the crisis of growth ('growing pangs') to disappear. The system is not responsible (if it were one would have to break off the dependence and, as the only solution, marginalize oneself from the world capitalist system); certain reforms must be carried out ("Alliance for Progress", a "Marshall Plan" for Africa, the "vietnamization" of the conflict) which will destroy the "feudal" structure (read here, primitive, traditional, pre-capitalist) and which will permit civilization to flourish. Lincoln Gordon writes: ". . . the already significant nuclei of industrialization, the gradual consolidation of the middle class and the formation of a group of firms full of vitality, although often undisciplined, are realities which give the hope that, through a well organized effort of cooperation, the greater part of Latin America may match the modern world economically in the space of ten years or so".[16] He wrote this in 1959-60.

This theory, as marxist sociologists have demonstrated,[17] reinforces the ties of domination, intensifies exploitation. You must have patience, the dominators suggest: when a mature middle class emerges, the "adolescent" phase of the underdevelopment will be over.

The idea that countries change like organisms, that they follow the same stages of growth as human beings (birth, childhood, adolescence, maturity etc.), afflicted with the same types of difficulty and problems (violence, sickness, domination, instability, etc.) as a product of growing up,[18] helps us to find the key which permits us to appreciate the basic structure of Babar and that of almost all the children's literature of our time. To summarize it in a word, the basic form of ideological domination must be the use of *innocence* to de-realize and reconcile the contradictions of the system.

We have already said that through the elephants the traditional values are incorporated pedagogically in the child. Not only are we informed in what beneficial way Africa (or any other primitive sector) has been brought up by civilization, but also it is demonstrated in what way innocent beings, playful, ignorant, affectionate, ingenuous — in short, children, in short, elephants — are confined in the world of grown-ups and have a place in it. Parallel to the historical scheme of the land of the elephants, a psychological-social message is developed: just as the elephants have adapted to the world, and have grown up, thus the child must do so as well. And he is assured that he has nothing to lose; he can be an adult without renouncing his child condition, just as in the utopia of Babar one can be African and European, man and animal, developed and underdeveloped, working without exploitation or money. ("Before going to sleep Babar thinks about this beautiful day. We will work happily, he tells himself, and thus we will continue being contented".) It is possible to enter the responsible world of adults, without denying ourselves the rights of childhood. It is possible to be initiated in the European world without losing one's nature.

The space in which this literature is perpetuated appears as essentially innocent: living tribally, without money, the relationships between people are simple and Edenic, dwelling proximity to the natural (also understood as ingenuous, immediate, without artifice or complexities) and all this is connected with one of the great human myths, that of the golden age, a uterine space, a paradisical womb. A scenario is fostered, which corresponds to infancy, and within it the animals make possible the necessary identification and projection. The child learns thus — through an alter ego elephant, but which could be a dog, bear, lion, bird — to admire the paternalistic civilized forms, work, education, etc., as though he were also another animal (another colonized being), another little savage who must come to fruit. The customs of the world are learned imitating the evolution of the elephants: the latter begin in a primitive state, crawling (four legs), start to mature, put on clothes, then work, acquire responsibilities. The changes in the child's world, in the stages of each individual's growth, coincide with the transformations in the same world of the elephants. But by means of this identification, of this innocent bridge, he acquires a pseudo-historical vision, he is introduced to a pre-existing scheme concerning the dialectic, to a prioristic way of understanding the world in which he lives (prejustification of a history which he doesn't yet know, but which he now has located, interpreted and snugly fastened in its place).

Innocence is therefore the habitual substratum which makes ideological domination possible: the stages of colonial penetration, the stages of the native's assumption of western civilization as the norm of perfection, the same stages in which the child legitimizes that civilization and allows himself to be encaged within the limits of its system, form an indivisible whole, confusing through the process of innocence, economic innocence, sexual innocence, almost metaphysical, natural innocence. The child does not suspect the animal (nor the adult): the confidence which the animals place in the system is translated into confidence which the children feel with respect to the animals.

The world of adults can conserve, while being permeated with ingenuousness, all its essential dominating characteristics, can be transferred to the child and internalized without creating anti-bodies of rejection. The child swallows *en bloc* the world itself, the system and its necessary kindness, the forms of its functioning, and this will permit him to flow through the ducts of socialization: the child prepares himself to function, to be an adult, to be Babar; to learn that this colonization (by his parents, by the most advanced nations) is highly beneficial to those who receive it, that those primitive nations (one of which may well be his own) are in a submissive and excellent relationship with mother-Europe, and that whatever type of dependence (his, on the values of his parents) is equally magnificent, and that he — elephant — will continue gloriously and without interruption the labor started by his ancestors, the old lady, grandma, the governess, mother church. Individual psychological life has been confused with the historical life of nations, and the result is a parallel structure of domination in both. Just as he has been treated like a child for his own good, thus the natives have to be, thus the backward nations . . . . . . The underdeveloped are children (and not a consequence of a world imperialist system), who only needed education, only needed technology to accede to the western, Christian, adult world. The contradictions and the changes are explained thus by biologizing the stages in society. The way in which the child grows up, will foster in him the idea that the maturing of the peoples-identical-to-children will be similar, will follow the same auspicious channels: the colonial and family systems reinforce each other mutually.

The innocence of that world appears in this way as the framework which makes possible all the other inversions and concealments. In animals the history of men — without its contradictions — can be developed; society moves within the limits of the "natural". The child is positioned at just the right spot of removal and closeness with respect to the models: he senses they are human beings, but at the same time knows they are not. This first fusion of nature and society, of animality and history, is the introductory step to the later simplification of the real tensions, the unity of city and country, development and underdevelopment, Europe and Africa, order and liberty, work and happiness. The contradictions have been resolved, we have arrived at the end of human history: it is not essential for socialism to realize *through the dialectics of change* the overcoming of the antagonisms, their synthesis, because in reality — just as men are elephants and elephants men — there is no such antagonism, no irreconcilable tension exists.

And hence the name of the protagonist: *Babar* recalls the childlike (the babble, the stutter, the naive repetition of syllables, but it is also a way of referring to Papar, to the father, to the admired future model. And as if it were small matter the idea is attached of baba-rian ("babare" in French), a barbarian missing an *r*, a quasi-barbarian, a semi, a perhaps, a who knows. And likewise the script in which the story is written appears equally naive: rounded, a little hesitant, careful, almost archetypal in a young child who has already learnt to write.

There are many other methods of preserving the innocence of that paternal figure. Among them, the most notable is a constant fluttering of birds around Babar, a gentle spiritualization of his character, a benediction of wings. It is something like — excepting the distance — the circle of violins about the illuminated head of Christ in Bach's *Passion According to Saint Matthew*. The story is always commenting on the message, reaffirming it pictorially.[19]

But the story is not over yet. There remains a final stage, which will last forever. In the anniversary parade of Celesteville the elephants are seen dressed up in costumes from all ages and countries: musketeers, Napoleonic Roman soldiers, lancers, boyscouts, etc.

Let us remember that the elephants do not have a cultural past of their own, since before the arrival of Babar they lived primitively and ingenuously in the haven of cyclical nature, they breathed paradise without time and without problems, in which one day was identical to the next. But on receiving a present modelled on Europe, on the commencement of colonialization and assimilation, they jump to another stage: they must attach themselves to the European past, invent an elephantine *history* which may be human history. The land of the elephants loses its essence of colony, its dependence on annulling the consciousness and knowledge of its peculiar situation: it now desires to be totally assimilable to Europe, for on erasing the past of the elephants and substituting it with a European one, the whole previous stage is cancelled, it eliminates all reference to the fact that an elephant once fled to the city and returned Prometheus-like with civilization and that they had a war with the rhinoceroses and were caged in and all the rest. The land of the elephants is not a mere orbit of Europe; it is one more of the centres which consider themselves heirs to the universality of western culture. It is not enough to adopt the present conditions of Europe (i.e. industries, etc.), but rather it is imperative to abolish its own history and to live that of the colonizers.

And therefore, simultaneously (out of the blue, so as to avoid questions) Babar's three children are born; the first generation conceived in the civilized ambit. This fictitious past is constructed for the children, for the hiers to the kingdom. It is a European world, radically removed from Babar's infancy: their mischief, accidents, toys (they have miniature lions and giraffes), are those of human beings. On the way to Belletrompe Castle a completely European landscape is seen: A tractor, a plane, a latest model stationwagon, a lorry. The mechanization of the land of the elephants implies — for the author — the suppression of the past, the fading out of primitivism.

"In the majestic hallway, the children admire the ancestors' portraits. Oh what an elegant musketeer, says Arthur. I prefer the Roman, says Zephyr". But we know that, given the progress of Babar from a primordial state to great worshipper and importer of civilization, it is impossible for their ancestors to be Romans, or Renaissance or Eighteenth Century people. They were simply elephants. Just as western history is imposed on subjugated races as their own , as *theirs*, when in reality their history is that of pitiless socio-economic domination, similarly the tracks left by the elephants in their march towards this civilized state are wiped out. It becomes impossible for the little elephants (and the equally little children) even to glimpse the process of *changes* which were necessary for "progress" to arrive in that land. The earlier books are erased, even that fictitious pseudo-history remains subsumed within the temporal European canons. The falsification which Babar verifies from his own past, which in turn was already an idealization (the rosy history of the conquest and exploitation), corresponds to a dependent bourgeoisie which ends up perpetuating, detemporalizing, the roots of the real. Babar's children (and the readers) learn the history of Europe as their own, but from this recollection has been eliminated all reference to the rest of the world, by the domination of which capitalism developed some countries and stunted others. The elephants become men, and do not wonder about their strange hybrid being of elephantman. We are "the English of South America", "the Switzerland of America". This need has been brilliantly described by Fanon and by Cleaver: the neo-colonial and racist mentality wishes to establish a dependent relationship in which the exploited behave as children and are loved as such, as . . . elephants. "Every colonized people", writes Fanon, " — in other words, every people in whose soul an inferiority complex has been created by the death and burial of its local cultural originality — finds itself face to face with the language of the civilizing nation; that is, with the culture of the mother country. The colonized is elevated above his jungle *status* in proportion to his adoption of the mother country's cultural standards. He becomes whiter as he renounces his blackness, his jungle."[20](Italics added). At the back of Babar one feels, then, the racist theory with which capitalism has justified anthropologically its superiority: the coloured man needs the white man, there is a subconscious desire to be squashed and to surrender their personality. As woman needs man and wishes to be subjugated, possessed; as the child renders the father indispensible. All relationships which recur in the books and reiterate the central thesis.

Thus Babar, his family and his realm enter the territory certain of lasting stability, of progress without change. From now onwards, the world will be immutable. On assimilating completely the bourgeois normativity, all possibility of transformation is lost, since not even the falsified roots exist: each incident, as in TV series, as in picture stories, as in comic stories, as in the majority of the products of alienating mass consumption, resembles structurally the following and the previous one, it is one more in a concatenation of identities within a static totality. The whole evolution of Babar has been created with the ultimate intention of acting as though he did not exist, to arrive at an ideal situation, identical to that of other characters, like Donald, Porky, Woody, etc. In the case of Babar it is especially interesting: he covers a path which other storybook animals have not covered (there are atemporal, asexual, their country neither advances nor deteriorates, they were never born, they have no father or mother), to finish up the same as them: in not knowing his history, the stages of his genesis, he is absorbed into Donald Duck or whoever, he becomes identical to him, and therefore the tales which are going to be reproduced in this mythical, ahistorical space, will not differ from those which occur in other storybooks. In this way, Babar can be transformed into a monthly magazine, a television series.

The miracle has been completed: the elephants are Europeans and they have Greek mythological statues, cherubims, satyrs, sirens, in pachyderm shape. *Africa* has been forgotten. But without doubt the elephants continue being innocent, good, and a little marginal, since therein rests their particular value. The author will focus from now on those moments when the elephants adopt such and such a specific western value, and which thus serves as a way of teaching the child-reader to accept, to learn, that characteristic as well. The primitive is erased insofar as historical stage, but not where a substratum which facilitates the learning of the apparatus and the processes of domination.

An example: *Babar* and *Father Christmas*. The little elephants discover how the children in other countries celebrate Christmas. "Don't you think we could write to him (Father Christmas) so that he might come to our houses in the land of the elephants?" But Father Christmas does not reply and Babar has to intervene: "Why didn't it occur to me before? I will go myself and ask Father Christmas to come to the land of the elephants". He follows the trail until managing to have a word with the Christmas visitor: "Babar asks him to go to his kingdom to distribute toys to the little elephants, just as he does with the children of men". After bringing the Old Man to the land of the elephants, where he relaxes in the sun, the reward comes: the responsibility is delegated to Babar. "Do you know what there is inside this bag? A Father Christmas suit of your size! A magic costume, which will enable you to *fly* (my italics) through the air, and a basket always full of toys. You will substitute for me on Christmas Eve in the land of the elephants. I promise to return when I have finished work and bring you a beautiful Christmas tree for your children." Babar imports, and then embodies the foreign model, which naturally is sought by all children (elephant and human) since it carries with it benefits and gifts. Paternalism is accentuated, the international habit is internalized: the attainment of happiness and wellbeing comes from imitating "the land of men" until there is no distinction. The great White Father fuses with the Great Father King and they mutually glamorize each other. For the children (for the elephants) the representative of Father Christmas, and therefore of magic, of control over the air, of the paradise of presents and profit, of power, the representative of foreign charity and the channel through which it arrives, the one who assures the continuation of childhood forever, is Babar, chief, father, civilized being, thrice powerful. God.

Babar is and isn't Father Christmas: he bestows presents but his suit is a foreign disguise. The children intuit that the true strength of Babar rests in maintaining an adequate, affectionate relationship with the land of men. The creatures who come from outside become indispensible, as much for the economic progress of the land of the elephants, as for the psychological wellbeing of the reader, who has already appropriated his role in the power structure (father-son, metropolis-satellite, rigidity-instinct) and who expects to see concretized and verified at all times the same system. Repetition creates a mental habit and everything converges to create a neutralized child — and, in the future, man.

Thus, from "outside" Professor Grifaton arrives, brother of the old lady (the gerontocracy continues): he brings a series of novelties, each one more marvelled at by the elephants. He goes out to catch butterflies for his collection: he is the intellectual (or technocrat) who comes to tell the natives about the riches they have and how they should exploit them. The drawing we see now shows books, a microscope, a series of scientific instruments, geometric designs on the wall and a Picasso reproduction. This space is of Europe, but always a little behind the times, always faintly animal: sufficient to always import the technology, science, the art, the progress of Europe, the latest model citroen. The young readers, themselves a little behind the times, will identify themselves with the elephants, especially the children of the elephants, and will also find those ideals admirable, the constant need to modernize themselves, to be up-to-date; technocracy as a solution to problems.[21]

A cave is discovered. It is Professor Grifaton, with his enterprising spirit, who leads to it being explored. "This cave interests me a great deal", says Professor Grifaton. "Do you not also think, my dear Babar, that we should explore it?" And they set out on an expedition, provided with modern equipment (helmets, lamps, etc.). But the affair does not end here. On discovering an underground river, "Dear commandant", says Professor Grifaton (note the politeness, a certain paternal condescension, distance and affection, a certain patience in the professor's voice), "wouldn't it be marvellous if all the elephants could sail up and down the subterranean river in motor launches? I have had an idea to build a pleasure boat". The ideas are always accepted with a "Bravo", "Long live", "Yes, yes", fixed interjectional forms which reaffirm assent and imposition. The result is a boat: "atomic propulsion with paddle wheels". Once again the most advanced technology (the atomic) is blended and made innocent, with the nostalgia of an earlier age, of an uncontaminated and placid world (the paddles).

But the ulterior aim of Professor Grifaton is *tourism*; the out of the way place is hitched to the world economic system, being transformed into a retreat for happiness and relaxation. Without industrializing the country, and furthermore maintaining it in an "exotic" state, "conserving" it, its nature and ancient traditions are traded on. It is *developed*, certainly, but it is a photographic development: the country is sublimated within a postcard, a *souvenir*, a "memento of Chile", and the inhabitants — in order to extract the tourists' money — must fit in with them and adjust their landscapes (their natural resources) to the demands of the travel agencies, must read about themselves through almanacs, encyclopedias, guidebooks, handbooks (for Junior Woodchucks).

The plan is a success. "And in the evening, in the amusement hall, Cornelius decorates Professor Grifaton, with the order of merit, as benefactor of Celeseteville". The hospital and educational services of the old lady, already received their reward; now it is the turn of the bearer of the Scientific Word.

The form of domination — as time passes — is modernized. "The latest ideological invasion", writes Gunder Frank, "proposes that North American know-how and technology can resolve all the problems of the peoples of the world, with simply allowing the Yankees to apply them without meddling. In industry this means foreign investments and a higher degree of monopolization . . . and unemployment. In agriculture this means methods of cultivation, seeds, fertilizers and machinery, etc. from the United States . . . and the production of fertilizers and machinery by Standard Oil and Ford. For the population, it means birth control through contraceptive pills, and medicines . . . and pharmaceutical companies. For culture it means 'the American way of life' in everything, through the media of mass expression, 'popular' education, through 'science', through electronic statistics, etc. The great Latin American bourgeoisie accepts all this on the basis of lesser partner. The 'nationalist' elements in the bourgeoisie and part of the petty bourgeoisie reject North American participation, but accept the technology, saying they will apply it themselves . . . and better."[22]

And the children, what do they say to all this? "At home, the children watch the fete (the decoration) on television, in the company of the old lady. They are very excited and clap loudly."

Thus, the Babar books never miss a chance to accentuate paternalism and even if occasionally the grown-ups come out slightly ridiculed, generally there is a tendency towards adoration of the fathers and their civilization. A divine transcendence is affirmed (God) which grants validity and meaning to the world. Liberty, non-dependence, is rejected.

But this means that the ties of domination can be made clear without much problem: the very rebelliousness of the child will end up disproving the relationships which are established in Babar's world, however innocent may be the unending jargon of submission.

Therefore, before ending, it would be interesting to show, although briefly, a form of domination in children's literature which proves to be more hidden and subtle, and consequently more dangerous: a complete ideological inversion. I have chosen, for this comparative effect, an episode in the hazardous life of Donald Duck (No. 434 of *Disneyland*).

In the first picture we are presented with a meeting of the "prudent parent club of Duckland". "It is the duty of all parents to watch for the safety of their children", asserts a mastodontic and old fashioned woman from a platform. Among the audience, Donald Duck stands out, assenting: if his nephews were in danger, "I would resort to my great strength and skill to rescue them". And now he will have an opportunity to put into practice his knowledge and precautionary measures: they are about to travel to South America ("full of dangers"). It appears we are dealing with a paternalistic attitude similar to that of Babar. However, the world of adults is already satirized in the first scene, and Donald above all. All the grown-ups are ridiculous, cross-eyed, archaic, falsely solemn; they smile idiotically, sit in rigid postures, gathered together for a plainly absurd, grotesque reason. They are caricatures of parents, pigs, dogs, human beings intermingled. And the worst is Donald: everything he proposes (boasts, cliches, "correct" answers) is ridiculed in his imbecilic face, in his fixed obsession.

In effect, the next pictures confirm this intention to criticize the adult world: while the nephews calmly contemplate the wharf moving away, Donald (shouting out that he will save the children if they run any risk) sways on the deck railing. When Donald falls, it is the children who save him. This situation is repeated *ad nauseum*. Donald is stupid, foolhardy, cowardly, mistaken all the time, lacks forethought, is selfish and disorganized, and the children have to rescue him from the most unlikely situations. It is an upside-down world, emphasized by the four or five occasions when Donald appears drawn with legs in the air falling, floating half-drowned, etc.). The adult is good for nothing, in spite of his words, his grandiloquence, his outward gestures. It is the children, in this world, who represent goodness and intelligence.

The structure of the story therefore coincides apparently with the criticism which present-day children and young people direct at the adult world. In all of Disney's work the little creatures (Chipmunks, the Big Bad Wolf, Dumbo, the mice Gus and Jaq, the little pigs, Scamp the dog) are more mature than their elders and always come out victorious. The readers, consequently, may feel that here the ideal adventure of the marginalized is played out: those who have the power are eccentric, extravagant, failures, hardheaded, foolish. One of the intentions of the comic form[23] is to make the social burden weigh on those who do not fulfil their duty, who are a pure phantasmagoria.

However, having achieved the identification of the reader with the little ducks, it is necessary to ask oneself, in effect, from where is the criticism of the stupidities of Donald Duck exercised, from what objectivity and norm? First, from his very intentions which are not discussed, and which are not fulfilled: the necessity of an order to protect the defenceless from danger. And secondly, from the responsible actions of the nephews: they are all that he should be. Rational, cautious, generous, wise, foresighted, brave, responsible, in a word, paternal. It transpires that Donald Duck, in the form of adult, is in reality a child, and that the young ducks, in the form of children, are in reality adults. The child attacks Donald Duck who represents all the childish characteristics; the child identifies with the nephews who symbolize all the adult characteristics. The nephews, for example, have to their credit the Junior Woodchuck Handbook, where all reality (amid that reality is South America) is defined and prescribed. There is nothing to discover in the world: everything is already written,[24] everything has already been met. It is sufficient now to apply the pre-established nomenclature, technocratize the universe, find the page of an encyclopedia in order for the problems to disappear. Chance (the great adventurous protagonist of these comic strips) remains subordinated to rationality and order: if Donald ascribed to these categories it would no longer be laughable, there would be no further discordance in the world. We could continue enumerating characteristics. But what is urgent is not deep analysis in this instance. It is important to note how an *inversion* has been brought about.

The child participates in the domination of himself, in the criticism of his axoims, and validates the paternalistic features in the universe when he identifies with children who are in reality the adults. The energies which tend to be rebellious, and which should destroy the existing order, inquiring into the contradictory sense of the world, are taken advantage of to neutralize an unruly being, are channelled so as to reaffirm the dominating categories in society. It is permitted that Babar criticize the old lady, make himself independent, live his own life, his country be liberated; but always provided he does it in the surreptitious name of the values represented by the old lady, provided he assumes the authentic representation of the western and Christian world. In favour of the existing order, Donald's little nephews should manage the situation. When they are adults, when they grow up, they will not repeat the wild errors of their elders. They will continue to progress, rising from sergeant to commanding officer, to general of Disneyland Club, from Junior Woodchucks, climbing *en masse*, small but reliable.

Behind Babar, behind Donald Duck, behind the multiplicity of children's literature in the capitalist countries, there is a single bourgeois vision, a single clear aim: to convince the dominators and the dominated of the goodness of the system, and to legitimize the forms in which it may be changed without threatening the existing order. In our dependent countries this literature acquires a particularly harmful function, since its preconceptions coincide with the way in which we were colonized, the way in which our economy is organized, our culture, our institutions. The bourgeoisie of the "advanced" countries educates its young with these models and the same do for our nations, because we also must be integrated into the scheme, repeat it by heart, just as it is done by the children and adolescents of the dominators and beneficiaries. This form of literature penetrates the whole functioning order, the whole theory of the universe and is reinforced by society as a whole.

A mere denunciation, a substructural, idealistic endeavour to replace these forms with others is not enough. If there is no change in the system of economic, political, cultural domination, if there is not a revolution, the new children's forms conceived will be branded as mere propaganda, and will be rejected as such. Precisely, the dominating ideology is not obtrusive because it *flows with* the system, because it reinforces and does not break the ties in force. Nobody takes notice of Babar because Babar is a part and echo of the accepted reality. The moment that Babar should start to do mad things, to stand on the side of the proletariat, to educate his children in a different way, to use another (poetic) language, the defence mechanism would end up expelling him, he would make himself too conspicuous. The struggle against current forms cannot be done surreptitiously, because the break with the order calls attention to itself. While every emphasis, every justification, inversion, is camouflaged in the environment, is dissolved in the set-up.

The new forms of children's literature will have to emerge in the struggle for a new society, they will become necessary in that combat. Only the destruction of the capitalist system, the gradual defeat of economic and mental neo-colonialism, can guarantee that one day, finally, Babar may risk killing the old lady and, by the loss of his innocence, hit upon the first step on the road to complete liberation.

Translated by John Lyons

---

1. Cf. among other texts by Althusser, *La revolucion teorica de Marx*, Siglo XXI, 1967; Lucien Sebag, *Marxism y estructuralismo*, Mexico, Siglo XXI, 1969, and the studies by Armand Mattelart, published in the CEREN.
2. Babar emerged in 1939 and reached its widest distribution after the Second World War. Thus it coincided with the neo-colonialist thesis regarding the African colonies which were gaining independence. Without being simplistic we may observe that the children who read Babar in France were the same ones who fought in Algeria; that those who read Babar in England support the Labour and Conservative line on South Africa and Rhodesia; as for the North Americans, we know very well where they have been, are, and will be. When Babar is translated into Spanish in 1965 and imported into Latin American countries, there is an acceptance of the process of ideological domination of the children of dependent bourgeoisie, which proceeds to interpret *their own countries* with the patterns and concepts of imperialism. This coincides, furthermore, with the reformist policy of the 'Alliance for Progress'.
3. "Myth does not, then, lend significance to an object which before the myth was lacking; on the contrary, it derives from the signs which make up social reality and superimposes a second meaning . . . This second *superimposed* meaning is presented in the myth as the *unique* meaning, and causes the first one to disappear, or if you prefer, 'eclipse it'' Eliseo Veron, *Conducta, estructura y communicacion*, Buenos Aires, Jorge Alvarez, p.234, 1968.
4. "Writing being the spectacularly compromised form of the word, contains simultaneously, through a rich ambiguity, the being and the semblance of power, what it is and what it would have believed of it." R.Barthes, *El grado cero de la escritura*, Buenos Aires, Jorge Alvares, p.26, 1967.
5. This is not the place to go into the geographical mystifications which occur in children's storybooks. However, I cannot resist the temptation to go a little deeper into this reference to Aztecland. On the one hand this place is an abstraction, remote, non-existent, incredible; consequently, any adventur could take place there, and there would be no other order than that brought by the characters. But, on the other hand, it is obvious that this country is Mexico and no other. There is a tendency to judge the real country (Mexico) as exotic, primitive, having external categories of the fictitious country it represents. The caricature substitutes the face itself. The poverty of these countries, their backwardness, do not have causes: it is a mere superficial eccentricity. This implies that to solve their problems it is sufficient to *technologize* them (underdevelopment is a lack of modernity); and that the inhabitants of these very places, or similar places, become self-aware within the terms of the dominant ideology. The peculiar characteristics of the marginal country (a way of creating new sensations) distinguish themselves among nations which occupy an equal position of dependence and which continue judging each other mutually according to the models lent by the dominators, making fun of themselves when they think they are doing it of others.
6. Cf. Gaston Bachelard, *El aire y los suenos, ensayo sobre la imaginacion del movimiento*, Mexico, Fonda de Cultura, 1958. Also my essay 'To Fly? A study of the narrative of Jorge Edwards and Antonio Skarmeta, *Revista Chilena de Literatura*, 1, pp.59-78, autumn 1970. Cf. Ensayos Quemados, Ediciones de la Flor, Buenos Aires, p.133, 1974.
7. Cf.Wolfgang Kayser, 'Origen y crises de la novela moderna', *Mapocho*, year II, vol.III, No.3, vol.9, pp. 58-80.
8. Cf. Ian Watt, 'Robinson Crusoe as a Myth', in *Eighteenth Century English Literature*, New York, Oxford University Press, pp.158-179, 1959. The pages of Marx's *Capital* are too well-known to be quoted; here also occurs a production of goods in isolation, a fiction of the *homo economicus*.
9. In *La Diana*, by Jorge de Montemayor; in the pastoral comedies of Shakespeare; in the plays of Lope de Vega; in Sannazaro's *Arcadia*; in *Astree* by Urfe, this division within nature proclaims its ambiguity: a generous and basically rational and courtly (shepherds) nature, opposed to a passionate, unrestrainable nature (Machiavellian characters, horrifying wild men who disavow the law of God to base themselves on their instincts).
10. Everything happens by chance in this world. There is a concept of changes as catastrophic, random, and in general unpredictable: the mother's death, meeting with the kindness of the old lady, the king's death, and now the war of the elephants. There are never reasons why anything happens: it is clouded in magic, in the inexplicable, the harsh day-to-day of facts.
11. Cf. Erik E.Erikson, *Childhood and Society*, Penguin, 1965. Apart from this, the other characteristics of the old lady permit her relationship with the real world to be traced. In France, her figure acquires vaguely recognisable features: the effigy of Marianne, of Joan of Arc, of the Statue of Liberty (given to a country which is shaking off its colonial ties), but subjected to an aging, possibly a result of the well-being and the refraining from too close relationships. Furthermore, the neo-colonialist theory accentuates the neutral and mediatory role of the state regarding the conflicts between the monopoly which operates from its own country and the interests of the conquered nations. Her austere benevolence appears thus uncontaminated by those perverse elements.
12. The elephants are always dancing. According to the racist theory concerning negroes, that is what they are good "at that", that they excel in music and sport. Cf. Eldridge Cleaver, *Soul on Ice*, Dell, 1968.
13. Albeit, Babar plays tennis with Pilophage and his wife, that is to say, he keeps on good terms with the military and no one else.
14. 'What's wrong with Africa?', in *International Socialist Journal*, Milan, 1, 4, August 1964, and by the same author, *The Search for a New Society, Which Way Africa?*, Penguin, 1964.
15. Davidson, op.cit., p.482.
16. Lincoln Gordon, 'Abrazo versus Coexistencia. Otros comentarios', in *Contraversia sobre Latinoamerica*, directed by Alberto O.Hirshman, Buenos Aires, Editorial del Instituto di Tella. Rostow's book, *The Stages of Economic Growth: A non-Communist manifesto*, London, Cambridge University Press, 1960. The stages he distinguishes are: "the traditional society; the preconditions for take off; the take off; the drive to maturity; the age of high consumption". The relationship between biology and economy are evident, as are the terms extracted from aeronautical jargon. Babar flies with Rostow's wings.
17. Gundar Frank, Cockcroft, Johnson, *Economia Politica del subdesarrollo en America Latina*, Buenos Aires, Signos, 1970; Petras and Zeitlin, *Latin America: Reform or Revolution? A Reader.*, Facett, 1968. Theotonio dos Santos, *El nuevo caracter de la dependencia*, CESO, Univ. of Chile, 1968.
18. "From the newly constituted league of Nations they accepted the duty of governing them [the African countries] as a 'sacred trust of civilization' until such time as they were able to 'stand on their own feet' in the arduous conditions of the modern world"; and Page, *A short History of Africa*, Penguin, p.210, 1962. Cf. also Romano Ledda, 'Africa: a stage of transition, Social classes and Political Struggle'. *International Socialist Journal*, Milan, IV, No.22, pp.560-580, August 1967.
19. Cf. Umberto Eco, *Apocalipticos e integrados ante la cultura de masas*, Lumen, the section 'El lenguaje del comic', pp.169-176, 1968.
20. *Black Skin White Masks*, Paladin 1970, London; p.14.
21. On technocratic models. Cf. Armand Mattelart, Carmen Castillo, Leonardo Castillo, *La ideologia de la dominacion en una sociedad dependiente*, Buenos Aires, Signos, 1970.
22. 'Subdesarrollo capitalista o revolucion socialista', in *Pensamiento critico*, La Habana, No.13, pp.3-41, Feb., 1968.
23. For an analysis of the comical see my study, 'La muerte como acto imaginativo en Cien Anos de Soledad', in *Imaginacion y violencia en America*, Santiago, Universitaria, 1970.
24. The world would be pre-coded signs where mythology is possible. Cf. Michel Foucault, *Las palabras y las cosas*, Mexico, Siglo XXI, 1968.

quiry violence. Mr Chris Ball, London quar
ashes. area organiser of APEX, alleged day,
and that one of the organisers of Geor
who the strike, Mr John Patel, aged publi
that 23, had been repeatedly hit by time,
bruta- a policeman who called him a the
"Paki bastard." his 2

"PAKI BASTARD"
(Portrait of the artist as a black person)
a live event with slides and sound by
RASHEED ARAEEN

"Paki Bastard" is the 2nd part of the trilogy (art events) which was conceived in 1976-77 as part of **Preliminary Notes for a BLACK MANIFESTO** published in **Black Phoenix** No.1 and which deals with the relationship between the Third World and the West. "Paki Bastard", first performed on July 31 1977 at the ARTISTS FOR DEMOCRACY, London, specifically reflects upon the predicament of black people in Britain; showing also how a black artist, uprooted from his original environment in the Third World and rejected by white society in the West, eventually comes to terms and identifies with the reality of his people. The 1st and 3rd parts, called "Noble Savage" and "Blood Sausages" respectively, will, it is hoped, be performed later this year.

N O T E

The following 6 photographs is a selection from 50 sequences. The text is not exactly the interpretation of the images here, but contains some of the thoughts that went into the making of the work. And although it contains autobiographical references, it would be wrong to read it at personal level.

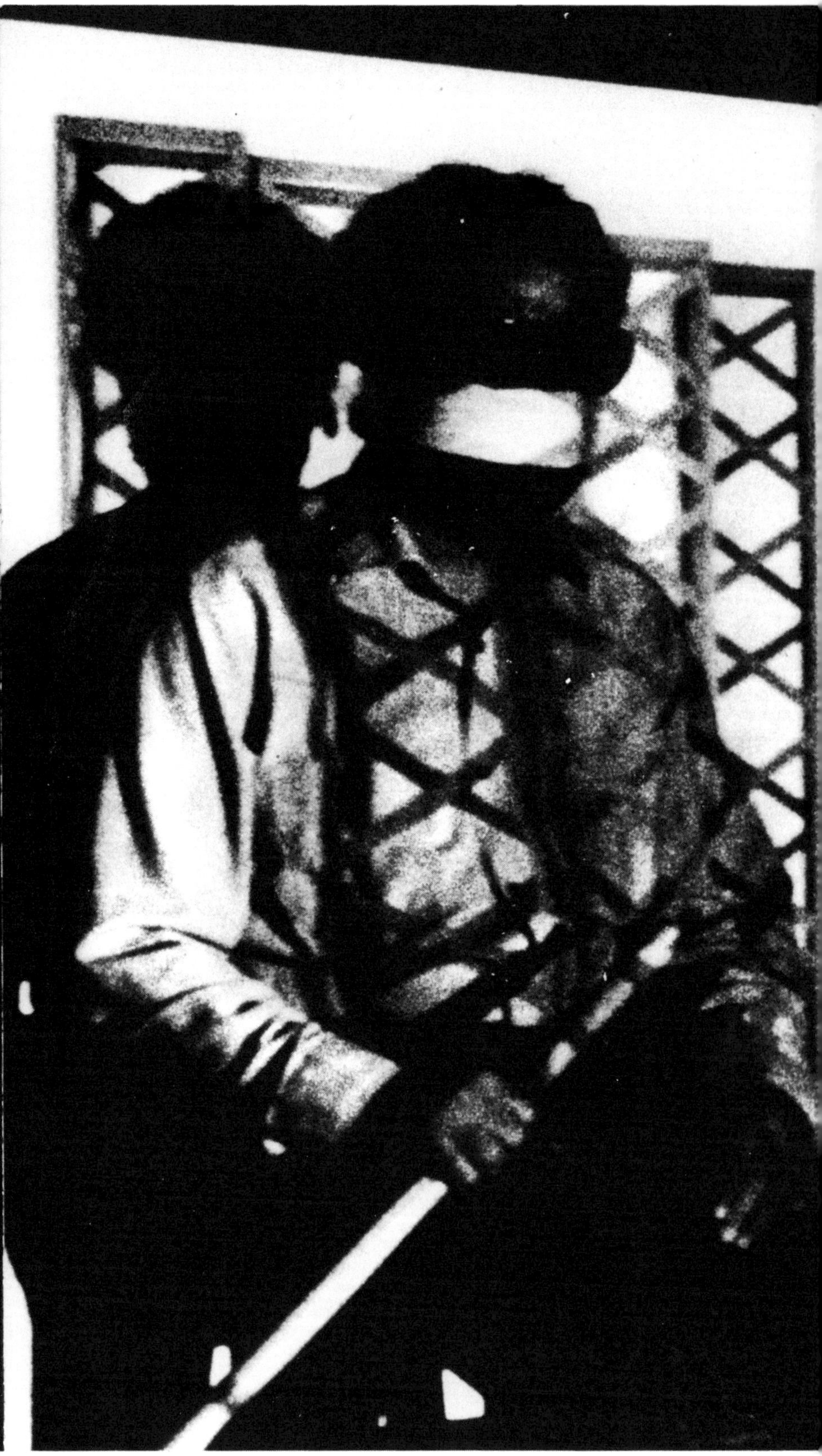

He sits there facing a slide projector, blind and gagged, holding a broom that defines his role in the contemporary world. In the background is the flute sound he made some time ago when he was very depressed. (He can't play 'music'.) The projector projects on him the image of one of his earlier works, the purpose being to create an artistic identity which is used throughout the piece in various manners. It also alludes, at a different level, to the mythical space, which is elevated, privileged and universalised, and in which the artist of the bourgeois world ends up cocooned and incarcerated. It is the mythical space within which the bourgeois 'freedom of artistic expression' manifests, and which is inversely proportional to the real space at the bottom of the hierarchical pyramid. The black, Third World, person thus remains outside this space confronted with reality.

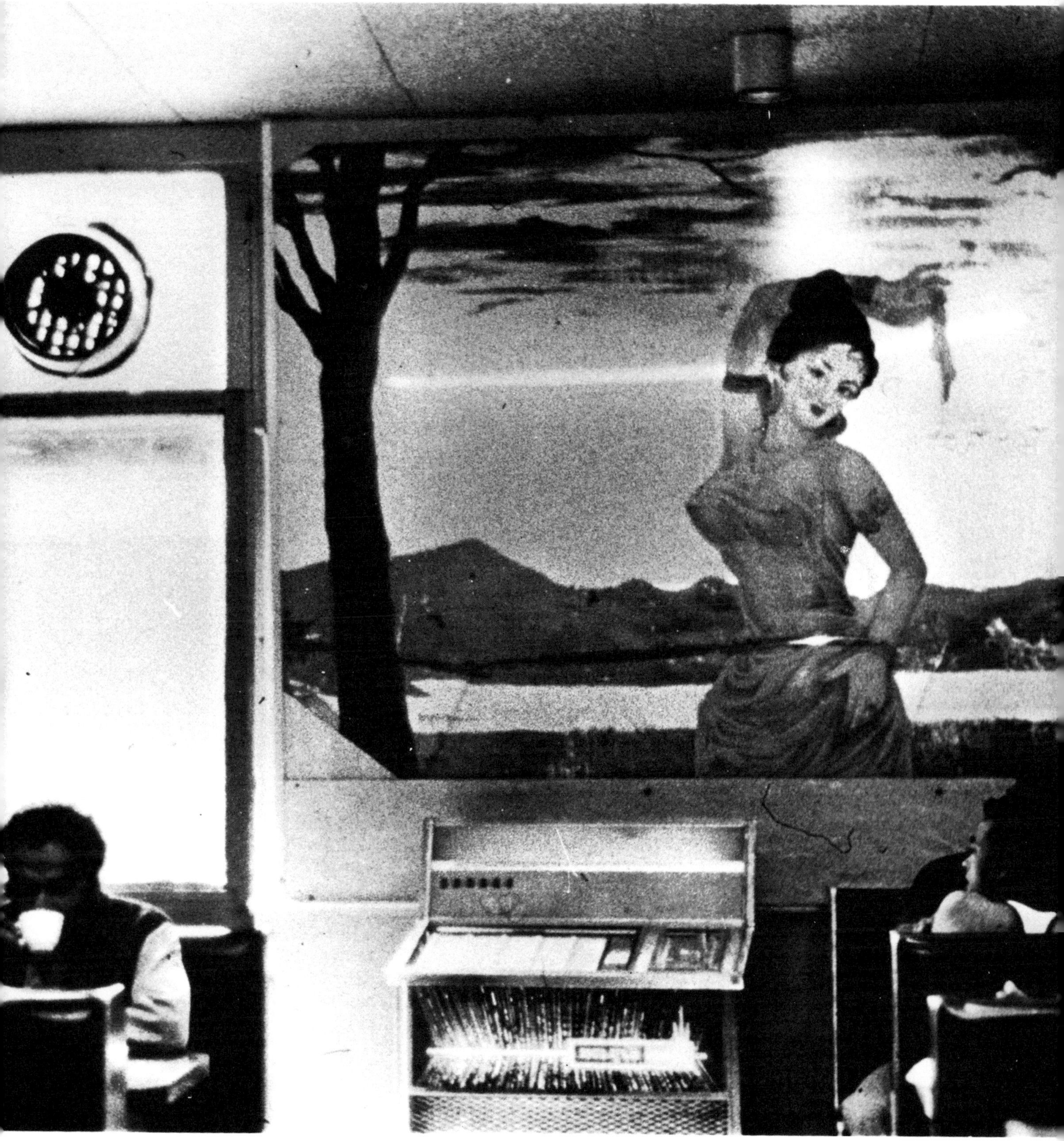

Sitting alone in a café in Brick Lane, he listens to the sexy, jazzy, romantic, sugary, vulgar, ... Indian film songs that pour out continuously from a jukebox. He is overtaken by nostalgia... He thinks of the time, his youth, when he himself secretly entertained the thoughts of becoming a film hero... He remembers his friends with whom he went to school/university, with whom he spent long evenings sitting in cafés and quite often talking about what was new from the West - literature, art, films, etc. How they all longed for the free and bohemian life in Paris, London, New York,... He thinks of his mother, father, brothers and sisters, who are still waiting for his return. They thought that their eldest son, their eldest brother, would one day be a successful engineer - after all he did complete his graduation. He would have been the pride of the family! But he had the crazy idea

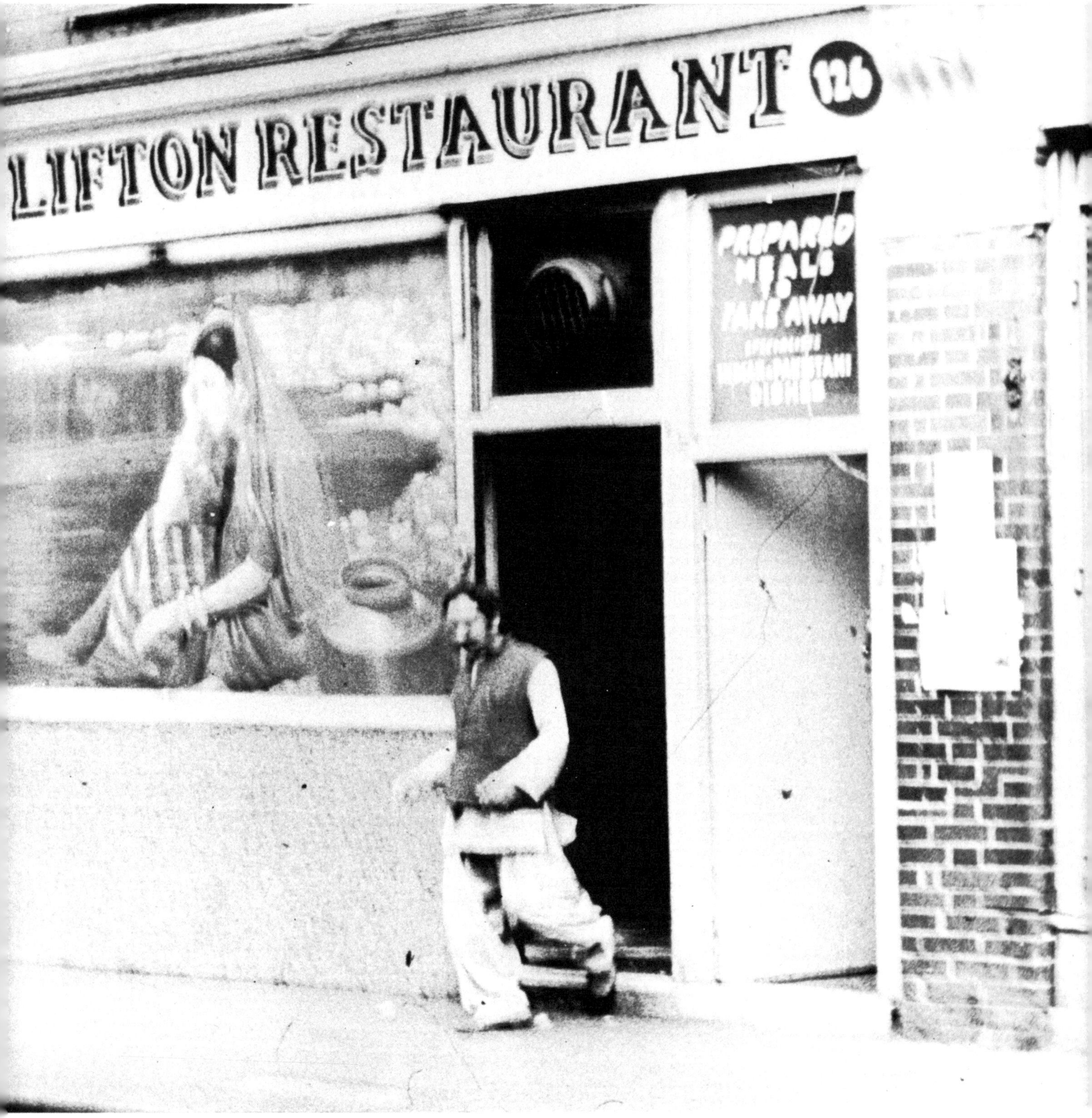

of going to Paris and instead becomimg a famous artist. They wouldn't understand. He had to tell them a lie, that he was going abroad for higher education... He remembers the day when he left. The whole family came to see him off at the harbour. How his two youngest sisters refuse to leave the ship... About three weeks later he was actually in Paris, lonely and homesick. He thought Paris was the centre of civilization... He thought of going back home, but he couldn't face the idea of being called a coward by his friends.... Instead he took train to London... Fourteen years is a long time... How could he come to terms with his 'failures'...

He exits. He leaves behind the fantasies, his own memories, his old dreams, and enters the world of real. It took him some time to realise that his own predicament is not unique. He is in fact part of the people who have been colonised, dominated and uprooted. He finally comes to accept the fact that he is part of the humanity which is being denied its own history, its culture and civilisation being undermined and plundered. He begins to under-

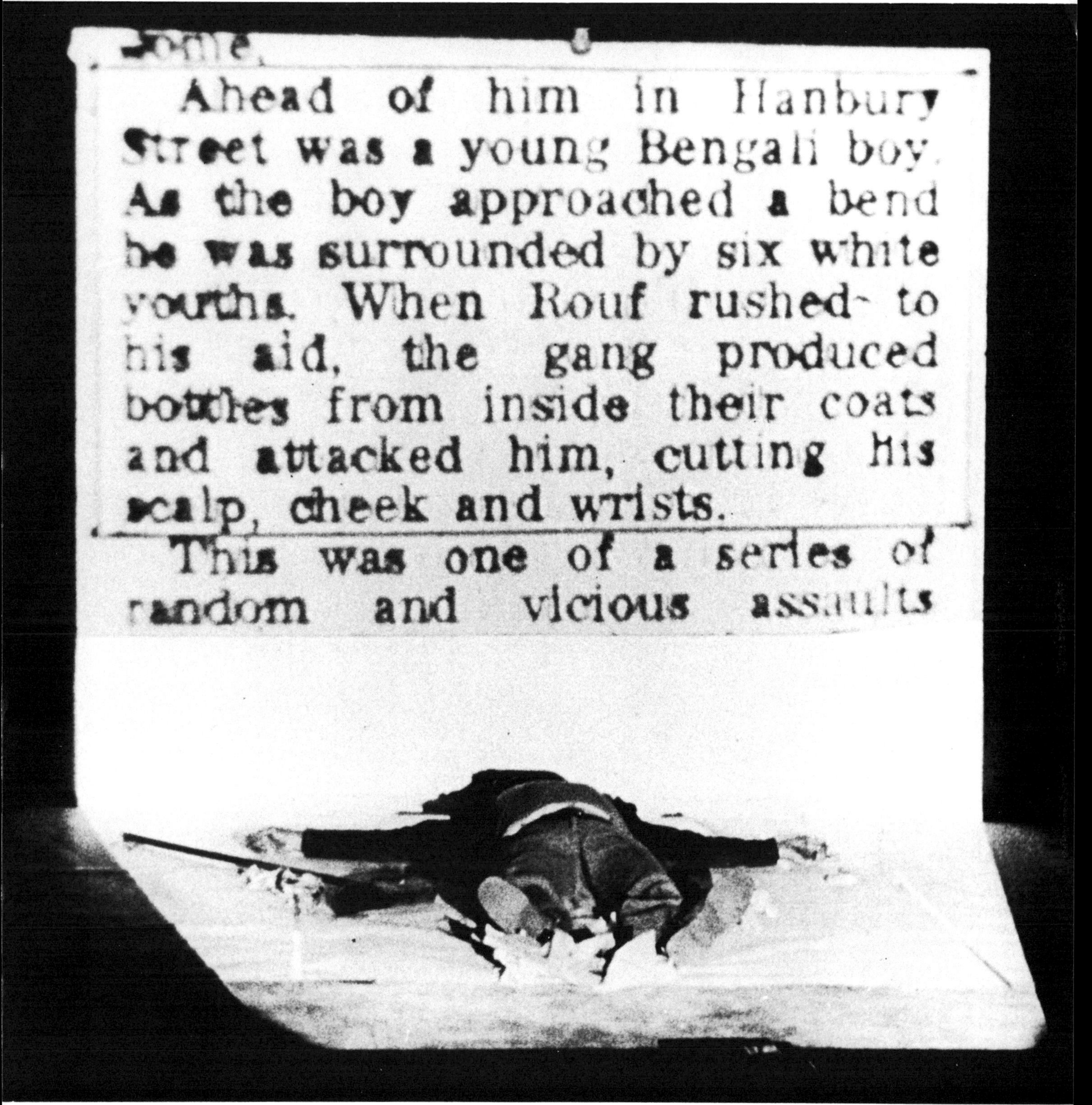

stand why he left his own country; why people leave their own countries and seek livelihood in the hostile and aggressive environment of Western cities. He can now see that the violence which is being inflicted upon people, whether it is physical violence or mental,

April 20 1978	May 4 1978	June 26 1978
KENNETH SINGH	ALTAB ALI	ALI ESHAQUE
MURDERED	STABBED TO DEATH	MURDERED

is the violence of the international economic system that has reduced most of the mankind to poverty and starvation. He can see now the true face of the civilisation that he once cherished. But confronted with all this violence and miseries he feels helpless again.... He thinks of the wretched of the earth, of his own 'wasted' life... Depression overtakes him again........

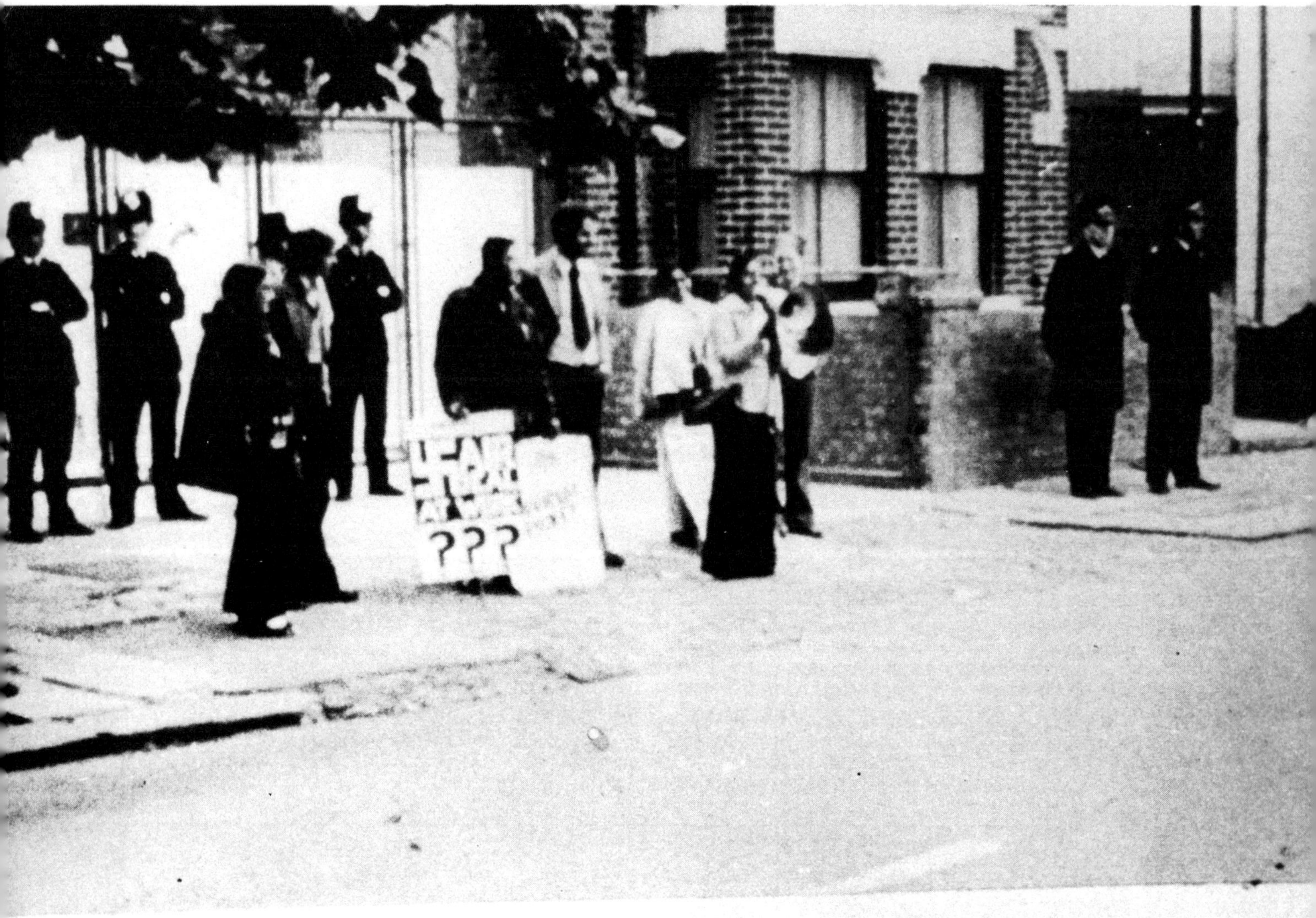

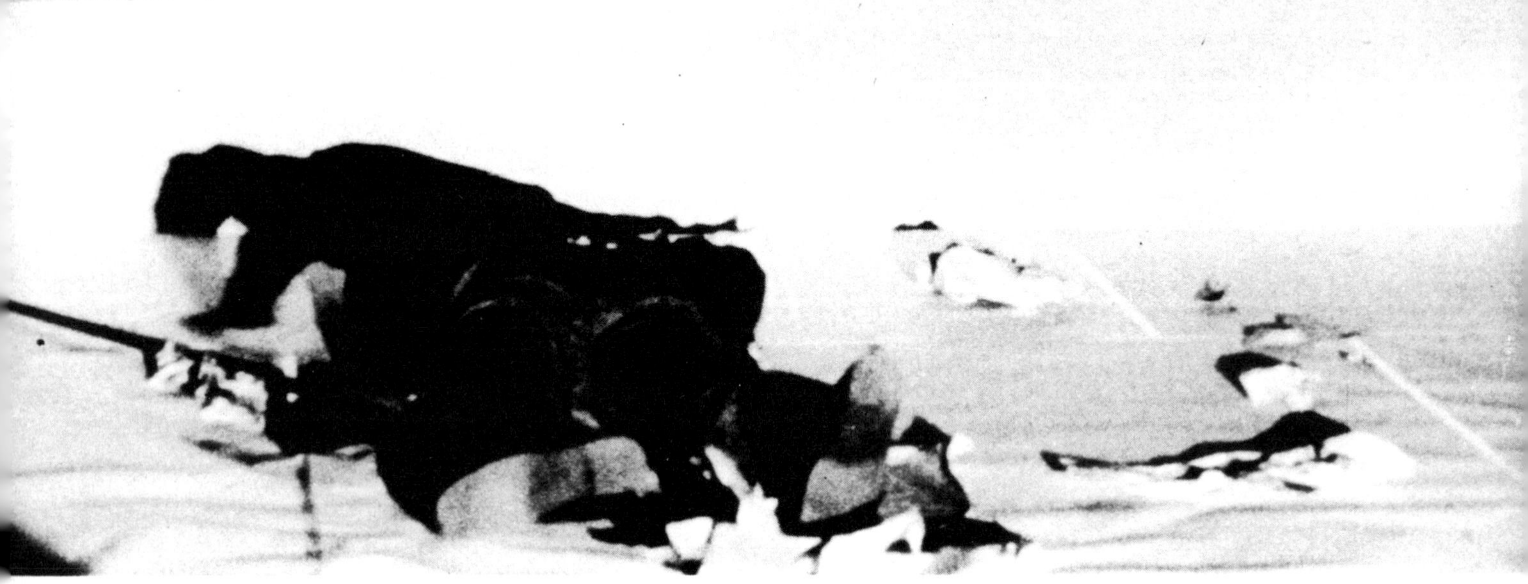

But fallen men and women rise up again with the call of liberation. Remember Algeria, Vietnam... The sound of early morning at Grunwick, perhaps the longest strike (690 days) in the history of working class struggle, wakes him up from his sleep, from his apathy. The struggle of the people all over the world against all kind of domination, physical as well as mental, gives him hope and courage. He gets up to join the people: they in turn become part of his new consciousness...
(The role of art in human struggle perhaps needs a comment here. Should art become an instrument of a political struggle in a mechanistic and functional way, or it should maintain its specific function vis-à-vis ideology. If we truly accept the dialectics of the process of transformation, the dialectical interaction between different human activities, taking into consideration both the collective and individual levels of conscious-

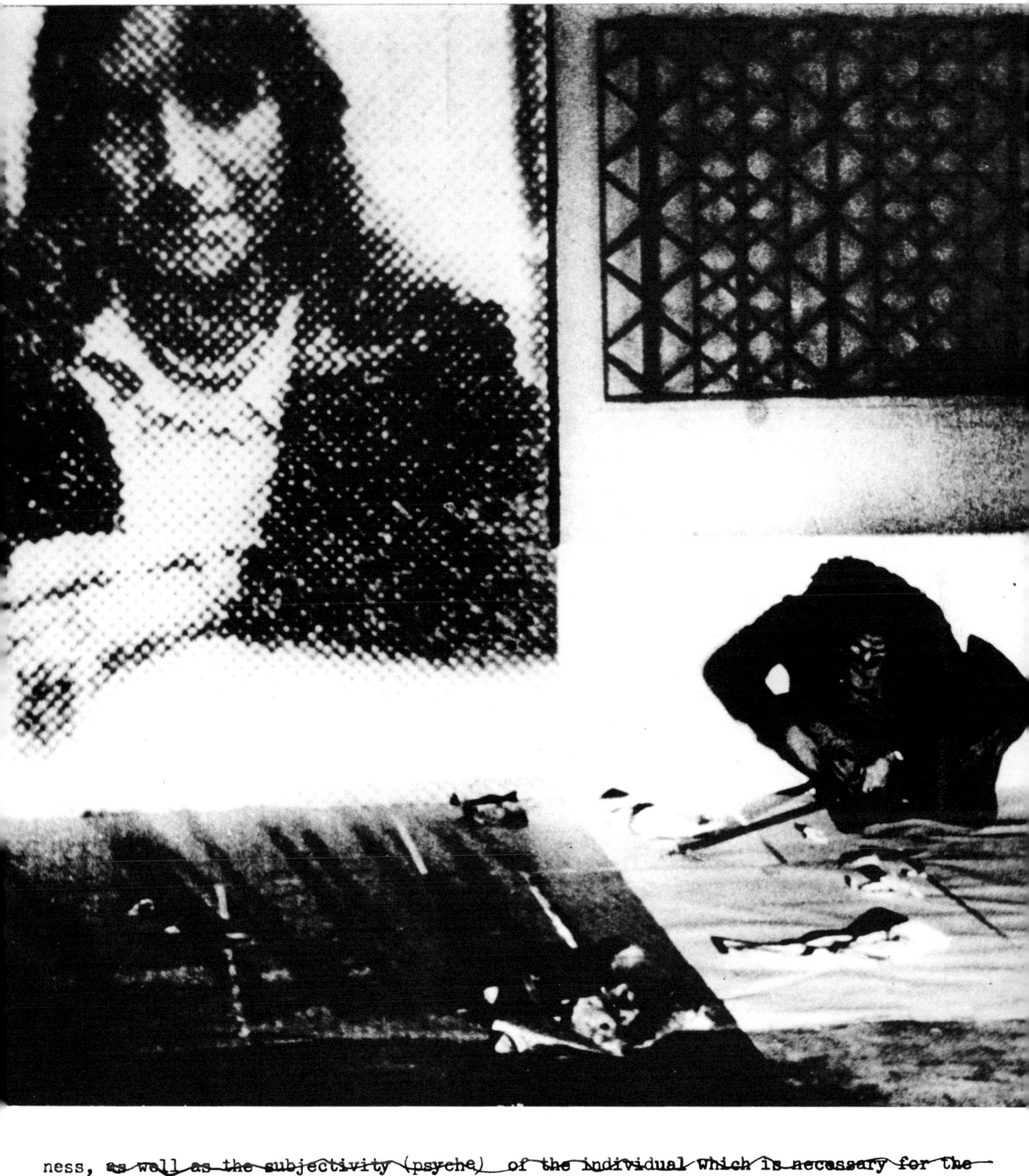

ness, ~~as well as the subjectivity (psyche) of the individual which is necessary for the critical reflection of the system in which one is living~~, then any prescription that marginalizes the role of the art must be rejected.)

However, the piece ends with a synthesis (above photograph): The top left is the face of an Indian woman who, after the big demo at Grunwick in which 10,000 people took part and in which many people were injured as the result of police violence (according to a Time Out report people received injuries on testicles and breasts), stands alone outside Grunwick holding a playcard that reads AN INJURY TO ONE IS AN INJURY TO ALL. The word INJURY appears on the floor next to the artist cutting the broom into pieces. The top right is a sculpture done a few years ago by cutting the wood into pieces and then structuring them together........... ....

SOME GENERAL OBSERVATIONS ON THE PROBLEM OF

CULTURAL COLONIALISM

Kenneth Coutts-Smith

This paper was offered to the Congress of AICA held in Lisbon, September 1976. We are reprinting the paper here as the author's contribution to the debate initiated by 'BLACK MANIFESTO' published in our last issue, with due acknowledgement to ARTERY in which the paper was first published in winter 1976-77. The two illustrations are our own choice.

Traditionally, historians of culture in general and art-critics in particular have tended to base their analyses and their theoretical platforms upon the assumption that art somehow represents the embodiment or the concretization of basic values and fundamental truths that exist somewhere outside of history, beyond social mutation, external to political and economic reality.

The complex of ideas that is clustered around the interrelated notions of the essential spirituality of art, the sublimity of the creative experience and the passion of genius, has served as a central nexus in the vast majority of thinking concerning matters of aesthetics since the inception of that area of inquiry as a specific discipline down to the present point in time. The validity of this position is, however, currently being severely questioned; though from the great majority of published art-criticism in specialist books, in art journals and in catalogue prefaces, it would not seem that our discipline has yet begun to take much note of a major shift in focus that is now occurring in the broad spectrum of world culture.

The present commentator himself is no longer able to accept the idea of the extra-historicity of art and the notion that artistic events take place in some manner in a continuum that is divorced from social and political dynamics. It also appears evident to him that when (in the vast majority of instances) we speak of a world-wide 'high' culture, a significant part of which is formed by the whole spectrum of the Fine Arts, we are actually speaking of a tradition that is largely restricted to the European cultural experience. Even a cursory glance at recent issues of the various 'international' art journals, or at museum and major exhibition catalogues, whether they emanate from Europe, from North America, Latin America, Soviet Russia, India, Japan or wherever, reveals a homogeneity of thought which fails utterly to question the Eurocentricity of most contemporary art-critical assumptions.

The two phenomena, the notion of the extra-historicity of art and the Eurocentric bias of our thinking on culture, are not merely in a clear reciprocal relationship but would seem to be mutually dependent one upon the other. In the present writer's opinion, they would also appear to be central aspects of a total attitude towards art which cannot, in clear honesty, be defined as anything less than Cultural Colonialism.

The stated theme of this present Congress is **Modern Art and Negro-African Art, Reciprocal Relations.** Such a subject obviously presupposes an examination of the relationship between African culture in terms of its national and regional heritage and its present manifestations on the one hand and the historically-defined edifice of European culture on the other. This inquiry cannot possibly avoid the issue of Cultural Colonialism, and the following observations are offered in the hope that they may be found to be of some value in this debate.

These observations, however, can only serve at this point in time as a sketch outlining the problem in broad strokes and thus attempt to define the general areas in which research and analysis is indicated. This specific inquiry is currently of an extremely pressing nature for obvious moral as well as historical reasons; but the scope of the question is very wide and far-reaching, penetrating as it does into every corner and crevice of our cultural superstructure, into every assumption and belief that helps to support our identity and self-esteem, into every facet and aspect of life that we regard as justifying our individual roles and activities.

In the broadest sense, what we regard generally as culture and specifically as art is the continually mutating end-product of a process that is basically mythic in nature, that is to say, a process in which beliefs and assumptions gain substance, become validated. But the dynamics of culture do not only lead in this way towards the fluid identification of a collective identity within a society, they also tend towards the freezing of concepts supportive to the interests of a dominant minority within that society.[1] Ideas which are at first the products of historical necessity are thus transformed into absolutes that are cited in justification of attempts to arrest the historical process, to maintain the status-quo.

The need to examine our present cultural assumptions in the light of the above contention cannot be emphasised strongly enough. It would seem that in the present majority view, there is hardly a single facet of that complex structure which we refer to as 'high' culture that is understood to remain conditional upon historic necessity; rather, the whole cultural superstructure appears to be generally regarded as constituting a self-enclosed system obedient only to the exigencies of 'art-history'—a different matter altogether. The discipline of art-history has never, until now (excepting in the work of isolated individuals regarded, institutionally, as tangential) been required to submit itself to the historical rigours of social and political fact, but has been nourished in the main on poetic insight and metaphysical speculation.

Art-history has been, since its inception in the late Renaissance, ultimately little more than a scholarly elaboration of myths inescapably engendered by the twin concepts of the essential sublimity of the creative process (which logically defines art as an experience located in the sphere of the ideal rather than the actual) and the centrality of style (which predicates the sequential development of an art whose central subject-matter is restricted to its confrontation with previous art rather than with real experience taking place in history).

The notion of the extra-historicity of art is, however, clearly a false one—not even, but *especially*—in terms of the class who do not only defend this idea, but who have also raised it to an ideological imperative. The bourgeois insistence upon the idealist nature of the whole creative process can be seen to serve, on the one hand, as justifying the view held by that class that its understanding of the individualistic, competitive and acquisitive nature of man is not a class-view but an absolute human condition, and, on the other hand, to obscure the almost total appropriation of 'high' culture as both the private property and preserve of a privileged group and as the spiritual vindication of their continuing economic and political domination.

Enough has been written elsewhere upon the question of a dominant class appropriation of cultural institutions to dispense with arguing this point in the present context: it is hoped that it will be here accepted that the possession of a broad culture and of a liberal-humanist education is not merely the privilege of the bourgeoisie but that it also comprises the structure of the code signals by which individual members of the class recognize each other and consolidate their own private identities. The institutions in which the transference and acquisition of cultural property take place are set up in such a manner as to perpetuate existing class privileges and to restrict the entry of extra-class individuals to those whose status is considered in terms of necessary recruitment, that is to say, as candidates for indoctrination into the bourgeois value system.

It might be stated that is is not our purpose here to consider the still-existing, though possibly eroding, bourgeois class dominance other than where class hegemony relates to colonialist assumptions. But this finally would be a meaningless statement since it is not possible to separate either, historically, the development of bourgeois consciousness from the development of colonialism, or, socially, the bourgeois value-system from racist and imperialist assumptions of superiority. Very little that is fruitful can be achieved in attempting to think of imperialism as a phenomenon divorced from the class assumptions of capitalism; this is an error frequently made in the past by many writers concerning the internally-colonialist status of the Blacks in North America and elsewhere, and, more recently, in regard to the Amerindians and internally-colonialized aboriginal peoples. The 'whites', as a collective and political undifferentiated mass, rather than the capitalist system which produces the alienation requisite for racist attitudes, are seen as the oppressors.

In our present context it is absolutely crucial to recognize that the two questions of cultural colonialism and class appropriation are interrelated and interdependent; and, although space clearly precludes that this paper should attempt an analysis on these lines, it must be emphasized that the dimension of class contradiction be borne in mind throughout the remainder of this exposition.

We have intimated that culturally colonialist attitudes and assumptions permeate the whole domain of 'high' culture, and that this is nowhere more evident than across the spectrum of the Fine Arts. The reason for this may well be related to the reason for the apparent pre-eminence in our present culture of the visual mode in the arts over both the musical and the verbal. Up until the end of the 19th century it would appear that musical and verbal culture were more highly regarded than was plastic culture, which, with few significant exceptions, essentially was considered as being the province of mere artisans. Indeed, in Anglo-Saxon countries, such an attitude has persisted until very recently, whereby literature might, under certain circumstances, be considered a fit occupation for a gentleman, while, at the same time, there was something suspect, indeed disreputable, in the idea of making a career as a painter.

It is interesting to observe, over a period of time, the changing social attitudes of the European and North American middle-class towards the Fine Arts. This process is perhaps due less to the fact that financial profit was possible in both production and speculation than to the supposition that painting (and sculpture to a lesser extent) was the art-form that best objectified bourgeois ideals, since the individual picture could become property *in the absolute sense*, since it could uniquely embody both the status and the aspiration of its owner in a manner that was obviously denied to the poem, the novel, the play or the opera.

That direct financial potential was not a factor to be taken into serious account becomes clear if one is to remember that only twice in the history of art during modern times was there a brief situation of boom and speculation in which art production and marketing could be said to approach a sufficiently high temperature of speculative potential to interest the serious investor or financier. One of these booms was in late Victorian genre painting, but this cannot in any way be considered a phenomenon of visual culture since it was, in essence, the sentimental and moralistic subject-matter exemplified by the work of such painters as Landseer and the late Millais that was at issue.

It is not possible, in this instance, to regard the art work as a cultural product designed for the consumption of a visually literate public, nor is it possible to see the individual painting operating as a special *objet de luxe*. The whole phenomenon was more in the nature of an early construct of mass-media soporific, one designed as a placebo for a restless lower middle-class and upper-proletariat. The vast prices that were paid for individual works, the aura of gossip and fame, the celebrity status awarded such artists as Watts, Alma-Tadema, Leighton and Poynter, as well as to such support-system mandarins as Ruskin, would seem to make it obvious that, if parallels were to be drawn with more recent times, then this extraordinary period should be related to the extravagance of Hollywood at its zenith, at a point when a later and only slightly more sophisticated generation of the articulate deprived were clearly persuaded to submerge their claims in a vicarious participation in constructed glamour.

The art boom, now substantially deflated, of the immediate past was a different matter altogether. It was the product of two forces; first, a direct and every lucrative dimension of speculation whereby industrial and corporative marketing techniques allied to sophisticated promotional methods were applied to the merchandising of art, and, secondarily, the recently initiated and still-ongoing 'canonisation' of culture whereby the arts have, to a certain extent, been required to fill a role of secular spiritualization in the vacuum left by the demise of religion within an increasingly alienated consumer society.

It is, however, not in respect of, but rather despite these two art 'booms', both resulting from forces extraneous to art itself, that we note the progressive ascension of the Fine Arts from a somewhat lowly status to a position of pre-eminence among other cultural pursuits to a point whereby the word 'art' became synonymous with the visual experience and connotes a dimension of sublimity only previously associated with mystical and divine visitation. The hypothesis that this process represents the development of the cultural symbol-system most appropriate to a society increasingly geared to profit and consumption would seem to be supported by a historical juxtaposition of the events in art during the last 150 years or so and the parallel emergence to social confidence, to political and to economic power, of the bourgeoisie.

If there is any virtue in the above line of thought, then one would expect to discover a more clearly impacted and more deeply ingrained structure of colonialist assumptions in the domain of the Fine Arts than in other parallel disciplines. Literature, certainly in the past maintained a clear allegiance to a tradition whereby it sought to locate itself in an 'academic' stream of liberal-humanism which restricted the definition of verbal culture to the European experience; however, on the threshold of the modern period, as we shall see, it abandoned this specific structure of collective civil value for a general structure of subjective and regional value.

The notion that culture comprises a humanizing body of values and concepts through which the *educated* both recognize each other and communicate with each other (through the common possession of a vocabulary of metaphors and historical or classical references) was an invention of the High Renaissance. There is an incontestable logic in the fact that, during the first years of evolving imperialism and condensing European identity, the emerging mercantile society should have

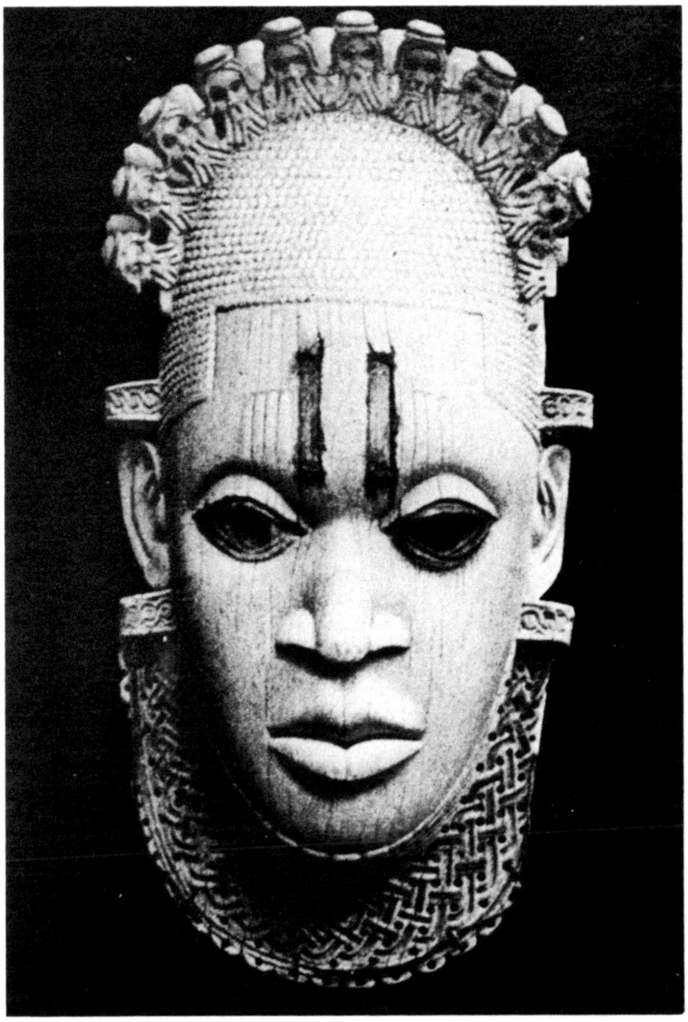

Ivory Mask brought back by Sir Garnet Wolseley from the Ashanti war in 1874, and now in the British Museum. Nigeria has been trying in vain for its return. It was even refused for the exhibition during the international 'Black Art' festival in Lagos, FESTAS'77, which had its image as its emblem.

regarded itself as both a historical and cultural nexus, and, in order to justify itself by initiating a claim upon predecessors and exemplars, should have projected value and *virtu* onto a mixed tradition that was part historical fact and part legendary construct.

The appropriation, in this manner, of a past that was an amalgam of myth and actual event was in essence the cultural dimension of a European expansionism that had its mental dimension in the developing scientific approach towards the natural world and its political and geographical dimensions in the mercantile and maritime explosion which took place at the crumbling of the Aristotilean universe. The birth of Europe was not only achieved in relationship to the twin forces of emergent science and emergent capitalism, but it was also fixated with a profound conviction of the fundamental centrality and manifest pre-eminence of the new political and social structures, and this event was accompanied from the very first by a deeply ingrained process of appropriation.

Colonialism did not appear in the modern world with the forays of Cortez into Yucatan, or with the destruction of Tenochtitlan, but with the claim of historical cozenage extended by Renaissance mercantile republicanism towards the exemplars of a dimly-remembered Roman *polis* observed through the roseate lenses of political ambition and swiftly-consolidating class interest.

It is from this point that we can note the development of a body of cultural property that was later to be defined as the tradition of liberal-humanism. At the beginning this represented simply the collective self-identification of a small but enormously self-confident mercantile class in Florence and elsewhere; but as time went on, the idea of 'humanism' was to be identified with civilized value itself, it was to become the prerequisite base of culture and education. In this way, the special interests of a specific class and the broad sweep of absolute cultural value were seen as synonymous. This claim upon history initiated the process of cultural mystification from which we are still suffering, and, as we may now perceive, it relied for its continued expansion upon a process of cultural appropriation.

Culture, in the new post-Renaissance understanding, was henceforth to serve the interests of a class rather than those of the collective; as the new economic imperatives penetrated the feudal world they inexorably mutated the relationships that exited in that world, transforming the co-operative *gemeinschaft* of the collective of Christianity into the competitive *gesellschaft* of economic, and later, of industrial man. Furthermore, the new concept of culture, as in the very nature of capitalism itself, demanded both a continually expanding lode of resources and a continually-expanding 'market'.

In opposition to the static and genuinely 'absolute' value of feudal culture, it was in essence dynamic and relative (though, of course, it pretended claims to the absolute) and thus could only function in a condition of permanent expansion. Since its subject-matter was not *realist* in the feudal sense, that is to say, one not reflecting the existant and, internally to that society, self-evidently timeless and eternal values subscribed to by that society, but, rather, was *idealist* (in that its motive was to project the poetic and the conditional, to project metaphorical allusions to a universe that did not yet exist but which might possibly be brought into being through the powers of the imagination) then, clearly, it was constrained to look outside of the general body of symbols and concepts that made up the common heritage of the society.

The culture of the feudal world, in terms of the understanding of that world, was far from a metaphysical one, for despite the totally Christian nature of its symbolism, the basic concept of the universe was of a hierarchical continuum rising vertically upward from the lowest peasant through the ranks of the nobility, the ranks of the church, through the Pope to the empyrean, to Christ and, finally, to the Godhead. The structure of medieval thought, just like the content of medieval religious painting, was essentially one which was concerned with things as physically present in both time and space as was man and his daily mundane activities and aspirations. Paradoxically, it is with the development of pictorial realism in the purely technical sense that we first note the shift towards the depiction of a metaphysical and idealist universe.

It would not seem to be coincidental that the Medici and their successors should have chosen and reinforced the medium of the visual arts to express and confirm the justification for their vision of a new, fragmented, and competitive structure of human social relations, since this medium could perhaps best embody the dimension of subjective idealism with the notion of individual 'genius', and thus help to salve and obscure the paradox engendered by the necessary opposition between usury and charity, between competition and co-operation, between the possession of economic power and privilege by a minority and the requisite resignation to poverty and to subservience demanded of a majority.

The new idea of the creative power of the imagination as the prime assumption within the domain of culture was, in so raising isolated and personal actions to a fundamental principle, without doubt engendered by the need to vindicate the moral ambiguity of individual economic and entrepreneurial aggression. Similarly, the claim upon precedent raised by the delineation of parallels between the 15th Century mercantile reality and an idealized view of Roman republican virtue was conditional upon the need to legitimize a social stance that was based upon fiscal manipulation in a society that had for centuries regarded usury as a cardinal sin.

A concept of appropriation that is soon to declare itself as colonialist in nature can thus be seen to have initiated its central role in European culture from the very point of the emergence of a continental 'European' consciousness. Though the first phase of this phenomenon can be seen to have operated almost exclusively in the domain of 'history', we must be clear at this point that the force that was working in this context was far from what we understand by the concept today.

An understanding of history as a continuum of events whereby the occurrences of the past to a great extent logically preclude the patterns of the future is dependent upon the possession of accurate records or plausible speculation together with an objective analysis of the evidence. History, until the end of the 18th Century at least, was as much, if not more, a matter of projection as it was of research and analysis; the separation between legend and fact was not accomplished until the comparatively recent past. Bishop Ussher's widely-accepted chronology, for example, whereby the world was understood to have been created in scriptural totality upon a specific day in February 4,004 B.C., or the fact that Isaac Newton was himself ultimately more interested in his theological and his historiographical speculations than in his scientific observations, demonstrates a profound ambiguity in regard to the past existing as late as the Enlightenment. At that time it was still imperative to somehow equate the literal and revealed truth of biblical text with the virtual and observed truth of archaeological and palaeontological evidence.

Even on the threshold of Romanticism we may observe William Blake alternately swinging between, on the one hand, his 'modernist' response to the injustices of industrial society and to the revolutionary aspirations of an awakening political consciousness and, on the other, his residual, but deeply intuitive, conviction of scriptural and his intellectual debt to Swedenborg and Jacob Bryant; indeed, it is from the very tensions of this paradox that his poetic inspiration depended.

The Romantic period, however, was not simply the major cultural response to the developing technological dimension of the industrial revolution and to the emerging social dimension of class-consciousness; it also marked the shift of central emphasis in the ongoing process of appropriation from the historical domain directly to the geographical, and, ultimately, to the colonial domain.

The conflict between Classicism and Romanticism that marked the closing decades of the 18th Century as well as the opening ones of the 19th Century, was not the result of simple stylistic or scholastic rivalry, it was not even primarily the expression of antagonism between the waning, closed society of post-Restoration aristocracy and the social forces unleashed by the French Revolution. Rather, it was much more the expression of the fact that a developing body of scientific knowledge had begun to render history opaque to the penetrations of capitalist appropriation. History had become, itself, a science, and, as a result, the possibility of a reinterpretation of the past in favour of an elite began to recede in the face of the increasing availability to a wider public of clear and unambiguous information.

In the light of the archaeological discoveries of Wincklemann and others, the ancient world took on the clearly defined lineaments of real life. The Classical antique, revealed at last to the scrutiny of daylight, thus lost the ambiguous and problematical dimensions which alone made it malleable to the idealism of appropriation. The Classical mutated into the neo-Classical; and, as the distinction between legend and fact was clarified, so images in art became more archaeologically 'truthful' and progressively less and less able to support the process of mystification.

In a final and spectacular burst of historical appropriation, the French Revolution itself claimed justification from the ancient world; but the brief paganism of the divinity of Reason was soon to fade, and by the time of Napoleon we note the sudden shift of focus, first to a non-Classical past, then, directly, to the double perspective of a geographical and colonial dimension balanced by the obverse invasion of purely mental territories.

Napoleon's colonial adventure into Egypt was the first one since the imperialism of the ancient world to return in triumph bearing cultural spoils as proof of conquest and territorial sovereignty. During earlier phases of colonialism, during the Spanish domination of Central and South America, for example, or during the British and French expansion into North America, artefacts, usually of a religious or totemic nature, were sometimes brought back to the colonizing metropolis. But it was not *cultural property* that was transported in this way as much as evidence of the spiritual and religious domination and subsequent conversion of the barbaric heathen. Conquistadors, gentleman-adventurers and merchants had no interest whatsoever in artefacts as cultural property, only in their possible value as precious metal. Neither did priests have any interests in such objects beyond exhibiting them as proof of their missionary zeal and as examples demonstrated before their ecclesiastical superiors of the thousands of pagan idols they have burnt and smashed in the name of the propagation of the faith.

The Napoleonic campaigns were innovative in that cultural property *was* accounted among the spoils of war; and not merely physical objects and artefacts either, but also the intangible and abstract property of artistic style. Together with the obelisks and statuary looted from the Nile valley, the victorious returning army brought back an artistic *style* that was to be rapidly adopted as the formal and official visible hallmark of the moral and political authority of Empire.

At the very point when the mother lode, as it were, of the Classical antique dried up as a resource for historical appropriation, a new pre-Classical civilization was offered as substitute. Yet, just as a transition was being made in the matter of resources, so parallel transition was also affected in terms of needs. The Egyptian civilization, dying as it did during the Classical period, turns out to be one-dimensional; there are, apparently, no decipherable records, no historic personages save a few vague shadows, no heroes, no exemplary legends, merely the single dimension of visual style.

Style alone, it quickly became apparent, cannot long fill the role now being proffered it—a radical departure, incidentally, to any previous response in regard to visual culture, and one crucially in need of proper analysis. This new aesthetic relationship clearly places style under the constraint of consumption; without subject-matter, without a moral or exemplary dimension, there must now be initiated a process of mutation, of change, novelty, surprise.

In this way, a specific element attached to the new imperial Egyptian style becomes first isolated, then made central; it is an element that seems at first to be capable of near-infinite variety, of almost continuous mutation, the element of strangeness itself, the element of *exoticism.*

The Romantic movement now has its *leit-motiv*, its theme; it is, however, to expand the search into the exotic into two essential and different directions. One, which is our direct concern here, is to result in the conscious attempt to appropriate and to incorporate into the body of European culture the diverse cultures, not only of the whole world, but also of the whole of history. It is here that the tacit historical appropriation that we have attempted to define becomes a clear and overt programme of colonial appropriation throughout the whole of world culture. There would seem little doubt that the expanding European military and economic imperialism in the early 19th Century

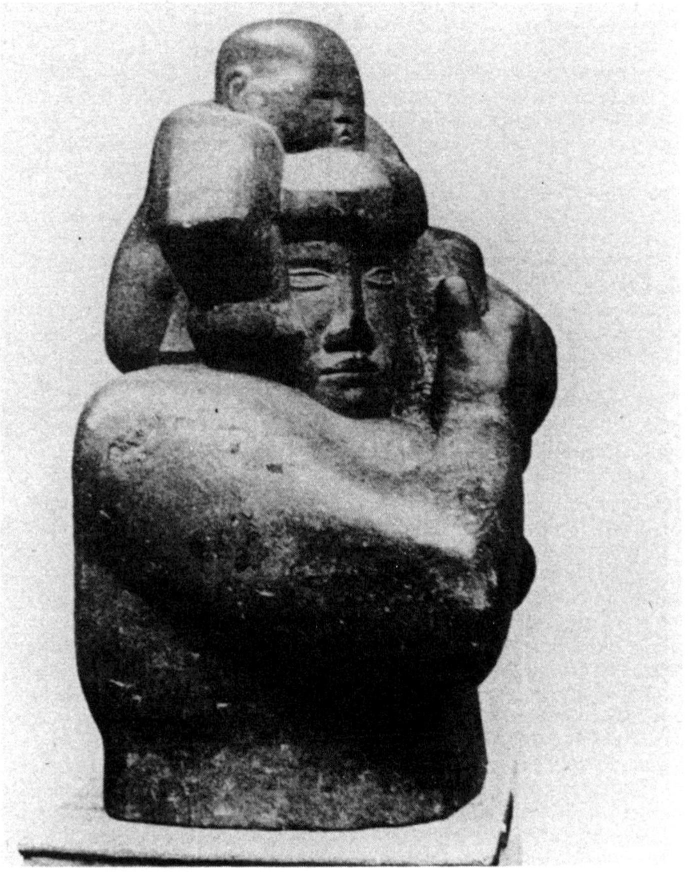

Mother and Child by Henry Moore, or an Eskimo sculpture?

onwards is paralleled and echoed with a developing structure of cultural colonialism.

The other direction taken by the Romantic movement in general constituted a similar expansion, but one that operated inwards, towards a 'colonization', as it were, of subjective mental territory. As the first force can be observed as co-opting the cultures not only of the non-European peoples but also of the vanished peoples of the past, so the second force may be seen to launch an attempt to appropriate the whole twilight territory of the mind, the landscapes of dreams and fantasies, the preserves of psychology and psychopathology, the primitivism of childhood, the bizarre territories of superstition, magic, folklore and the absurd.

It is not within our scope here to enter into an inquiry concerning the subjectivist space that the arts have invaded and which has become so firmly a characteristic of artistic modernism; suffice, at this point, to briefly remark on two points. Firstly, during the early years of the Romantic movement, the visual arts entered the subjectivist area with considerable vigour. In a spectrum that might include Fuseli, John Martin and Caspar-David Friedrich at one pole and Gericault's fascination with abnormality at another, we could stretch out the whole band width of the sublime and the picaresque, particularly in terms of landscape, and even include the gentler Wordsworthian echoes to be found in such celebrators of the spiritual in nature as Constable.

However, despite the dramatic intensity of the period, the theme of mental space in painting is, after a short time, to be almost completely abandoned until it is picked up once more, at a later date, in a minor key by the Surrealists and by various introspective individualists such as Paul Klee. Secondly, in considering subjectivist appropriation, we may here return to a point that was earlier intimated concerning the relationship between the visual arts and other creative areas of activity. A simple glance at the events of the Romantic movement and after will reveal that it is verbal culture in general and literature in particular which has most consistently explored the subjectivist arena. During the Renaissance and the Baroque, literature naturally expressed the Classical structure that we have defined (witness Spencer or Racine) but for some reason, perhaps partly because pre-Renaissance writing (Chaucer, Dante, Petrach, Villon, Rabelais) retained more direct links with the antique world, it never objectified Renaissance and Baroque society as eloquently as did the plastic arts.

Similarly, at the point of the Romantic movement, literature, and to a similar extent, music, was to concentrate almost exclusively on the subjectivist view of society, of the world, and of nature. This may also partly explain why present-day literature, though obviously by no means totally free of colonialist assumptions, stands in a less crucial position in this regard than do the plastic arts.[2]

As we have remarked, the subjectivist position exhibited in early 19th Century painting was not to hold centre stage for more than a brief period. Such subjectivism demands *content* in painting, even if it be no more than that found in Turner, for example: the flux of the individual artist's emotions in the face of nature. It was not Gericault, with his deeply humanistic response to man, who was to survive and to condition the future, but Delacroix, the flamboyant and brilliant master of style, the inaugurator of pure painting, the dynamic colourist, the anticipator of expressionist abstractionism, and the artist who, above all, defined the ideal subject matter of painting as the *exotic*.

It was Delacroix who travelled North Africa in the wake of a colonizing Embassy and, in observing the picaresque Bedouin, the harem *odalisque*, reified them into exotic and glamorous objects. He painted people as if they were guitars, and personally inaugurated the long process through which European art was to attempt to appropriate the visual culture of the whole planet into its own self-conceived 'mainstream'.

Can we here isolate an imperative within the general structure of capitalist social relations? A subjectivist artist, even if his overt motivation is that of an egoic sensibility who desires his personality to expand to the dimensions of the universe, still observes and recognizes his fellow creatures. But if the necessities of capitalist society require art to maintain its appropriative roles in the real-time world, having lost its hegemony over the 'historical' world, then it could hardly be expected to observe and recognize *real* fellow human beings; too many contradictions could result and inhibit the process.

If the visual arts were to be about *modern life*, if painters were to anticipate Baudelaire (or at a slightly later date, to follow him), they would find themselves in a different position from the poet and outsider who was comparatively more free of social claims. It seems plausible to envisage a situation of pretending a more profound bohemianism than is accepted as commitment, and, subsequently, avoiding conflicts by reifying the subject matter. The logic of the situation demanded that people had to be treated as still-lives (or, more eloquently, as *nature-mortes*), the logic of the situation also revealed that the imperative towards abstractionism was inevitable.

We can note with the Barbizon painters a swing not only against the commitment of content in painting but also the first intimations of the idea of a pure painting of style. The landscape, in their hands, began to become the starting point for an essay into pure visual sensibility, and was thus the initiation of a process later to be explored by some of the Impressionists into the point of negation. For the individual artist, this represented the threshold of an exciting and passionate voyage into the potential of the eye, and despite their conscious intentions (even, paradoxically, in opposition to a stated allegiance to content, to a search for rural innocence), the hegemony of style over content was inaugurated.

The later landscape painters of the pre-Impressionist period were already committed to the pure visual adventure. In their conscious understanding, as well as in their visual intuition, the separation between narrative painting and pure painting was achieved. Both the creative experience and the artistic product were thrust firmly into the sphere of the aboslute, and from that point onwards we began to become used to thinking of 'high' culture in general and the Fine Arts in particular as operating in some sort of mental and moral space totally divorced from any but the most abstract and tenuous relationship with social realities.

The present world climate of thought, however, now obliges us to begin to reassess the relationships that obtain, historically, in regard to the arts; there is a current tendency to query whether it is possible for any event to take place in isolation from the social domain. If this is so, then the initial commitment to pure painting represents not merely the cultural echoes of an attempt to reify the world, but also a significant factor operating towards this end. It could be said that the *plein-airistes*, developing commitment to style, reversed the image celebrated by such of their predecessors as Constable who envisaged a coherent and humanized landscape, and in this way projected an image of an absolute, fragmented and dehumanized landscape.

Immersed in their narrow stylistic concerns, the individual artists, many professing liberal, humane and even 'socialist' affiliations, nevertheless acquiesced in a restructuring of man's relationship with his environment which, ultimately, was profitable to restricted political interests. The capitalist social relations that were consolidating at the peak of the Industrial Revolution demanded a divorce between man and his natural environment in order that the masses might better accept the artificial environment of the industrial milieu.

It is possible that an earlier stage of this process was initiated during the period of the Gothic Revival, for, with the idea of the picaresque, we can observe the first intimations of the transformation of the natural environment (the basic arena for man's presence, identity and social interaction, the archetypal space in which man labours and humanizes the world and himself) to a product, a commodity designed to be consumed. It is capitalism, rather than the technological exigencies of the modern world, that required our present almost total alienation from natural phenomenon, and it would simply not seem plausible to regard a major cultural event, such as the process of developing abstraction in 19th Century landscape painting, as being socially unrelated to capitalism's achievement of this aim.

In this context, we are obliged to observe the developing hegemony of 'style' and pure painting as not merely a series of events taking place in the domain of 'art-history', but as events taking place in real history, events taking place in respect of the continually mutating structure of social relations. In substituting style for content, the visual arts were suddenly launched, as we have seen, upon a process of reliance on external resources. The speed with which art, as it were, consumed landscape, eroded its stylistic potential (the rapidity of the voyage between Barbizon and, for instance, Monet's *Haystacks*) was remarkable.

Most of us are culturally and historically conditioned to regard the intense burst of activity that took place largely in Paris between the 1860s and the 1920s, to consider that period of roughly half-a-century which begins with the mature work of Manet and which climaxes with Surrealism, Constructivism and the Bauhaus, as a peak in terms of human dignity and freedom. We usually think of this as a point where the human race compares favourably with its more common idiocies and barbarities. The only cloud that occasionally shadows this myth is a Pompidou-like French chauvinism that would claim national credit for this wonder which, in reality, belongs to the world; but that does not seem serious, since we are all, apparently, proud to claim passports to the moral citizenship of the Parisian *avant-garde*.

There would seem to be no question that we would have to regard this period in art as a unique and positive moment in human history if the version proposed by art-history be correct; if it really is true that a group of the most talented people that the world has ever seen congregated almost by accident and created, *in vacuo*, as it were, a dazzling perspective of images so multitudinous and so fruitful that, for half-a-century style succeeded style, concept displaced concept, in a variety and complexity that historians and curators have hardly been able yet to begin adequately to comprehend and classify the wealth of cultural material thus placed to our common heritage.

However, it is questionable that this is what happened. It is questionable that a great and fruitful stratum of creativity was suddenly brought to light in this manner. A doubt would appear to be raised if we are to regard the whole phenomenon of modern art in the context which we have here attempted to define; for thus we would note the centrality of *appropriation* rather than that of creation. An art structure that is rapidly expanding, both in terms of its audience and in terms of its practitioners, develops a pressing need for nourishment. And an art restricted to style, as we have seen, cannot feed from its own social and historical reality, but demands a constant supply of raw forms for its survival.

When the potential of landscape was 'consumed' some time in the 1880s, a brief foray into the twilight territory of the Parisian *demi-monde* was undertaken, but this alone did not appear to provide substantial fare. A more solid source of material was required; and this was provided just at the point of most pressing need. At various levels throughout late 19th Century society, from the academic ethnologists and anthropologists, guardians of brand-new sciences, to the frivolity of salons and dinner tables, an awareness of extra-European culture was penetrating. Peoples in distant countries and in 'primitive' societies began to take on a substance more solid than that of the undifferentiated native. Suddenly, with the possibility of an almost apparently limitless material ripe for stylistic adoption, the vertical take-off of modern art was assured.

The process of co-option and appropriation was extraordinarily rapid and complete, beginning jointly, and perhaps hesitantly, with Degas and Whistler staking out claims in the Japanese, and with Gauguin grasping first the 'primitive' of Breton folk-art, then that of Melanesia, the pattern was set. Every artist, from the most significant members of the cenacle at *La Lapin Agile* to the most obscure dauber in the *Place du Tertre*, attempted to secure for himself some sort of cultural territory to exploit. Within thirty to forty years not one corner of non-European culture remained untouched as a source of imagery either, geographically, to the most obscure tribal totem, or, temporarily, to the most shadowy Celtic dolman and palaeolithic cave.

Despite the ransacking of time and space, the individual artist by himself, the painter in his studio, did not, of course, personally appropriate the complete cultures of non-European space and extra-modern time. However, both by his adaption of aspects of these cultures to contemporary idioms and by his elevation of style to an absolute principle, he was responsible for permitting the European and Eurocentric institutions of culture to consummate the appropriation totally.

For in this way was laid the justification for the process first described by Walter Benjamin in **The Work of Art in the Age of Mechanical Reproduction** and ultimately formalized by Malraux in his invidious concept of **The Museum Without Walls**, wherein the whole of known culture is placed on terms of neutral and negative institutional equality, divorced from function, divorced from meaning, divorced from human use, divorced from any social dimension whatsoever.

Any lingering doubt concerning the now almost total acceptance of this view of art, of the world-wide *bourgeoisification* of culture, may be laid to rest by visiting at random any fair-sized Fine Art museum *in any city in the world.*[3] Inevitably, one will there observe cultural artefacts from diverse societies and from diverse historical epochs torn out of social context and presented in a manner where the only standard of comparison or relationship is similarity or divergence of style. Further, one will see these cultural artefacts displayed peripherally to a central collection of European or Eurocentric painting (usually covering the period from the International Gothic to the latest in Conceptual Art).

We are so conditioned to this relationship, we are so ingrained to the central imperative of style, that the implications of the display usually escape. Only a certain type of analytical approach (such as has been attempted here) whereby art is regarded primarily from the point of view of its social role, is capable of revealing an assumption so arrogant as to stagger the mind: the assumption that the whole existing body of world culture from the very dawn of human time must be conventionally understood and appreciated *in the light of the European visual experience of the last 500 years!*

It has been the intention of this paper to propose that it is a plausible idea to regard the assumptions of modern art and the traditions that have led up to these assumptions as being neither international in scope nor absolute in nature. On the contrary, it is suggested that the assumptions of modern art are fundamentally of a Eurocentric character and are ultimately limited to a specific world-view that is defined by the nature of the dominant class in the capitalist world.

It would seem that there is evidence to demonstrate the possibility that the Fine Arts have, historically, long been (though, no doubt, unwittingly) in a position of service to social interests that are inimical, both economically and politically, to its own well-being. It would also seem that the Fine Arts have, historically, fallen victim to a myth concerning the absolute and metaphysical nature of its activity, as a result of which its actions and its products have been used to justify not merely a criminal structure of social relations but also the world-wide edifice of imperialism upon which this structure still depends.

Should this line of thought be found in any way to be a viable one, then the ramifications to the artistic community in general, and to the art-critical community in specific, are enormous. We may currently observe significant factions of the academic disciplines of Anthropology and Sociology questioning whom they serve in terms of the conventional and accepted methodology of these sciences. Art-criticism deserves to do no less than to examine the nature of its own role in this regard.

The whole question of cultural colonialism needs desperately, for obvious reasons, to be placed under scrutiny. To the best knowledge of this present commentator, this task has yet to be initiated; and this current paper may well be the first tentative attempt in this direction. The moral obligation of the European critical community to clarify their position is uncontestable. The pressing need for the Third World countries, presently struggling for economic, political and cultural independence, to dispel the myths obscuring the true social nature of culture, goes without saying.

The scope of the question is vast, and the implications penetrate into most levels of local, regional, national and international political relations wherever cultural differences are either a significant factor or where cultural autonomy is being threatened by more forceful neighbours. The problem does not only reside primarily in the emergent Third World countries, but everywhere. One crucial area, for instance, is located in the clear policy of cultural genocide through assimilation that is currently being practised in North America and elsewhere in regard to the indigenous peoples. A sub-section of this area is the ambiguous cultural activity residing in the artificial 'airport-art' constructs of Navajho jewellery and Eskimo stone-carvings, whereby bureaucratic political institutions are *inventing* art-forms on behalf of subservient and internally-colonised peoples.

It is not within the scope of this paper to chart, at this point, the enormous task of analysis ahead of us. However, should some debate which might lead to the commencement of this analysis result from this thesis, then the author will feel that its primary purpose has been achieved.

---

1. Roland Barthes speaks of myth as being 'depoliticised speech', *Mythologies*, Paladin, London 1972, p.142. I am using the word 'mythic' here in an analogous manner. See also (ibid) ". . . myth is a type of speech . . . a mode of signification (p.109) . . . [it] is an inflexion . . . it transforms history into nature." (p.109).
2. Naturally, the very subjectivist bias that the mainstream of the literature of the last 100 years or so (e.g. since Rimbaud's *Lettre de Voyant* of 1871) seems to justify the bourgeois contention that extreme individualism and competitiveness are the "natural human condition", thus, in turn, appearing to vindicate a political and economic system that accords priority to competition over co-operation.
3. We should clearly remark here that this would be at the present time with the obvious exception of China. It remains to be seen what forms the art institutions of that country will take in the future. In this context, it is perhaps as well to emphasize here that this *does not except* Soviet Russia and other Eastern European socialist countries who remain European chauvinists in this regard.

The phrase 'Fine Art Museum' has been used in this paragraph. It is possible to remark here upon a tendency that is occasionally observable in certain so-called Ethnographic or Anthropological Museums where cultural artefacts are displayed as if they were 'art', defining them minimally in a social context. The bourgeois assumptions concerning culture are very insidious indeed.

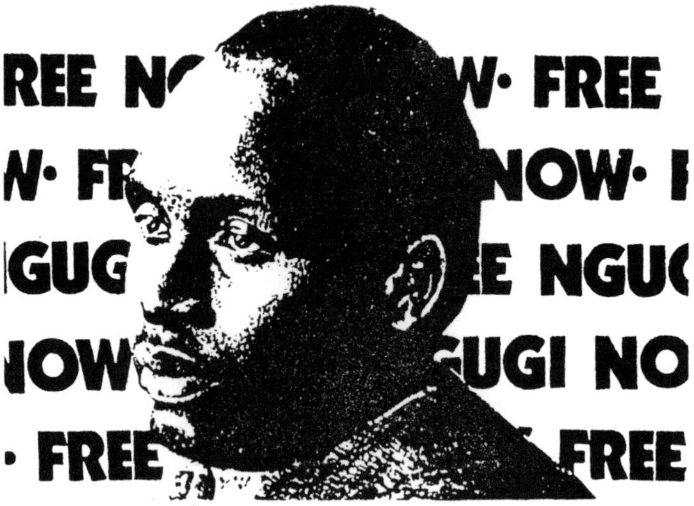

Where is Ngugi?

Since the arrest of Ngugi wa Thiong'o by the Kenyan Government on Dec 31st 1978, nobody has been allowed to see him, not even his wife and children. Nobody knows where he is being kept or if he is alive. The reason for his not being put on trial is obvious. He has committed no crime. It is not a crime to speak up openly about the continual misery of one's people or to oppose foreign domination. One can see why those who are making loud noises about 'human rights' have not come forward to comment upon the plight of Ngugi. It is therefore the duty of progressive people all over the world to demand the immediate release of Ngugi. Those who wish to help must contact NGUGI DEFENCE COMMITTEE, 28/29 Southampton Street, London, W.C.2.

The following report, by Chris Wanjala, sent soon after the arrest from Nairobi, is being published here with acknowledgement to THIRD WORLD MEDIA, London. The quotes in the boxes are from Ngugi's interview which he gave to THE WEEKLY REVIEW, Nairobi, after the publication of PETALS OF BLOOD.

Evenings are calm in Limuru, Ngugi's home village some 15 miles north-west of Nairobi. The traffic from Limuru is heavy. On one of our visits to Ngugi's family we stopped at a shop to buy some soda. The shopkeeper was an ex-freedom fighter. 'Limuru was the centre of fighting during the Emergency', he put in with pride. For him the shop meant a lot for Kenya's independence from the British. We asked him about Ngugi. 'Ngugi stays at the University of Nairobi where he teachers', the old man said cowing. 'He comes home in the evening, and we do not see him here'. This feeling of suspicion pervades the way people receive visitors to the area since Ngugi's arrest. The people dodge questions put to them about the play.

Although children in Ngugi's house eventually talked to us when we visited his home, the house-girl ran into the kitchen and she remained in hiding while we were there. Ngugi's third child, one of the five, told us that his mother was away in town. Ngugi's mother stays at her eldest son's home in Kawangware ten miles away from Limuru.

In the morning people in the area hurry through the early mist on their way to their various places of work. The watchmen can be seen trekking home after their night's work. You have to keep your car lights on lest you run over the little girls and boys trotting feverishly to school. Unlike the workers they seem little aware of the arrest of the Kenyan novelist. The play, *Ngahika Ndenda,* is about these workers. It was co-authored by Ngugi wa Thiong'o to help *Kamiritho Community Centre,* the local educational and cultural centre for integrated rural development. Initially the play was envisaged as the follow-up to a highly successful literacy scheme run by the centre. The hope that its success would put the centre on its feet seems doomed after its closure by the authorities. The future of the centre as 'the soul of the village' once again looks dim.

The other co-author of the play is Ngugi wa Mirii, a specialist in adult literacy. He is free and at work as a research assistant at the University of Nairobi's Institute of Development Studies.

The play owes its success to many songs collected from the people by the authors. These songs were sung by the people themselves acting in the play. The play pokes satirical comments at religion and the accumulation of wealth, focusing on the way the owners of small plots of land easily lose their land to richer people in the process of seeking to improve their lot. Kiganda, the 'hero' but also the victim, is the worker who is swindled into asking for a loan from the bank using his title deed. The land is taken away from him when he fails to repay the loan.

The play also shows the misuse of church by the rich. 'Ndini . . . ndini . . .', says Njaki, a character in the play, 'Ndini ni uriu wa ngoro. Ni urogi wa meciria' (religion intoxicates and bewitches the brain).

> **"I have always thought of Christianity itself as part and parcel of cultural imperialism. Christianity, in the past, has been used to rationalise imperialist domination and exploitation of peasants and workers. It has been used to blind people to the reality of their exploitation because religion as a whole wants to tell people that their lot is God-given, as opposed to being man-conditioned. So if you see that you are poor because God has willed it, you are more likely to continue to pray to God to right your conditions. But if you know that your poverty is not God-conditioned, but it is socially conditioned, then you are likely to do something about those social conditions that are assuring that you be poor."**

The Director of the play, Dr. Kimani Gecau, recalled that the people had enjoyed the play immensely, and indeed, where the script fell short of the message the play wanted to put across, the players themselves suggested changes. They, for instance, suggested a more rigorous questioning of the acquisitive values which had come with Western culture. In a way it was their own play.

As one of the papers in Nairobi has put it, '(the play) was certainly (Ngugi's) most radical, in form if not in content. *Ngaahika* was a play written in Kikuyu, the first piece of literature by any major author which tried to interpret for its audience society's workings in one of Kenya's ethnic languages . .'

Ngugi has moved from the English tradition of literary criticism and sunk deeply into the collective spirit of the countryside. He is the only professor at the University of Nairobi who operates from his home in a village. The play itself is the result of his growing desire to communicate through his work with the people of Kenya rather than the 'international' English language audience at home and abroad who so admired his work.

> **"In the course of writing the novel, I became more and more attracted, as I said, to the national songs, songs like those of the Mau Mau which are national songs. Songs which were sung in the 1930 s against the British which were also national songs. Of course, they form a very important part of Kenya's national literature.**
>
> **The language issue is a slightly different one, although it is related to the novel in the sense that it was in the course of writing the novel that I came to be more and more disillusioned with the use of foreign languages to express Kenya's soul or to express the social conditions in Kenya. I think the people should express their national aspirations and their national history in the various national languages of Kenya, including the main national language which is Swahili."**

Ngugi was picked in the small hours of December 31st from his Limuru house, and subsequently detained. It is not clear whether or not Ngugi's arrest was related to his play. But by taking this play to the people, Ngugi has elicited a lot of reaction from the theatre-goers. People have read what they wanted from the play. Its producer, however, says: 'The government has always called the people to develop their indigenous culture, so the play is very much pro-government'.

'In the absence of an official statement, it is difficult to know precisely what Ngugi was detained for', as a paper in Nairobi has put it. *The Weekly Review* in Nairobi, on the other hand, has said that the writer might have been detained because of Chinese and other communist literature (in his possession) which is banned in Kenya.

People in Nairobi have reacted in many different ways to the arrest of and detention of Ngugi: 'We cannot sympathise with Professor Ngugi', says one academic between sips of beer at the Nairobi University Common Room. 'He was arrested outside the precincts of the University at his own house in the village'. For this academic Ngugi was not covered by academic freedom unless he was operating from a University house.

Students, however, have reacted to the arrest differently. *The Anvil,* a student newspaper at the University of Nairobi, reports: 'Crowd-pulling notices appeared last week referring to the arrest and subsequent detention of Prof. Ngugi wa Thiong'o.' It goes on to say: 'The note also condemned the government's action and Ngugi's critics'. *The Anvil* also reported how graffiti referring to Ngugi's arrest was hastily removed by the authorities. One of the graffiti showed, 'a courageous Prof. Ngugi being whipped'. The students have thus joined Ngugi's well-wishers in Kenya and abroad in their demand for the immediate release of Ngugi.

"History is very important in any people. How we look at our past is very important in determining how we look at and how we evaluate the present. A distorted view of a people's past can very easily distort our views and evaluation of the present as well as the evaluation of our present potentials and our future possibilities as a people. Our history up to now has been distorted by the cultural needs of imperialism, that is, it was in the interest of the imperialists to distort Kenyan history with the view of showing that Kenyan people had not struggled with nature and with other men to change their natural environment and create a positive social environment. It was also in the interests of imperialism to implement missionaries and other agents of imperialism in bright colours, and they did all these things using the terms of apparent objectivity. Now I feel that Kenyan writers, intellectuals, historians, political scientists, must be able to show us Kenya's past which correctly evaluate Keynan people's achievements in the past, in the present, and at the same time, pointing out their creative potential in the future.

Sometimes when I look at Kenya's history, I ask myself what about all those Kenyans who so resisted the Portuguese intrusion into Kenya in the 16th Century to the extent that the Portuguese were forced to build one of the strongest forts in the world, Fort Jesus? Or rather put it this way: Isn't the strength of Fort Jesus a comment on the ferocity of the resistance by the Kenyan people. What about all the Kenyan people that fought against Arab slave owning and slave hunting classes, and for many years successfully made sure that the Arabs were unable to penetrate into the interior of Kenya? What about all the fierce wars of resistance by Kenyan people in the Nineteenth Century against British imperialism? What about the wars fought by heroes like Waiyaki and others? What about all the fierce wars fought by Kenyan people around Mount Elgon?

We, as writers, as historians, as Kenyan intellectuals must be able to tell these stories, or histories, or history or heroic resistance to foreign domination by Kenyan people. Doing so, we shall not be looking at ourselves as people who were weak in the face of foreign domination, threats, aggression, but as a people whose history shines with the grandeur, if you like, of heroic resistance and achievement of the Kenyan people. That's why I think history dominates PETALS OF BLOOD so much. I feel that Kenyan history, either pre-colonial or colonial has not yet been written. . . . It is important because we are still not yet free of imperialist domination and exploitation. The Kenyan people must know their history in order to face up to the challenge of imperialism."

"The question of what is international itself needs to be questioned very seriously because there is a tendency of imperialists, capitalists, thinking of their own culture as being international, and this includes their languages. Often, what they mean by this is that they want their language and culture to hold sway in all those areas under their exploitation. What this means is that if you learn a people's language, and you adopt their culture, you are more likely to see yourself in terms of their world outlook, their aspirations. And you are not likely to see their system as an enemy system, but as a friendly system with one or two possible anomalies. So, the term international depends upon the base from which you look at it. So, why don't we look at internationality from the point of view of the needs of the peasants and workers of Kenya? Our national languages are international and national to the extent that they are able to stress the aspirations of the vast majority of not only the Kenyan people but also of peoples the world over. It is the content of internationality whether a language or not is expressing the needs that affect the mass of the people the world over. In Kenya, to the extent that national languages are the ones which are used by the vast majority of the people, . . . then those languages should be used, utilised, and developed; and a literature ought to develop in those languages so that there will be a vital relationship between the writer and the mass of Kenyan people."

Notes on ART & LIBERATION STRUGGLE

N. Kilele

These notes have two aims.

Firstly, to distinguish artistic practice (AP) from political practice (PP), since they are often confused and substituted for each other, so as to increase the effectiveness of AP. I shall primarily concentrate on painting, sculpture and drawing — although they constitute specific spheres within AP owing to their peculiarities. I hasten to add that I am not making a claim for the 'independence of art', as will be clear in the course of these notes. The production of art is in fact a social activity and is determined 'in the last instance' by the existing social relations.

After having outlined the first. I shall examine the tasks of AP with regard to a specific reality, that of Tanzania. I shall try to show that the development of 'national art' is a necessary component of liberation struggle.

The production of art is relatively an autonomous activity; for although it can be situated within the ideological level, it is partly determined by the economic level. The elements of which art is composed of are specific to it and most of them do not exist in the various spheres that constitute the ideological level, which in turn exists within a specific socio-economic formation.[1]

An indication of the specificity of the practices in general is the phrase 'red and expert' used by many revolutionary leaders. If all practices were reducible to PP, if PP were to be the only practice, then one would only speak of 'red'; painting a mural would then equal political agitation. This phrase further indicates that every specific practice must be informed by political criteria. Although general criteria are required to judge whether an artistic product is in the interest of the majority of the people, an additional criterion specific to each practice, whether AP or PP, is needed since each practice uses different materials in a particular manner.[2] This will be clear if we briefly examine the nature of PP and AP and the relations between them.

PP has as its object the social relations of a society upon which it acts in order to transform them. It is guided by a correct political line which necessitates a revolutionary theory, a proletarian party that works out the political line and implements it, depending on the relations between classes. The correct political line is worked out from experience in the struggle itself.

PP involves itself not only with economic struggles (wage demands) but also raises political demands (e.g. equal rights for minorities); its strategic aim being the seizure of state power and the transformation of social relations.

AP differs from PP by having a different mode of operation and in having as its object the ideology of the spectator and/or participant. The mode of operation varies in the materials used, the manner of the usage of materials even when common to both, and the conditions necessary for the usage of the materials.

AP shares with PP, as their object, the ideology. The ideology is only a means for PP, a channel for it to act upon social relations. Whereas for AP, the ideology is its main object; and this affects its mode of operation.

Being a specific practice, AP is informed by a theory of art which provides an understanding of the history of the production and consumption of artistic products. In this manner it also contributes to the effectiveness of AP by providing tools of analysis for the present. This theory of art is in turn informed by the science of historical materialism and the philosophy of dialectical materialism, both of which provide the former with some of the necessary categories and concepts.

Marxist theory in conjunction with PP maps out the road which AP has to travel upon; it points out the enemy at this historical juncture: the prevailing bourgeois capitalist class and its ideology.

It should be made clear that aesthetic elements do not contain ideology(ies) in themselves; it is the latter that arranges the aesthetic elements in a specific manner. Often more than one ideology may be present in an artistic product and these may manifest themselves in different or even the same type of aesthetic elements. This explains why art that embodies bourgeois ideology may also appeal to our senses, for it is the aesthetic element(s) that may attract us. On the other hand, aesthetic elements used in revolutionary art could be appropriated and used in works whose dominant ideology is reactionary or used in such a way that perpetuate bourgeois ideology. The use of the aesthetic elements of Chinese revolutionary posters by ***The Sunday Times*** in its publicity ads to boost its circulation is such an example of bourgeois appropriation. The aesthetic element(s) exudes a particular ideology depending upon how it is arranged, the use made of it, and the manner of its production, reproduction and consumption.

A few brief examples of AP will clarify the above and indicate the differences between the various practices based on the materials they use and their mode of operation. These differences also influence when and how one uses a particular practice.

A painting or a novel cannot convey all the contradictions in their changing form — their simultaneity and determination — and their historical development.

Cartoons, for example, can attack the ruling order, but they must be transmitted through a material (paper or a wall for the graffiti) whereas poems can be transmitted orally — very useful in countries with high literacy and/or where political activities are banned. Similarly, watching a film necessitates a degree of darkness, equipment, and the audience has to remain stationary — often exposing themselves to retribution from the oppressive state machinery.

Consider the design of two badges: one aimed at making the people in Britain aware of massacres in another country and the other to show that there also exists a revolutionary movement in the country concerned. A badge is usually worn on the lapel. It has to have an image that is immediately understood so that the message is comprehended in the few seconds that a passerby has on a bus, in the street . . . it cannot explain how and why such a situation exists; it can only state that there are massacres. Pamphlets, meetings, etc. can then explain why these massacres have taken place and by whom they have been committed

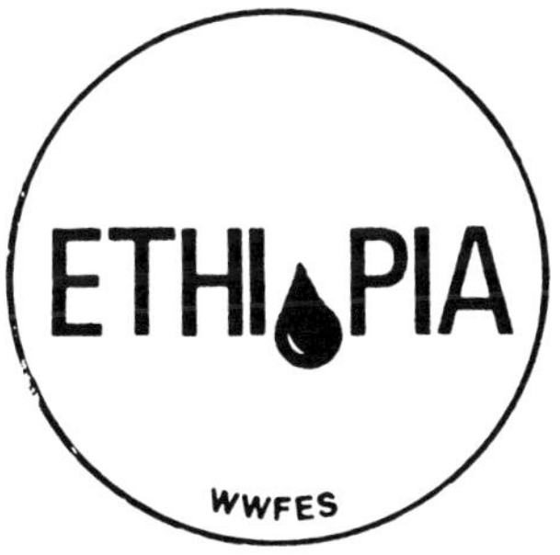

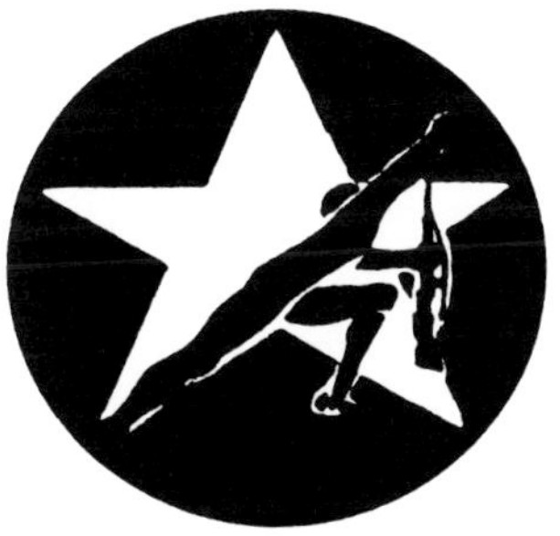

The other badge can only state that a revolutionary movement exists. But its programme, how it arose, its stage of development, can only be explained by other means.

Certain incorrect positions are held by artists as a result of the confusion between AP and PP.

Some hold the position that 'my art is my politics and my contribution towards changing society is my AP'. This position, partly a result of the complete separation between AP and PP, often leads the artists from withholding him/herself from PP.

Another position is that 'I participate in PP and that is my contribution to changing society. My art is my work as an artist'. This position, again a result of separation between AP and PP, ignores the ideology embodied within artistic products.

Finally there are artists who are primarily concerned with celebrating the marginal achievement of socialism in a capitalist society instead of questioning and criticising the ruling ideologies — a task that comes before the portrayal of the 'achievement of socialism'.

AP and artistic products are in the final instance determined by the existing social relations, by the concrete situation, for not only does ideology exist within a definite social formation but the production and consumption of art takes place within such a formation. The class position and the ideology of the person who commissons/buys a work, the relationship of the ideology embodied within an artwork to the other prevailing ideologies, and the level of development of the productive forces, are among some of the factors that affect the artistic product.

However, while one can speak of an advanced mode of production or a higher level of productive forces, one cannot pass such qualitative judgements on aesthetics. It would be incorrect to say that African aesthetics are more advanced than European or vice versa. There cannot be one 'correct' aesthetic, nationally as well as internationally. The nature of perception and aesthetic values vary according to different cultures and historical periods.

Artistic products can, however, hold different meanings for different societies — this appropriation depends on the ruling aesthetic ideologies and the prevailing material conditions.

The specificity of AP, its mode of operation, enables it to carry out certain tasks that PP would find difficult in conditions where overt political activities are banned, and where the revolutionary struggle is young. In these conditions one has to use all possible means to spread the truth (the truth about who exploits whom and how . . .). In his essay of 1932, 'Writing the Truth: 5 Difficulties', Brecht mentions cunning as one of the skills necessary in spreading the truth.

AP can then play an important role in national struggle, especially since by its very nature (that of being *unable* to advance prescriptions to political contradictions) it usually has more leeway. It can help to raise the consciousness of the masses, even though only to a certain level. Additional use of other means (pamphlets, study classes, meetings and other forms of communication available) can raise the consciousness to a higher level. This should be clear since very few forms of AP can advance prescriptions. (Novels or poems that try to do this lose their effectiveness by straddling between AP and PP.) It is enough to show that things are wrong and that they should be changed . . . 'How?' can be dealt more effectively by other practices.

I shall now consider the tasks that face AP in a concrete situation, that of Tanzania.

At the end of the 19th century, Tanzanian society came under the rule of colonialism, The primary aim of colonialism was profits which were realised through the extractions of raw materials, the production of agricultural products, and the selling of manufactured goods. This was achieved by the military, political and cultural subjugation of the Tanzanian people. In practice this meant the shattering of the incipient division of labour that was developing and the hindering of the growth of the productive forces.

Artistic products were stolen or destroyed. Tanzanian dances, songs and art were frowned upon and repressed. Craftsmen were instead 'taught' the making of chairs etc. according to European norms. Education was to impart 'a sound knowledge of German customs and patriotism'. The aim of drawing classes in the government schools was clearly expressed in a German report (1911): Pupils drew 'illustrated pictures of German history from Germany's greatest era (which) deepened their grasp of Germany's strength and greatness!'[3]

At the present time, Tanzania is a neo-colonial state under the rule of the bureaucratic native bourgeoisie allied with imperialism which maintains the backwardness of peasant production by various methods including outright state repression. It also represses the workers and the lower sections of the petty-bourgeoisie.

Thus the present stage of the Tanzanian revolution is to prepare the ground for a socialist revolution by establishing the dictatorship of the proletariat in alliance with the peasants. This requires the overthrow of imperialism and its allies to pave the way for the building of the national economy and culture.

One of the means of maintaining the bureaucratic bourgeois rule in Tanzania today is through the ideological state apparatus. It controls the only two national newspapers and the radio station; the latter is regarded as the main instrument for spreading its ideology since the majority of the population is illiterate and newspapers do not reach all parts of the country. ' . . . the radio has been used as an educational medium, for it reaches further and more quickly into our villages than any other form of communication' — Nyerere in *10 years after the Arusha Declaration.*

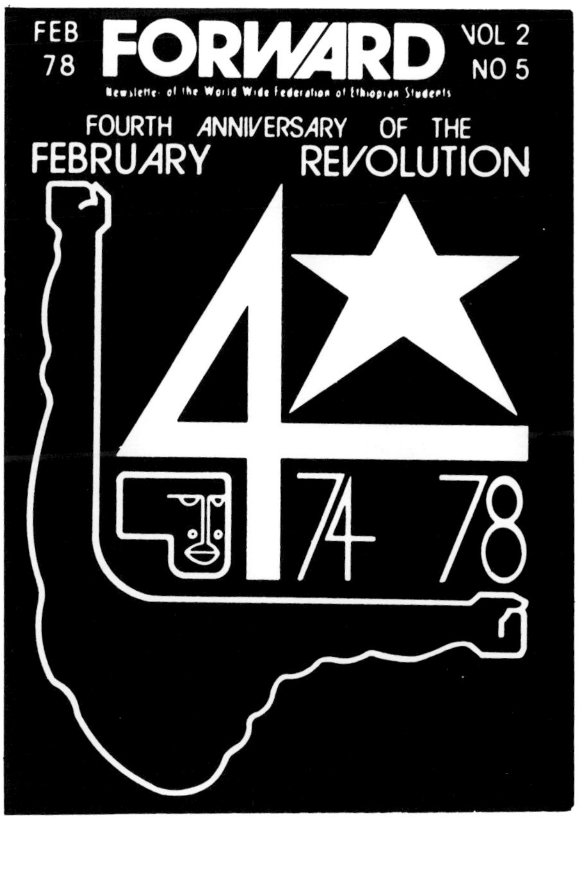

It propagates its ideology through the educational system strictly controlled by the government. Further, any form of cultural activity has to be approved first by an organ of the ruling party (which is the only one allowed).

The ideological hegemony of the bureaucratic bourgeoisie in Tanzania does not preclude the existence of other ideologies. In fact, in spite of its anti-imperialist noises, the ideology of world imperialism dominates certain spheres. The few cinemas that exist in the towns show a steady diet of 'Kung Fu' and 'Westerns'. African films or films from socialist countries are not shown since, as the Tanzanian Film Board puts it, 'they do not make money'. The rural areas are sometimes rewarded with films about technology or the few productions that espouse the ruling class ideology. Imported cheap novels and magazines (from the West) monopolise the bookshops.

The sphere of production of painting/sculpture is underdeveloped in Tanzania today. Even then, the State tries to monopolise whatever exists. It also promotes tendencies that are to its benefit. The parastatal SIDO has set up centres that produce 'sculptures' for sale to tourists who are the main buyers. In fact the Tanzanian Arts Council has a catalogue from which they order large series of sculptures based on one model. These are usually copies of traditional art produced in the past under a different mode of production, embodying the dominant ideology of the remote past and serving a different purpose. Just as pre-capitalist relations of production are reinforced, are utilised by imperialism, the pre-capitalist aesthetic elements are promoted to serve a different (imperialist) ideology.

An example of this is the promotion of the 'shetani' (spirits) Makondi Art since the mid 50s whose ideology is dominantly mystical. It gained its popularity because the 'customers in the art shops seemed to find it attractive . . . and more carvings of strange spirit shapes were created in the shed. Today shetani carvings are produced in most of the craft communities'.— Jorn Korn in *Modern Makonde Art.*

As a result, that section of the art of Makonde people that commented upon the issues which concerned the Makonde people and, in some cases, that of the whole country, has declined. Contemporary political satire, birth and death, and other social issues do not interest the tourist.

Contrary to this, the Makonde Art produced recently in Mozambique deals with the dominant issues of the time. The liberation struggle helped strengthen the elements that dealt with social function and thus provided it with a new dynamic for a genuine development, in form as well as content.

The production of art that has to pander to the buyers' conceptions is a problem that faces artists in all capitalist countries. African artists have an additional handicap, for the market that allows them to survive is located outside the continent *in all respects.* The fact that they have to produce for those people who in most cases do not have any knowledge of the African reality (neither are they concerned about it) totally alienates them from their own contemporary reality. The art objects are usually sold or taken to the West where private collectors or museums hoard/display them as examples of 'primitive' art. The second or third-rate objects that are generally stocked in 'art galleries' in Africa are also mostly bought by Western tourists who usually see them as momentoes of a holiday.[4]

The dealers who control the production of these objects, and in some cases the artists themselves, have no scruples about imitation or pandering to the tourists' demands; new objects are deliberately broken and then mended and/or in other cases new objects are buried in the ground for some time in order to give them the appearance of antiques. The extent to which the market dominates the production of artistic objects in Africa today is illustrated by the fact that Hausa metalworkers now produce the famous Ashanti goldweights.

Furthermore, one of the consequences of large numbers of best past works being stored in museums in the West is that the contemporary African artist often has to work in a complete vacuum. And since information about Western art is more easily available, he/she is more likely to be influenced by it, and, as a result, often turns out bad copies of it.

There are two reasons for the encouragement of such 'artistic' products by the Tanzanian regime. Firstly, it is a source of profits (foreign exchange). Capitalist relations encroach upon all spheres of production and these products are no exception. They have become commodities and hence are subjected to the market forces.

Secondly, the Tanzanian regime uses the ideology located in the past to negate the dynamic of the present struggle by positing the idea of one united nation as the dominant one. It also presents itself as the inheritor and the protector of the peoples' culture for all time. This is in effect achieved by taking the past works out of their historical context so that the question of the ideology(ies) of the works is ignored. (It is for this ideological purpose that the Tanzanian regime, like other African governments, is demanding the return of past works which were stolen by colonial powers. One supports the call for the return of all the works to their land of origin, but at the same time it is essential to expose their ideological use under reactionary regimes).

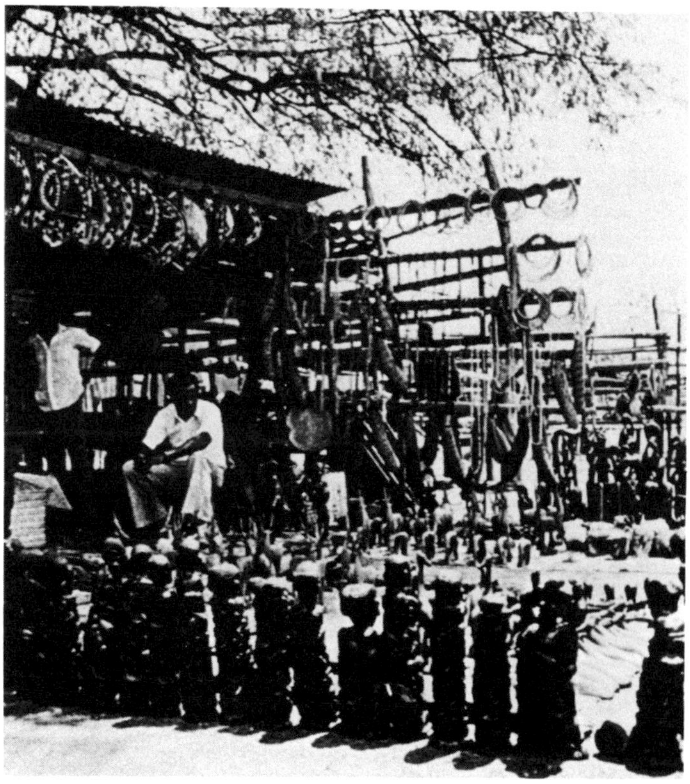

The idea that the past works represent the African reality for all times hinders the development of an AP that has its roots in the contemporary social reality, a practice that probes the issues that concern the majority of the people and exposes that which is not in their interest.

Another ideology within AP in Tanzania is the ideology of naturalism. This ideology was part of the emergence of the bourgeiosie in Europe but was imposed on the rest of the world during colonialism. In Tanzania, being under the heels of imperialism, this ideology still dominates the country. It can be found in illustrations of all sorts (advertising, posters, stamps, books, painting, etc.). Students were, and are still, taught to portray things exactly as they saw them — a methodology that has nothing in common with African aesthetics (and a task that is impossible anyway).

What then are the tasks that face Tanzanian artistis today? These are, as stated before, governed by the political tasks which have already been outlined. They are: 1) To combat the specific form that cultural imperialism takes within the sphere of artistic production in Tanzania and cultural imperialism in general; 2) to look at the dominant ideology (of the ruling class) crticially and expose its real function in the context of the present reality of the oppressed Tanzanian masses, and thereby assist them in their struggle. Both tasks are interrelated.

Before tackling the question of how to achieve this, the question of style within artistic production must be clarified. By style I mean specific elements and a specific combination of these elements (motifs, forms). Thus a national style would comprise of elements, and their relations, indigenous to Tanzania, Owing to historical factors, some of these elements and their specific combinations are common to many parts of Africa; since there still exist similar combinations are common to many parts of Africa; since there still exist similar modes of production and the division of one people into different countries as a result of boundaries imposed by colonialism. Therefore the national style of Tanzania would have a lot in common with that of the surrounding countries.

Such a style would combat the encroachment of the 'international' style, which is rooted in the West, and would enable us to develop our culture according to our needs and the concrete situation. However, we cannot imitate our past or other cultures.

If life as a whole were built on the basis of imitation only, then there would be no development or human progress but a mere repetition of a phenomenon.

The ideologues of imperialism argue that the development of the peoples (whether material or cultural) who are 'late' in entering the road of progress has to tread the paths of the advanced nations. We totally reject this.

We do not oppose utilising the experiences of other peoples provided we are in a position to utilise their positive aspects and learn lessons from the negative ones. We have to bear in mind the concrete conditions that exist within our own country in applying these lessons.

The historical development of Tanzanian society has been disrupted by imperialism. One of the present tasks of AP is to forge a link with the past, to establish a continuum to serve as a basis for the leap into the future. In order to do this, attitudes to past works must be re-assessed: they must be analysed in the context of the fact that they were produced in a different time and served different purposes. However, the traditional forms (whether from the remote past or prevailing in the present) can be used to express the present realities without losing the identity of their specific aesthetic.

I shall now try to illustrate one method of using the past to create the new. A study of past works will show that the elements are used in a specific manner. That is to say, the elements and their inter-relationships are of a specific order; and it can be shown that this specific order relates to specific socio-economic relations. It is now possible to isolate the elements and by reconstituting them in a different order, create a new relationship between them to reflect the new reality of our different age.

Consider the following illustration as an example:

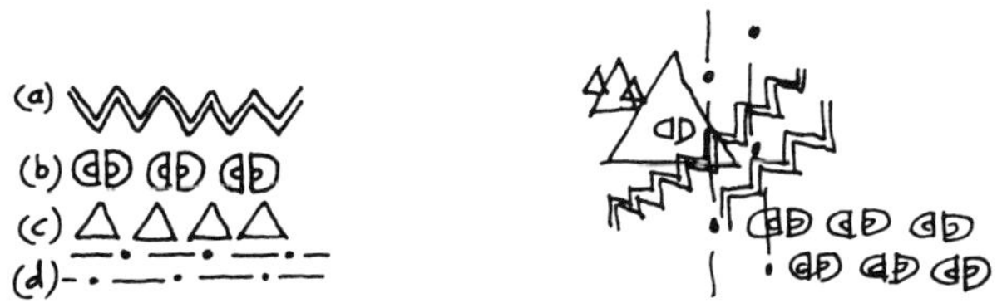

a, b, c, and d each denote a different element, Each element is made up of sub-elements. Line c is made up of a number of triangular elements. There also exists a definite hierarchy: a is above b, and b above c, and so on. This hierarchy is one relationship between the elements. There are others.

We have now destroyed the previous relations of the sub-elements of c by placing one above the other, by enlarging them to varying degree, and so on. The relation of c to the other elements is no longer the same; d is now to the right of c and not below c as before. The relationship of the sub-elements of line d has also changed.

The drawing above is that of a mask. The drawing below it shows how it is possible to 'extract' elements from the mask. The two-dimensionality of the drawing is emphasised by the lines crossing each other. Nor is the nose symmetrical any longer.

In other words, the aesthetic elements of the past have been separated from the ideology that arranged them in a specific manner, and they can now be used in a different manner reflecting another ideology. The relations between the elements may go on changing/evolving as society evolves. There will come a time when the elements themselves are outmoded and replaced. This 'replacement' will not occur at a single moment. As the relations change, so do the elements. New elements may have to be introduced for task for which there are no precedents and which the elements of the old order are unable to satisfy.

However, much research needs to be done on the past works, not only at isolating their elements or their specificity but also situating them in their original context, including the relationship of the aesthetic elements to the dominant ideology(ies) of that time.

There exist many nationalities within Tanzania: many of them have different art forms. This may result in the national aesthetic having different tendencies within it. Some artists may prefer to work with a certain number of aesthetic elements. All this (and much more) can only be 'tested' in practice.

Production implies consumption, for only when it is consumed does a product become a product. Production and consumption are united by the fact that consumption determines the ideal object of production. However it is production that is the primary determinate. It is not possible to consume a product unless it exists and the product determines the manner of consumption by shaping or creating the object in a definite manner (painting can only be seen and not heard).

National art can and must struggle against the ruling ideology within the sphere of artistic production and thus combat the ruling ideology of the native bourgeoisie which is not in the interest of people. It can expose the actions of the ruling class (e.g. through cartoons). But ideology cannot be struggled against solely at the ideological level. The deterioration in the living conditions of the masses will increasingly dent the hegemony of the ruling ideology, resulting in economic and political repercussions and affecting the ideological level..To a certain extent, this is already happening in Tanzania.

The development of national art will also help combat the increasing influence of cultural imperialism. Care will have to be taken that the national art does not advance too fast in isolation from the people or so that it loses its connection with the past, for the attempt to bridge the gap will not be perceived by the majority of the masses and the national art will be in a danger of becoming an alien art form again.

If art is to avoid becoming sterile, if it is to avoid 'talking' to itself, if it is to gain acceptance by the majority of the people, then it will have to deal with the issues that face them. This will also work to its advantage for it will then gain mass acceptance, it will be understood by the people. The artist then has to become a part of the vanguard, not only in the political sense but also in the realm of his specific practice.

We have only dealt with the sphere of artistic production. Other practices also face similar tasks; to struggle against bourgeois ideology (within their specific domains) in such a manner that the struggle is located within the concrete situation of Tanzania, e.g. old myths and stories can be turned 'upside down'; instead of God being the cause of the misfortune that befalls a family, the same story can be used to show the material causes behind the poverty of the people.

Though every practice and every possible means should be utilised in the struggle, the actual circumstance will determine the particular practice that will be the most effective.

However, the specific tasks of various practices at all times will be defined by the political analysis/situation. It should be clear now that the artist cannot content him/herself with AP only, for it can never be a substitute for PP. As the Senegalese film director, Sembene Ousmane, has pointed out, '. . . it is impossible to make a revolution with a film no matter how progressive it is'.

---

1. The relatively autonomous nature of artistic production has often been indicated by various revolutionary leaders: ". . . [the] question of right and wrong in the arts and sciences should be settled through free discussion in artistic and scientific circles and in the course of political work in the arts and sciences" — Mao Tse Tung in *On the Correct Handling of Contradictions among the People*. "There is no question . . . that in this field [literature] greater scope must undoubtedly be allowed for personal initiative, individual inclination, thought and fantasy, form and content", and that the "literary side of the proletarian party cause cannot be mechanically identified with its other causes" — Lenin in *Party Organisation and Party Literature*..
2. Mao, who was a poet himself, is explicit about this. After listing political criteria that can be used to judge whether actions and words are in the interests of the people, he continues: "Naturally, in judging the truthfulness of scientific theories or assessing the aesthetic value of works of art, other pertinent criteria are needed . . .", ibid.
3. K.F.Hirji, *Colonial Ideological Apparatuses in Tanganyika under the Germans*.
4. For a long description of this, see "The Contemporary-Traditional Art Market in Africa" and 'The West African Art Market Revisited' by Daniel Crowley in *African Arts*, Autumn 1970 and Summer 1974.

an introduction to RADICAL URDU POETRY

Mahmood Jamal

Urdu poetry has for centuries played an important role in the cultural life of northern India.* Originating in the courts of nobles and princes, the *mushaira* or poetry reading has developed into a regular cultural event providing a platform for poets to show their mastery of the art and to come in contact with their audience in a far more direct way than is possible through books.

Before this century, the bulk of Urdu poetry consisted of *gazals* or love lyrics. There was very little which could be described as political or social; nonetheless varied subjects of philosophical and psychological importance were dealt with in great depth and with astounding beauty of expression. The *gazal* has the added advantage of being very musical and many are easily sung by poets themselves or by singers. As a result their popularity has remained undiminished.

In the earlier part of this century, Urdu poetry reached a turning point; poets facing the trauma of colonial oppression began to reflect this in their poetry. Mass politics were also taking shape in the form of the Indian freedom movement. Poets began to forge new poems to meet the changed and changing reality that faced them.

The inspiration no longer came just from cruel red lips and dark eyes, nor from ancient kings and queens; although some poets in a nostalgic delirium started to sing in praise of old ideas and values, took to reviving dead themes that modern man had long left in the museums. (Granted that a vigorous re-appraisal of history is required by all nations struggling to liberate themselves from colonial domination, but that in itself is not enough and future too must be charted to avoid sinking into the mire of obscurantism and mystification.) The inspiration for the progressive poets came not from some abstract promise of palaces in the skies nor from rivers of milk and honey nor from the exploits of ancient warriors or reformers. It came from the concrete possibilities which were opened before mankind by the revolution of 1917, by the struggles of freedom fighters in India and around the colonised world.

A much needed dynamism had at least been injected into Urdu literature and a new era had begun in Urdu poetry, different both in content and form though traditional forms also continued and the *gazal* still flourishes.

Those who supported national independence have seen their dream go sour with the collaborationist attitude of their native bourgeoisie and with the advent of neo-colonialism. They want the promised freedom; they only get new forms of repression. They hoped that a new dawn would break upon their land with the departure of the hated colonisers; instead the night grows ever darker:

This is not that dawn with longing for which
the friends set out . . .

Then the brutal realisation that the struggle is not yet over:

Where did that fine breeze, that the wayside lamp
Has not once felt, blow from—where has it fled?
Night's heaviness is unlessened still, the hour
Of mind and spirit's ransom has not struck:
Let us go on our goal is not reached yet.

— *Faiz Ahmad Faiz*

The real face of the rulers is exposed. The mask of democracy was inadequate. The guns had to come out backed by tanks, planes, and AID programmes. A single spark here! A poem can have the force of a storm. A banner placed in the mental landscape, a symbol of revolt, a terrifying scream against oppression, a rallying point for revolution.

The writers and intellectuals, poets and artists have all been radicalised in varying degrees by being witness to a systematic denial of humanity to the people around them. They are intensely aware of this and their works reflect this awareness. But the rulers can survive only by keeping the people in ignorance. So, inevitably, the poets come in conflict with the rulers.

Poetry and imprisonment seem very incongruous indeed to someone who lives in a culture where poets have become mere entertainers playing with worlds usually to a small audience of academics. But if we cast a glance at the important names of Urdu poetry, we can hardly think of any poet who has not been to prison or has been threatened with worse. **Faiz** has been to jail. **Sardar J'afri** has been to jail. **Habib Jalib** went to prison several times in Pakistan. **Hasrat Mohani** was imprisoned by the British in India. Other forms of restrictions have been imposed on those who stayed out: **Josh's** famous poem *To the Heirs of East India Company* was banned by the British.

Those who went to jail did not stop writing there. In fact, many of them came up with their best poems: like **Yanis Ristos** in Greece, **Kim Chi Ha** in Korea, **Saeed Zahiri** in Singapore, **Denis Brutus** in South Africa, **Nazim Hikmet** in Turkey, many Palestinian poets in Israel, and numerous others around the world.

How much frustration they must have caused their captors! To see the unbroken spirits lighting up flames in the darkness of their oppression, sending out sparks to light prairie fires!

---

* In 1947, the Indian sub-continent was partitioned into two independent countries and so was Urdu poetry, so to speak. Of the poets presented here **Faiz Ahmad Faiz** and **Habib Jalib** live in Pakistan while **Sardar J'afri** and **Sahir Ludhianavi** are from India.

A GIFT OF BLOOD

Searching for a garden in my world
you will find fiery winds, not spring.
No rainbow colours here, in this grey afternoon;
from one end to the other swings the noose.
Once again they go towards their gory end
those leaders who have lost their way so many times!

Behind the veil of their democracy,
they build prisons they make whips.
In the name of peace they conjure wars
In the clamour for justice they produce disparity.
Fear guards the heart and lips are sealed;
Overhead, the tents of iron bars stretch out.

Yet have they ever feared cruelty and oppression
those ideas that have given strength to the imagination.
No mercenary army can ever break
that glass that holds the people's wakened spirits.
At each step, life gives a gift of blood
to the lamps that entangle with the darkness.

Onward moves the caravan of human progress
shaking the heart of tyrants
All around the drums of revolt are sounding
young people walk around like lighted flames.
The whole earth is a boiling ocean
the mountains and the forests are alive!

It's easy to stifle my scream
but who will stop the challenge of life?
The wall of steel and fire may be high
but who will stop the force of changing times?
You who block the way of new ideas
who will stop the sword of rising masses?

From the very place of darkness where you seek refuge
the armies of morning will emerge!
In the air unfurl the red flags
The east and west converge!

Sahir Ludhianavi

ONE YEAR

What is the meaning of imprisonment?
What the significance of jails?
O year now asleep in times graveyard
on your shrivelled shadow
barking jaildogs weep.
I look at all this and I laugh.

Those venomous stings of moments past;
the blood-soaked sharpness of the morning's sword;
that blackness left in the evening's eye
by gunpowder,
and those riders of weeks on the months' backs
who came to crush my revolt;
All those I've left sleeping
by your side O passing year.

Blood drips from the eyes of sentries.
The rifles speak through iron lips;
and bullets sting with tongues of brass.
And LAW, that chain of property,
extends its links and gathers more
within its deceptive embrace.
Year after year the snake changes its form.
Inside the charmers basket
poisonous cobras lurk upholding the rule
of LAW and JUSTICE
while his flute hides the hissing
within its waves of melody.

Still the proud hearts of selfless
fighters are beating,
the throb of struggling veins resounds;
and through time and history's streets
pass the processions.

(ii)

How many youthful yearnings bled in China
to adorn the face of the new dawn?
And how many hearts the free beauties of Greece
have sown in anticipation of spring!
The tears that rained down
from the eye of Spain are restless
to become pearls and dewdrops.
Like a bright banner the blood of martyrs
from Vietnam and Malaya
is shimmering in the mirror of the sky.
The fire of revolt in Tilangana
rushes to burn the fields of slavery.
The wounded spirit of Bengal
has recovered its might.
Pain and cries for mercy
have found the fiery language
of slogans demanding demanding.
From each corner the bursting force of floods;
from each particle the dance of emerging light.
Pain of death, terror of slavery
and against them,
WAKING AND RISING HUMANITY!

What is imprisonment?
What is the significance of jails!

(iii)

What are days and nights
but milestones on the roads;
months and years are dust left
by travellers.
Imprisonment comes and passes.
We meet mountains of trouble
valleys of ignorance;
hearts burning in deserts of starvation,
life burns in the boiling river of blood.
And in the thorny wastes and plains
footsteps become red lines of blood.
Yet the caravan moves towards the destination.
Eyelids unveil the scenery
dreams erupt with flowers.

(iv)

I am not lonely here
for so many yearnings are imprisoned with me.
So many youthful faces bred in mountain valleys
So many sons of the green fields
So many workers that drive trains and machines
So many fragrances from kisses
So many curls of lovely hair
So many sisters' lotuses of hope
So many Mothers' lamps of fulfilment.
So many storms, gusts of wind
So many mutilated hands of strikers
So many banners of revolt!

The higher the mountain to climb
the greater the courage we muster;
soaring like eagles of Himalaya
tearing through the skies
our endless courage!

And the old prisoners, wise friends
whose wrinkles are pages of historical events;
the laughter in their sparkling eyes
the wrinkles of their smiles,
are a mockery of the system's cruelty.
In this night of slavery
the silver of their hair foretells
that morning is approaching.
And those passionate poets and story tellers
melt the chains of worry
with the warmth of their song.

Each verse they write the story of heroism.
Each song they sing shakes these walls!

The flames of voices rise with such force
that they set fire to the dark dungeons
and our destination glimmers in the arches
of Time, rays from the morning sun.

If I have companions like these
then the purpose of travelling is great!
If the night is so bright
how much brighter the dawn!

— Sardar J'afri, *Central Jail, Nasik, India, April 1950.*

MY DAUGHTER

Thinking that it was a toy,
When she saw the chain around my wrists
my daughter jumped with joy.

Her laughter was the gift of morning,
Her laughter gave me endless strength.
A living hint of a free tomorrow
gave meaning to my night of sorrow.

ON THE BANNING OF A BOOK OF POEMS

In my hand I hold a pen
In my heart the light of consciousness
How can your forces of oppression
Ever win?
I, concerned with peace for all mankind
And you just out to save your precious skin.
Into the world I dawn, the rising sun;
Into the ocean of oblivion you shall sink!

Habib Jalib

MY CITY

What is the latest fashion in my city now?
What price the spring extorts these days?
Are they in lonely streets
tearing out their hearts;
or inside the dungeon their empty
morning starts?
Are they in dreary houses
deep in wine?
Tell me! Tell me what my friends are suffering
in these troubled times!

Faiz Ahmad Faiz

A PRISON NIGHTFALL

The night descends
step by silent step
down the stairway of stars.
The breeze goes by me
like a kindly whispered phrase.

The homeless trees of the prison yard
are absorbed in making patterns
against the sky.

On the roof's high crest
the loving hand of the moonlight rests.
In dust is drowned the starry river
and the sky is glowing silver with moonlight.
In the dark foliage
shadows play with the wind
as a wave of painful loss
invades the heart.

Defiantly, a thought tells me
how sweet life is at this instant.
Those that brew the poison of cruelty
will today nor tomorrow win.
They can put out the lamps
where lovers meet;
they cannot blind the moon!

Faiz Ahmad Faiz, *Lahore Jail, Pakistan.*

All the poems are translated from Urdu by Mahmood Jamal

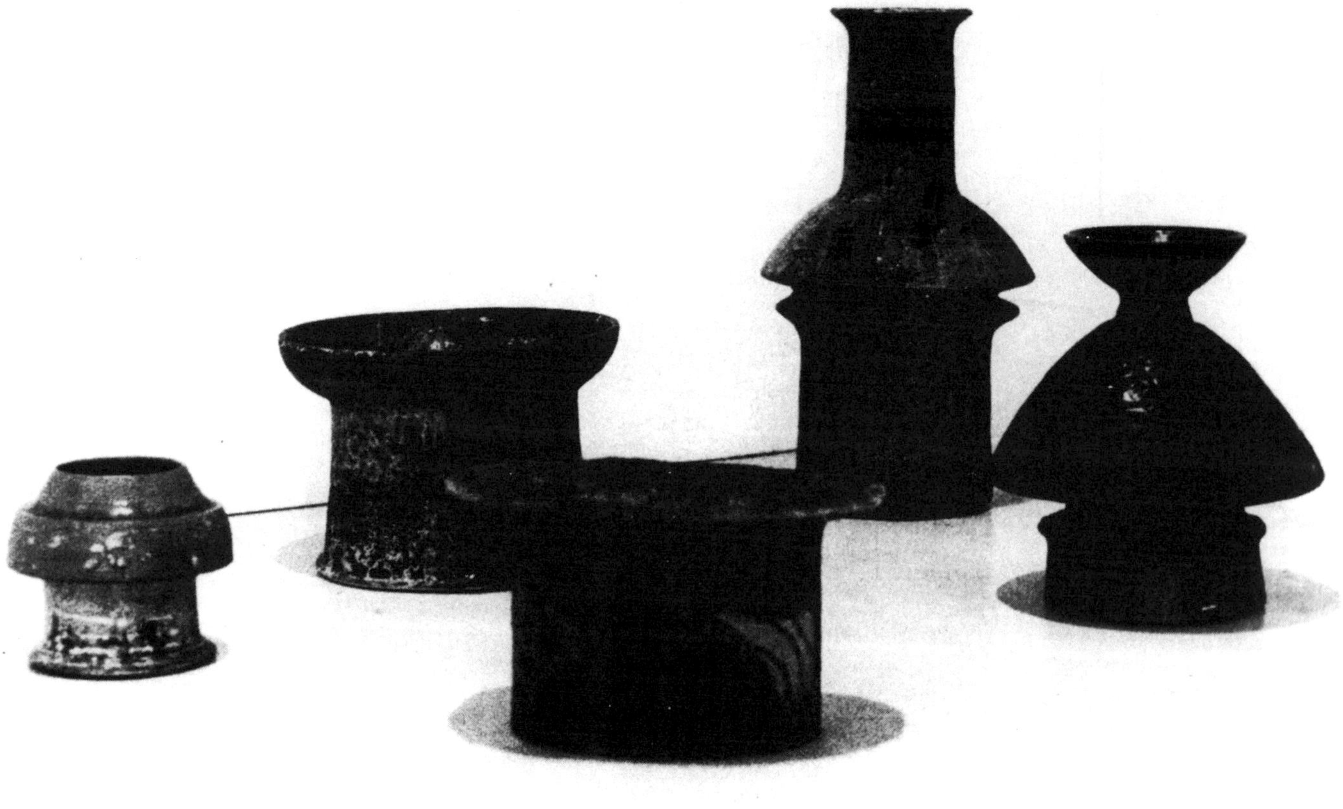

Group of Ceramic Pots by M.A. Abdalla

Afro-Caribbean Art

An analysis by Rasheed Araeen

In May 1978, Drum Arts Centre, an organisation formed in 1974 in order to encourage and promote the artistic and cultural interests of Afro-Caribbean people in Britain, presented this exhibition at the Artists Market (sometimes called Warehouse Gallery as well), London. The exhibition comprised of painting, sculpture, pottery/ceramics, photography, etc. ..... produced by black artists (of Afro-Caribbean origin) in Britain.

In the introduction to the exhibition Drum's Executive Director, John Mapondera, says, "The rarity of such exhibitions underlines the lack of opportunity for these artists to expose their work to genuine criticism and evaluation. For it is only when this can happen freely and often enough that Afro-Caribbean Artists in Britain could be expected to make a meaningful contribution as part of the 'main currents' in the common artistic endeavours. Some of the artists whose work is included in this exhibition are already making a significant contribution to art in Britain and even internationally. We include their work in order to focus on the enormous scope for development which exists when opportunities are available.

But what is Afro-Caribbean Art? is *the* question one cannot help asking after seeing the exhibition. And in fact one wonders if there really is such a thing as Afro-Caribbean Art. The question can be answered in two different ways, affirmatively as well as negatively, depending upon how one would like to look at things. Whether one is just happy to see *some* black artists exhibiting together under *some* title, or one is seriously concerned about the nature and content of the work beyond liberal sympathy and sentimentality.

The reality which qualifies an art as 'Afro-Caribbean art' is to be there. Just because an art is produced by somebody who is of Afro-Caribbean origin, or for that matter from Africa or the Caribbean, does not itself lend to that art an Afro-Caribbean particularity unless that particularity is expressed in the work, unless the work reflects upon or deals with a reality which in turn necessitates the work to be called Afro-Caribbean Art. This is particularly essential for an art produced by Afro-Caribbean people living outside Africa or the Caribbean.

In other words, the work *must* express or show different aesthetic characteristics, not necessarily in the deployment of different techniques or/and material but in the essence that separates it from its non-Afro-Caribbean contemporaries. It must have a content which, in some way, is reflective of Afro-Caribbean experience, in this case, in Britain.

African Art, for example, clearly distinguishes itself in its specificity; not only because it has been created in Africa, not only at its formal level, but because it *also* expresses the African world-view – and it expresses it very profoundly indeed. It *communicates* the socio-economic, cultural, as well as political, reality of its people(s) in various periods in its history, through a specific sensibility which became known as African aesthetic sensibility expressed in a variety of formal innovations. (It was this African sensibility that was injected into, if not appropriated by, the mainstream of European culture in the beginning of this century, and as a result we had the development of Cubism and so on.)

Looking at the exhibition, however, one finds little that is distinguishably Afro-Caribbean in its contemporary context. There is little which is distinctly different, in form as well as content (if any), from various Western styles. Here one is not necessarily looking for a formal criteria that may remind one of Africa or the Caribbean, or that looks 'African'; and in fact there are works in the exhibition (by Taiwo Jegede, Adesose Wallace, Cyprian Mandala ..... and the pottery/ceramics) that have a traditional African quality. The important thing here really is what is that which is being *expressed*, its specificity and aesthetic quality, as well as its social relevance.

The work, with a few exceptions, lacks an originality and a sense of purpose. It shows no guts for an original experimentation and search for a methodology necessary for the communication of its supposed specificity. Nor does it bother to address to its social reality. Most of the works are either art-school exercises (amateurish, naive and childish) or bad imitations of various Western styles developed in this century but now outmoded. There are no surprises and the painting section is particularly bad.

Three works by Frank Bowling, who is supposed to be

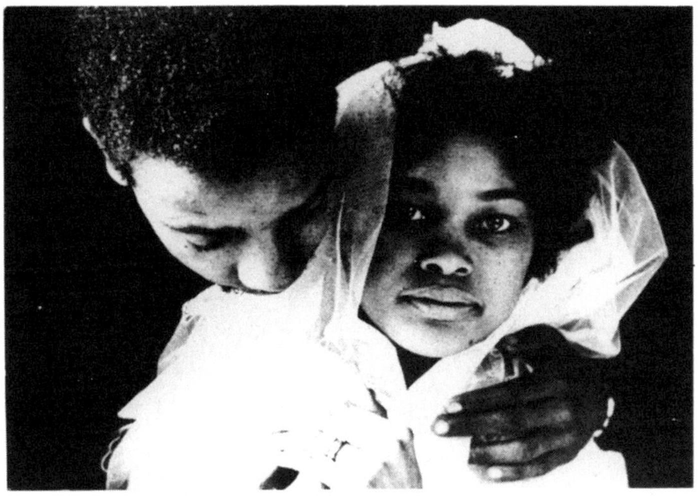

Portrait by Bill Patterson

internationally known, might have impressed us twenty years ago. In fact we would have certainly credited him if he had innovated this method of throwing paint directly on the canvas or contributed further to its development. Now one has to be ignorant, or pretend ignorance, to appreciate what is no more than a decorative pastiche of the outmoded styles of post-abstract expressionist period in New York. They might look beautiful in somebody's house or office but have nothing to say. (This criticism, in fact, applies to many artists today, black and white, who are dabblingly pursuing a kind of mannerism.)

However, *Carnival Dancer* by Merdelle Irving, *When the Albino Comes* by Reynold Duncan, *Trophies of Empire* by Donald Locke, are interesting works and show skill and some originality. Donald Locke's other works, like *Seed Pot*, show his competence as a craftsman. One would, however, like to see him coming out of the cocoon of his sexual fantasies and come to terms with the world outside as well.

Groups of Ceramic Pots by M.A. Abdalla shows a real professional dedication of a craftsman; the scuptural arrangement — which does evoke a feeling of an African village—would have been more effective spatially if the pots were slightly bigger. *Four Ceramic Plates* by Siddig El N'goumi have also been beautifully done.

The photographic section shows professional talent, but the content of the works suffers from stereotyped themes. It lacks boldness in the choice of the subject and misses so much of the social reality of black people in Britain. It is particularly disappointing to see the work of Lance Watson comprising only of a few Nigerian portraits, which are technically impressive. He has been actively involved in the community and has done a lot of work that is particularly related to Afro-Caribbean reality.

In this respect, one is also reminded of the important work done by Errol Lloyd in book illustrations, particularly storybooks for black kids. One wonders why this work was not included.

The exhibition was perhaps a celebration for its liberal supporters who look to such an occasion or a venture to show their paternal concern for the predicament of black people (there were in fact some faces from the art establishment present during the opening) and absolve their guilty conscience, but for those who are seriously concerned with the state of art of black people in Britain it was a big disappointment. The exhibition in fact conforms to the general and erroneous notion about the level of development of the non-white artist.

One could say, and perhaps rightly say, that we are being harsh in judging this exhibition, since it was the first chance for many to show their work. If there had existed equal opportunities, an opportunity for the black artists to develop and show their work along with their white contemporaries, and thus subjected to open criticism and analysis, we would have seen a better standard. Very true. In fact, we were the first ones to put forward an analysis of the difficulties faced by black artists (here we include Asians as well) in Britain (see 'Black Manifesto' in our issue Number 1) and we have pointed out that there has been a deliberate policy on the part of the art establishment to ignore black artists or marginalise their status. But that does not mean that all black artists were defeated by the difficulties and produced compromisingly third to fifth-rate works. We are particularly pointing out this because there is a general impression that this was "a survey of black artists in Britain" (Time Out No. 422); which is not true.

The point is that this kind of exhibition, at this particular time in the history of black people in Britain when there is a widespread ignorance about their actual contribution (vis-a-vis art) of the last thirty years or so, does not serve any real purpose. On the contrary, by gathering some amateurs and mediocres under some *convenient* title, it could perpetuate the myth of marginal black artist. The issue

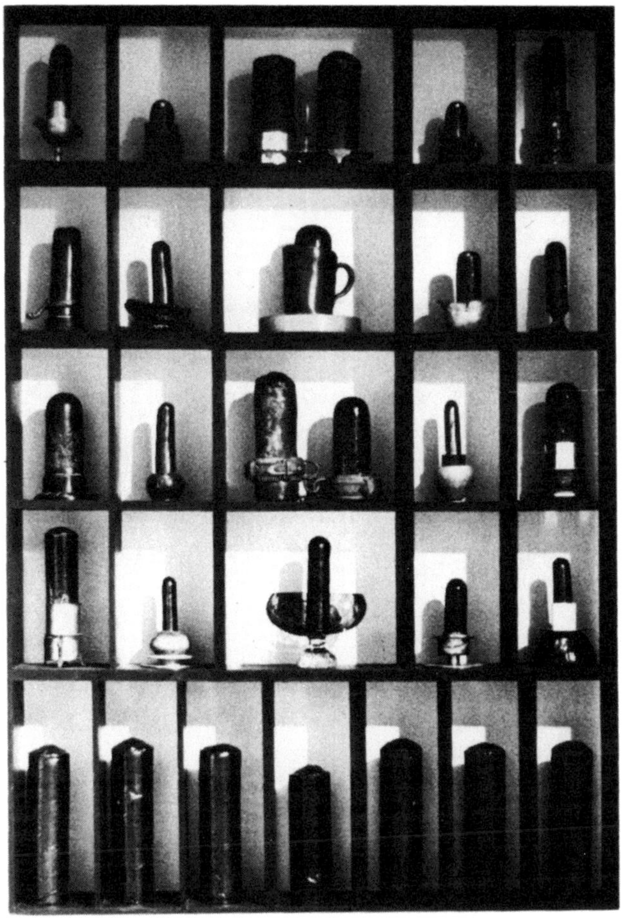

Trophies of Empire by Donald Locke

here really is of *Black Artists in Britain* and not of 'Afro-Caribbean Art', and it ought to be dealt with seriously outside the superficial limits of ethnic categories. That does not imply that Afro-Caribbean particularity ought to be suppressed but that it ought to be dealt with within the larger context of black predicament.

This brings us to the *context* of the exhibition, which in fact reveals the real issue. It is not coincidental that the work (in the exhibition) resembles so much of the kind of work being done today in most Third World countries, the work that fails to question the reality of neo-colonialism but *accepts* it, resulting into its subordination and marginality to the 'mainstream' art created in the West. It is this marginality created by cultural imperialism that is also evident here.

Neo-colonialism is now being 'brought' home to the metropolis of the capitalist world, for there exists a people within the Western world that must be neo-colonialised and marginalised. That means an intermediary class must be created, a counterpart of the *native* bourgeoisie in the Third World, an *ethnic* bourgeoisie in the West — exotic and subservient.

A black middle-class leadership (with white liberal advisors) is now being created in Britain. It would supposedly look after the interests of its respective people but in reality serve the dominant ruling ideology. A class of ethnic intermediaries will help contain and submerge the consciousness of black people and thereby *try* to destroy the potential radical role of the sub-proletariat class, by channelling its energies and frustrations into the field which is considered (by the bourgeoisie) safe, neutral and non-political: art and culture. It would therefore be natural for the 'ethnic minority' artists, who *accept* the intermediary role of their respective middle-classes, to incorporate the middle-class view of the world in their work. 'Afro-Caribbean Art' exhibition betrays such a tendency.

This is however not an unexpected occurrence. There will in fact be many such exhibitions, supported by the establishment, taking place under various ethnic titles during the coming years, including exhibitions of neo-colonial art (see again 'Black Manifesto') imported from various Commonwealth countries, which will attempt to *re-ethnicise* the *black* artist and thereby marginalise further his/her role in this society.

The choice for us is clear. Either we accept our marginalised separate categories or reject them. The rejection will entail hard thinking and commitment. It would require us to look deep into our reality as black people in this country, as well as in the world at large, and unless until we incorporate critically this reality in our creative work we would have nothing to say or contribute. Art is not merely a craft, decoration or entertainment, but means of expression through which one asserts one's own humanity.

BLACK PHOENIX : NUMBER TWO : SUMMER 1978 : EXTRACTS

To say that "this country might be swamped by people of a different culture" at a time when the whole world is being viciously dominated by the West, is to perpetuate imperialist lies; lies which must be exposed and denounced. — BLACK PHOENIX

The new form of children's literature will have to emerge in the struggle for a new society, they will become necessary in that combat. Only the destruction of the capitalist system, the gradual defeat of economic and mental neo-colonialism, can guarantee that one day, finally, Babar may risk killing the old lady and, by the loss of his innocence, hit upon the first step on the road to complete liberation. — ARIEL DORFMAN

It is not possible to separate either, historically, the development of bourgeois consciousness from the development of colonialism, or, socially, the bourgeois value-system from racist and imperialist assumptions of superiority... the Fine Arts have, historically, fallen victim to a myth concerning the absolute and metaphysical nature of its activity, as a result of which its actions and its products have been used to justify not merely a criminal structure of social relations but also the world-wide edifice of imperialism upon which this structure still depends. — KENNETH COUTTS-SMITH

While one can speak of an advanced mode of production or a higher level of productive forces, one cannot pass such qualitative judgement on aesthetics. It would be incorrect to say that African aesthetics are more advanced than European or vice versa. There cannot be one 'correct' aesthetics, nationally as well as internationally. — N.KILELE

Neo-colonialism is now being 'brought' home to the metropolis of the capitalist world, for there exists a people within the Western world that must be neo-colonised and marginalised. That means an intermediary class must be created, a counterpart of <u>native</u> bourgeoisie in the Third World, an <u>ethnic</u> bougeoisie in the West - exotic and subservient. — RASHEED ARAEEN

BLACK PHOENIX

THIRD WORLD PERSPECTIVE ON CONTEMPORARY ART AND CULTURE No 3 SPRING 1979 60p

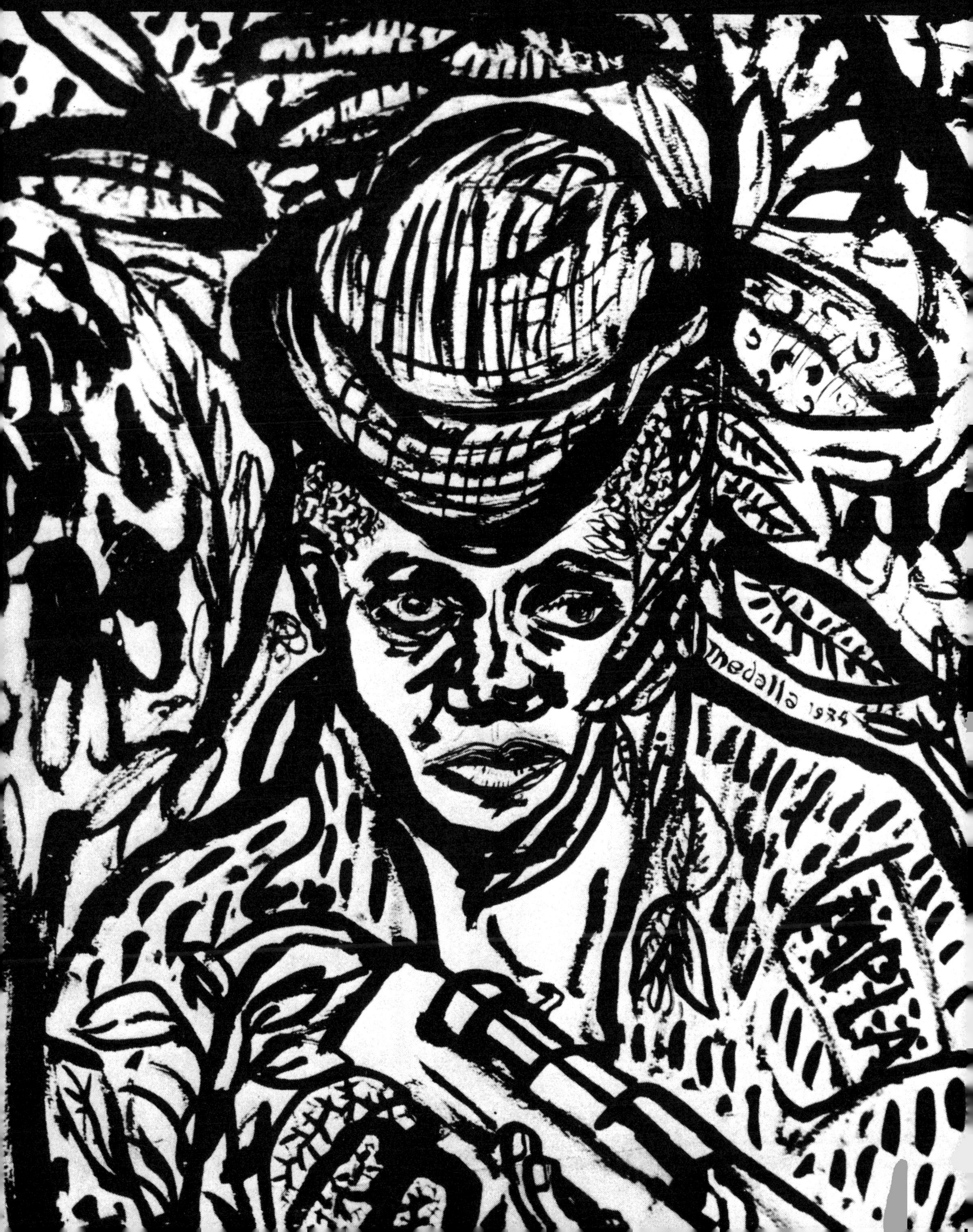

BLACK PHOENIX

Third World Perspective on Contemporary Art & Culture

No 3 SPRING 1979

Edited and published by:
Rasheed Araeen, Mahmood Jamal

BCM BLACKPHOENIX
LONDON WC1V 6XX

Tel: 01-624 7185

Subscriptions: 4 issues p&p included.
UK £3 EUROPE £4 OTHERS £5
Make cheques payable to *Black Phoenix*.

Typeset: Bread 'n Roses (TU) 01-485 4432
Printing: Blackrose Press
Distribution: Publications Distribution Co-op., 27 Clerkenwell Close, London EC1.

CONTENTS

ISSN 0141-9080

Cover: David Medalla *A Freedom Fighter* ' 1974

CONTRIBUTORS

Rasheed Araeen was born in Karachi (Pakistan), but since 1964 has lived in London. Although a civil engineering graduate, he has devoted himself to art and cultural activity. His main concern has been with the dialectical aspect of transformational processes. His first 'sculpture' comprised of *burning of bicycle tyres*, Karachi 1959. Since early '70s he has been involved in activities, both artistic and political, which are related to his own subjectivity as a black person living in Britain and the predicament of the Third World. In 1975-76 he wrote his major statement, **Preliminary Notes for a BLACK MANIFESTO**, which questions the pretended universality of Western Art and its international role in the world today, published in *BP* issue No 1.

Guy Brett was formerly Art Critic of *The Times*. He contributes to many art journals and has organised exhibitions, including *In Motion* (kinetic art) for the Arts Council of Great Britain (ACGB) 1966, Helio Oiticica (Brazilian environmental artist) at the Whitechapel Gallery 1969; *Peasant Paintings from Hu County, Shensi Province, China* with the ACGB 1976, *Patchwork Art of Resistance from Chile* 1977. Currently he is working on a study of the transformations of some indigenous popular art forms in the 20th century.

Kenneth Coutts-Smith is a British art critic/historian, now residing in Canada. He is the author of many articles/reviews, as well as two books: *Dada* (Dutton-Studio Vista, 1970) and *The Dream of Icarus, Art and Society in the 20th Century* (Hutchinson, 1970). At present he is holder of a Senior Arts Award from the Canada Council, in order to write two books: one on *Art & Politics*, and the other a study of *Cultural Colonialism*.

Eduardo Galeano, a leading Uruguayan writer and journalist, was chief editor of the weekly *Marcha* (1961-64) and founded the magazine *Crisis* in Buenos Aires. He has written several books, among them is his famous *Open Veins of Latin America* (Monthly Review Press). He is now living in exile in Barcelona, Spain.

Susil Sirivardana describes himself as a 40 years old Sri Lankan who throughout his working life has combined interests in development work, social science research and writing on culture. He is one of the editors of the progressive Sinhala language cultural quarterly *Mavatha* (The Path), which in recent times has played a vanguard role in the struggle for a people's culture in Sri Lanka.

We acknowledge the financial assistance (£480) from the Arts Council of Great Britain in respect of this issue.

SEVEN YEARS ON

Eduardo Galeano

"What is the use of writing if not to defy the blockade which the system places around the dissident message?" - Eduardo Galeano. Yes, indeed, what is the use? What is the point in writing, or making art, if not to denounce the inhumanity of the system, and of our time?

It is true though that art and literature decorate life, by celebrating its moments of leisure. It is true that the function of art and literature, of poetry and music, is to enhance our pleasure of living, to make our relationship with each other more intense, harmonious and meaningful... But how could one celebrate the world in which most of the people only <u>exist</u> for the sadistic pleasure of a privileged few? How could one be in harmony with the system that constantly sucks the blood from the open veins? The open veins are not only of Latin America but indeed of the whole Third World.

For us it is really a moment of crisis, not a time for celebration ! It is a moment for looking at our reality, for critical reflection, not a time for mystical contemplation. It is a time of struggle, and in struggle we need a voice which exposes the oppressive system and denounces its inhumanity, and which offers us a hope for the future. Eduardo Galeano is one such authentic voice, which speaks not only for Latin America but for the whole Third World, and indeed for all mankind.

We are printing here Galeano's <u>Seven Years On</u> in place of the editorial.

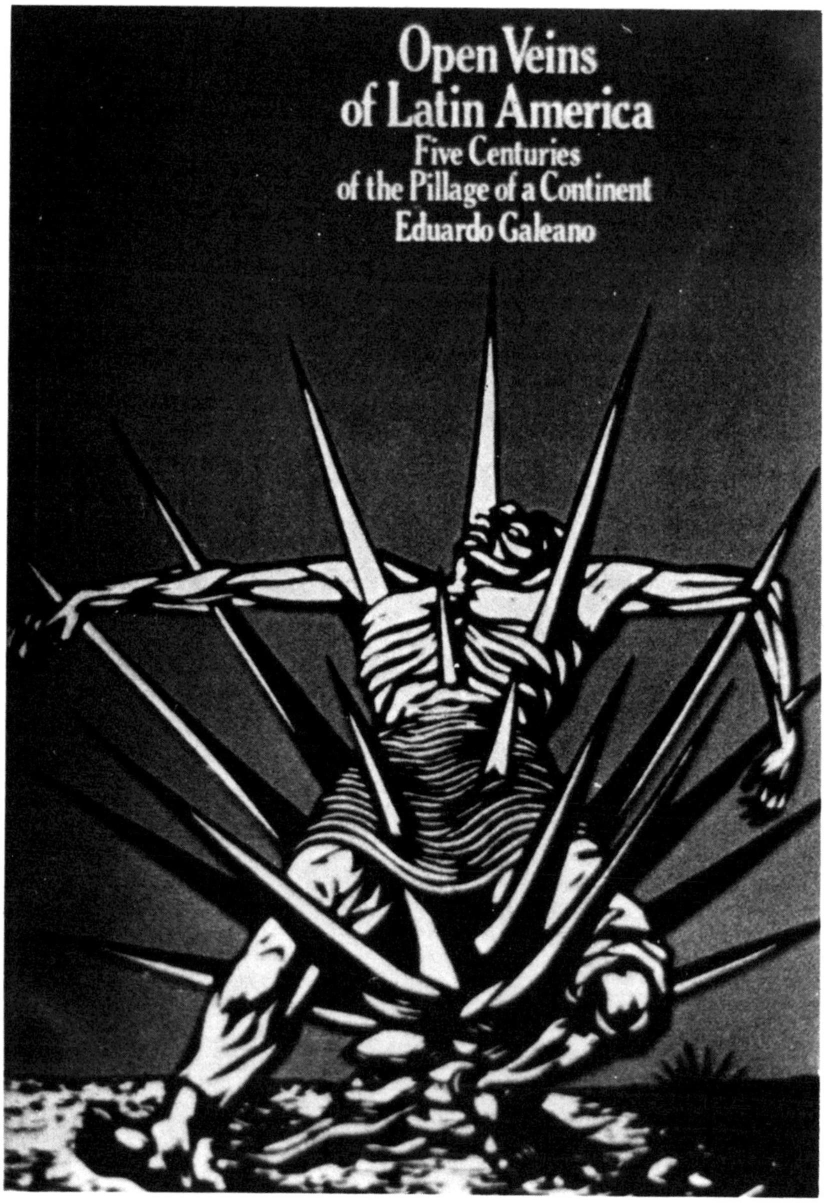

1 Seven years have passed since *Open Veins of Latin America* was first published. The book was written in order to converse with the people. A non-specialist author addressed a non-specialist public, with the intention of revealing certain facts which the official history, the history told by the victors, conceals or falsifies.

The most stimulating response did not come from the literary pages of the newspapers but from real life, in the form of some episodes which took place in the street. For example, the girl who was reading the book to her friend in the seat beside her ended up standing and reading it aloud to all the passengers while the bus crossed the streets of Bogota; or the woman who fled from Santiago de Chile, during the days of the killings, with this book wrapped in the baby's nappies, or the student who for a whole week went through the bookshops on Corrientes Street, in Buenos Aires, and read it bit by bit, from bookshop to bookshop, because he did not have the money to buy it.

In the same way, the most favourable criticism which this book received comes not from any famous critic but from the military dictatorship who praised it by banning it. For example, *Open Veins* cannot circulate in my own country, Uruguay; nor in Chile, and in Argentina the authorities denounced it, on television and in the papers, as an instrument for the corruption of the youth. "They don't allow what I write to be seen", Elas de Otero would say, "because I write what I see".

I believe there is no vanity in the joy of asserting, when all's said and done, that *Open Veins* has not been a book without voice.

2 I know that it might have seemed sacrilegious that this handbook of revelations should discuss political economy in the style of a romance or a pirate novel. But I have to admit, for me it is an uphill task to read some worthy studies by certain sociologists, politicologists, economists or historians, who write in code. Hermetic language is not always the inevitable price of profundity. It may simply, in some cases, conceal an inability to communicate, elevated to the rank of intellectual virtue. I suspect that boredom frequently serves in this way to consecrate the established order; it confirms that knowledge is a privilege of the *elites*.

Something similar usually happens, it may be said in passing, with certain militant literature aimed at a converted public. In spite of all its revolutionary rhetoric, language which mechanically repeats, for the same ears, the same readymade phrases, the same adjectives, the same declamatory formulae, strikes me as conformist. Perhaps this parochial literature is as far removed from the revolution as pornography is from eroticism.

3 One writes to try and answer the questions which buzz in one's head, persistent flies which disturb the sleep, and what one writes can take on a collective meaning when in some way it coincides with the social need for an answer. I wrote *Open Veins* in order to disseminate different ideas and personal experiences which might help a little, in their realistic character, to clarify certain question marks which have always bothered us: Is Latin America a region of the world condemned to humiliation and poverty? Condemned by whom? The fault of God, the fault of nature? The stifling climate, the inferior races? Religion, custom? Isn't the misfortune a product of history, made by man and which through man may, therefore, be unmade?

Veneration of the past always seemed to me reactionary. The right chooses the past because it prefers the dead: an untroubled world, untroubled times. The powerful, who legitimize their privileges through inheritance, cultivate nostalgia. History is studied as one visits a museum; and that collection of mummies is a confidence trick. They lie to us about the past as they lie to us about the present: they disguise reality. The oppressed is obliged to take as his own a memory fabricated by the oppressor, alien, dissected, sterile. Thus he will resign himself to lead a life which is not his own as though it were the only one possible.

In *Open Veins*, the past always appears summoned by the present, as a live memory of our time. This book is a search for the keys of past history so that they may contribute to explain the present which is also making history, working on the basis that the first condition of changing reality is to know it. We are not presented here with a catalogue of heroes dressed as though for a fancy-dress ball, who on dying in battle utter solemn and exceedingly long sentences, but rather examine the sound and the tracks of the multitudinous paces which predict our present-day steps. *Open Veins* derives from reality, but also from other books, better than itself, which have helped us to know what we are, in order to know what we can be, and which have helped us to ascertain from where we come so we can better guess where we are going. That reality and those books demonstrate that Latin American underdevelopment is a consequence of foreign development, that Latin Americans are poor because the soil we tread is rich, and that places privileged by nature have been cursed by history. In this world of ours, a world of powerful centres and subjected suburbs, there is no wealth which does not prove at least suspicious.

4 In the time elapsed since the first edition of *Open Veins* history has not ceased to be, for us, a cruel mistress.

The system has multiplied hunger and fear; wealth continued to become concentrated and poverty to spread. It is recognized thus in the documents of the specialized international organisations, whose aseptic language calls our oppressed provinces 'countries in the process of development' and names the implacable impoverishment of the working class 'regressive distribution of income'.

The international machinery has continued functioning: countries in the service of commodities, men in the service of things.

With the passage of time, they continue to perfect the methods of exporting crises. Monopolistic capital reaches its peak of concentration and the international domination of markets, credit and investment makes possible the systematic and growing transfer of contradictions: the suburbs pay the price for the prosperity of the centres, without major upsets.

The international market continues to be one of the master keys of this operation. There the multinational corporations exercise their dictatorship – multinational, as Sweezy explains, because they operate in many countries, but well and truly national, of course, in their property and control. The world organisation of inequality is not altered by the fact that today Brazil exports, for example, Volkswagen cars to other South American countries and to the distant markets of Africa and the Near East. After all, it is the German Volkswagen company which has decided that it proves more convenient to export cars, for certain markets, from its Brazilian affiliate; the low production costs, the cheap hands are Brazilian, and the high profits are German.

Neither is the straitjacket broken by magic when a raw material manages to escape the curse of low prices. This was the case of oil since 1973. Is oil not an international business? Standard Oil of New Jersey, now called Exxon, Royal Dutch Shell or Gulf, are they Arab or Latin American countries? Who takes the lion's share? Otherwise revealing was the scandal unleashed against the oil producing countries, who dared to defend their price and were immediately turned into the scapegoats for the inflation and unemployment among workers in Europe and the United States. Did the most developed countries at any time ever consult anyone before raising the price of any of their products? For twenty years the price of oil had been falling and falling. Its ignoble quotation represented a gigantic subsidy to the great industrial centres of the world, whose products, on the other hand, grew ever more costly. In relation to the unending price increase of North American and European products, the new oil quotation has done nothing more than bring it back to its 1952 levels. In 1973, crude oil simply recuperated the purchasing power which it held two decades before.

5 One of the important episodes which took place in these seven years was the nationalisation of oil in Venezuela. The nationalisation did not break Venezuelan dependence in matters of refining and commercialization, but it opened a new area of autonomy. Shortly after its coming into being

the state company, *Petroleos de Venezuela*, held first place among the 500 most important companies in Latin America. It began the exploration of new markets beside the traditional ones and *Petroven* rapidly gained new clients.

As always, however, when the State becomes the owner of the principal wealth of a country, it is apposite to ask who is the owner of the State. The nationalisation of basic resources does not imply, in itself, the redistribution of the income for the benefit of the majority, nor does it necessarily jeopardize the power or the privileges of the dominant minority. In Venezuela, the economy of wastefulness continues to function, intact. In its centre, illuminated by neon lights, a squandering multi-millionaire social class glitters. In 1976, imports increased 25 percent, in good measure to finance articles of super-luxury which flood the Venezuelan market in a cataract. Fetishism of merchandise as symbol of power, human relations reduced to competition and consumption: in the middle of the ocean of underdevelopment the privileged minority imitates the way of life and the fashions of the richest members of the most opulent societies in the world; in the ostentation of Caracas, as in New York, the 'natural' assets *par excellence* – the air, light and silence – become more and more costly and scarce. "Careful", warns Juan Pablo Perez Alfonso, patriarch of Venezuelan nationalism and prophet of the recuperation of the oil: "One can die from indigestion", he says, "as much as from hunger".[1]

6 I finished writing *Open Veins* during the final days of 1970.

In the final days of 1977, Juan Velasco Alvarado died on an operating table. His coffin was carried shoulder-high to the cemetery by the largest crowd ever seen in the streets of Lima. General Velasco Alvarado, born in a humble house in the dry lands of the north of Peru, had headed a process of social and economic reforms. It was the most far-reaching and profound attempt at change in the contemporary history of his country. Beginning with the uprising of 1968, the military government was the driving force behind a true agrarian reform and opened the path for the recuperation of natural resources usurped by foreign capital. But some time back, even before Valasco Alvarado died, the funeral of the revolution had already been celebrated. The creative process had a brief life: it wound up suffocated by the blackmail of the moneylenders and the dealers and by the implicit fragility of any project which is paternalistic and without an organised popular base.

On the eve of Christmas '77, while the heart of General Velasco Alvarado was beating for the last time in Peru, in Bolivia another general, who bore no resemblance to him whatsoever, brought his fist down sharply on his desk. General Hugo Banzer, dictator of Bolivia, was saying *no* to the amnesty for prisoners, the exiled and sacked workers. Four women and fourteen children, from the tin mines, came to La Paz and began a hunger strike.

"It is not the moment", the experts judged. "We'll give you the word when . . ."

The woman sat on the floor.

"We are not consulting", said the women. "We are informing. The decision is taken. Up there in the mines there is always a hunger strike. No sooner born and already the hunger strike begins. Up there we're also bound to die. More slowly, but we're still bound to die."

The government reacted punishing, threatening; but the hunger strike unleashed forces pent up for a long time. The whole of Bolivia shook and bared its teeth. Ten days later, it was not four women and fourteen children: one thousand four hundred workers and students had risen in hunger strike. The dictatorship felt that the ground was opening beneath its feet. The general amnesty was obtained.

In this way two of the countries in the Andes crossed the line between 1977 and 1978. Further north, in the Caribbean, Panama was waiting for the promised liquidation of the colonial statute of the canal, at the end of thorny negotiations with a new government of the United States; and in Cuba the people were celebrating the socialist revolution, were feting, unconquered, their first seventeen years of life. A few days later, in Nicaragua, the people burst furiously onto the streets. The dictator Somoza, son of the dictator Somoza, was peeping through the keyhole. Several firms were burned by the wrath of the people. One of them, called *Plasmaferesis*, razed by fire at the beginning of '78, was the property of Cuban exiles, which dedicated itself to selling Nicaraguan blood to the United States. (In the blood business, as in all the others, the producers receive little more than the tip. The firm *Hemo Caribbean*, for example, pays the Haitians three dollars for each litre which is resold at twenty-five dollars on the North American market.)

7 In August '76, Orlando Letelier published an article proclaiming that the terror of the Pinochet dictatorship and the 'economic liberty' of the small privileged groups are two sides of the same coin.[2] Letelier, who had been a minister in the government of Salvador Allende, was exiled in the United States. There he was blown to pieces a short time after.[3] In his article, he argued that it is absurd to talk of free competition in an economy like that of Chile, subject to the monopolies which play at will with the prices, and that it is laughable to mention workers' rights in a country where the real trade unions are outlawed and the salaries are fixed by the military junta. Letelier described the extensive dismantling of the conquests gained for the people of Chile during the Unidad Popular government. Of the industrial monopolies and oligopolies nationalised by Salvador Allende, the dictatorship had returned half to their former owners and had put the other half up for sale. Firestone had bought the national tyre factory; Parsons and Whittemore, a huge plant for paper pulp . . . The Chilean economy, Letelier said, is now more concentrated and monopolized than on the eve of Allende's government.[4] *Free Negotiations as never before, people arrested as never before: in Lating America, the liberty of companies is incompatible with civil liberties.* Freedom of markets? Since the beginning of 1975 the price of milk is 'free' in Chile. The result was not long in coming. Two firms dominate the market. The price of milk increased immediately, for the consumers, by 40 percent, while the price for the producers was lowered by 22 percent.

Infant mortality, which had been reduced substantially under the Unidad Popular, leapt up dramatically after Pinochet took over. When Letelier was assassinated in a Washington street, a quarter of the population of Chile received *no* income and survived, thanks to outside charity or to obstinacy itself and people's own wits.

The gulf which opens in Latin America between the well-being of a few and the misfortune of the many is infinitely greater than in Europe or in the United States. The methods necessary in order to safeguard this distance are, therefore, much more savage. Brazil has an enormous and very well-equipped army, but designates five per cent of the national budget to education. In Uruguay, half the budget is at present absorbed by the armed forces and the police: a fifth of the active population has the function of keeping an eye on, pursuing or punishing, the rest.

Without doubt, one of the most significant events of the decade in our lands was a tragedy: the military insurrection which on the 11th of September overturned the democratic government of Salvador Allende and plunged Chile into a bloodbath.

Shortly before, in June, a *coup d'etat* in Uruguay had dissolved the Parliament, outlawed the trade unions and had forbidden all political activity.[5]

In March '76, the Argentinian generals returned to power: the government of the widow of Juan Domingo Peron, rotten to the core, collapsed unmourned and without glory.

The three countries of the south are, now, a sore on the world, a perennial of bad news. Torture, abductions, assassinations and enforced exile have become daily customs. These dictatorships: are they tumours to be extirpated from healthy organisms or the pus which proclaims the system's infection?

There always exists, I believe, a close relationship between the intensity of the threat and the brutality of the response. What is happening today in Brazil and Bolivia, cannot be understood, I believe, without bearing in mind the experience of the regimes of Jango Goulart and Juan Jose Torres. Before their fall, these governments had put into practice a series of social reforms and had carried forward a nationalist economic policy, during a process halted in 1964 in Brazil and in 1971 in Bolivia. *Similarly, it could well be said that Chile, Argentina and Uruguay are atoning for the sin of hope.* The cycle of deep changes during Allende's government, the flags of justice which mobilized the masses of Argentian workers and fluttered high during the shortlived government of Hector Campora in 1973 and the rapid politicization of the youth of Uruguay, were all challenges which a powerless and crisis-ridden system could not bear. The violent oxygen of liberty proved fulminating for the ghosts and the praetorian guard was called in to preserve order. The clean-up operation is a plan for extermination.

8 The records of Congress in the United States frequently register irrefutable testimonies concerning the interventions in Latin America. Stung by the acids of guilt, the consciences affect their catharsis in the confessionals of the Empire. In these recent times, for example, official admissions of the responsibility of the United States in various disasters have multiplied. Extensive public confessions have proved, among other things, that the government of the United States participated directly, by means of bribery, espionage and blackmail, in Chilean politics. The strategy of the crime was planned in Washington. From 1970, Kissinger and the intelligence services carefully prepared the fall of Allende. Millions of dollars were distributed among the enemies of the legal Unidad Popular government. It was thus, for example, that the truck owners were able to sustain their long strike which in 1973 paralyzed a good part of the economy of the country. The certainty of impunity loosens tongues. At the time of the *coup d'etat* against Goulart, the United States maintained their largest embassy in the world in Brazil. Lincoln Gordon, who was the ambassador, admitted three years later, to a reporter, that his government was financing for a good time back the forces which opposed the reforms: "What the devil", said Gordon. "That was more or less a habit in those days . . . The CIA was accustomed to handling political funds".[6] In the same interview, Gordon explained that in the days of the *coup* the Pentagon positioned an enormous aircraft-carrier and four tanker-ships alongside the Brazilian coast "in the event that the anti-Goulart forces should request our support". That support, he said, "would not be merely moral. We would give logistics back-up, supplies, weapons, oil".

Since president Jimmy Carter initiated the human rights policy, it has become customary for the Latin American regime, imposed in the first place by North American intervention, to formulate declarations against North American interference in their internal affairs.

The United States Congress resolved, in 1976 and 1977, to suspend economic and military aid to various countries. The greater part of the external aid of the United States does not pass, however, through the filter of the Congress. Thus, in spite of the declarations and the resolutions and the protests, the regime of general Pinochet received, during 1976, 290 million dollars in aid direct from the United States without 'parliamentary' authorization. After completing the first year of its life, the dictatorship of general Videla had received 500 million dollars from private North American banks and 415 million from two institutions (the World Bank and the Inter-American Development Bank) where the United States wield a decisive influence. The special drawing rights of Argentina on the International Monetary Fund, which were for 64 million dollars in 1975, had risen to 700 million a couple of years later.

President Carter's concern over the butchering which some Latin American countries are undergoing seems salutary, but the present dictators are not self-taught: they have learned the techniques and art of governing in the Pentagon courses in the United States and in the Panama Canal zone. Those courses continue to this day and, as far as is known, have not altered their content one iota. The Latin American military men who today constitute the source of scandal for the United States, have been good pupils. Four years ago, when the present president of the World Bank, Robert McNamara, was Secretary of Defence, he spelled it out: "They are the new leaders. I don't need to elaborate on the value of having in positions of leadership men who have previously learnt at close range how we Americans think and do things. To become friends with those men is invaluable".[7]

Can those who created the paralytic offer us the wheelchair?

9 The bishops of France speak of another type of responsibility, deeper, less visible: "We, who belong to the nations which claim to be the most advanced in the world, form a part of those who benefit from the exploitation of those countries in the process of development. We do not see the suffering which this provokes in the flesh and in the spirit of entire peoples. We contribute to reinforcing the present division of the world, in which the domination of the poor by the rich, of the weak by the powerful, stands out. Do we know that our squandering of resources and raw materials would not be possible without the control of international trade by the Western countries? Do we not see who profits from the trafficking of arms, of which our country has provided sad examples? Do we even understand that the militarization of the regimes of poor countries is one of the consequences of the economic and cultural domination exercised by the industrialized countries, where life is ruled by the desire for profits and the powers of money?".[8]

Dictators, torturers, inquisitors: terror has its officials, like the post office or the banks, and is applied because it proves necessary. It is not a question of a conspiracy of evil men. General Pinochet may resemble a character in Goya's *Black Paintings*, a feast for psychoanalysts or the heir to a truculent tradition from the banana republics. But the clinical or folkloric traits of such and such a dictator act as a condiment to history; they are not history. Who today would dare to claim that the First World War broke out because of the complexes of Kaiser Wilhelm, who had one arm shorter than the other? "In the democratic countries the character of violence which economics has is not revealed; in authoritarian countries, the same happens with the economic character of violence", Bertolt Brecht wrote, towards the end of 1940, in his working journal.

In the southern countries of Latin America, the centurions have occupied power to serve a function of the system, perpetrating state terrorism when the dominant classes can no longer carry out their business affairs through any other means. *In our countries torture would not exist were it not efficient; and formal democracy would persist if it could be guaranteed that it would not slip out of the control of the owners of power.* In difficult times democracy becomes a crime against national security – or rather, against the security of internal privileges and foreign investments. Our machines for mincing human flesh are geared to an international mechanism. The entire society is militarized, the exceptional state becomes permanent and the apparatus of repression assumes hegemony as soon as there is a tightening of nuts from the centre of the imperialist system. When the shadow of a crisis lurks, it is necessary to increase the plundering of the poor countries in order to guarantee full employment, civil liberties and the high rates of development in the rich countries. *The relationship of victim and executioner, a sinister dialectic: there is a structure of successive humiliations which begins on the international markets and in the financial centres and ends in the home of every citizen.*

10 Haiti is the poorest country in the western hemisphere. There are more feet-washers there than shoeshine boys: children who for a coin wash the feet of barefoot clients, who do not have shoes to shine. The Haitians live, on average, little more than thirty years. Out of every ten Haitians, nine can neither read nor write. For internal consumption, the rugged mountain slopes are cultivated. For export, the fertile valleys, the best lands, are given over to coffee, sugar, cacao and other produce needed by the North American market. No one plays baseball in Haiti, but Haiti is the world's leading producer of balls for that game. There is no shortage of workshops in the country where children work for a dollar a day assembling cassettes and electronic goods. They are, naturally, products for export; and, naturally, the profits are also exported, after deducting the cut due to the administrators of terror. The slightest hint of protest, in Haiti, implies prison or

death. Incredible as it may seem, the salaries of Haitian workers have lost, between 1971 and 1975, a quarter of their extremely low real value.[9] Significantly, during that period a new flow of United States capital entered the country.

I remember an editorial in a Buenos Aires newspaper, published a couple of years ago. An old conservative paper stormed angrily because in an international document Argentina appeared as an underdeveloped and dependent country. How could a cultured, European, prosperous and white society be measured by the same yardstick as a country as poor and as black as Haiti?

Undoubtedly, the differences are enormous – although they have little to do with the Buenos Aires oligarchy's categories of analysis. Yet, for all the dissimilarities and contradictions there may be, Argentina is not free from the vicious circle which strangles the Latin American economy as a whole and no effort of intellectual exorcism can remove it from the reality which is shared, to a lesser or greater extent, by the other countries of the region.

After all, General Videla's killings are not more civilized than those of *Papa Doc* Duvalier or his heir to the throne, even though the repression in Argentina may be on a higher technological level. Essentially, both dictatorships function in the service of the same objective: *to supply cheap labour to an international market which demands cheap products.*

No sooner had it taken power, Videla's dictatorship hastened to prohibit strikes and decreed the freeing of prices at the same time as it was clamping down wages. Five months after the *coup d'etat*, the new foreign investments law placed national and foreign companies on the same footing. Free competition, thus, brought to an end the situation of unfair disadvantage in which some multi-national corporations found themselves compared to local firms: helpless General Motors, for example, whose volume of world sales is equal to no less than the entire gross national product of Argentina. Also free now, with lax restrictions, are the remittance of profits abroad and the repatriation of invested capital.

When the regime was one year old, the real value of wages had been reduced to forty per cent. It was a feat accomplished by terror. "Fifteen thousand disappearances, ten thousand imprisoned, four thousand dead and tens of thousands exiled is the raw figure of this terror", the writer Rodolfo Walsh accused in an open letter. The letter was sent on March 29th 1977 to the three leaders of the government junta. That same day, Walsh was abducted and disappeared.

11 Reliable sources confirm that a tiny proportion of new direct foreign investments in Latin America actually comes from the country of origin. According to a report published by the United States Department of Commerce,[10] scarcely 12% of the funds derives from the US matrix, 22% corresponds to earnings made in Latin America and the remaining 66% emanates from the internal credit sources and, above all, from international credit. The proportions are same for investments of European or Japanese origin; and it must be borne in mind that frequently that 12% of investment which stems from the head offices is no more than the result of the transfer of worn out machinery or simply reflects the arbitrary price which the firms impose for their industrial *know-how*, patents or brand names. *The multinational corporations, therefore, not only usurp the internal credit of the countries where they operate, in exchange for a rather questionable capital contribution, but furthermore multiply their overseas debts.*

The Latin American overseas debt was, in 1975, almost three times bigger than in 1969.[11] Brazil, Mexico, Chile and Uruguay devoted, in 1975, approximately *half* of their export earnings to the payment of amortizations and interests on the debt and to the payment of the profits of the foreign firms established in those countries. The servicing of the debt and the remittance of profits swallowed up, that year, 55 percent of Panama's exports and 60 percent of Peru's.[12] In 1969, every inhabitant of Bolivia owed 137 dollars abroad. In 1977, he owed 483. The inhabitans of Bolivia were never consulted nor did they ever see a single cent of those loans which have tied a noose round their necks.

The Citibank does not figure as a candidate on any list, in the few Latin American countries where elections are still held; and none of the generals who practise the dictatorships is called International Monetary Fund. But which is the hand which executes and which is the conscience which ordains? He who lends, rules. In order to pay, more must be exported, and more must be exported in order to finance imports and in order to cover the hemorrhage of profits and *royalties* which the foreign firms drain off to their head offices. The increase in export, whose actual returns continue diminishing, brings starvation wages. Mass poverty, the key to success of an economy turned over to outside interests, impedes the growth of the internal consumer markets necessary to maintain a harmonious economic development. Our countries become echoes and gradually lose their own voice. They depend on others, they exist insofar as they respond to the needs of others. In turn, the re-shaping of the economy in the service of external demand brings us back to the original stranglehold: it opens the doors to foreign monopolies' plundering and compels the contraction of new and larger borrowings from the international bank. *The vicious circle is perfect: the overseas debt and foreign investment dictate an increase in exports which they themselves are continually devouring. The task cannot be achieved with nice manners. In order for Latin American workers to comply with their function as hostages of foreign prosperity, they have to remain prisoners – on the inside or the outside of the jail bars.*

12 The savage exploitation of manual labour is not incompatible with intensive technology. It never was, in our lands: for example, the legions of Bolivian workers who left their lungs in the Oruro mines, in the time of Simon Patino, worked in a regime of salaried slavery but with very modern machinery. The *tin baron* managed to combine the highest levels of technology of his era with the lowest level of salaries.[13]

Furthermore, in our time, the importation of the technology of the most advanced economies coincides with the expropriation of the industrial businesses, set up by local capital, by the almighty multinational corporations. The movement of centralizing capital is accompanied through "a merciless *burning off* of *obsolete* business levels, which not by chance are precisely those state owned".[14] The rapid de-nationalization of Latin American industry brings with it a growing technological dependence. Technology, the decisive key to power, is monopolized, in the capitalist world, by the metropolitan centres. The technology comes second hand, but those centres charge for the copies as though they were originals. In 1970, Mexico paid double of that in 1968 for the importation of foreign technology. Between 1965 and 1969, Brazil doubled its payments; and a similar rise occurred, in the same period, in Argentina.

The transplanting of technology augments the very heavy debts overseas and has devastating consequences on the labour market. In a system organized for the draining of profits to the exterior, the labour force of the "traditional" company continues to lose scope for employment. In exchange for a questionable dynamic impetus upon the rest of the economy, the little islands of modern industry sacrifice workers as they reduce the working time necessary for production. The existence of a swollen and increasing army of unemployed facilitates, in turn, the killing off of the real value of wages.

13 Even the documents of the United Nations Economic Commission for Latin America (ECLA) are talking, now, of an international re-division of labour. Within a few years from now, as the hopeful experts venture, Latin America may possibly be exporting manufactured goods in the same quantity as today it sells raw material and food abroad. "The disparity of wages between developed and developing countries – including those in Latin America – may induce a new division of activities among the countries shifting, for reasons of competition, their industries, in which the labour costs may be very considerable, from the former to the latter. Labour costs in the manufacturing industry, for example, are

generally much lower in Mexico or Brazil than in the United States."[15]

The impetus of progress or neo-colonial adventure? Electrical and non-electrical machinery now features among the leading export products of Mexico. In Brazil, the sale abroad of vehicles and armaments is increasing. Some Latin American countries are living a new stage of industrialization, to a great extent induced and directed by foreign needs and foreign owners of the means of production. Will this not be another chapter to tag onto our long history of "externally oriented development"? On the international markets, the prices that are continually rising do not correspond generically to the "manufactured goods", but to the more sophisticated articles with greater technological make-up, which are exclusive to the more developed countries. *The leading export product of Latin America, whatever it sells, raw materials or manufactured goods, is its cheap labour.*

Has ours not been a continual historical experience of mutilation and disintegration disguised as development? Centuries ago, the Conquest razed the land to plant crops for export and annihilated the native populations in the mine-shafts and the placers in order to satisfy the demand for gold and silver overseas. The diet of the pre-Columbian population that managed to survive the extermination, *deteriorated* along with the technological progress. Today, the people of Peru produce fishmeal, very rich in protein, for the cattle of the United States and Europe; yet protein is conspicuous in its absence from the diet of the majority of Peruvians. The Volkswagen in Switzerland plants a tree for every car it sells there, an ecological courtesy, while Volkswagen's Brazilian affiliate razes hundreds of hectares of woodland which it sets aside for the intensive production of meat for export. The Brazilian people – who rarely taste meat – are selling increasingly more meat abroad. Not long ago, in conversation, Darcy Ribeiro was saying to me that a *volkswagen republic* is no different, essentially, from a *banana republic*. For every dollar produced by the export of bananas, barely eleven cents stay in the producer country,[16] and of those eleven cents a trifling portion goes to the plantation workers. Do the proportions alter when a Latin American country produces cars?

The slavers no longer ply the ocean. Now the slave-traders operate from the Ministry of Employment. African wages, European prices. What are the *coups d'etat*, in Latin America, but successive episodes in a war of plunder? Immediately, the brand new dictatorships invite the foreign firms to exploit the cheap and abundant work force, unlimited credit, tax exemptions and the raw materials within arm's reach.

14 The employees of the Chilean government's emergency plan receive wages equivalent to thirty dollars a month. A kilo of bread costs 50 cents. They receive therefore two kilos of bread a day. The minimum wage in Uruguay and Argentina at present is equivalent to the price of six kilos of coffee. The minimum wage in Brazil is sixty dollars per month, but the *boias frias*, itinerant countryside labourers, earn between 50 cents and a dollar a day on the plantations of coffee, soya and other export crops. The fodder eaten by the cattle in Mexico contains more protein than the diet of the peasants who look after them. The meat from these cattle is destined for a few privileged mouths within the country and principally for the international market. Under the protection of a generous policy of official credits and easy terms, export agriculture is flourishing in Mexico, while between 1970 and 1976 the amount of protein available for each inhabitant has *decreased* and in the rural areas only one in every five Mexican children is of normal height and weight.[17] In Guatemala, the rice, maize and dry beans, which are for internal consumption, are abandoned to the will of God; yet the coffee, cotton and other export products corner 87% of credit. For every *ten* Guatemalan families engaged in the cultivation and harvesting of coffee, the leading source of foreign currency in the country, barely *one* is fed according to the minimum adequate requirements.[18] In Brazil, only 5% of agricultural credit is channelled into rice, dry beans and manioc – which make up the staple diet of the Brazilians. The rest pours into produce for export.

The recent collapse of the international sugar price did not unleash, as before, a wave of hunger among the Cuban peasants. In Cuba malnutrition no longer exists. Conversely, the almost simultaneous rise in the international price of coffee in no way lessened the chronic poverty of the workers in the Brazilian coffee plantations. The increase in the quotation of coffee in 1976 – a chance euphoria brought about by the frosts which wiped out the Brazilian crop – "was not materially reflected in the wages", as a high-ranking official of the Brazilian Institute of Coffee admitted.[19]

In reality, export crops are not, necessarily, incompatible with the wellbeing of the people nor do they contradict, necessarily, "internally oriented" economic development. After all, the sale of sugar abroad has served as a lever, in Cuba, for the creation of a new world in which all have access to the fruits of development; and solidarity is the crux of human relationships.

15 We already know who are those condemned to pay for the crisis of readjustment in the system. The prices of the majority of products which Latin America sells inexorably drop in relation to the prices of the products which it buys from the countries which monopolize technology, commerce, investment and credit. To compensate for the difference, and to face up to the obligations vis-a-vis foreign capital, *it is necessary to make up in quantity what is lost in price.* Within this framework, the dictatorships of the Southern Cone have halved workers' wages and transformed each centre of production into forced labour camps. *The workers also have to make up for the fall in value of their labour, which is the product they sell on the market. The workers are obliged to compensate by working more hours, for what they lose in the purchasing power of their wages. The laws of the international market are reproduced, thus, in the microworld of the life of every Latin America worker.* For those workers who have the 'luck' to hold on to a permanent job, the eight-hour working day only exists in the dead letter of the law. It is common to work ten, twelve, even fourteen, hours, and more than one has lost his Sundays.

Accidents at work, in turn, have shot up, human blood offered on the altar of productivity. Three examples from the end of 1977 in Uruguay:

a) The railway quarries, which produce stone and gravel, double their output. At the beginning of spring, fifteen miners die in a gelignite explosion.

b) Lines of unemployed outside a factory which makes rocket fireworks. Several children on the production. Records are beaten. December 20th, an explosion: five workers dead and dozens injured.

c) December 28th, at seven in the morning, workers refuse to enter a fish canning factory, because they sense a strong smell of gas. They are threatened: if they won't go in, they lose their job. They still refuse. They are threatened, we are going to call in the soldiers. The firm has already summoned the army on other occasions. The workers enter. Four dead and several hospitalized. There was an ammonia gas leak.[20]

16 Maria Carolina de Jesus was born in the midst of rubbish and vultures.

She grew up, suffered, worked hard; loved two men, had children. In a little notebook she jotted down, in poor handwriting, her chores and her days.

A reporter read these notebooks by chance and Maria Carolina became a famous writer. Her book *Quarto de despejo*, "The shanty town", a diary of five years' life in a sordid suburb in the city of Sao Paulo, was read in forty countries and translated into thirteen languages.

Cinderella of Brazil, the product of world consumption, Maria Carolina de Jesus left the shanty town, travelled the world, was interviewed and photographed, won awards from the critics, was feted by gentlemen and received by presidents.

And the years passed. At the beginning of 1977, one Sunday at daybreak, Maria Carolina de Jesus died in the midst of rubbish and vultures. Nobody now remembers the woman who had written: "Hunger is the dynamite of the human body".

She, who had lived on leftovers, managed to become, fleetingly, one of the elect. She was allowed to sit at the table. After the dessert, the spell was broken. And as her dream elapsed, Brazil continued being a country where each day a hundred workers end up maimed in work accidents and where out of every ten children, four are born to become beggars, thieves or magicians.

Although the statistics smile, the people are buggered. In systems organized back to front, when the economy grows social injustice also grows with it. During the most successful period of the Brazilian "miracle", the rate of infant mortality in the suburbs of the richest city in the country increased. The sudden prosperity from the oil in Ecuador brought colour television instead of schools and hospitals.

The cities are swelling to bursting point. In 1950, Latin America had six cities with more than a million inhabitants. In 1980, it will have 25 millions.[21] The vast legions of workers, driven off from the countryside, share, on the edge of the great urban centres, the same fate which the system reserves for young city-dwelling 'leftovers'. The artful forms of survival of these 'scavengers' are perfected in picaresque Latin America. "The system of production has shown over a time a visible incapacity to generate productive employment to absorb the growing work force in the region, in particular the large contingents of labour in the city . . ."[23]

A study of the World Labour Organisation indicated not long ago that in Latin America there are more than 110 million people in conditions of "acute poverty". Of this number, 70 million can be considered "destitute".[23] What percentage of the population eats less than is necessary? In the language of the experts, 42% of the population of Brazil, 43% of Colombians, 49% of Hondurans, 31% of Mexicans, 45% of Peruvians, 29% of Chileans, 35% of Ecuadorians, receive "income less than the cost of minimum balanced nutrition".[24]

17 In our lands, the terror industry pays dearly, like any other, for foreign *know-how*. North American technology of repression, tried out across the four cardinal points of the planet, is bought and applied, on a large scale. But it would be unfair not to recognize a certain creative capacity, in this field of activity, among the Latin American ruling classes.

Our bourgeoisies were incapable of independent economic development and their attempts at creating a national industry took off like a hen, a short and very low flight. In the course of our historical process, the owners of power have given, also, more than enough evidence of their lack of political imagination and of their cultural sterility. In exchange, they have managed to set up a gigantic machine of fear and have made their own contributions to the technique of extermination of people and ideas. The recent experience of the River Plate countries is revealing, in this respect.

"The task of disinfection will take us a long time", warned the Argentinian officers, on taking over. The armed forces were called in successively by the ruling classes of Uruguay and Argentina to crush the forces of change, to tear out their roots, to perpetuate the internal order of privileges and to generate economic and political conditions enticing to foreign capital: the land cleared, the country in order, submissive and cheap labour. There is nothing more ordered than a cemetery. The population was immediately transformed into the enemy within. Any sign of life, protest or simple doubt, constitutes a dangerous challenge from the point of view of the military doctrine of national security.

Thus, complex mechanisms of prevention and punishment have been formulated.

A profound rationality lurks beneath the appearances. *In order to operate efficiently, repression must seem arbitrary.* Apart from breathing, any human activity may constitute a crime. In Uruguay, torture is applied as a standard system of interrogation: *anybody may be its victim*, and not only suspects and those guilty of acts of opposition. *In this way the panic of torture is spread among all the citizens, like a paralysing gas which infiltrates every household and takes root in the soul of every citizen.*

In Chile, the hunt took a toll of 30 thousand dead. But in Argentine, they don't shoot: they abduct. The victims *disappear.* The unseen armies of the night carry out the task. There are no corpses, no one to take the blame. Thus the slaughter – always officious, never official – is carried out with greater impunity, *and in this way the collective anxiety is radiated more powerfully. No one gives account, no one profers explanations. Each crime is a painful uncertainty for those people close to the victim and also a warning for all the rest. State terrorism sets out to paralyze the population through fear.*

In order to obtain work or to keep it, in Uruguay, it is imperative to be in the military's good books. In a country where it proves so difficult to get work outside of the barracks and police stations, this necessity does not only serve to drive into exodus a good part of the 300 thousand citizens filed as leftwingers. *It is also useful to threaten those who remain.* The Montevideo newspapers are accustomed to printing public repentances and declarations from citizens who beat their breasts, just in case . . .: "I have never been, I am not, nor shall I ever be . . ."

In Argentina it is no longer necessary to ban any book by decree. The new Penal Code punishes, as always, the writer and the editor of a book it considers subversive. But furthermore it punishes the printer, so that no one may dare print a text that is merely suspect, and also the distributor and the bookseller, so that nobody dares sell it, and in case that is not enough the reader is punished, so that nobody dares read it let alone hold on to it. The consumer of a book thus receives the same treatment which the law reserves for the consumer of drugs.[25] *In this plan for a society of deaf-mutes, each citizen must become his own Torquemada.*

In Uruguay, not to denounce your neighbour is an offence. On entering the University, the students swear in writing that they will inform on anyone who undertakes, in the university ambit, "any activity foreign to the performance of study". The student makes himself co-responsible for any episode which might take place in his presence. *In this plan for a society of sleepwalkers, each citizen must be his own policeman and that of the others.* However, the system, quite rightly, is distrustful. Police and soldiers in Uruguay add up to a hundred thousand, but informers also add up to one hundred thousand. Spies work on the streets and in the cafes and on buses, in factories and secondary schools, in the offices and in the University. Whoever complains aloud, because life is so expensive and hard, is going to wind up in jail: he has committed an "offense against the morale of the armed forces", which is paid for by three to six years in prison.

18 In the referendum of January 1978, a vote for *yes* to Pinochet's dictatorship was marked by a cross beneath the flag of Chile. A vote for *no*, on the other hand, was marked beneath a black rectangle.

The system wishes to be taken for the country. The system is the country, says the official propaganda which day and night bombards the citizens. The enemy of the system is a traitor to the fatherland. The capacity for indignation against injustice and the will to change constitute the evidence of the desertion. In many Latin American countries, those not exiled beyond the frontiers, suffer exile in their own land.

But at the same time as Pinochet was celebrating his victory, the dictatorship was calling the strikes which were breaking out all over Chile inspite of the terror, "collective worker absenteeism". The great majority of those abducted or who disappeared in Argentina is made up of workers who were developing some trade union activity. Unceasingly in the inexhaustable imagination of the people, new forms of struggle are hatched, *go-slows*, *non-cooperation*, and solidarity finds new outlets to avoid fear. Many all-out strikes occurred in Argentina during 1977, when the danger of losing life was as certain as the risk of losing the job. The power of a working class, organized and with a long tradition of struggle, to answer back, is not destroyed at the stroke of a pen. In May of the same year, when the Uruguayan dictatorship drew up the balance of its programmes of brainwashings and collective castrations, it felt obliged to admit that "there still remains in the country thirtyseven per cent of citizens interested in politics".[26]

We are not witnessing in these lands the savage infancy of capitalism, but rather its bloody decrepitude. *Underdevelop-*

ment is not a stage in development. It is its consequence. Latin American underdevelopment arises from foreign development and it continues to fuel it. Impotent through its function of international servitude, moribund from birth, the system has clay feet. It postulates itself as destiny and would like to be mistaken for eternity. All memory is subversive, because it is different, and likewise any future plan. It obliges the *zombie* to eat without salt: salt, dangerous, could wake it up. The system finds its paradigm in the immutable society of the ants. For this reason it does not get on well with the history of man, however much it changes. And because in the history of man, every act of destruction finds its answer, sooner or later, in an act of creation.

Calella, Barcelona, April 1978.

Translated by John Lyons © 1979

Notes

1. Interview by Jean-Pierre Clerc in *Le Monde*, Paris, 8-9 May 1977.
2. *The Nation*, 28 August 1976.
3. The crime occurred in Washington on 21 September 1976. Several political exiles from Uruguay, Chile and Bolivia had been assassinated, before, in Argentina. Among them, the most notable were general Carlos Prats, a key figure in the military scheme of Allende's government, whose car blew up in a garage in Buenos Aires on September 27, 1974; general Juan Jose Torres, who had led a shortlived anti-imperialist government in Bolivia and was riddled with bullets on June 15, 1976; and the Uruguayan legislators, Zelmar Michelini and Hector Gutierrez Ruiz, abducted, tortured and murdered, also in Buenos Aires, between the 18th and 21st March, 1976.
4. Also the land reform, which was started by the Christian Democrat government and was intensified by the Unidad Popular, was scrapped. Cf. Maria Beatriz de Albuquerque W., "La agricultura chilena: modernizaction capitalista o regresion a formas tradicionales? Comentarios sobre la contra-reforma agraria en Chile". *Iberoamericana*, vol. VI:2, 1976, Institute of Latin American Studies, Stockholm.
5. Three months later, there were elections in the University. They were the only elections which survived. The candidates of the dictatorship polled 2½% of the votes. Consequently, in defence of the democracy, the dictatorship imprisoned a lot of people and handed over the democracy to that 2½%.
6. *Veja*, No 444, Sao Paulo, 9 March 1977.
7. US House of Representatives, Committee on Appropriations, Foreign Operations for 1963, Hearings 87th Congress, 2nd Session, Part I.
8. Declaration of Lourdes, October 1976.
9. *Le nouvelliste*, Port-au-Prince, Haiti, 19-20 March 1977. Information quoted by Augustin Cueva in "El desarrollo del capitalismo en America Latina", Siglo XXI, Mexico, 1977.
10. Ida May Mantel, "Sources and uses of funds for a sample of majority-owned foreign affiliates of US companies, 1966-1972", US Department of Commerce, *Survey of Current Business*, July 1975.
11. United Nations, Economic Commission for Latin America (ECLA), "El desarrollo economico y social y las relaciones externas de America Latina", Santo Domingo, Dominican Republic, February 1977.
12. Money, which has little wings, travels without a passport. A good part of the profits generated by the exploitation of our resources finds refuge in the United States, Switzerland, West Germany or other countries where it takes a round turn to come back to our countries in the form of loans.
13. Agustin Cueva, op. cit., note 9.
14. Ibid.
15. United Nations, ECLA, op. cit., note 9.
16. UNCTAD, "The Marketing and Distribution System for Bananas". December 1974.
17. "Reflexiones sobre la desnutricion en Mexico", *Comercio exterior*, Banco Nacional de Comercio Exterior, S.A., Vol.28, No 2, Mexico, Feb. 1978.
18. Roger Burbach and Patricia Flynn, "Agribusiness Targets Latin America", NACLA, Vol.XII, No 1. Nueva York, Jan-Feb. 1978.
19. Ibid.
20. Datos de fuentes sindicales y periodisticas, published in *Uruguay Informations*, Nos. 21 & 25, Paris.
21. United Nations, ECLA, op. cit., note 11.
22. Ibid.
23. International Labour Organization (ILO), "Empleo, crecimiento y necesidades essenciales", Geneva, 1976.
24. United Nations, ECLA, op. cit., note 11.
25. In Uruguay, the inquisitors have become modernized. A curious mixture of the Middle Ages and capitalist business sense. The military no longer burns the books: now they sell them to paper mills. The paper mills shred them, turn them into paper pulp and put them back on the consumer market. It is not true that Marx is not within the reach of the public. He is, not in the form of books but as serviettes.
26. Press conference given by President Aparicio Mendez, 21 May 1977, in Paysandu. "We are saving the country from the tragedy of political passion", said the president. "Decent men do not talk of dictatorships, do not think about dictatorship or demand civil rights".

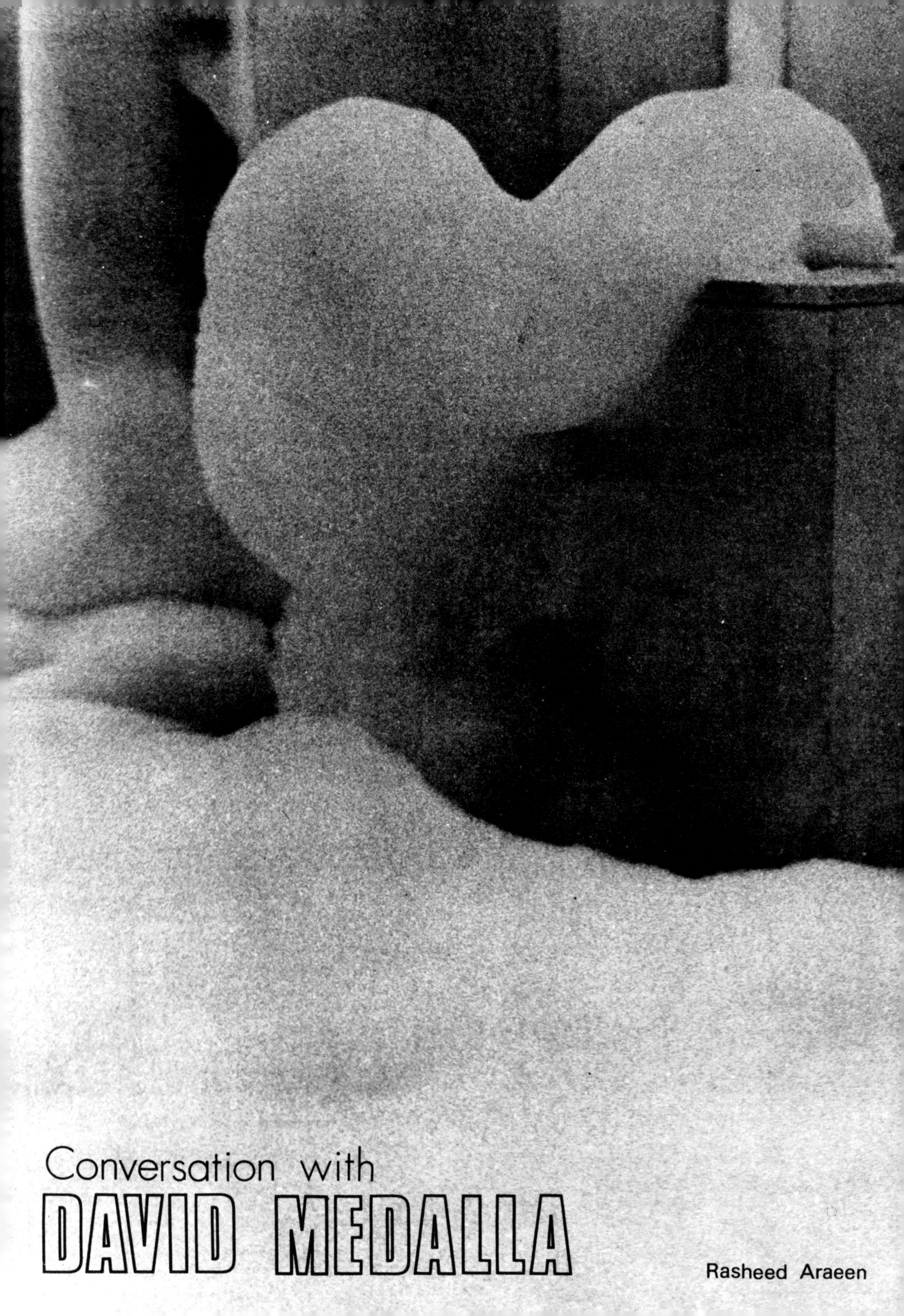

Conversation with DAVID MEDALLA

Rasheed Araeen

Rasheed Araeen: Before you became known as a visual artist in the mid-60s in London you were, I believe, more interested in poetry. What made you switch on from poetry to visual arts?

David Medalla: I was in America in the mid-50s and it was actually there that I started to paint. Before that when I was 9 years old I did a work. Well, I didn't realise then that it was art. It was a participation propulsion whereby I invited farmers and fishermen to sculpt an island . . . But I have always believed in myself as an artist. Not once did I think I was anything else. I didn't have a professional ambition though, like I was going to put a sign saying: "I'm an artist". I think it was in London that I started becoming more visual than literary, and again it was a circumstance. You see, when I arrived in London in 1960 I was writing poetry. I spent most of my time going from one coffee bar to another, mostly in Soho, Chelsea and Hampstead, and in these places I met many English poets. But they were chauvinists; I wrote better poetry in English than most of them did, and they would never publish me. So, I said to myself that there's no hope. I was never published in England until Susan Hiller printed a portion of one of my poems some years ago in *Wallpaper*.

RA: Really!

DM: You see, England is such a provincial and cliquey place. In America things are slightly different. The funny thing about America is, because of the multiplicity of ethnic groups, that you can actually get your poetry published there more easily. In England it's much more difficult . . . I have never given up poetry, but I realised that since I wanted to communicate certain things, it's much easier to do it on the visual level; because visual art transcends verbal language.

RA: But how much this realisation that your poetry wasn't going to be published here made you decide to take up visual arts more seriously?

DM: Very much, I think.

RA: The first important work that you did here in Britain, in 1964, were bubble mobiles, *Cloud Canyons*; and I think they were very important part of the new developments then that challenged the status quo. To paraphrase Guy Brett: they expressed the energy which before had not existed in mechanical sculpture . . . However, I wonder how much you felt being part of that newly emerging art scene then in Britain?

DM: I don't think I was part of the British scene. I was always part of the Paris scene. It's only in the last 5 years that I have become English — Anglicised you know. I lived three months in London and then three months in Paris. The three months I was here I was writing poetry. I mixed up with the poets; I went to poetry readings; I went to pubs and drank with them — that's why I know many of the poets around here. But in Paris I was with visual artists; that's a whole world of difference. So, I didn't know much about the art scene here. What I came across here then in the visual arts was very naive and amateurish, and I didn't like the painting and sculpture very much.

RA: What inspired you then actually to make works like *Cloud Canyons*?

DM: Memories, I suppose; and my love of science. I have always liked the scientific approach to things. I think the scientific approach is better than any other approach. I really like reading about physics and electronics, about matter and energy; and at the same time I would think about writing poetry. I actually wrote a poem called *Shepherds of Clouds* — it was published in 1963 in the Philippines. I wrote the poem when I was in Paris. I was invited to a dinner party by Arp. There were a lot of people from his generation, the Surrealists. I never liked Surrealism as a movement though. The only Surrealists I like are Bunuel and Meret Oppenheim. Anyway, many Surrealists were there, and it was the time, I think, when Arp started dribbling in his mouth . . . And suddenly I was looking at a cloud through the window and I kept on remembering the clouds I grew up with in the Philippines; and I said to myself, "it's an incredible thing". You see, I did not see the cloud as a static thing. I saw it something that was moving, which brought rain and made the rice field become fertile. It was good for rice; it was nourishment. It was energy. So, I created *Cloud Canyons* not only because I was interested in art. I was interested in seeing how matter could be transformed into energy.

RA: But you said you have been doing art before and that must have contributed something to their realisation . . .

DM: No, I wasn't thinking of art when I was doing *Cloud Canyons*. I just wanted to see how normally invisible forces could be made tangible, visible to the naked eye.

RA: You didn't see them as an artistic proposition then?

DM: No, not initially, not at the conceptual stage.

RA: It looks very Duchampian, isn't it?

DM: Well, may be. But there was an aesthetic thing to what I was doing, because when I began constructing the actual work I knew what I was going to produce. For example, the structure containing the machines were based on relations derived from proportions of my body.

RA: I wonder how much you were conscious of the so-called art-historical forces of the time. Were you not looking for something new in the context of avant-garde? You know, the way the contemporary artist works: most of his energy is spent frantically looking for something new, something unique, something which has not been done before. Did you also have that kind of drive or motivation?

DM: No. In fact, I wanted to do something that was old. I would rather be related to the Tung Huang cave paintings of Buddhist China, to Moghul architecture, to Bernini, to Cellini, to Leonardo da Vinci, to Michaelangelo, to Velasquez. . . And this is really true, then and today, as far as my artistic aspirations are concerned.

RA: But how would you see then your work in terms of the social and artistic context of our own time?

DM: Well, I did see the work as they evolved in an artistic context, but only secondarily. The first consideration was social. In my *Sand Machine* I was looking into the possibility of deserts being reclaimed with energy that's available from the sun, to produce food. I was really interested in solar energy at that time . . . If we can use our resources constructively we all can have freedom to live and enjoy life. It was maybe naive of me; because I thought if people could see how with a very little effort we could all have food, clothing and houses. This was really the essence behind my work.

RA: But how does the *Sand Machine* relate to solar energy?

DM: Well, I thought it could, because there's a lot of sun in the desert. I thought it could be a way of utilizing that energy and with that energy we could cultivate the desert . . .

RA: But how?

DM: It's only a poetic statement, you know; a visual metaphor, a presentiment of things to come. The trouble with artists is that we are only visionaries. But the important thing is that the visions are there; and it's up to all those other non-visionaries that we humans become a little bit systematic. We need analytical and practical brains to transform these visions.

RA: But there was an artistic content within which your work was accepted, or shall we say that your work of that time ought to be seen within an art-historical period?

DM: Yes. There was this Kinetic Movement.

RA: And it was the time when people like Metzger were doing similar things . . .

DM: Yes. Metzger was actually the first person to praise me, but for the wrong reasons. He thought I was into auto-destruction; we had a row over that. I don't believe in auto-destruction. I believe in auto-creation, you know, as a continuous spiral. I was very obviously skeptical about auto-destructive artists. I actually said to him, "look, I never did an auto-destructive work; all my works are auto-creative". I mean they were creating themselves till the moment their destruction became essential. So, maybe it was only a misunderstanding between us.

Lament: Sand Machine, 1964. Photo by Clay Perry

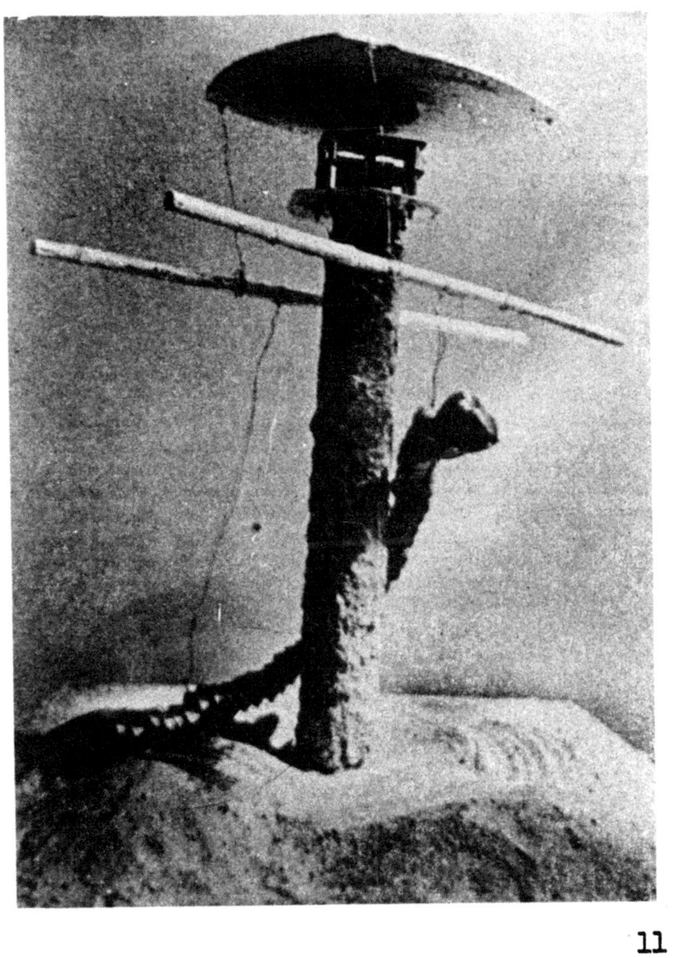

RA: I think it's better we move on now from your earlier work, which I think was an original and important contribution, to the Exploding Galaxy which you co-founded in 1967.
DM: That's fine.
RA: Well, tell us something about the Exploding Galaxy. What made you move on from making individual works of art to collective manifestations like the Exploding Galaxy?
DM: You see, I had a kind of horror of consumer society. Perhaps it wasn't really a horror; maybe it was just my indifference to it. I mean, I consume things — like I smoke cigarettes, I drink Coca-Cola, but I don't need my life to be determined by a consumer society. Maybe it's very retrograde on my part, because it's the aristocratic part of me; but I can't imagine myself going around and buying cheap furniture. I would rather live without any furniture, if I can't have real good furniture, like Chippendale, you know . . . (laughs). I have always had this attitude. I would rather have an environment where I had beautiful sculptures and paintings, which I did have for a long time.
RA: Since you can't be a king, you'd rather live like a beggar . . .
DM: Yes. Maybe that's one of the weaknesses of my character. It's very hard for people to take that . . . However, I was horrified by the power of money, the bourgeois money. Look at Soto now! He was such an amazing artist when he was a peasant playing his guitar in Paris in the '50s. I'm not trying to be romantic, but there has been a real qualitative change since he has been accepted by the art establishment. He was taken over by Denise René, by Marlborough . . and look at him now. It's worse than being a mummy.
RA: But he made a very original and important contribution to the Kinetic Art movement. In fact he was one of the pioneers of the post-War developments. Perhaps now he is only repeating himself, churning works one after another for the art market . . .
DM: They are not even works of art now. They are just expensive decor. They are things that clutter the space; and an artist is supposed to be a poet of space.
RA: And you thought then this was going to happen?
DM: I saw it then happening. It wasn't only my instinct, it was an analysis. I was at the Venice Biennale when they gave the major award to Le Parc, which disappointed poor Soto; and when I came back to London I just felt the whole art market was so horrible . . . At that time I also read the writings of Lygia Clark. She was the first person to understand participation art. Her insights really moved me. I was also amazed by the objects she was then making — those articulated sculptures. I admire Takis' kind of audacity — it's like someone from the Third World grasping science and technology to express something original and prehistoric. But I was more intrigued by Lygia Clark. There's a very sophisticated technology involved in her work.
RA: The fact that Lygia Clark is from the Third World, from Brazil, do you think that has anything to do with her work?
DM: I think so, very much. It was actually before concepts like 'Third World' came into being . . . One day I said to myself: "How come Lygia Clark is a much better constructivist than the people who are from Paris or London?" So, I started to look at her work more seriously. Then I read an article she wrote on participation art, and another one on multiples. She wanted to make her work available to everybody in a democratic spirit. And then, inspired by her writing, I was all for multiples. But you also had people, like Denise René, Jeremy Fry, business people, who were also all for it, for multiples. Their whole concept of it went utterly against my idea of multiples. For them they were the objects to be produced in multiples, marketed and consumed as an elitist thing, as a kind of expensive decor for your home. So, I just didn't go with this. At that time Signals Gallery was also going through financial crises, and they could have only continued with it by having a very expensive set-up in the West End — a sort of thing which Denise René eventually did with her gallery in Paris. So, I said to myself: "I'm not going to do this. I will do something else".

David Medalla, along with some other members of the Exploding Galaxy, being arrested by the police, for no reasons other than that they were wearing unusual clothes and thus were only attracting public attention, in Kings Road, London, on 22nd July 1967.

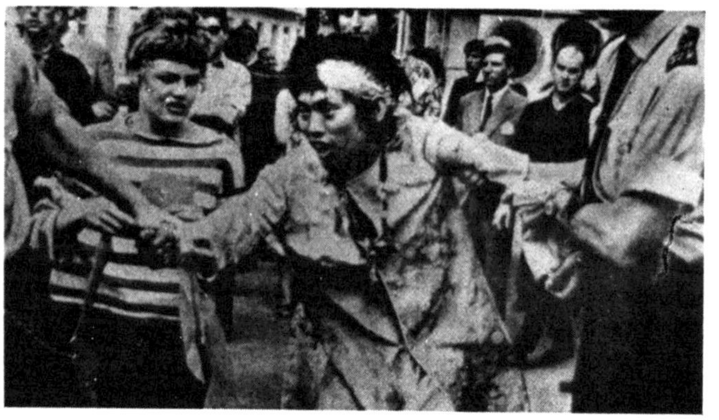

And I started the Exploding Galaxy, which I thought was fun. It was a kind of laboratory, to see how people behaved collectively. It was very anarchical, which is, I think, my main criticism of it. I don't like anarchy, you know; not in practice. Maybe it is very good as a concept, but not in practice. Anyway the Exploding Galaxy days taught me a lot.
RA: But it was very important for you then to move on to something in which people could develop their artistic potential collectively . . .
DM: Yes.
RA: It was also the time when the so-called flower people movement emerged and the Exploding Galaxy fitted very well into it.
DM: Yes. But, you know, that's the sad part of it. All these things get fitted in, because of the way the media operates.
RA: So you think it was the manipulation of the media that gave the Exploding Galaxy an eternal image?
DM: Yes, I think so. But that was not with my knowledge nor with my collaboration. Each time the popular media was around doing something about the Exploding Galaxy, I wasn't there. I was either away from the place or away from England. And all of a sudden I saw it in the newspapers, or heard that they were making a film about it. I was actually one of the many people who participated in the Exploding Galaxy who did not want to be in the newspapers or to be on the TV.
RA: But then what actually was your role in the Exploding Galaxy?
DM: I don't know exactly. Maybe it was something to do with the personality cult . . . I initiated the entire thing, one evening in January 1967 in my room at Balls Pond Road . . .
RA: You mean you were the main personality in it?
DM: Yes . . . also Paul Keeler, who was very powerful in it. Paul is a very gifted administrator and organiser. The external aspect of the Exploding Galaxy, I must say, was Paul Keeler more than I. He organised many things . . .
RA: Paul Keeler actually closed down his gallery, Signals, in which you were also involved, at the end of 1966. How much do you think this played into you going into something which was not related to the gallery situation? The sort of dance-dramas you were doing in the Exploding Galaxy didn't really need a gallery space.
DM: We could have had another gallery. I was at that time actually doing some work that could be exhibited in a gallery space. But by the mid-60s all the galleries were really dead. There was no point in going to them. It's rather like the so-called community arts thing now. By this year it would all be finished. I mean, there's no point in going to places like the Camden Arts Centre . . . They are all dead. And I don't know what it is. I think it's a 20th century urban phenomenon; these places are only interesting in the beginning. They soon run out of steam. This is the thing that art establishment people don't understand in England. They keep on propping up institutions like the ICA which is now dead. In the early '60s the ICA was incredibly wonderful. You could then sit down in the ICA in Dover Street, play the one-arm bandit machine, have a cup of coffee, and meet interesting people. But can you meet anyone interesting at the ICA now? So, I think by the mid 60s art galleries in London were really dead. They really were. You couldn't revive them, no matter how much money, anything, you put into them. It's a dead structure.
RA: But they are still showing works and doing a lot of business . . .
DM: Well, churches are also doing business. They are selling candles and images of saints. It's the same thing, you know. It's nothing to do with reality.
RA: Do you see any alternative to the present structure?
DM: At the moment, no. I think the only alternative is the mobility of the artist, physical mobility; because now one moment you can be in the most technologically advanced situation, like in Berlin or London . . ., and the next moment in Africa or Asia. I think that's the next stage — the physical movement of the artist.
RA: But that's already been happening. Western artists like Richard Long have been going around . . .
DM: Is he really going around? No, he is not going around all over the world. He is just going around in art magazines. It's one thing to go around the world, and it's another to go from one art magazine to another . . .
RA: But they do physically travel. Don't they?
DM: Do they? I have no idea. That's what they say. Anyway I don't mean just physical travel. I mean both physical and psychological.
RA: Are you suggesting that artists should really travel to meet different peoples?
DM: Yes. That's what I mean.
RA: And these artists are just going around the world, doing the kind of art which does not touch or concern with the reality of the world. They are just using faraway places and sites to do the so-called conceptual art and bring it to the capitalist metropolis. It's really an advanced kind of appropriation.
DM: Yes. It's rather sentimental.
RA: But they do make a point; and I think this must be understood within the context of the imperialist world-view of corporate capitalism, which is different from the old colonialist world-view. The present instrument of appropriation and exploitation is advanced technology. Some Western artists are now going around with their cameras in

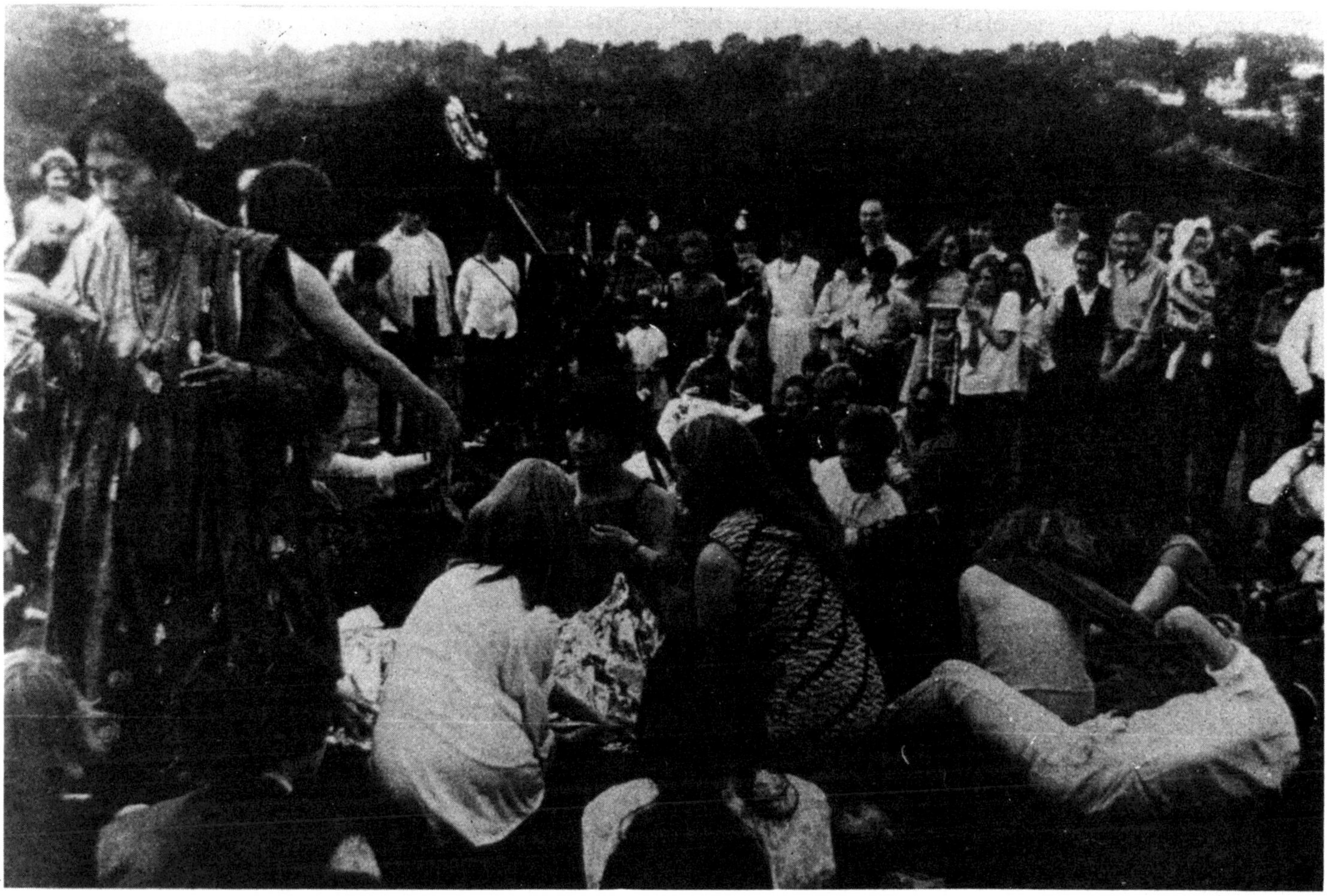

The Exploding Galaxy at Hampstead Heath, London 1968. David Medalla, standing left, is reading a story as part of the performance of ***Buddha Ballet.***

perpetuation of their claim to the whole world, by marking and recording their presence wherever they go. It may look a bit naive on their part, but it is nevertheless symbolic in the sense that their attitude coincides historically with the imperialist world-view.

DM: The British artists doing all these sorts of things, it's funny to me. It's like dressing up as kings and admirals and what-not, but knowing fully well that they have no battle-ships and aeroplanes. So that doesn't really disturb me. I'm more conscious of the new and growing forces, because we must be aware if these new forces are going to benefit humanity or they are going to benefit a small section of people. So what people like Richard Long are doing is rather touching. You can expose this kind of work and ridicule it, but I want to reserve my strength for that which is really real, potentially more obnoxious and dangerous . . . Now, to give you an example, when the cross was the cross, you see, the cross was something that meant the Inquisition, the destruction of many cultures. Now you see a cross between the breasts of a young girl. It's just a kind of seduction piece. Nobody would take that cross seriously; I mean, you don't tremble before the cross. You can see the Pope on TV, may be blessing people with plastic rosaries. It hasn't any power any longer.. Even a small dictator like Marcos is not intimidated by the cross. He will be only intimidated by President Carter, by the American Eagle — it's got a signification. So, it's a toothless lion, the British kind of signification about their imperialist past. It's good to ridicule it though, because it will stop the new lions from thinking that they can have the run of the show.

RA: But don't you think that's the trouble with most of the British intelligentsia? I'm sometimes really surprised by the extent of imperialist mentality here. You come across so many nice people and then suddenly you discover that deep down inside they are still the old lot. They would still play the old game, you know, as if the world is their Empire.

DM: Yes. That's true. That's when they are so absurd. It's really pathetic. To play the game when you don't even have the cards to play it with is really pathetic. They should have made a transition like the Greeks did: the Greeks became the teachers to the Romans.

RA: Now let us go back to your own story. After the Exploding Galaxy, I believe, you went on a long tour of Africa and Asia. And when you came back in the early '70s your way of looking at things was somehow changed, in the sense that you became overtly political in your artistic practice. Is it because of what you saw in Africa and Asia, or you were influenced by what was happening then in China, I mean, the cultural revolution?

DM: Before I answer that, Rasheed, I will go back to something I think I must record here now. My most memorable experience in coming over from Asia via Africa to Europe occurred in Djibouti about 20 years ago. I remember arriving at the port of Djibouti on a boat which I took in Bombay. I had a shock of my life when I reached the town. Right in a desert I saw a small French provincial town, you cannot imagine, right in Africa. It had an *Avenue du Marechal Foch*, something with two rows of vulture-infested trees. They had *Hotel de Paris, Cafe du Place Vendome*, etc., all the elements of French culture. I said, "where am I?" It was like a bad dream. And I couldn't find a room to sleep. Wherever I went they said, *"tout complet"*. So I slept outside in the square. That was my first politicisation.

RA: Why do you think they didn't let you a room?

DM: I wasn't French. Yes, that was the main reason.

RA: That was the first time you came across racism . . .

DM: That was the first time. I never came across racism when I was in New York. Although New York is full of different peoples — Jews; Puerto Ricans, Chinese, blacks — and there must be racism there, I never personally felt it. But I really did feel it in the middle of this desert. So, long before I went back to Africa and Asia I knew there was a real kind of contradiction between the colour of your skin and one's reality as a human being. And the colour of one's skin is purely to do with who has the power; it has to do with a socio-economic and political thing . . . When I came back to Europe in the early '70s what I was really interested in was what Lenin called the popular and democratic forms of culture; because I think the world's masses will one day create a new kind of world civilisation. It's actually happening now: you are from one culture and I'm from another, and Oriol over there is again from another, but we are now beginning to learn how to see all these different cultures together. The thing is not to trust the politician, politicians and bureaucrats, although up to a certain point we are at their mercy. I think it's very easy for the artists to have the kind of illusion that they have the power. I don't think they really have. We can make signs, we can make metaphors, we can even make programmes for other people, but we will still be dependent on many factors beyond our control. Look at what happened in Russia: after the revolution all the progressive artists were suppressed, and the bureaucracy introduced an official art — the so-called Social Realism. Russian Social Realism is retrograde, because the tenets of Social Realism are neither artistic nor revolutionary. Paradoxically whenever a progressive movement gains political power, there is the other tendency to make it as conservative as possible by suppressing progressive thinking — look at China today after the death of Chairman Mao. On the other hand when in 1871 the Paris Commune lost, the proletariat lost, and yet in spite of this, it was possible for artists who were progressive to gain a foothold in history. I'm here thinking about the Impressionists, many of whom supported the Commune. Had the Commune succeeded, you know, Courbet would have become the head of the Cultural Commission. And if after him a painter like Courbet had succeeded, which was very likely, do you suppose that people like Lautrec and Cezanne have had any chance?

RA: Do you mean to say that . . .

DM: They would have been put in jail.

RA: You mean to say that there is a contradiction between political power and artistic practice?

DM: There is. There has always been. This is the thing that we, who are interested in art and politics, must look into very carefully. Another good example is the so-called Spanish Century of Gold; you know, the famous *siglo de oro*. This was the time of Velasquez. It was the period of decadence of the Spanish Empire and, at the same time, it was the epoch which saw the flowering of the best Spanish art and literature. It's very peculiar; I mean, I don't see the clear connection. Whether it's the world of imagination compensating for reality or the other way round. It is a very strange contradiction; you have to admit that.

RA: Since the early '70s you have been involved in radical politics as well as art, and quite often combining both together. Do you think you have now retreated from that position?

DM: No, no, no, . . . I never retreat from political positions. No. I think if you do, you lose your true orientation.

RA: No, I didn't mean that. I only meant your position regarding art. Do you still believe that art should be explicitly political?

DM: I think one should do some retreat tactically. If I have retreated at all, it's only because the forms I had explored were not functional. Do you understand? But I do believe my art has become even more political.

RA: Let's go back and tell us what you did in the early '70s?

DM: Well, I did things about the repressive situation in the Philippines, and about the industrial struggle of miners here in Britain. I did a lot of political posters . . . In answer to your previous question I would say if I did retreat at all, it's because I found the forms I was using were not correct. In other words, they were not functional, they were therefore not effective. Like, if you were leading a struggle in the battlefield and you start losing men, and then if you retreat that doesn't mean you are defeated. You have to try again and try another form. Maybe it's incorrect sometimes to use artillery, you know. Maybe it's incorrect to use posters or slide-shows, etc.

RA: How about Artists' Liberation Front?

DM: That was very ultra-left.

RA: And it was then you did a lot of political poster work?

DM: Yes. But I didn't see that as art. It was propaganda; it was not art.

RA: You mean to say that there was only a political function behind that kind of work?

RA: But the politics is finished for that. It was mainly for the struggle in Guine-Bissau, Angola, Mozambique . . . Well, they have now gained their political independence.

RA: You mean it was necessary for you at that time to do propaganda work?

DM: Yes, because those people needed one's help. Like if you saw somebody outside in the street being beaten up you'd go out and stop your dinner. Dinner may be the most beautiful thing you're cooking, right, but you must stop your dinner and go out and see what you can do. When a country is fighting for its liberation from colonial rule, it needs international support. After they have gained independence it's their internal problem, whether they are going to follow a socialist path or not. You know what I mean? It's now their problem, and the only thing then you can do is to become a critic rather than a supporter . . . I support all genuine struggles for liberation. Incidentally, many of them are made by people who speak a wide variety of languages. It reminds me of a Spanish poet I met recently. When I asked him if he was still writing poetry, he said: "well, to some extent; but for me the Spanish language will only be viable if it becomes a dialect again". And I said, "what do you mean?" He said, "well, at the moment, Spanish is spoken not just in Spain but in Latin America as well. But it doesn't have the power of English, French or German. The Spanish language must therefore play its role as a dialect, and it's only then that I will begin to find my bearing as a poet". He has this theory that the real language that is spoken by people must be a dialect. That is, there will be an emergence again of dialects all over the world, because the major international languages — like, English, French, German, and probably Russian and Chinese as well — are not the languages of real feeling and real insight. They are the languages of exploitation and oppression. I'm not a linguist, but I was very amazed by this concept.

RA: Can you apply this as an analogy to visual arts?

DM: Probably, yes. The so-called marginal art forms — not the marginal artists — may express a deeper reality better than the major accepted art forms.

RA: It reminds me of the French art critic Pierre Restany who once described you as "the marginal artist *par excellence*". I wonder why he said that? Do you understand why he described you as a *marginal* artist?

DM: Well, he knows that I cannot be situated in the context of French art, or English art, or European art in general.

RA: Why couldn't you be placed in French art or British art?

DM: First of all I'm conscious of not wanting to be placed in . . . Never!

RA: You have been living in Britain since 1960, and that has been your social reality . . .

DM: That's true. But, on the other hand, I may be living in Britain, and I have to be honest about this, many of my friends are not British . . . I do have British friends, but they are a handful. The artists among them, the British ones, do not belong to the art establishment here. So, I mean, being placed or not in this context has never bothered me. The thing is I'd rather not be part of . . . (long pause). I don't want to be a British artist, whatever that means . . .

RA: You have spent most of your life, over 20 years, in the West. How could you then avoid being part of this reality?

DM: I'm part of the reality here, in so far as I take part in the struggles here. But the question of being part of British art or not, I do not see as part of the struggle.

RA: Wouldn't you like your art being discussed, you see, in the context of the social reality in which it has been created?

DM: No, because . . . No, no, Rasheed, you see there is an aspect of me, but maybe you won't agree with this. I'm sure you won't . . . (pause).

RA: Let's come back to your 'marginal' position: I don't think it really depends how you see yourself, whether you want to be placed in the context of European history or not

DM: I don't want to be part of only European history. I want to be part of world history. My art belongs to the world at large, to the people in London as well as to the people in Kathmandu.

RA: I agree with you there; but that's an entirely different thing. The way Pierre Restany or somebody else in the West looks at you is another thing. . .

DM: Yes. That's true. But I don't know . . . (pause).

RA: You see, your 'marginal' position is not inherent in your work, and it shouldn't therefore really matter whether you are European or not. Yet you are seen in the West as marginal, because you come from part of the world which has been colonised and marginalised. Your 'marginality' is, in fact, the reflection of a common Western attitude towards those who are not of European origin.

DM: That's true, but not vis-a-vis Pierre Restany. He was just stating a fact . . . He is an intelligent and perceptive art critic, one of the few I've met and respect; although I don't agree with all his ideas.

RA: And what is that fact?

DM: Well, whether I like it or not, I'm not going to be part of that central tradition of European culture. But that's not really my problem; that's a problem for Europe. This may sound arrogant on my part, but it's never been my problem . . . Having worked here off and on for nearly 20 years, I don't even have my one drawing in an English art-collection. That's not my problem; it's their problem.

RA: You mean, you really see yourself not being part of . . .

DM: Do you want to be part of something that's dying? The cultural scene here is really moribund; except that I like the idea of a few of my friends showing their work here and there, like in the Hayward Gallery, and then one can go there and see them. But, on the other hand, if the whole gallery was offered to me I wouldn't accept it. I'm not saying this out of pride. It's simply because: what is the point? It's to me like a casket, you know, it's something dead. If there was a possibility of destroying, say the Hayward Gallery, that would have been another matter. It's only earth underneath that and you could change it.

RA: I still don't understand why you are denying your work its historical context. Why wouldn't you like your art to be discussed in the context of which it has been developing?

DM: No. Because, *they* wouldn't have the criteria for discussing me. Would they?

RA: What do you mean by that?

DM: Can you talk about my art, say, in the line of Turner and William Blake . . and all those people. I'm talking here specifically about England. I mean, I may like a painting by Hogarth, or a sketch by Constable, but I'm not that keen about the recent schools of British art. There are some British artists I like and they are also ignored by the British art establishment.

RA: But wouldn't you say that your work has been part of the avant-garde movements in Europe since the early '60s?

DM: Not really European, but an international movement. What would you say about artists like Lygia Clark, Helio Oiticica, Soto, Otero, Li Yuan-Chia, yourself Rasheed, and all those artists who're not European. Even someone like Takis who is from Greece is marginal to Western Europe. The progressive aspect of kinetic art is definitely international; and most of the pioneers of the kinetic art movement were not from Western Europe.

RA: Yeah. But their work could have only matured in the context of metropolis, rather than in Latin America, even in Hungary or Greece . . .

DM: That's true. It's metropolitan. That I agree with you, but it was

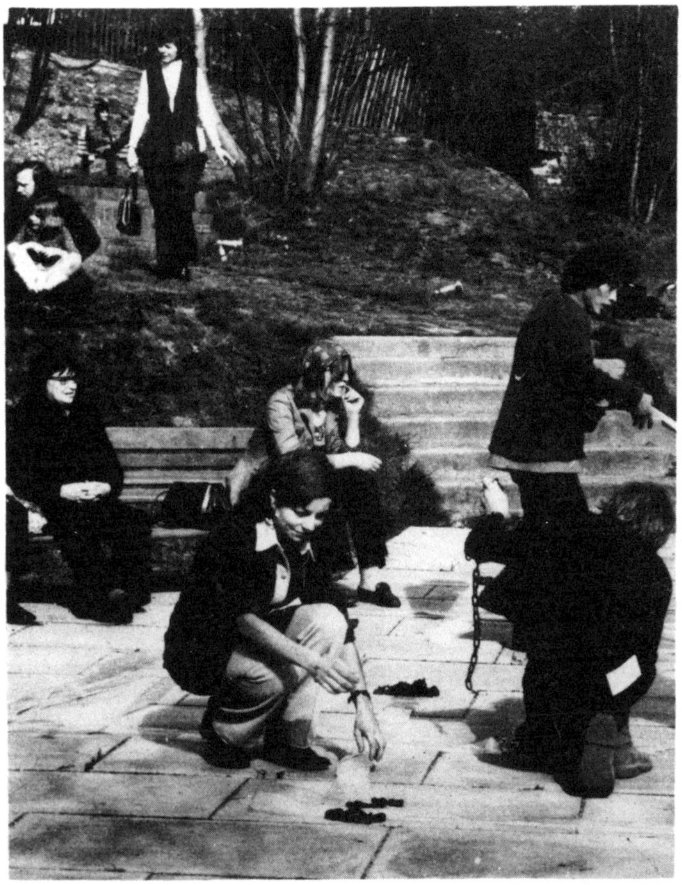

Down with the Slave Trade, London 1971 Photo by Rasheed Araeen

not European in its roots.
RA: While your contemporaries have accepted the metropolitan context, you are denying yourself that context. Why?
DM: Some of them have accepted this context, you know, and they have just destroyed their art. Haven't they? I'm one of the few who really rejected it; Lygia Clark and Helio Oiticica did as well at the same time.
RA: But you cannot deny the fact that your contemporaries from Latin America, from Greece, from Hungary, from Romania or Poland, are recognised in the metropolitan centres of Paris, London or New York, without being considered marginal. Why should it be different in your case? Isn't it because you are Asian?
DM: Yes, I think so. Maybe it's also to do with the fact that Latin Americans who are living in the big cities see themselves as Europeans. Is that not true? But, on the other hand, their problem really is greater than mine. While they can see themselves as Europeans, they know very well, even when they have accepted European culture and in turn they have been recognised as part of European history, they are not really part of Europe.
RA: Okay, I do recognise this problem. But I think there are many people in Latin America now who are questioning their European identity, Western influence and domination. Aren't they? However, I want to come back to the question which is specific to you, about your position as an Asian artist who has lived in Europe for nearly 20 years. Well, I don't really believe that it's totally true that your non-recognition here has got something to do with your rejection of the metropolitan context. It's actually because *they* have rejected you. . .
DM: I'm glad. I mean, take an analogy about love. You can be in a room with someone who looks fascinating. So, you may make a little attempt at making some contact. But there's nothing really that fascinates me in contemporary British art or culture. I never was fascinated about anything here. So it's not a matter of rejection. You can only feel rejected by something that really fascinates you . . .
RA: I wasn't really being specific about British art or culture. I was actually thinking of your position within what you yourself describe as international. So, even when I'm considering the British situation it's within that larger context . . .
DM: Ah, no . . . But the British are considered only a distant outpost of continental tradition. Now, this may be illusion, or delusion, but when I go to Paris or even to some place like Amsterdam, I don't feel rejected by the French or Dutch artists.
RA: But you do feel rejected here in Britain?
DM: Well, not rejected; 'ignored' is more the word.
RA: Okay, yes.
DM: And I ignore them too. There is no feeling, either way. If I went to Paris and started to live there and I felt ignored there I would really get furious; I would really feel, "my God!". I would rather measure myself by the Parisian standards, you know, by the Dutch or Italian, rather than by the British. I'm here talking about only visual arts. I have never been attracted to the modern British art. Not once have I looked at a Henry Moore sculpture and said, "this is magnificent". But I look at a Brancusi sculpture, or a Julio Gonzales, or even a Gabo, or a Vantongerloo, and I love what they did. And I would really feel rejected if I was rejected by these people. And since there's been very little contact between me and the continental people — I see them only when I go there occasionally, I don't feel rejected by them.
RA: But surely it's not totally true . . .
DM: It's true. I mean, I wouldn't want to be in an exhibition with, for example, Anthony Caro.
RA: You once complained that you were not included in the exhibition of British art, *Arte Inglese Oggi*, in Milan in 1976, while many of your students were there.
DM: It's only because there was money involved; and being a materialist I would have liked a trip to Milan. And I could have seen my friends there. I wouldn't really mind representing Britain abroad if I could get money from the British Council.
RA: But how could they send you abroad to represent Britain if you have nothing to do with Britain?
DM: That's it. I mean, that's why I'm not aggravated when I'm ignored here. I get angry when they have exhibitions representing various tendencies in art — like the survey exhibitions of kinetic art or performance art — and they reject me. That's what happened with the Hayward Gallery show of kinetic art in 1971. They didn't include me in it, and that made me furious; not because I was an artist working in Britain, but I was an artist working in kinetic art.
RA: Why do you think they rejected you?
DM: Well, it's a racist thing, whoever organised the show. I think it was a guy from South Africa. Wasn't he? It must be that or it was his ignorance, you see.
RA: But that's a simplistic explanation, isn't it? I mean you are looking at the whole racial issue by pointing your finger at one particular individual, rather than examining the whole ideology of racism and how it operates vis-a-vis art.
DM: There is an ideological context to it. Yes, I agree with you there. But there's a difficulty in my case which I can't quite understand. The thing is I was at the Kassel Documenta in 1972 and I was seen as an artist from Britain . . .
RA: But you were not officially representing Britain there.
DM: No. I was actually invited by the organiser of the Documenta — Harald Szeeman. He's a friend of mine; he is Swiss, you know . . . What I'm trying to say is that there is also another problem in art, which we mustn't ignore. That is, if you are doing some kind of original work you can be rejected even by your own compatriots. I'm thinking about somebody like Mondrian or Duchamp. So, that's also the problem . . . For the Milan show they had this section about performance art, and I'm sure that I wasn't the only performance artist who was rejected. They rejected a few other artists as well who were indigenous British. So, it's very difficult to make a generalised statement. I think it's also because many of those who organise exhibitions are incapable of understanding art.
RA: Yes, that's true. But the kinetic art exhibition wasn't the only time when you were ignored. I don't remember seeing a single exhibition, an official survey here, in which you have been included and given due recognition.
DM: No. They did a multiples show here a long time ago and I was in it. I was then actually living in Paris. Hugh Shaw of the Arts Council organised the multiples show — he is one of the few officials I know who are genuinely interested in art and artists . . . There's a racial aspect to many art events here. But there's also an aesthetic problem which we mustn't ignore. That is, if I were doing a work that's not entirely original I would have much better chance to be recognised. Do you understand?
RA: Yes, I do. And also if you were following some so-called ethnic style in your work, so that you were clearly defineable in terms of your past traditional culture in Asia or Africa, you would be acceptable. In other words, if you as a black artist could be categorised separately at a level which is below the so-called mainstream you would be less of a problem for the art establishemnt.
DM: Yes. Well, that's why it is a two-fold thing. It's both a political and an artistic thing. And that's why it acts twice against my position as an artist. But at the same time we mustn't forget that there are white artists who are not recognised. Takis lived here in London; they rejected him too. He is white, you know. A lot of artists from the continent are not recognised here. The question really is: who does the recognition? Well, with all due respect, I don't believe that people in a position of power when there are still class divisions will use objective criteria for evaluating art works, whether we are living now in China or here in Britain.
RA: I think you are being elusive now . . .
DM: No. This is the most philistine country in the world. Even the English artists will admit this . . .
RA: But, David; let's not confuse the issue of the position of black

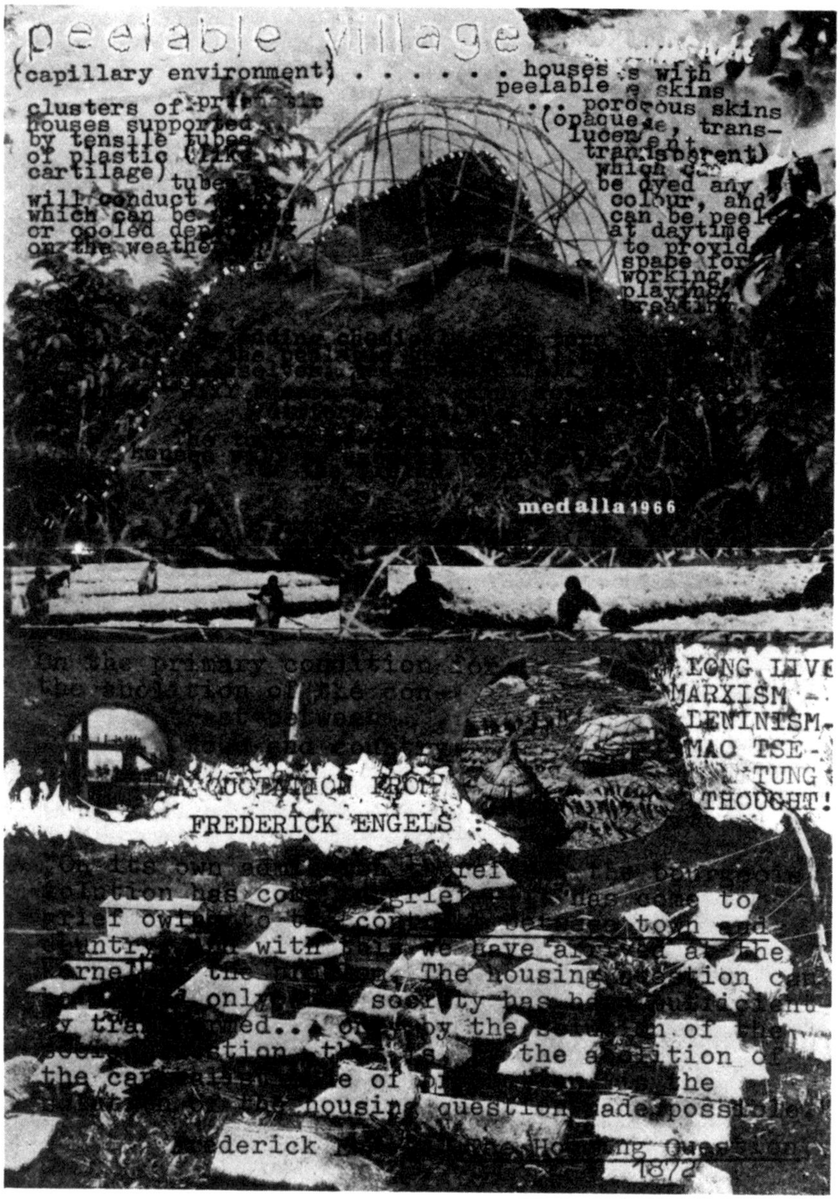

Peelable Village 1966

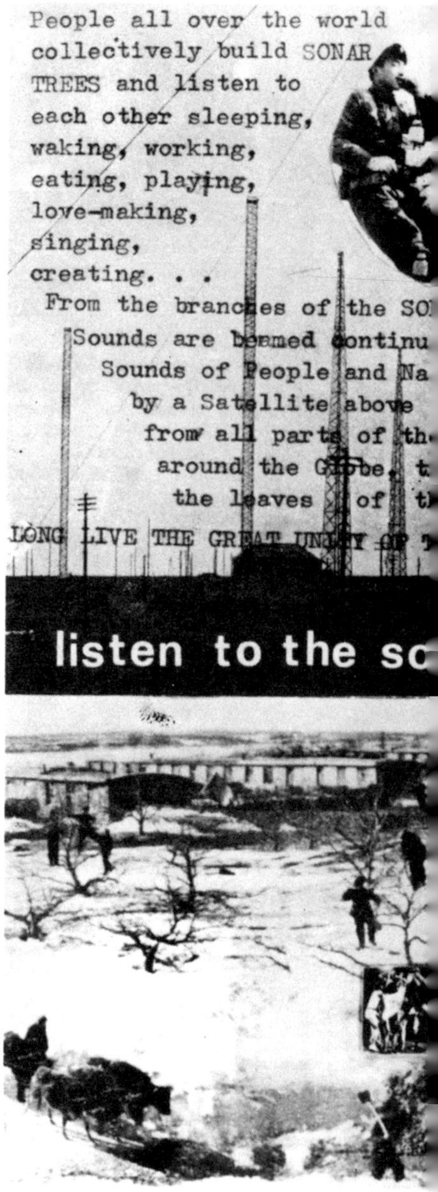

Listen to the Sonar Trees! 1969

artists here.
DM: I'm not confusing the issue. I'm trying to make this very clear: I think we should fight for our rights as artists and as black artists, and against the philistinism of this society as well. This is the most philistine society I've come across. The art bureaucrats and many art critics just don't have any sensitivity. They only have gross appetites, you know, the English middle class. Many of them don't feel the necessity to read a poem or hear a piece of real music or look at a work of art. They turn on the television to see the most horrific programmes; they are happy with the telly whether they are Cabinet Ministers or shopkeepers or all the way down to the bottom, the working class. They are smug and complacent with the visual diet they get from their TV sets.
RA: I agree with you about the philistinism, but there is something more to it. I mean, if you are a black artist, philistinism is not the only thing that you come across. Won't you agree with that?
DM: Ah, but that's why the black artists are a bit more privileged. The British philistinism towards their own people is so pervasive that they don't even know what's killing them. Do you know what I mean? That's why your art, my art, can be so integral. We can really go on developing, you know. I do feel very privileged here, in a negative sense of the word; and I feel the white British artist is not really privileged . . .
RA: Come on, David . . .
DM: No. I really mean that . . .
RA: Privilege of being at the bottom of the pyramid!
DM: That's it. We are at the bottom of the pyramid, may be outside of it altogether, and we can see it. But the white artists, the best ones among them who are also discriminated against, can't see it . . .
RA: I agree with you there, but . . .
DM: . . . that's the sad part of it. That's why my polemics is really to convince them that a capitalist society is definitely anti-art, and I'm so glad that people like Derek Boshier and Conrad Atkinson are seeing this reality. Since they are the majority, I want the white artists to see the class contradictions, because they will have to do the fighting, mostly; and I will be in the sidelines. I will be watching the whole thing, you see. They are the majority, not me. I don't want to confuse the issue by pointing and seeing that the contradiction is me. I want to say that the contradiction is in *their* society, between the bourgeoisie and the proletariat. For every one Indian or Pakistani or West Indian, Filipino or Turkish, worker here there will be a hundred, or maybe a thousand, white British workers. I want these British workers to see that reality inside their society. For every black artist here there are 200 products of Chelsea School of Art every year – white artists. But they still don't see it. It's a pity that so many of them still have illusions. They still don't see that it's an exploitative, oppressive and repressive society. WE SEE IT: that's what I'm trying to say. In paradoxical terms, we are rather privileged because we can see it right away. And, you know, when you can see the danger right away, you can take precautions. . . They really don't see it. They are being poisoned, they are being manipulated, and they don't see it.
RA: What is then your actual role, as a black artist and a radical from the Third World, in this capitalist metropolis?
DM: Well, a subversive role; that's all. Subversion is different from revolution. You can't be revolutionary here because you're part of a minority. You can only be subversive. You can be a carrier of new ideas, revolutionary consciousness. You can be a catalyst for all the latent creative forces.
RA: But don't you think if your ideas were recognised here in the West, and since the West is influential all over the world, you would be in a better position to influence the things as well internationally?
DM: The fucked up capitalist system is so manipulative and subversive. Do you see what I mean? You will end up becoming an integral part of its structure.

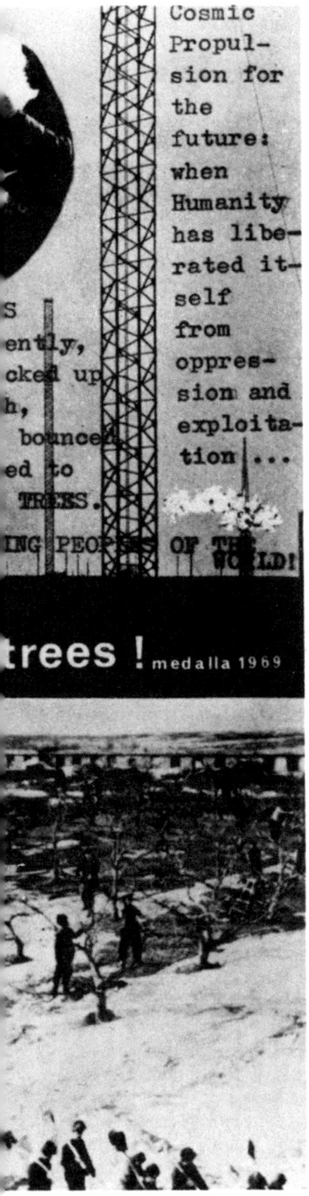

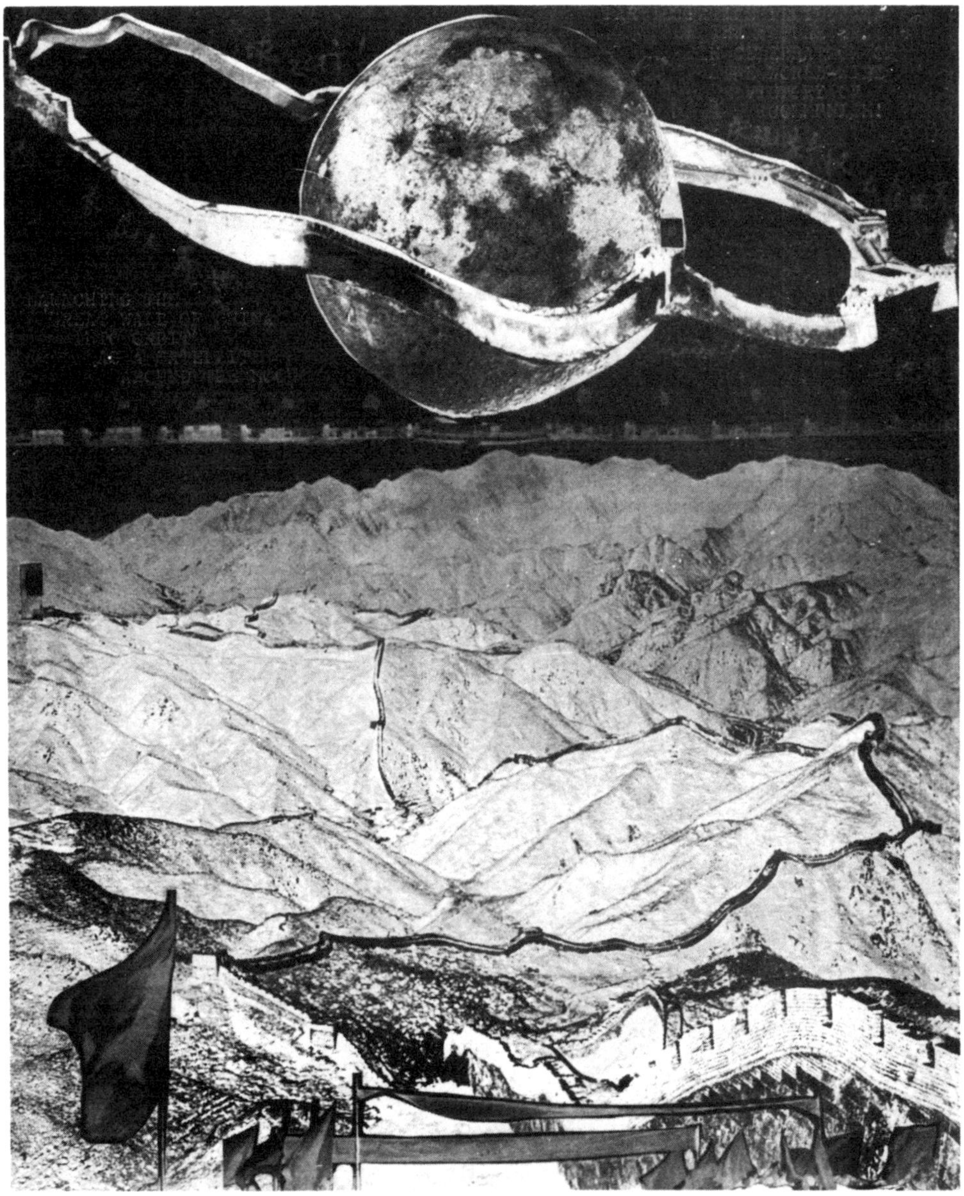

The Great Wall of China around the Moon! 1969

RA: You mean you will have to fight always from outside?
DM: No, not really. But I don't want to have a retrospective at the Tate Gallery, for example. Can you imagine? That would be the worse thing that would ever happen to anybody . . . (general laughter).
RA: Are you serious about that? You are not just laughing?
DM: No, no. It's utterly true, you see, Rasheed look . . .
RA: Come on, David. Last week you said to me that you would like to have a retrospective at the Hayward Gallery, London . . .
DM: Ah, that's a different thing. I would say 'yes' to a Hayward show if I had the whole Gallery for a year to try out my ideas.
RA: So, you would like to have a bigger recognition than a token
DM: Exactly. That's what I was coming to . . . (laughter).
RA: I think we have been talking in such terms that may not be very clear to the readers in the Third World; because it's becoming very internal. So can we . . .?
DM: No, no, they are not. I think people in the Third World are always curious about what happens in London. They do want to know what goes on in the English art scene . . . (laughs).
RA: Or in the so-called international art scene.
DM: Yeah.
RA: Now tell us something about Artists for Democracy (AFD). What were the motives behind AFD? And looking back do you think it was a successful venture?
DM: Well, it grew out of the Artists' Liberation Front, which was then becoming a masonic thing. A group of young artists started meeting at my place and talking about changing society, and all that idealism of youth. Then we saw the possibility of starting an organisation which, by its activities, would support liberation struggles in various parts of the world, particularly in the Third World. We actually started AFD, in 1974, with an arts festival at the Royal College of Art in support of Chilean struggle against the fascist junta there. Then in early 1975 we moved into a premises, which we squatted, at Whitfield Street. There we held many exhibitions of art as well as of documents, poetry readings, films/slide shows, discussions etc, in support of liberation struggles in Africa, in the Middle East... We organised an especial art festival in support of Vietnam, and in fact to celebrate her victory over American aggression. We also held an important exhibition in support of the American Indian Movement . . . In general we also showed the works, as individual exhibitions, of many artists. And I think as a whole it was a successful venture.
RA: As you know, I was also an active member of AFD, at least for some time. I got interested in AFD because of its orientation towards the problems of the Third World. But I think, AFD became merely a sort of support organisation and it didn't really address itself to the basic and essential ideological issues regarding the cultural relationship between the Third World and the West. Don't you think it was the failure of the AFD not to deal with this question, of cultural imperialism, particularly vis-a-vis radical artistic practice?
DM: Yes. I think it was a failure. But you see the failure had to do with the material conditions. I thought it was a failure even before the question was posed. It's like this: if people can't grasp what your question is, how can you expect an answer? We had many cultural workers, the artists, who would support all those struggles but had little knowledge of actual politics. On the other hand, there were the political radicals who came to the AFD; but they had no desire whatsoever even to look at a drawing or a painting or listen to a poem. It's the most amazing contradiction, and I saw it all the time. You see, when we had artists who did exhibitions, some only exhibited their work in the AFD because there was no other place for them to exhibit; but they were not really interested in what was happening in Brixton (London), let alone Mozambique.
RA: I want now to come back to your own work with that period, from Artists' Liberation Front to AFD. Most of the time the context of your work was China, or shall we say your work was orientated to

Mao Tse-Tung Thought. I would have thought that it would have been more appropriate for you to relate your work to the Third World as a whole or to the Philippines. I wonder how you would explain your orientation towards China, particularly in the context of you actually living in Britain. Was it due to purely a political identity or can you also explain it at a psychological or subjective level?
DM: It was purely political. It was never artistic. The Chinese supported all the liberation struggles at that time. They were really progressive. But when they started moving to the other camp, I became very critical.
RA: You mean to say that during that period you were more of a political activist than an artist?
DM: No, no. I was both. I mean, the artist was always there, but I was also trying to find out what politics were . . .
RA: How politics could relate to art or vice-versa.
DM: Yes. It's actually like this: I don't think politics is everything of humanity. It's like religion which is not everything of humanity. In the Exploding Galaxy epoch I was interested in religion, because religion is part of humanity. It's not all humanity. And this is what's so fucked up about most human beings, because they are either religious or political or artistic or scientific or something else rather than human. To be truly human one must be all of these at every instant of one's life. To substitute one feeling for another would be alienating and ridiculous.
RA: Okay. In terms of relationship between art and politics what would you say you have achieved yourself?
DM: I think the artist is usually the victim of nitty-gritty politics; and it's not the other way round.
RA: Would you then say that your own work suffered because of politics?
DM: No. My work did not suffer because I did not serve any political party or group. I was interested in politics the way Rembrandt was interested in Christianity. He was not a Protestant or a Catholic. He made sure he was not claimed by one camp or the other. He was interested in the progressive aspect of Christianity.
DM: Most of your activity of that time overtly showed your interest in the Chinese. Didn't it? And I think it was after your disillusionment with the Chinese change of world-view in the mid-70s that you started shifting your position . . .
DM: The world-view of the Chinese then was a brilliant one, guided by Marxism-Leninism-Mao Tse Tung Thought, and I'm not really disillusioned with them or with what I did. But I was, I think, more sympathetic to the Vietnamese. My present position is that I support the small against the big. I don't think I have really shifted my position.
RA: Let me explain what I meant by your shift of position. About two years ago, I think, you did the performance called *The Dialogue between Tatlin and Malevich* at the Acme Gallery. Later on you did another one with Oriol de Quadras, the young Catalan artist, at the Acme Gallery again. I saw both of them; and what surprised me most was the absence of explicit political material and references in these works. That is, while you previously often had an external orientation, the new works displayed a sudden and total shift towards subjectivity. You started dealing with your *own* life, your own place in the world around; and I saw this as an important change in your work...
DM: Yes. I think it was important.
RA: I wonder how you really see yourself that transition from objectivity to subjectivity?
DM: I don't see it completely yet. You see, Rasheed, at that time I was beginning to see the concept of the state. It's like this: you have an idea, a new idea, and it has to fight its way. But when it seizes power it becomes a state, and the people who were fighting for that idea, all of a sudden, become the victims of that idea. I was looking at the most spectacular artists of the Russian Revolution, Tatlin and Malevich, because both became victims of the art bureaucrats after the Revolution became consolidated.
RA: Are you implying now that the artist shouldn't get involved in political issues or align to a particular movement in his or her artistic practice?
DM: Oh, no. I think you should. You see, it's a matter of time and space. The thing is that after the first stage has been achieved, the artist must find what he or she must do next. I think if we were now in a revolutionary situation I would certainly fight for the revolutionary forces.
RA: So you still believe that your priority as an artist is to function at a political level rather than to deal with questions which are inherent in art at socio-cultural, ideological and subjective levels?
DM: Yes. The contradictions only become overt at certain critical moments, and one must be prepared to take sides.
RA: Like we had during the Algerian War, Vietnam War, and various liberation struggles in the Third World. Even in Europe we had two wars which shattered the human complacency of normal times. But I personally believe these moments were only acute moments of eruptions, and the human conflicts that lead to these tragic moments are still there with us. The conditions which would create crises in any sensitive and aware human being are still there today. That is, we are continually facing a state of crises, particularly resulting from the human conditions in most parts of the Third World. And I'm sure you must be continually affected by this state of crisis, as I am, as thousands and millions of human beings must be, physically as well as psychologically. The question now really is: how do we as artists from the Third World deal with this crisis? While coming to terms with our own subjectivity, shouldn't we also develop a specific and constant ideological position in our artistic practice in the context of our critical condition resulting primarily from imperialist domination?
DM: That's fascinating, Rasheed. This is really interesting. I must say that you have twice before made me really think. Once when you spoke about the importance of the subjective in art; you had a great insight there which helped to clarify my ideas . . . (pause). I'm now thinking about a world-view, you know, materialism. The world is round, right. We have a history of the world which we are only beginning to see synchronistically. Looking back into history we see certain static focal points — like Rome, Mecca, Peking, etc. — which are the centres of certain static ideas and then there are other ideas that go against the focal points. How come these centres are persistent in their domination? I think I really want to do a lot of reading and study this problem . . . (long pause).
RA: So, you don't want to answer the question, David?
DM: No. I can't answer it as yet, let's put it that way. I can's answer it because I'm still thinking and reflecting about it. But let's go back

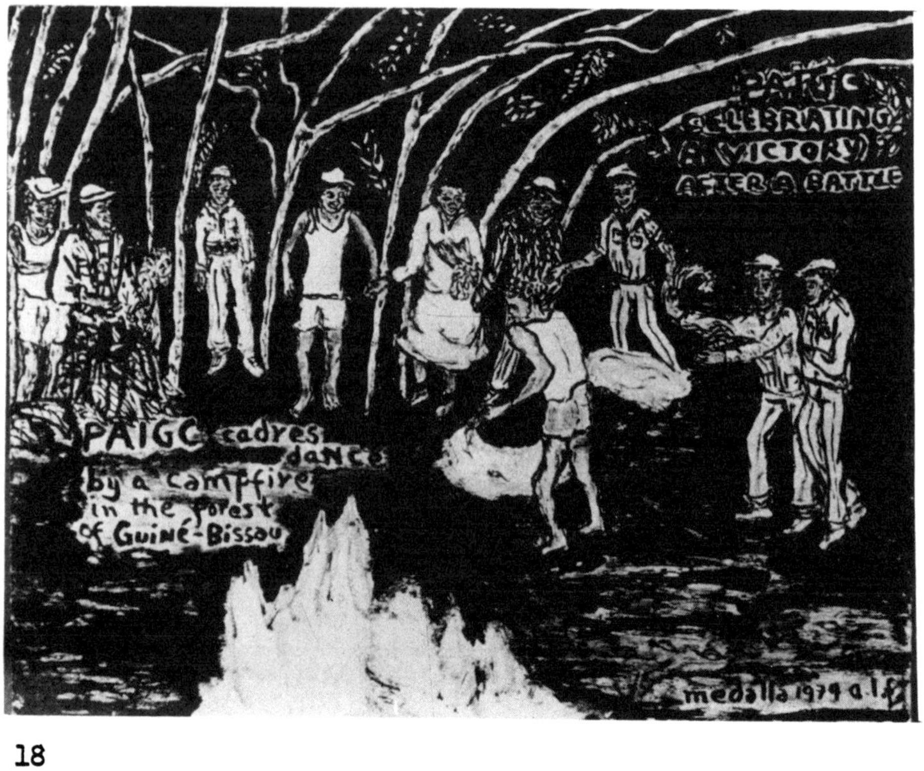

***PAIGC celebrating a Victory after a Battle*, 1974**

Photo by Rasheed Araeen

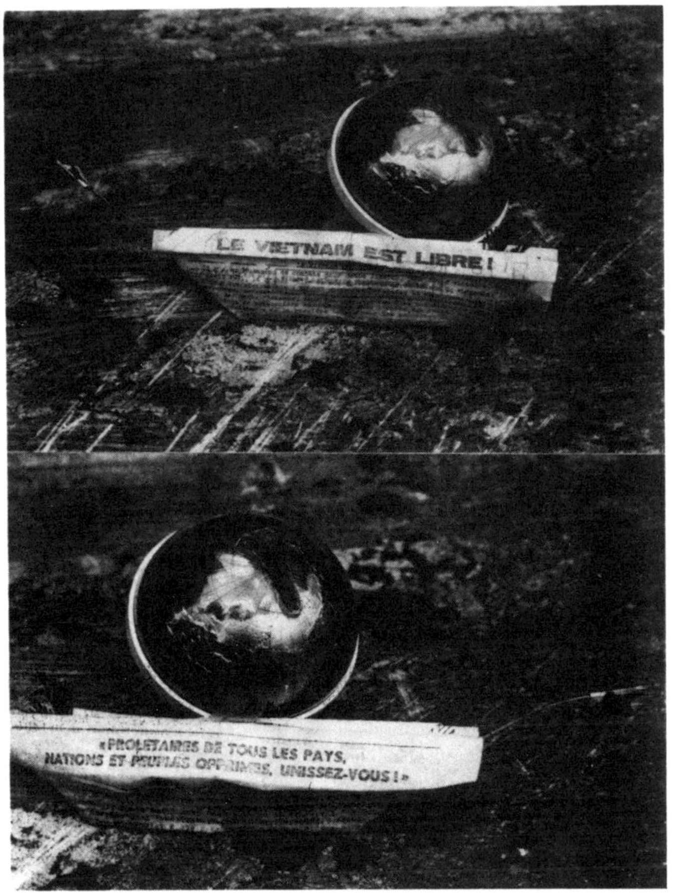

Le Vietnam est Libre! 1975

again to history. History is a good way of looking at things . . .
RA: You know, this question has been bothering me myself for some time. I have posed the same question in *Black Manifesto*, which I think you have read, and I have also tried to suggest how this question might be radically dealt with. I'm therefore wondering how much you agree with my position?
DM: Well, I can't.
RA: You mean we can't maintain a constant ideological position vis-a-vis the Third World, rather than taking actions only at what you call critical moments?
DM: That's just what I mean. You see, you're positing for me something which I don't yet agree with . . . Let's go back to history and see who was going to carry the culture after the Arab and Christian fight in Spain, between the Moors and the Spanish. The hedonistic Granada lost to the ascetic, puritanical Castilians. And in the passage the Greek culture, along with all other knowledge, went back to Europe and created the Renaissance. But the peasants in Andalucia remained just as oppressed as in Castilia, and so were they in Italy. Had the artists of the Renaissance any real choice? They had to work either for the Pope or for the Medicis . . . It's really a fascinating problem and I don't really know the answer.
RA: You mean to say that we can't develop a world-view which is non-European?
DM: Well, no. Not at the moment, not from where we are now. Because, you see, Europe is the dominant ideological thing, although its dominance is now subsiding.
RA: Can't we have an antithesis to that dominant thing?
DM: But where is this antithesis? China was the one which I thought was going to be the antithesis. Now China herself has turned to Europe and; even worse, America. Vietnam could have been the antithesis, but it's turning to Russia. These are two focal points and both are bad. And that's why I'm really shocked by the whole thing, by the recent events in Southeast Asia where I originally come from.
RA: But why do you need a country as a base from where to look at the world?
DM: Because people are part of countries, and it's masses of people who try out new ideas . . . Look, the Philippines are pro-American today. If the revolutionary struggle wins there, we will have to make a decision whether to turn towards China or Russia, whether we like it or not. It's a matter of power. Either way I would be horrified. Do you see my point? The Russian model is horrific; it's linear, monolithic, patriarchal, and theocratical . . . What is the other model? One would have thought that the liberation struggles were models, but they are not as yet. A struggle is not a model; it's a movement. Once the movement has expressed a certain direction it will have to define a form. There has been no form yet. Cuba could have been one, but look where it went . . . Truly the problem of culture is the one we will have to think most about. We don't want Western capitalist garbage, but the other garbage is just as bad.
RA: Can I come back to what I meant by an antithetical world-view. You see, we are today living in a world which is dominated by an imperialist world-view, which is hierarchical and Eurocentric. It offers and perpetuates a universal monolithical pattern of human development based on the exploitation of one human being by another, and the art and culture that springs from it must carry its reflection. Now, you mean to say that we cannot develop a world-view, manifesting in our art, which is opposed to this imperialist world-view?
DM: That's it. You have to have a model first. I was hoping China would create a model based on Mao Tse-Tung Thought, and it tried. The cultural revolution was on the whole good. Today there are really only two other models: Russia and the West.
RA: But does art necessarily require or offer a model . . . ?
DM: Oh, no, no, no, ... But politics first, you see. Look, Angola is a beautiful example. Where Agostinho Neto go now? He has to have Cuban troops there to consolidate the power. That is the fact, isn't it? And now he is also making peace with the US. And yet, Agostinho Neto is a man of intelligence, imagination, and he is a real revolutionary and a great poet. I trust and hope that Agostinho Neto will succeed in inspiring his people to create a new living culture in Angola.
RA: So, if I may conclude, you are in a limbo.
DM: I think most of the world is in a limbo for the time being. It's a kind of limbo until things change radically.
RA: What you are really trying to say here, I think, is that there is no totally independent country in the Third World today, with its own cultural values, and which is also sufficiently developed economically to provide a base for the Third World artists to operate from and develop a world-view reflecting what I have described as antithetical. And therefore there is very little choice for artists like you and me . . .
DM: Very little. I mean, it's also a geographical choice as far as the immediate moment is concerned. If I happen to be living in London I'm more in contact with Western artists. I have to know all that's happening in the European and American art scene . . . What I want to say is this, vis-a-vis the politics of one's art: we must always work on behalf of the exploited and oppressed. The majority of the exploited and the oppressed are in Asia, Africa and Latin America. But there are quite a lot of exploited and oppressed people here in England, immigrant as well as native workers.
RA: You mean your subversive role which you mentioned before — the radical role of the Third World artist in the metropolis — cannot be extended to the Third World via the so-called international communication channels.
DM: No, because you're not operating there. If you were an artist and you happen to live in a peripheral region between the Muslims and the Christians at a time when they were in conflict, you would do something either for the mosque or for the cathedral or you would just refuse to do anything at all.
RA: So, you mean to say that you cannot be really effectively functioning as a Third World artist living in the West, neither from the Third World at this moment for different reasons?
DM: Yes.
RA: But the Western artist, who never leaves his studio in New York, London or Paris, is able to exert a great influence all over the world.
DM: Yes. Simply because they are part of the dominant forces, and we are not. We are part of the periphery. The power has not yet moved to the Third World; but it will happen and we must be ready for it, with all imagination and intelligence.
RA: So your subversive role is really very limited.
DM: It will have to be, for the time being. You know, one has to see one's limits and then work from those limits and then try to extend oneself . . .
RA: I don't think I can agree with you here that the Third World artist, the black artist, has no choice but to accept a marginal role. He or she may not be *acceptable* otherwise is another matter; after all subversive ideas are not easily acceptable. However the limitation of space here does not allow us to discuss this any further. But to conclude, David, could you tell us what are you doing now? Are you doing any new work?
DM: Well, I'm doing this new work with Oriol de Quadras who is from Spain. It's called *The Circumnavigation of the World*. I'm very interested in the moment when humanity, or one section of humanity, developed a universal concept. We have been doing performances and events and studies and all kinds of art works. I don't know what the end result will be. We hope to start a data-gathering expedition around the world in 1980. Although I agree with you about this subjective thing, at this particular stage we are just looking at an objective reality. We are trying to find out what happened when the white Western civilisation entered non-European areas. I hope we come out with a certain kind of ideas. It would really be interesting to find out what happened to all those places where Magellan went.

September 1978

The Myth of the Artist as Rebel and Hero

Kenneth Coutts-Smith

We agree with the central contention of this article, which was delivered to the Caucus for Marxism and Art, at the Conference of the College Art Association, New York, January 1978, since it is imperative to separate myth from reality and expose its ideology; and this is particularly important now when the hollowness of the recent avant-garde has become more and more evident. But there are some points in the article which are ambiguous, perhaps due to the fact that all the points could not be dealt with elaborately in such a small space. However, since we see this article as a starting point for a wider discussion, it is important here to spell out what these points are.

While recognising the futility of perpetually innovatory processes, which are detached from social consciousness, how are we to look at the vast amount of knowledge generated by the avant-garde art in this century and which now lies behind us as part of human history? While casting a critical look at the avant-garde and rightly seeing it as belonging to a bourgeois epoch, which, as suggested by Coutts-Smith, has reached its end, how are we to face up to the new reality of the corporate state of international monopoly capital?

Is it really possible, and necessary, to abandon all that has been associated with the avant-garde, and look for new alternatives? Or is it only a question of different orientation, which may help redefine its premises, so that it may be possible to radicalise the methodology of avant-garde and reject its bourgeois ideology and concepts inherent in its literal meaning?

Although The Myth of the Artist as Rebel and Hero is not yet entirely applicable, specially in the domain of visual art, to the black, Third World, artist (we shall explain why this is so in the future issues), the question of avant-garde is an important issue, not only in the West but for the Third World as well where, paradoxically, there has been a movement towards the objectification of art in the form of painting and sculpture based on the concept of purity in style and material. Our own view is that art should not be restricted by formal, stylistic or/and material boundaries, and we shall use all the media at our disposal.

However we hope that the continuation of this debate in Black Phoenix will be able to make some contribution towards the understanding of this complex issue; and we invite you to participate in this discussion.

I do not propose to present for your consideration a paper in conventional form exploring a defined and specific problem in the broad area of our professional interest. This is not to imply that I personally have any *general* objection to a focused art-historical scholarship; though I do have a specific one. The latter, of course, is towards that form of "research" which depends upon an idealisation of culture, upon severing the art event from its social context (or, at best, admitting merely a simplistic and vulgar determinism) – ostensibly in order to provide an objective historical detachment, but, effectively, to justify a particular class view of culture.

Also, my own preoccupations have always been those of an art *critic* rather than of an art historian; though, perhaps inevitably, given our present social reality, criticism (being structurally less institutionalised than academic art history) both demands and achieves a more complex sense of historical relations. My personal attempts at analysis, frequently confused though they may be, have been for some time now of a dialectical nature. By this, I do not mean that I simply attempt to observe events in a dialectical relationship of influence and progression, but that I also struggle to develop not merely my thought, but the form of my analysis in dialectical terms.

Marxism is not simply a way of explaining the human social experience, it is also a way of thinking about it, and, ultimately, of living it. The dialectical position, seeking as it does, to develop new and unexpected relationship of thought, is obviously in conflict with the traditional art-historical impetus towards the accumulation and stockpiling of inert information. The difference is analogous to that between the development of a body of lived human experience on the one hand and the accumulation of property on the other.

The method of my discourse will consist, then, of an interim report (for dialectical thought is never finished, always provisional) of some of my thinking concerning what appears to be a central task now facing a *social* criticism of art: namely, the dismantling of a structure of myth and assumption concerning the nature of art (and the self-view of the artist) that tends to obscure our present understanding. An inevitable drawback, however, in such a context as the present one, is that the attempt to develop what Frederick Jameson has called "thought to the second power" lies, as he says, in its "holistic *totalizing* character: as though you could not say one thing until you had first said everything; as though with each new idea you were bound to recapitulate the entire system".[1]

Inevitably, therefore, I shall raise points that you may well consider in isolation as self-evident, even simplistic. The risk is taken, however, not merely in the hopes of achieving a dialectical exposition, but also in terms of the fundamental teleology of the dialectical method. It is taken for a "tactical" reason, if you will; since, as I understand it, a Marxist perspective on either the criticism or the history of art (as on any other area of human activity) implies a praxis, a transcension of passive scholarship into the active and on-going process of inventing the world.

I do not imagine that anyone would now question the fact that for some time there has been a widespread and developing attitude of *refusal* on the part of a significant number of contemporary artists towards the basic institutions of the capitalist art market. What is debatable, however, is the extent to which this tendency represents a social (indeed a *socialist*) analysis of the institutions and cultural ideology of capitalism despite a vociferous quasi-Marxist rhetoric. What is also debatable, though less obviously so for reasons that I trust will shortly become apparent, is the extent that this tendency springs from a collective rather than an individual motivation, from a shift in the consciousness of the art community rather than from the re-affirmation (though no doubt an unconscious and last-ditch one) of the old bohemian imperatives of personal creative volunteerism.

Though largely an inchoate phenomenon (mingling, at its extreme, social utopianism and a sort of disillusionment engendered by the recognition of failed promises – idealist anarchism and sour grapes), this current has, over the last decade, peaked in various ways across a spectrum that stretches from organised demonstration and confrontation to various sequential attempts at formulating fora for debates and introspective analysis.[2] I have said: "over the last decade . . .", and it would not seem to be insignificant that we are now at a point exactly ten years after the confused events that ran like a cultural bush-fire through the capitalist world and climaxed in Paris, in May 1968.

It has taken *that* long for the unformulated and reflexive refusal towards a certain structure of ideological assumptions to begin to develop effectively into an analysis of the nature of culture and the role of art at this present stage of the evolution of capitalism. This Spring will doubtless provide a focal point for both the re-assessment of the "meaning" of 1968 and for the consolidation of strategies that are applicable to the realities of late capitalism.

The word *realities* is here emphasised, since it seems in retrospect that 1968 may have indicated only the *apparent* rejection of a socio-cultural system that concretized and justified the commodicisation of culture. One reason for this suspicion, in the broad arena, lies in the remarkably rapid breakdown of "The Movement", in the apparent *volte-face*, the withdrawal, in many cases into quasi-mystical subjectivism and ecological mystification. One would rightly expect any serious critique of capitalist cultural ideology to have demonstrated more stamina in failure, and to have demanded in the first place a more solid reward than that of an "instant" political gratification.

Another reason for this suspicion may be observed in the field of our own professional interest. It has often been claimed that the phenomenon of the "dematerialization" of art springs essentially from a political response on the part of the artist

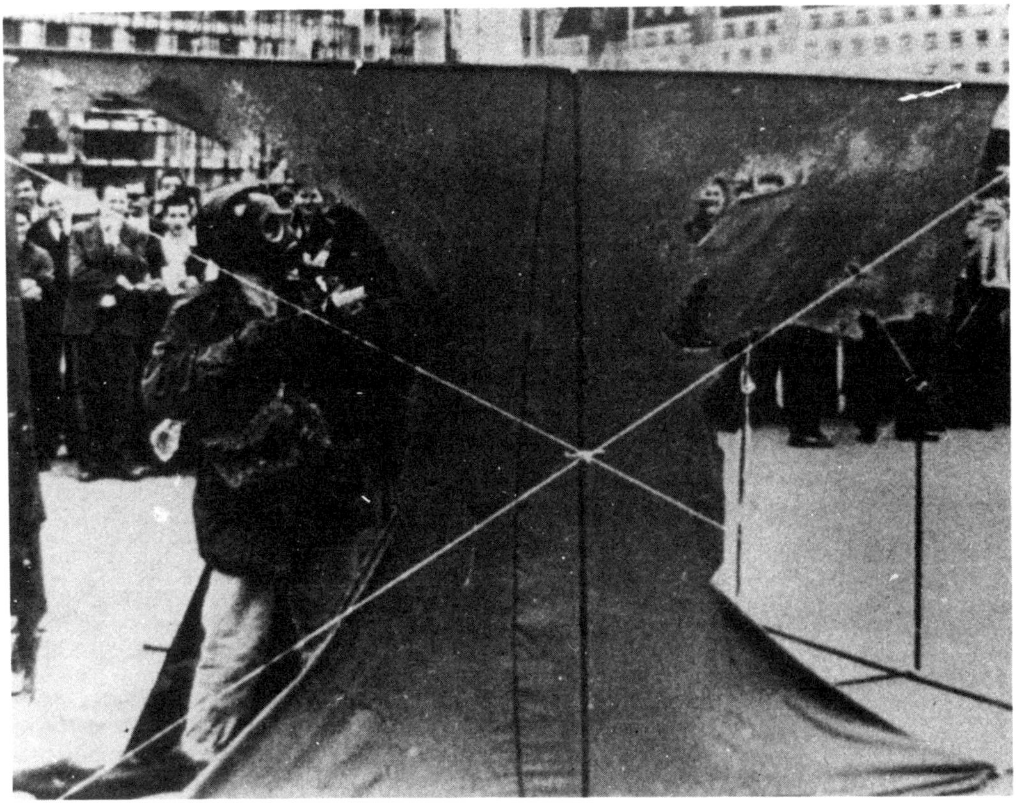

Gustav Metzger:
demonstration Auto-Destructive Art,
London, 3.7.1961

who, in rejecting the traditional and capitalist structures of the art market, opposes a "cabal" of dealers, critics and speculators, and, consequently, attempts to produce purely conceptual and non-material works of art that cannot be bought or sold. In this case, one would rightly expect to note the wide emergence of a political (or at least a *social*) content in the growing complex of concept-orientated work.

As is well known, with very few, though highly visible, exceptions (Beuys, Vostell, Metzger, Haacke – all European, incidentally)[3] this did not happen. Even the claims to have accepted the challenge of non-material art to provide, as Lucy Lippard would have it, "a drastic solution to the problems of artists being bought and sold so easily along with their art",[4] erodes quickly in the face of subsequent events. Rather than providing a defensive "block" of purely creative integrity, the de-materialized work of art was easily and quickly assimilated into the capitalist structure of economic relations.

This happened largely because, although the artist may have attempted genuinely for various reasons to withdraw the work itself, the physical art object, from the sphere and domination of the capitalist art market, he did not, at the same time, withdraw himself; that is to say, he did not withdraw his praxis, the process of conceiving, making and manifesting the art object.[5] By trying to transform the object of art and not the process of art, the individual artist found himself trapped in essentially the same relationship as before, isolated in the face of the whole complicated capitalist mechanism of exposure and communication, of audience-recognition, fame and identity. What had not been anticipated (in an attitude that was at best a naive stance, at worst a justification) was the fact that *prestige is also property*. Even the most transparent and rigorously de-materialized works remained stubbornly subservient to the special exigencies of the art market.

It would seem reasonable to observe in both the broad "cultural revolution" of the late 1960s and the specific phenomenon of the de-materialization of art a common reaffirmation of individual subjective imperative which, in terms of the historical fine-art community, has traditionally manifested itself in a particular structure of attitudes that define the fundamental self-view of the artist. This self-view has, of course, throughout the modern period, been essentially structured upon the basic notion of the artist as an individual axiomatically in *opposition* to established social and cultural norms, as representing, in fact, and in his person, the ideal of rebel and hero.

Recognising this fact, it may well be that an analysis of the myth of the artist as rebel and hero, and a further understanding of the dialectical relationship of this myth to what we must call the "ideology" of the avant-garde (for clearly such a myth dictates historical events as much as it illuminates them) can help clarify the specific problems that presently confront us; and do this not merely, may I add, in critical or socio-historical terms, but also in respect to the more central question of current studio praxis.

Obviously, a necessarily short and diverse paper such as this cannot possibly indicate even the flimsiest structural framework of such an analysis as I am here indicating. I merely hope in this instance to draw your attention to the potential that may lie in this direction, as well as to indicate (in the context of a rapidly changing social and political climate) that, though there appears to be a new understanding of the nature of the art work that is presently emerging, there would not yet seem to be a clear concomitant reassessment of the artist's self-view.

I assume that we may (here, at least) accept the fundamental notion that art is a social activity, and that the manifestations of art are relative – mutating in form and essential nature as the broad cultural superstructure resonates to the shifts and developments of the economic base. This perspective inevitably concludes that the *function* of art assumes different forms under different historical conditions, and that it operates (both in regard to the collective consciousness of society and the individual consciousness of man) at any one moment in a manner appropriate to the historical moment.[6]

This, obviously, is a direct contradiction to the generally-held view of the nature of art in our society. It is a negation, not merely of what might be described as an academic, conventional, popular or middle-class understanding of the function and nature of visual culture, but also, it would seem, of certain assumptions central to the most progressive and advanced elements of that culture.

It has become clear in recent years that there is now no longer any essential difference between a "bourgeois" view of art (using the word in its general and classical sense of "middle-class") and an "avant-garde" one. Indeed, the congruence now appears to obviate any effective contemporary use of the latter term other than in a strictly historical sense. We may state that, in a real way, the avant-garde came to an end at the point of this very congruence; and that the term may now only be effectively used in regard to a defined historical period.

The melding of the avant-garde and the middle-class viewpoints has arrived at a consensus concerning the nature of art and of artistic activity. In one sense it is possible to state that the previous minority view central to the advanced art community (which constituted the *ideology* of the avant-garde) has now been absorbed into the larger ideology of contemporary capitalism. As an aside I must remark upon the ambiguity of the term "bourgeois" in this context; as John Berger has recently pointed out, the cultural identity of the bourgeoisie is presently in erosion not before the forces of an emergent proletariat, but in the face of a rising corporate state.[7]

It is an obvious error, therefore, to regard the current demise of the avant-garde as being in any way the result of an appropriation in a manner analogous to the recent commercial appropriation of sub-culture value in the areas of popular music, style and fashion. The expansion and acceptance of modern art in the capitalist world is clearly not simply the result of a speculative process, of the cultural and financial penetration of the art market and the museo-critical complex. It is, rather, the result of a convergence of opposing value, and it would seem clearly to indicate the cessation of the previous mutual struggle between the bourgeois cultural world-view and that proposed by the avant-garde.

This, however, does not necessarily mean that the struggle has been resolved by an absorption, by the victory or ascension of one structure or value system. It does not even mean (as is suggested by the greater part of contemporary conventional and academic criticism) that abody of advanced ideas, long misunderstood, have now become accepted. What, in fact, has occurred is that one structure, the determinate one, has now ceased to exist, has finally eroded in the face of historical change, and has, consequently, negated the justification for the opposition.[8]

This process has been obscured by the fact that we consistently confuse two separate notions – the idea of *modernism* in the creative arts and the idea of the *avant-garde*. Art history demonstrates a sequential process of cultural development that may be regarded as being analogous to that of increasing technological complexity; there would seem to be little doubt that artistic events, since the point of the Renaissance, anyway, have formed, in effect, a cumulative structure.

In one sense of the idea, we can observe "the modern" existing at any arbitrary point during the last five hundred years or so; we can observe an on-going consciousness of fresh standards continually superseding even those of the immediate past. If we regard Durer, for instance, as being representative of certain aspects of the Northern Renaissance, we cannot help but also see him as a spokesman for a body of vanguard concepts, despite the fact that he seems to have largely misunderstood the ideas emanating from Italian sources.

The process of change in the visual arts, though obviously cross-linked dialectically to all the other domains of both mental and material culture, nevertheless demands and defines its own logic; the logic of a self-conscious and deliberate attempt at innovation. Yet, until comparatively recently, never was this activity at any time conceived in terms of an *opposition* to the cultural conventions of the period; though they were, of course, frequently thought of *in contrast* to the retardaire conventions that were in the process of being superseded.

Even Romanticism (perhaps, especially Romanticism) was an expression of the dominant currents of the period. The very emergence of the idea of the artist as hero – the Byronic ideal – is consistent with the developing exaltation of individuality resultant upon the social and political consolidation of bourgeois society. The Romantic artists were not at odds with the dominant value system, and, neither, essentially, were any of the other artists until comparatively late in the nineteenth century.

There have been many studies of the development of both bohemia and of artistic and social non-conformism, but, to my knowledge, no-one has adequately dealt with the fact that, though this phenomenon took place to a large extent in an artistic milieu, there was a remarkable lack of consistency between social rebellion and artistic innovation.

Indeed, bohemianism, in its earlier stages, remained a purely social response, one dependent, no doubt, upon the alienation experienced by artisans and decorative artists in the emerging industrial and mercantile society. There would seem to have been no correlation whatsoever between a self-view of the artist that did not, in fact, appear until the advent of Symbolism, for it was not until the last quarter of the nineteenth century that the concept *rebel* was to be added to that of *hero*.

Only with the full consolidation of the idea of *art for art's sake* (and how late that finally was may be emphasised by reminding ourselves that Manet disavowed the Impressionists since he still, at that late date, entertained hopes of academic salon acceptance) did "modernism" in art discover itself in total opposition to an established social and cultural value system.

The most striking transference that took place at this point was not so much one between style and content, between formalism and narrative, but one between pictorial culture and the artist's individual self-view. As the art object de-materialized (that is to say, in effect, as it was de-socialized) so the artist institutionalized his stance of rebellious opposition. From the very beginning, from say, as a convenient date, Rimbaud's *Lettre de voyant* of 1871, the new consciousness of the "avant-garde" was to be defined by the merging of two ideas: the commitment to a stylistic modernism increasingly dependent upon internal justification and the commitment to an intransigent opposition to the bourgeois cultural and moral value system.

This was, despite the fact that we are presently conditioned to regard it as a normal, even desirable, combination, a remarkable development, since at no time before has art ever sought values outside of the historically dominant ones of the period in question. The story of the avant-garde is as much the story of the search for these values as it is the story of mutating stylistic elements. With the rejection of historic reality, this search had obviously to be focused upon the various demands of the ideal, upon mysticism, hermeticism and the primitive.

We must now, as I have intimated, regard the avant-garde as a closed historical period. The apostolic succession which we have observed opening with Rimbaud, draws to a close with the generation of Pollock and Dylan Thomas. It is perhaps only in retrospect that we now notice a punctuation mark that divides us today from the heroism, the rebellion *and the confidence* of the Abstract Expressionists. We have certainly taken note of the changed role of art in contemporary society; our very presence here testifies to our disquiet with the concept of art as a simple commodity.

Yet, it is necessary to ask, are we not still looking, to a large extent at the world with eyes and minds conditioned by a self-view that no longer applies? For, quite simple, what application can there be in an ideology that remains based, in any form, in the idea of *epater les bourgeois*, when the bourgeoisie, as a distinct class, no longer exists?

Avant-garde culture, throughout its history, was balanced and opposed by what we can only describe as bourgeois culture. It is notable that this polarization vanished as the avant-garde drew to a close. What remained, for example, of bourgeois visual culture (I think here of an artist like Andrew Wyeth) was inexorably drawn by the new corporate institutions of art, the museo-critical complex, into the post-bourgeois mainstream. The rapid assimilation of avant-garde visual culture is a consequence of the emergence of a post-bourgeois society, of the emergence of the corporate state.

The paradox of the bourgeois world was that it required the artist to assume the role of rebel and hero in order to ritually justify the ideology of competitive individualism while it was necessarily scandalised by the artist as the antithesis of the social conformism required by mercantile society.

It is certain that a specific role was demanded of the artist during his co-existence with bourgeois culture, and the best of our predecessors handled that role with exemplary moral commitment. It is equally certain that this role has been for some time now a clumsy anachronism, devoid of moral scale.

Finally it is certain that we must clarify our individual and collective self-view if we wish to avoid being drawn, as passive agents, into the cultural institutions of the capitalist corporate state. In historically losing the rôle of the artist as rebel and hero, we stand at risk of being embarked upon the role of artist as bureaucrat.

Notes

1. Frederick Jameson, *Marxism and Form*, Princeton New Jersey, Princeton University Press, 1971, pp 306-307.
2. I am thinking here of a sequence, in New York for instance, that spans the period from the Art Workers' Coalition of 1969, *The Fox* and similar polemical journals, up to the formation of the Caucus for Marxism and Art and the present meeting. Similar developments may easily be observed in any developed capitalist country with differing degrees of intensity. The most advanced formulations of this critique (much more advanced than in the United States) have taken place in France and Germany.
3. Although Beuys, Vostell, Metzger, Haacke . . . were exceptions in the context of the emergence of conceptualism and process art, they are obviously not so now, since their example presently offers the basis for a tradition of its own.
4. "I think the art world is probably going to be able to absorb conceptual art as another 'movement' and not pay much attention to it. The art establishment depends so greatly on objects which can be bought and sold that I don't expect it to do much about an art that is opposed to the prevailing systems . . . The artists who are trying to do non-object art are introducing a drastic solution to the problems of artists being bought and sold so easily along with their art . . ." Lucy Lippard, *Six Years: The Dematerialization of the Art Object*, Praeger, New York, 1973, pp 7-8.
5. By and large (as an examination of the majority of artists' statements contained in Lippard's book) the motivation would seem to have been a subjectivist and personal one.
6. Care should be taken here to understand this in a dialectical context, not as a form of determination, not (most certainly not) as the type of reflective theory common to so many art-history text books which maintain a direct and vulgar relationship between events in art and the sphere of politics and material culture. I am thinking here of the banality (indeed the essential falsity) of the synoptic tables in Janson.
7. John Berger, *Ways of Seeing*, BBC and Penguin Books, London 1972, p 32.
8. The erosion of the struggle between bourgeois culture and the avant-garde raises an interesting and crucial problem. The determinate factor of that struggle was the imperative towards constant innovation. This process, traditionally, has always operated within the domain of style. The fact that there has been no significant *stylistic* 'jump' for some years would appear to bear out the central contention. Nevertheless, impetus towards innovation itself (just as the basic self-view of the artist as rebel and hero) does not yet seem to have cancelled out. Following upon the erosion of style (or the transcension of it, if you will) we note the imperatives of the new penetrating into conceptual and process areas. This 'innovation' would, in turn, currently appear to be giving way to a social dimension, a latter-day polit-art. It would seem that there is a very real risk that aspects of the new socio-political consciousness in the fine arts may be nothing more than a substitue for stylistic innovation. As an aside to this, we may also consider the following: if bourgeois culture has not been subsumed into the new culture of the corporate state, the old hostility of the avant-garde becomes irrelevant. Indeed, should this hostility even move from the social to the political plane, there would seem to be no real threat offered to the capitalist status-quo. As long as vanguard culture focuses its hostility upon the target of an effectively defunct bourgeoisie culture, it will be tolerated. Can we not therefore see that many aspects of the present developments constitute a permitted, even an encouraged, safety-valve? The fact that this phenomenon is operating so strongly within structured academic institutions would suggest that this might be so.

Back Cover: A poster by Juan Munoz, from the BAGHDAD INTERNATIONAL POSTER EXHIBITION '79 organised by The Iraqi Cultural Centre, London, where it was held recently. The exhibition will be shown in Baghdad in May 1979.

ART AUCTION

The African National Congress (the liberation movement of South Africa) is organising an art exhibition and auction sale to take place on Sunday June 17th at the Africa Centre, King Street, London WC2. The proceeds will go to help build and equip a school for South African students which is being built, largely by the students themselves, in Tanzania on land given by the Tanzanian government. The students, mostly in their teens, were forced to flee South Africa after taking part in the 1976 Soweto uprising against the enforced Bantu education and the system of Apartheid.

Any artist wishing to donate a work to the exhibition and sale, or participate in other ways, should write to the ANC at 28 Penton Street, London N1 9PR; or for further information, contact Nancy White (Tel: 01-607 4510). Works should be sent in, or be ready for collection, by May 21.

Parakrama Kodituwakku

A SRI LANKAN POET AND HIS PEOPLE

Susil Sirivardana

Behind the white faces
carrying the naked tots
giving biscuits and toffees
is only exploitation
swollen like molten metal
stinking like excreta . . .

cries out a man of the people, a worker, fighting the rape of a great forest, once a virgin, and the pollution of a local river, once a source of life.

A poor peasant girl, in love with learning, is torn by the tensions of not having a frock to wear for the school. She is absorbing the history of human struggle, is poising for a militant womanhood:

It's not on your wedding night
that you'll become a woman
but tonight when you learn human history
and come into our midst tomorrow!

A young farmer prays to the sun:

Give us time to roof the house
myriad the things yet to be mastered.

And the New Man, ideologically equipped to transform the villagers and the village, says:

Let us all come close to one another
let us all become equal
. . . let us build a new society
that will breed fine human ways and qualities

This is how the Sri Lankan poet Parakrama Kodituwakku *sees and identifies with* his people.

Although since independence, in 1948, Sri Lanka has been a neo-colony, the people themselves have been struggling to give a new content to the political, economic, social and cultural aspects of their life, with a national identity and new dignity. Today, when a large part of capitalist Asia is in the grip of dictatorships, Sri Lanka has been able to sustain its democratic institutions to a signficant degree. This is not to say that in recent times these structures have not been under pressure. Economically, while the country has staved off widespread starvation, it has dramatically failed to realize its vast agricultural potentials. Though a small island with 14.5 million people, both from a strategic and commercial point of view, she is sensitively located in the Indian Ocean. Thus it has been particularly exposed to imperialist influences.

It is this social reality of Sri Lanka, relations of exploitation and oppression — both internal and external, that Kodituwakku confronts and articulates in his work.

Before we deal with the work of Kodituwakku in particular, it would be useful to have a quick look at the historical background of Sri Lanka. Sri Lanka made a tremendous contribution to world culture, during the feudal times, through its great achievements in irrigation engineering, its Anuradhapura and Polonnaruwa cultures, its tradition of Therevada Buddhism and its indigenous Tamil Hindu culture. In later feudal times, its indigenous dancing and dance music, its folk literature, the masks of its exorcistic rituals and folk theatre, the folk theatre itself and the temple fresco paintings have made a distinctive contribution. It is important to realize here that the national history of Sri Lanka is composed of a *unified mainstream* drawn from the majority Sinhala community as well as the Tamil and Muslim minority communities.

Between 1505 and 1948, Sri Lanka underwent 350 years of respective Portuguese, Dutch and British colonial rule.

However, there has been a movement towards the development of a new culture, national in form and scientific in content, as part and parcel of the cultural mainstream of the last hundred years, with inputs from three equally indigenous traditions — Sinhala, Tamil and Islamic. As far as literature goes, the Sinhala people express themselves in Tamil. However, we will be discussing here only the Sinhalese contribution to the mainstream, concentrating on poetry but at the same time keeping a look on the whole cultural spectrum.

The period from the 1870s to the 1930s can be taken as a whole, as it has features of continuity and homogeneity. During this period, the political struggle against colonialism often expressed itself in a cultural form. The leading poet of this period, like Ariya Rajakaruna, G.H.Perera, Piyadasa Sirisena . . . , fully participated in a whole range of activities which were both cultural and political. They returned to the source of Sinhala poetry, revived the tradition and gave a valuable perspective to national history through their own poetry. However, while they were patently anti-colonialist and patriotic, their understanding of the nature of colonialism was not profound; and therefore they made certain concessions. But their success lay in channelling the anti-colonialist impulses of the people and helping to keep their consciousness focused on this struggle. They were also producers, in the sense that the developed the cultural productive forces — the readership itself, the printing presses, the theatres, the educational texts, newspapers, periodicals and new literary forms, like the short story and novel. There is no doubt that this mainstream served the interests and needs of the majority of the people.

The second period stretches from the 1930s to the 1960s. Internal contradictions begin to mature side by side the external ones. First, the literary mainstream was split up into a popular or populist movement and an elitist sub-stream. Secondly, the elitist sub-stream in particular, and sometimes even the whole mainstream, dissociated themselves completely from the political struggle. An important reason for this was that the working class movement at the time dramatically failed to understand the whole cultural question, and therefore it failed to positively motivate potential writers.

The leading mainstream poets of the second period, like Wimalaratna Kumaragama, Sagara Palansuriya, Alwis Perera, Mundisa Cumaratunga and Bhikku Mahinda, strived vigorously to grasp the social reality of their time. While they continued the mainstream tradition of the earlier period and introduced innovations in form and content, none of them attempted a fundamental critique of their society. Again, they lacked the consciousness to undertake that task. However, the achievement of the finest of them, Kumaragama, is substantial. He made a brilliant and sensitive examination of the travails of village life and then branched off into the scrutiny of individual relationships, reaching great depth and complexity. A man firmly grounded in the life and traditions of the country; even his studies of personal relationships are enriched by the context in which he situates them.

If the mainstream poets had their roots in the people, the substream poets had theirs in the mind. They drew substance from their university education and careers, and also from their absorption of modern European literature and criticism. Lacking the experience of developing expanding social relations with their people, they sought authenticity and identity in the psyche and foreign literary models. They individualised values and moral categories. The content of their work lies in a privatisation of reality, in a sick psychologism and a vision of loneliness and defeat vis-a-vis the mainstream of society. But by virtue of their access to power and preferment, they were able to obtain the key levers in the cultural establishment (the higher education centres, the press, the radio and the cultural bureaucracy). Thus, for a short time — from the early 1950s to the end of the 1960s, this sub-stream usurped the place of the mainstream. Gunadasa Amerasekera, Siri Gunasinghe, Wimal Dissanayake and G.B. Senanayake are some of the leading poets of this period.

Before moving on to the third phase to which Kodituwakku belongs, we should take stock of the nature of cultural underdevelopment in Sri Lanka. This is manifested in the relative or total inability of artists and writers to pose to themselves certain vital questions, about the relationship of art and culture with politics, about decolonization from colonialism as well as neo-colonialism, about the nature of bourgeois values, about the role of internal and external factors in national history and the great struggle for democracy throughout the Third World. And who makes history? One writer who did ask these questions is Martin Wickramasinghe, whose essays and novels offer a rich self-image of the contradictions in Sri Lankan society. Among the poets, we should also mention Mahagama Sekera as the one artist who came near to making a comparable effort.

The threshold of the third phase was the General Election of 1970, when the democratic movement reached a higher level of development. The new democratic forces that were released at the time, made many positive and relatively advanced demands in many spheres of national life. In the cultural sphere there was an intense debate, and during this debate the slogans like "A People's Culture' and 'A People's Art and Literature' were concretely formulated. Both, the demands as well as the subsequent struggle — the Insurrection of April 1971 included — reflect the fact that there had been a distinctive advance in the consciousness of the people.

The cultural history of the 1970s is the story of the growth of the "People's Culture" movement. There have been major changes of direction in almost every field of artistic activity. Many of the writers and artists who belong to this movement come from the petit bourgeoisie, but they have been trying to make a transformation in their consciousness; whereby they have been able to identify themselves with the struggles of the oppressed people. *Recognising this immense experience as their base, they have tried to define and express various facets of that social reality.* The first few years showed much spontaneity. Now the movement is in struggle to deepen and strengthen itself.

Kodituwakku and several other fellow poets are a fine index of this new direction. Poets like Monica Ruwanpathirana, Buddhadasa Galappaththy, Berty B. Kudahetty, W.A. Abeysinghe, Senerath Tennekoon, Denegama Siriwardena and Pushpa Ramalani Ratnayake have been producing some good work. Among the older poets, the achievement of Mahagama Sekera stands out as the case of an artist who transformed himself by carefully listening to the call of the people. Kodituwakku himself has come out to vindicate Sekera's place as a major poet who wrote for the people, and called his last work, Prabuddha (The sage, 1977), published posthumously, a great long poem. The other older poets like Gunadasa Amerasekera and Wimal Dissanayake were silent for some time, but they have been trying now to come to terms with the changed environment in their recent work.

To read Kodituwakku's poems is to encounter a fresh and distinctive content. The particular actions that sustain each of his poems are grounded in Sri Lankan social reality. In fact Sri Lankan society is, as it were, the chief actor of his work. In most of his poems the poet has boldly ventured out into the fields and experiences which, in an ideological sense, are crying out for recognition and redefinition. And he has expressed them in a variety of subjects: the inhumanity of feudal society (*Pina, the Pot-Seller*); the youth drain from the village (*For the Brother who went to the University*); revaluation of the role of woman (*Woman*); the responsibility of the artist (*Depict Reality*); the exploitation of the farmers (*Moving with the Water*); Sinhala-Tamil unity (*One of Us*); etc., etc . . . His intellectual approach and spiritual quest involve a continuous questioning and challenging of the received ideas, discovering of obscured achievements of working class people and unearthing their potentialities, keeping a balance between negative and positive, and, through a process of sharp analysis, coming up with answers and alternatives. *In fact on reading Kodituwakku's work one feels that here is a mind that is engaged in a thorough-going analysis and critique of his society.*

His poems have the quality of being saturated with the experience of society; and their specificity lies in the *social* quality of the experience treated. How is this done? This is done by a deft balancing of individual and social experiences, or by their intertwining in a state of mutual tension. Every subjective response is plumbed to its objective, social depth. In other words, nothing is privatised, nothing is treated merely on the plane of the individual. The individual experience is often the suggestion of something else or a point of departure, and it is probed and pressed out in an expanding exploration. This is not done in the manner of a sociologist, but by using the method of the poet — selecting experience, crystallising and compressing it, and then wroughting it into wholes where thought and feeling are fused. This probing has a definite direction: it is always moving outwards from the individual (the particular) to the social (the general). This discipline reaches its most developed practice in his third and latest book, *The New Man Has Come* (1975).

There are certain recurring perspectives that make up the content of his work. The first of them is struggle and liberation from oppressive structures. Here conventional wisdom is ruthlessly questioned. Second is the fact of change and movement, of a journey to a yet unrealised ideal but whose seeds have begun to germinate. Thirdly, the personalities in his poems are not simply mere characters, but are really social emblems. Fourthly, there is the awareness of building anew, construction and growth. Here it is very much the case of some suppressed potential being released or the promise of such a release. Fifthly, his poems have a parable-like didactic quality. The poems create consciousness. Finally, there is an immediacy and particularity of experience, the feeling that the poet has himself deeply felt what he is writing about. It is the combination of all these elements that make up the dynamic in Kodituwakku's poetry.

In the formal quality of his poems, Kodituwakku exhibits both craftsmanship and sensitivity. This lies behind the apparent simplicity. The formal aspects appear simple, because *the poet is very clear about for whom* he writes poetry. He would hate mystification and distraction. He uses a short lyrical form as well as a longer narrative form. In both, the form is emphatically determined by the content. While the lyric is used to crystallise and emblemize a theme within a limited compass, the narrative form is used to evoke a setting or a context, dramatising an action and then pursuing the tensions of a debate towards the resolution. Most of his work is written in free verse, using conversational speech rhythms, but he also uses selectively the numerous traditional metrical forms. *Pina, the Pot-Seller*, one of his finest short poems, is in rhymed quatrains. But he often interposes a rhymed verse in a free verse form for variety and enrichment.

His ample use of local imagery, allusions and myth is another aspect of his craft. This is very evident in *A Petition about the Sinharaja Worksite*. His clever use of very commonplace symbols for telling 'blow-ups' is noteworthy. In *Oh Sun, Please Stay A While* several preceding metaphors conjure up a whole village or region, and the final symbol of the 'roof' so clearly suggests the vast construction effort that the people have undertaken. Kodituwakku has also made a deep study of the formal features of the folk poem. His brilliant use of simile recalls the folk tradition. In his fine little lyric, named *Seenamalie* (like Kusumawathie, the name of a young girl), which is about the tragedy of a poor village girl who goes to the town to be a servant and who comes back home pregnant, he says, in the final lines, that when she left the village she was like the Botanical Gardens at Peradeniya but when she returned she was like the ruined city of Anuradhapura.

Kodituwakku's first book, *Younger Brother* (1972), was dedicated as: "Brothers and comrades! How can I tell you that all that is in these poems is imaginary? To whom else apart from you can I dedicate them?" Quite a few poems in this book are about psychological conflicts and themes, though they are placed within a wider context. The second book, *The World of a Disobedient Son* (1974), reflects a great concern about the social and political situation. In his third and latest book, *The New Man Has Come* (1975), he has further developed this trend; as he dedicates it to "The patriotic people — that this may be a weapon in their struggle against imperialism!" The movement from the psychological to specifically social and political, has heightened the interest of people in his work. It is not merely that the focus has been changed, but the whole outlook has matured to encompass the historical, the moral, the personal and the political in a developing national context.

Ever since he published his first book in 1972, Kodituwakku has been playing an influential and vanguard role as a critic and publicist. He has been taking clear positions on all subjects in the national cultural debate. In 1975 he sparked off a protracted debate on feudal literature in the main Sinhala language daily paper; and at the same time defining his conception of a people's culture:

> "I believe that in order to renew our village cultural inheritance, which went through a process of erosion because of the catastrophic impact of feudal culture and colonial aggression, the slogan 'A People's Literature' is the correct one for the time. . ."

and

> "That is the process of eroding the old society and building the new. In the 'People's Art' that is created out of these two processes, a revolutionary quality that was absent in the 'folk art' of feudal society should be present. That must be so because the basis for people's art which will really serve the majority of the people, is socialist humanism and socialist philosophy."
> (*On Feudal Culture*, 1976)

His other writings range from newspaper articles on literature and culture, his series of newspaper sketches on village life called 'A Voice from the Village', to his four articles in the progressive cultural magazine, *Mavatha.*

Being so firmly grounded in the reality of the people among whom he lives, Kodituwakku has been able to fertilise the whole debate about a people's culture, which commenced in the early '70s. Not only has he made significant contributions defining an ideology of a people's culture, he has been a practitioner of the imperative which seeks to link the cultural movement to the political movement. He has been able to bear witness to the experience of the village with a new authenticity.

He has also been searching for a new method of criticism, with a new set of concepts and values, which, while not mystifying or over-simplifying reality, will broaden and deepen the literary experience for the majority of readers. This has entailed not only the difficult task of introducing new concepts and categories but of testing them out in a practice, shaping Sinhala equivalents in such a way that they are also convincingly clear to the non-English speaking reader. He has thus been able to develop a totalistic outlook, which has enabled him to embark on a critique of whole society, with a combination of scholarship and creative writing, in addition to his life as a teacher and an active political worker.

To conclude, Kodituwakku is a poet and writer of the Third World. He and his progressive writer sisters and brothers join together in the community of the writers which is numerically the largest in the world, and which is historically and potentially the most pregnant for the future. The progressive writers of the Third World are identifying their art with the liberation struggles, and are thus creating new values and self-images, both equally revolutionary. Therefore Kodituwakku stands shoulder to shoulder and spirit to spirit with Kim Chi Ha, Said Zahari, Ngugi wa Thiongo's, Sembene Ousmane, Nicolas Guillen, Gabriel Garcia Marquez, to mention a few names, who have taken up parallel challenges in their own national situations. What is common to them all are the different cultural traditions and stages of development of the national struggles in their respective societies. However, they do perceive the responsibility of the artist in the same way, manifesting in their universality — human simplicity, humility, courage and labour.

Finally, a word about Kodituwakku the person. In his late thirties, he is married and has one son. He has been a teacher in the village areas all his working life; and he has sworn that he will never leave teaching in the village for anything else. Thus he has remained loyal to the countryside of Sri Lanka where he was born and bred. For a long time, he has been living and working in the District of Ratnapura, which is about 60 miles from the capital. In 1977, when a new left-oriented political party called the People's Democratic Party was formed, he was elected its Cultural Secretary.

Let us conclude with a farewell from the poet himself. The last poem in his latest book is called *To All Who Write To Me* and is addressed to his readers. It ends:

> **Priests and pundits**
> **never, never hold your cry.**
> **Your cry that muffles the thunder**
> **is the true cry of the people.**
> **From a hundred prisons**
> **unfailingly, I will answer you.**
> **Where the struggle is**
> **there we will surely meet again!**

****

OH SUN, PLEASE STAY A WHILE

Father is still working . . . . .
Tired out early
I was resting my head
on the grass floor in the *chena**
and gazing out afar . . . . .

Like silvery edges
the grass-blades stick up
along the shirt sleeve
a red ant strolls
bird beaks open
and a song drops down
splicing the earth's crust
the Bindu flowers hop out.

Bestowing alms with its saffron yolk
the sun approaches reverently.

Oh sun, stay a while
say my thoughts like a child's;
oh sun, please stay a while.

The roads are only half cut
the letters only half written
only half the song is sung
the book's unread pages still many
the journey's not over, the way's still long,
and the flowers only half bloomed.
Give us time to roof the house
myriad the things yet to be mastered.

Oh sun, please, stay a while.

* a shifting cultivation plot.

A NEW MAN CAME AND WENT

At dawn
when the sun
strikes the latched door
you came . . . . . .

WHO'S THAT?

In half-sleep we opened the door.

YOU.

You stood with a smile . . . . . .

To the village people come and go.
One of them, you too,
with a morose face —
that's what we thought.

But I doubted —
ruffled hair
drawn face tea-coloured
and deep-sunk eyes
had a strange significance —
the quivering brilliance
of a waterfall
illumined with a single thought.

During the day
we had here
the cry of the red-eyed cuckoo
path-blind and drifting:
we had here
only the wind's howl
rubbing the crevices of crumbling hills.

. . . . . . in their midst
your words had
a new vibrancy
never heard before
words as unpretentious
as a betel-chew.
Yet these words contained
an astringency that mined the mind.

You spoke to us
"Comrade-brothers"
such a warm and sympathetic word
never had we heard before.

". . . . . . Let us all come close to one another
let us all become equal
and to solve our problems
let us all work in a new way
with courage
with toil
overcoming obstacles
and go forwards . . . . . .
Let us build a new society
that will breed fine human ways and qualities"

That's how you talked
that's also how you acted.
Children trapped amidst desk bench and book
you led out
along roads and slopes and fieldbunds
up hills and under trees
with freedom to become birds
to see and absorb everything the world over.

Wherever there was a problem, trouble,
you were unfailingly there.
In the centre of our shadow you stood
our comrade
like an elder brother
one of our very own.

The day the village Youth Club started
with you there
we felt all the cells in our bodies
coming alive:
that day, we were wet with excitement
of rivers of electric young hopes,
of the great benedictory rains.

You are the one who taught us
to uproot the old weeds
and in their stead
plant
fertile new seed.

"To kindle a new fire
and cook
the first after-harvest rice meal,
let us work together."

Insults slanders abuses
from antagonists
were for you "mere trifles".

On the day
a foe
had felled and cut up hundreds of banana trees
in the farm
and they lay prone like corpses,
you bellowed out shaking with fury

"Reactionaries
deceivers
bastards"
insensate
fists raised in challenge.

The day after you yourself said
"To be emotional like that
is not the correct way."

"Withstanding everything courageously
let us readjust ourselves
and get down to work."

On every furrow of village soil
like oil
here there
were fallen
your ideas.
Amongst us you spread
like a fever
like a fragrance.

On the day you were going on transfer
"Let us meet again and again" you said
without any change in your voice.

And you went.

Though you have gone
we keep changing.
The wind's voice is now strange
trees embellished with fresh leaves
cloud-thick the village-sky is lovely
beneath the gloom, light appears here there
the radiance of your eyes has rubbed on everything.
Day after day
we meet you within us
as a new man
when we open the door to the sun
at dawn !

Poems translated by Susil Sirivardana © 1979

Cultural Colonialism: a discussion

Guy Brett/ Kenneth Coutts-Smith

Isn't really true that "the assumptions of modern art are fundamentally of a Eurocentric character..."? (Our emphasis). Guy Brett doesn't think so; and yet Kenneth Coutts-Smith find himself "in overall agreement with his basic position". How are we to resolve this contradiction or confusion? Coutts-Smith has, of course, clarified his position by reiterating his original thesis, but it would have been better if he had concentrated on what we beleive is the basic difference between their two positions.

The difference really is not of their different attitudes toawrds the development of truly international socialist art and culture, nor is it a question of different emphasis. It is really to do with the understanding of what constitutes Eurocentricity, how and from what angle one looks at it. While Coutts-Smith has penetrated behind the deceptive facade of European development since the Renaissance and has rightly put his finger on its real content as well as its historical dynamics, Brett is looking only at the formal transformations that have taken place in modern history. And since these formal transformations contain non-European material he has mistakenly taken this as a sign of something that has defied European ethnocentricity and offered a progressive outlook to the whole world. The fact is, while Europe uses material from all over the world in its transformation, its basic orientation remains beneficial only to Europe. In other words, its development is oriented towards its own centre and objectives.

Now let us take the analogy of science, which Guy Brett has himself put forward in favour of his argument. Here it would be important to differentiate between 'science', and for that matter 'art', as an objective knowledge, and the nature of its specific development in a specific period of human history. And therefore when we talk about modern science or art we should not see its development removed from its historical dynamics, and this is the only way to reach its essence.

There is no doubt that the scientific development in modern Europe was part of its progressive forces, and there has always been reactionary opposition to it, in the same way there has been reactionary opposition to the development of new and radical ideas in art; and in fact it was this conflict between the progressive and reactionary forces that provided a dynamic for its continuous development. However, in spite of the fact that the material source for this development did not, and does not, come from within but from Europe's relationship with the rest of the world which it has colonised, its progressive forces did not and do not necessarily offer a progressive outlook to the whole world. On the contrary the modern development in science or art is directly responsible for the lack of similar development in the rest of the world.

What do we then mean when we talk of internationalism and progressiveness of modern science and art? Of course we recognise that scientific, and for that matter artistic, developments contain within themselves aspects which are universal and which could be beneficial to all mankind. But that is not an argument here at all. The question really is: how does the progressiveness of an individual, contained by an ideology which is Eurocentric and imperialistic, offer a world-view which is truly international?

Now let us take a specific example. Gauguin was a 'progressive' artist. He spent most of his last years in Tahiti, in sympathetic relationship with Tahitans. He painted them, and perhaps he was genuinely in love with them. At the same time he also hated French colonislism. But what does his work of Tahiti say? Guy Brett says that "Gauguin's world-view must be judged by the plastic values of his paintings." What does this really mean? Can we really separate the plastic values of his work from the way he looked at and depicted Tahitans? Brett does not explain how Gauguin's world-view, expressed in his art, is different from the bourgeois world-view of the time? Is it not true, in fact, that Gauguin, in spite of his plastic innovations and progressiveness and his great sympathy for his subjects, conforms to the world-view that looked upon Tahitans as noble savages (perhaps he also considered himself a noble savage), living a paradisaical existence under the paternalistic and beneficent French colonialism? Was there no resistance, physical psychological, to the French rule? Were the Tahitans really so passive as they look in Gauguin's paintings?

It is not to denounce here an individual for his failure to offer a world-view which is truly in opposition to the Eurocentric imperialist world-view, but to look critically at the underlying causes of this failure. Therefore it is essential that we do not restrict ourselves to the formal level of a reality, which deceptively offers an international outlook, but we must examine its content, context and orientation, so that we can undersatnd the past and develop a truly international world-view that identifies the aspirations of the oppressed people all over the world.

The purpose of this short note, however, was not to deal with all the aspects of this issue. It was merely to introduce, and determine the direction of, this debate which we think is very imporatnt. We shall continue this debate in the future issues, depending of course on your response.

Talk about the 'internationalism' of modern art has been so facile, and has so often obviously hidden the imperialist motives of powerful countries, that it needs to be exposed, as Kenneth Coutts-Smith sets out to do in his article on *Cultural Colonialism* (which was first given suitably to an international meeting of art critics — and published in *Black Phoenix 2*). But this cultural colonialism in its turn also needs to be carefully defined, in order to help in the struggle for an internationalism which is really progressive and liberating. It seems to me that Kenneth Coutts-Smith's analysis is too crude and mechanical actually to provide weapons in this struggle.

Coutts-Smith lays it down that "the assumptions of modern art are fundamentally of a Eurocentric character and are ultimately limited to a specific world-view that is defined by the nature of the dominant class in the capitalist world".

This is to set the European world against the colonised world in a completely monolithic way. For Coutts-Smith, European artists without exception for the last 150 years or so share the outlook and values of the imperialist system. Their interest in the cultures of the colonised peoples, and in non-European cultures generally, can only be described with the metaphors of imperialist aggression. They "co-opt" and "ransack" other cultures, they only want to "secure for themselves some cultural territory to exploit". Really, he is using such metaphors with great insensitivity! He fails to make any distinction of attitude or stand taken in their work by different artists, and therefore supposes they all share, consciously or unconsciously, the world-view of the ruling class and of capitalism-imperialism. He fails to see that these questions of attitude towards "other culture" are intimately related to artistic and ideological struggles taking place inside the European powers themselves.

In many ways Coutts-Smith is repeating the old argument that modern art is *an expression* of the bourgeoisie in its period of decline, an expression of the decadence of the West. Despite his Marxist terminology he takes a position rather similar to Paul Valery's around 1919, as Max Raphael paraphrased it in his brilliant essay *The Struggle to Understand Art*: "European man, in whose mind the ideas, arts, and cultures of all nations and ages flow together as into a common market; European man, culturally rotten to the core, has become incapable of spiritual production: such is Paul Valery's View."

Max Raphael, who disagrees with this, goes on to say: **"It is a fact that since 1870 the dogma of the supreme or exclusive values of classical antiquity and the Renaissance has collapsed. Not only Gothic and Baroque art, but also the arts of China, Japan, India, Asia Minor, Egypt, the African Negro tribes, the North American Indians, Mexico, South America and the South Seas, are felt to be closer to us today than the art of the Renaissance . . . For the theory of art these new developments have been very fruitful . . ."**

Coutts-Smith presents this "confluence of cultures" in modern art *exclusively* as a reflection of cultural colonialism and bourgeois values. Actually it has two sides, and expresses two attitudes. One is reactionary, predatory and nostalgic. The other is revolutionary and treats this phenomenon as part of an emerging new world.

In order to consider the position of artists, I believe it is necessary to look at the situation first under 'classic' colonialism, the period of direct domination when the culture of the colonised people was despised (at the same time that its precious objects were plundered); and the more recent and contemporary period of neo-colonialism, where 'other cultures' are recognised but only within the framework of economic dependence.

It goes without saying that European artists were made aware of the art of other peoples as a result of colonial conquest and plunder. But their attitudes towards it were often different from prevailing opinion. There has always been to some extent an internationalism in art rather of the same kind that J.D.Bernal has described for science: **"The internationalism of science is one of its most specific characteristics. Science has been from the start international in the sense that men of scientific temper, even in the most primitive times, were willing to learn from others in different tribes and races."**

When Durer in 1521 saw the works of Aztec art brought to Europe as tribute to the Emperor Charles V, he didn't share the view that these were just fabulous metal or evidence of the savagery of the Mexicans, but his "artistic temper" was excited and he saw them as the works of brother artists for whom he had the most profound respect: **"And in all the days of my life I have seen nothing that has so rejoiced my heart as these things. For I saw among them strange and exquisitely worked objects and marvelled at the subtle genius of men in distant lands. The things I saw there I have no words to express."**

But of course, whatever Durer's sympathy, the Indian artists were not given the opportunity for such disinterested appraisal and exchange of ideas! they were forced to adopt Western artistic styles by the Spanish as an integral part of their own subjection.

In the 19th century, as colonialism grew and the diversity of non-European art was more and more revealed to Europeans, the attitudes of artists towards them also diversified and varied in a way which sharply expressed their differences of world-view. What distinguishes the attitude of a Victorian genre painter — a Poynter for example — who takes an exotic Eastern interior with marble and ferns for his upper-class pornography, and, for example, Gauguin's paintings in Tahiti is a world of difference and a difference of world-view. Of course Gauguin's position is complex and contradictory. His vision of Tahiti may be romantic, Rousseauesque; it may be the dream of a man escaping from cold, grasping, bourgeois Europe. But it is also the vision of a man who saw and hated French colonialism at first hand. He made no apology for it whatsoever. His hatred is not expressed directly (for no colonialist ever appears in his pictures) but indirectly by his love for the Tahitans and his efforts to move closer to them. Gauguin can be criticised for romance, for inaccuracy; but what does this mean? He was not making an anthropological 'case-study'. In fact, formally speaking, Gauguin's paintings "of Tahiti" are deeply influenced by his love of the stone reliefs of the buddhist temple of Barobadur in Central Java . . . Gauguin's world-view must be judged in the plastic values of his paintings. When one compares his work with that of the Victorian genre painter, one sees that the Victorian's artistic philistinism is closely connected with his Eurocentricity.

There are not only differences between artists, but there are differences within the work of individuals. One can see this if one looks at the paintings of Matisse at different periods of his life, especially in the way he made use of the influence of Islamic art. There is a clear difference between the paintings of the period of the *Red Studio*, for example, and paintings from his 1930s *Odalisques* period. The first is both more exploratory in terms of his own paintings, more emancipated, and also gives more insight into Islamic art, than the second where the Moorishness is a thing of decor, an accessory to a bourgeois life.

The more closely you look, the more it seems true that those artists and others more superficial in their attitudes to non-European cultures, more concerned with externals, with adopting what could be adapted to the lifestyle of the European ruling class, therefore more ethnocentric, were also artists who contributed less to the development of art; whereas the great innovators, stylistic innovators, were also those with a deeper understanding of other cultures. For them, the idea of 'modernism' seemed intimately connected both with the rejection of bourgeois academicism and the rejection of ethnocentricity.

Of course again it is contradiction, paradox. They were *European* artists, inheriting, and struggling against, their tradition. This is their

Paul Gauguan *Nafea Foa Ipoipo* 1892

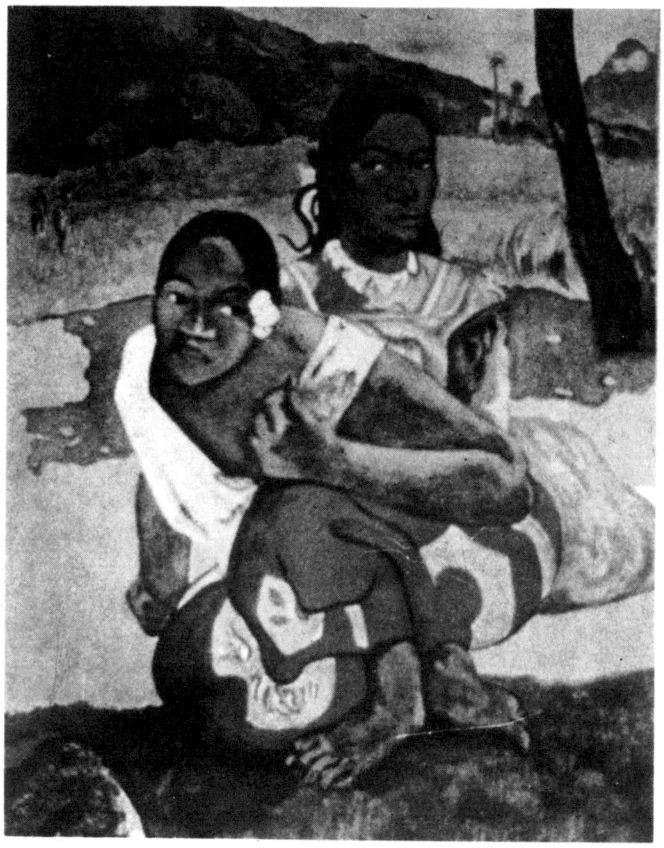

specific situation. I believe it is these kinds of tensions which help to explain the particular beauty of the work of certain pioneering modern artists — for example, the sculpture of Brancusi.

Brancusi broke in a decisive way with the tradition of European sculpture going back to the Greeks. Even his teacher, Rodin, had been still very much in this tradition. Brancusi scathingly referred to its modern practicioners as 'beefstake' sculptors. Philosophically this tradition saw God, the creator, as like a human sculptor, who moulded the inert clay (matter) and created the world out of it. The world was created by a great designer (a man of course) outside of it. But Brancusi, when he made his egg-shaped sculptures, like the one called *Beginning of the World* (1920), produced an image expressing creating by internal energies. Man is not created by God, he makes himself in history.

Brancusi also broke with the Greco-Roman aesthetic norm. It is hard to imagine today how much this ideal dominated the European consciousness. Even for Karl Marx, Greek art was in a sphere of its own, "in certain respects . . . the standard and model beyond attainment". For Brancusi there was no such ideal and he begins to treat sculpture as a common labour of mankind. His simple-composite forms are a kind of distillation of essential formal elements from European, Asian, African, Latin American art, as well as the folk art of his own country, Rumania. Brancusi plays with a world-wide vocabulary of artistic canons — not capriciously, though sometimes with humour and irony to remove the danger of pedantry. He finds in them certain common denominators, related to experiences of the real world. They are like seeds, alike but not identical, but with the energy concentrated in them that will turn into the blossom of the many different cultures.

Many of Brancusi's sculptures are based on animals. Why? Perhaps because he wished to refer to an earlier period of man's identification with animals, but at the same time find values there which were liberated from hierarchy, totem and myth. New values through animal forms, free, democratic, world-wide: the bird — soaring and flight; the cock — rising to greet the sun; the fish — traversing the oceans. It is very striking how his work seems to reach far back into the past and also to point to the future; and how, although he was the individualist and cosmopolitan type of artist of modern capitalist society, his work has a look of anonymity and seems to reflect collective values.

Another example of the connection between modernism and the attack on bourgeois and ethnocentric values would be the synthesis attempted by Leger in his paintings. Throughout his life Leger was inspired by the life of the modern urban working class and sought in his art to crystallise this energy. He drew on many sources in building up his pictorial language: classical French painting, the shapes and colours of the modern city and machinery, French popular prints, African sculpture, Indian Kalighat paintings as well as the experiments of his contemporaries. For Leger, the art of a colonised people linked up with the popular culture of his own people equally in the formation of his style. Both would equally have been despised (or patronised) by the ruling-class culture of his time — even in its mass forms of the film and the best-seller.

But these are particular syntheses, particular subjectivities. It is also a question of artistic movements, innovations and styles which are in the air and cannot be limited to particular individuals. If the "assumptions" of modern art were really Eurocentric, as Coutts-Smith claims, how could they be attractive to deeply anti-colonialist artists in the colonised countries themselves. Aime Cesaire, the Martinican poet and militant, said this of Surrealism: **"I have accepted it joyfully because in it I have found more of a confirmation than a revelation. It was a weapon that exploded the French language. It shook up absolutely everything. This was very important because the traditional forms — burdensome, overused forms — were crushing me."**

Coutts-Smith downgrades the whole question of style. He maintains that modern artists have been obsessed with style and that this itself is a reactionary trend that tries to remove art from life and society and place it in a pure and timeless realm. The rapid succession of styles he sees as closely connected with colonialist attitudes, which must find continually some new area to exploit. "An art restricted to style", he says, ". . . demands a constant supply of raw forms" — a metaphor in which "raw forms" is obviously the equivalent of "raw materials". The comparison applies well to consumerist eclecticism but is not exact at all if you try to apply it to, for example, Mondrian's art. Mondrian had no need of a constant supply of raw material. In fact this criticism begins to look like a revival in new terms of the old accusations of "formalism" which often implied that it was improper, almost indecent, to venture outside traditional norms.

The relationship between style (as the *visual* ideology) and other ideologies such as the political one, is obviously a complicated subject which cannot be dealt with in a summary way. A work may be colonialist or anti-colonialist in outlook without the artist having formed these concepts clearly in his mind. He or she may not come into contact with or may not have accepted the kind of intellectual formation which deals with these concepts and defines them clearly. Picasso, for example, began to refer directly to these movements after the Second World War when he joined the Communist Party and painted a large canvas protesting American aggression in Korea. Even so, he treated it much in the style of his earlier work. He never absorbed the Marxist intellectual method into his art in the way that Brecht did, or Eisenstein, or Joris Ivens in his documentary films.

One artist who did set out directly to paint (to find pictorial form for) concepts of "imperialism", "socialism", "anti-colonial liberation movement", among the earlier modern artists, was Diego Rivera. Rivera was an artist of a "Third World" country (Mexico); he was also a cosmopolitan figure who knew all the avant-garde trends of his day; he was a communist who tried to find a visual, painterly expression for the Marxist interpretation of society, both Mexican society and the world-wide problems of the 20th century. In the heat of the Mexican national revolution and with tremendous creative force, Rivera, along with others, evolved a mural painting style which drew on Renaissance European, Aztec Indian, Mexican popular and contemporary avant-garde sources, it aimed itself at the Mexican population which at that time was 80% illiterate.

Rivera studied and drew on the Indian art of Mexico in a way which was not colonialist because the "revindication of the Indian and his history is inserted into a revolutionary programme" (Jose Carlos Mariategui). The "Indianising" of Mexican art, the rejection of Spanish academic painting, has been part of the Mexican independence movement in the 19th century.

Rivera's use of Indian art could be described as "indigenist". The Peruvian critic Jose Carlos Mariategui (who was contemporary with Rivera) has defined the term in a way which, although he was speaking of literature, applies exactly to Rivera's art: "Indigenist literature cannot give a strictly authentic version of the Indian, for it must idealize and stylize him. Nor can it give us his soul. It is still a mestizo literature and as such is called indigenist rather than indigenous. If an indigenous literature finally appears, it will be when the Indians themselves are able to produce."

Rivera took this stand, but his work is quite contradictory too. If you were able to see all of his production of pictures together they would have no unified character. Rivera of the murals is someone quite different from Rivera of the portraits. If he "painted for the people" in his murals, he was entrenched in a more traditional role with his portraits than many painters who had no such political stand. His portraits (with a few honourable exceptions) were between personalising of glamorous and cosmopolitan figures, and a sentimentally naive depiction of the anonymous poor. It is only too easy to imagine his portraits of Mexico's poor on the walls of wealthy living-rooms. In fact official exhibitions organised by Mexico's establishment have always tended to emphasise this side of his work. There's no doubt that Rivera was capable of a plastic vulgarity which casts some shadow over all his work.

In our period today those early struggles of modern art have been won. The Greco-Roman aesthetic ideal no longer has a central place, it is just one among many, the relativity of subjects and styles is generally accepted. And yet Eurocentrism still flourishes. The forms it

Diego River's "idealisation and stylisation of the Indian". Detail from the 'Aztec Medicine'/section of Rivera's mural in the Hospital de la Raza, Mexico City, 1953—54.

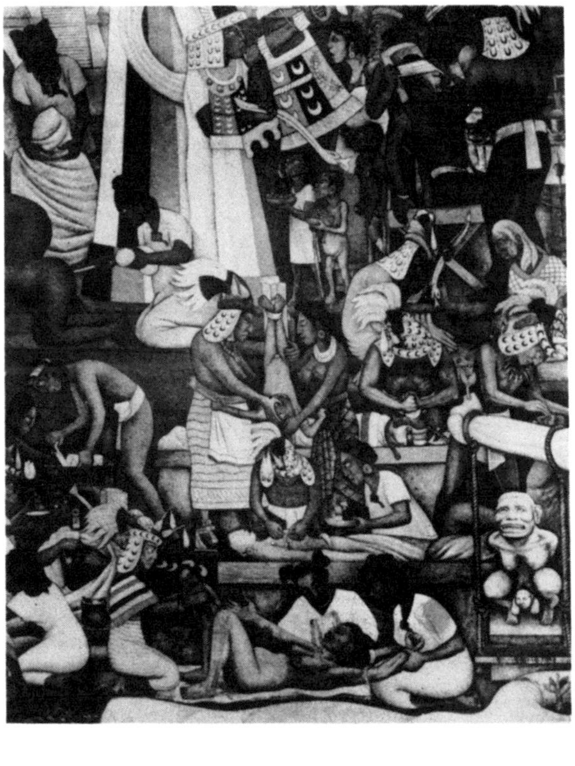

takes are more subtle, just as the forms of oppression are more veiled, though perhaps more pervasive than ever, under the system known as neo-colonialism.

Everyone is familiar with some of the cultural features of this neo-colonial period, which belong to a world which has grown much smaller. The pattern is still the same: riches, material and cultural, still flows from the poor to the rich countries. But the movement of images, sounds, words, works of art, and people about the world has become extraordinarily complicated. It divides not only along national boundaries but also and increasingly along international class lines, a situation which leads often to ironies so absurd that even a satirist would hardly think of them.[1]

The living indigenous art forms in the developing countries are no longer despised. In fact they are usually promoted as part of the tourist industry.[2] An extraordinary richness of indigenous art forms still survive in Third World countries, more perhaps than is suspected by art circles in the rich countries which think they have "seen everything". These arts are not, as some believe, "original" and timeless; they have often changed and are capable of change. But under neo-colonialism the kind of changes forced on them are those dictated by the demands of tourism. The pressure is to maintain the appearance — of a dance, a basket, a painting — while taking away the essence. (If the essence is taken away, the appearance of course changes.) When they become commodities, objects of consumption for people who have no links with their creators at all, their energy, their wit and dignity are drained away. They seem to express a kind of servility, for the production of the popular artists is linked with the fate of his people.

There are countless examples of this kind of thing, in capitalist and also in some "socialist" countries. Sometimes the mass-production of a piece of folk-art reaches maddening proportions; for example those Russian peasant-dolls which appear everywhere and now decorate the Aeroflot offices in London. A great industrial superpower projects itself to potential tourists in the image of the peasant-doll because it pays lip service to the idea of "popular art", the "expression of the people", while being completely alienated from the people's real existence. The official Soviet Union has stereotyped popular art in the static model of "folk art" partly because they have also stultified the high art of the past in an image of "cultural treasures" and long-bearded artistic father-figures.

The modern artists' response to other cultures has also been taken over by official museums and galleries in the rich countries in ways which subtly preserve ethnocentricity and colonial attitudes. The Arts Council's exhibition of North American Indian Art, *Sacred Circles*, London 1976, was a clear example of such an attitude. The catalogue patronisingly began: "The day when American Indian art could be dismissed as unartistic and provincial is over. It is beginning to receive world-wide attention, after centuries of neglect and much prejudice. The artistic evaluation of this art is still in its infancy (!) . . ." And it goes on to talk about Indian art at last joining "the mainstream of art history".

Only a few lines later the author is saying: "The Indian relic market of yesterday has become a sophisticated art market today. We admire collectors like . . .", etc etc. The attitude of snobbish superiority perfectly joined the attitude of the consumer! Needless to say, there was no mention in the exhibition of the present conditions and struggles of the American Indian. And that's why, however many masterpieces of Indian art it contained, the Hayward Gallery exhibition did not have the spiritual beauty of the small exhibition of art works, poems and documents mounted by the American Indian Movement at Artists for Democracy, London, at the same time.

There we had, in the middle of London, the neo-colonial, ethnocentric tourist culture, backed up by the apparatus of museum installation and scholarship — directly opposed by the culture of the Liberation Movement. And the subject of both was ostensibly the same. This is one form the conflict of appearance and essence, and the two different sorts of internationalism (or "world-wide attention"), takes place.

Never has the dialectical tension between international and local in artistic life seemed so crucial as today. The two terms are continually being confounded. "Local" suddenly becomes international; "international" suddenly takes on a sad parochialism. People talk of the "contemporary art world", but often without a real sense of the *world* or of *contemporaneity*. They reveal the equivalent of the *micro-nationalism* so sharply described by Jose Marti: **"The proud villager believes that the whole world is his village, and, so long as he's mayor, or he succeeds in mortifying his rival who took his girl away from him, or his savings mount up, the universe is fine for him the way it is; he knows not that giants are striding out and can stamp him underfoot or that there's a fight raging among the comets in the sky which flash through the still air gobbling up worlds . . ."**

Others talk of "quality" and feel themselves to be guided solely by the criterion of artistic quality. But so often this hides a dogged dependence on the artistic leadership of the economically powerful nations. If they really had a criterion of quality they would refuse to be dictated to by economic power, by technological level and literacy and would realize that Indians of an Amazon tribe, for example, are among the finest artists living today. They would feel the closest possible ties with them. But they would also realize that their art, and their lives, are threatened *because* of their economic powerlessness, their subjection to alien economies.

Bourgeois culture, which profanes everything sacred and turns everything into commodities, is bound to produce an opposite within itself which tries to preserve things in a static and ficticious state of purity. The business man will cross any barrier and modify anything in order to sell it; the academic compartmentalises and labels, saying that one thing must not interact with another (how could he do otherwise considering he is a specialist, and the world outside his specialisation tends to look to him fearsome, unknown). The striking thing is that neither the genuine popular artist nor the revolutionary artist have any such purism, both are open to any influence, any source (whether they understand it perfectly or not) which can answer their need to understand and express the new conditions of life. That's why I believe Kenneth Coutts-Smith is wrong to separate them with mechanical categories.

Guy Brett
London SW2

Footnotes

1. To take just one example: The Shah of Iran buys at an auction in New York, USA, for $180,000 an Iranian Tabriz carpet to decorate the royal palace in Tehran. (New York Guardian, October 11, 1978, p.20).
2. In Africa, tourism is an industry dominated by Western companies, and most of the tourists come from former colonial powers, according to an article in the New York Guardian (May 24 1978). The Guardian journalist Obi Bini writes perceptively that in the modern context tourism perpetuates the belief among Africans that all white people are rich, thereby blurring the existence of classes in the developed nations.

My initial reaction to Guy Brett's intervention was largely composed of bewilderment since I find myself in overall agreement with his basic position; yet, at the same time, he levels some extremely serious objections against me. It seems that either I didn't write the article that he read or that he didn't read the article I wrote.

The accusation that my analysis is crudely mechanical and that I attempt to structure my argument through the confrontation of monolithic characteristics is, I believe, both unjust and unfounded. In proposing, however, that Guy Brett (a critic whose ongoing contribution towards the emergence of a genuine socialist visual culture is unquestioned) has either misread or misunderstood my essential thesis, I must obviously accept responsibility for ambiguities in my text. I never question the fact that I frequently fail to express clearly what I intend to state.

Before dealing with the specific objections raised by Brett, it may clarify matters if I comment on my general argument as it appeared in the last issue of *Black Phoenix*.

The central structure of my argument was provided by the attempt to propose two different themes in such a fashion as to dialectically determine the actual flow and outcome of the argument. In parenthesis, it should be remarked that it is probably at this nexus that we would be most likely to be able to isolate either the misunderstanding of Brett's reading or whatever weaknesses there might be in my text due to opacity and ambiguity.

The two themes are: the process of appropriation and reification by bourgeois culture of artistic products and concepts, and the process of the development of the fluid body of ideas that provide the structure from which innovatory artistic products and concepts have sprung.

The one constitutes the dynamic of the broad network of tradition, myth and assumption that is (or has been, until recently) in a constant state of flux owing to the ongoing generation of innovatory concepts. This latter may well be coeval though it is not necessarily identical with artistic modernism; and it might well be defined for our purposes here (in terms of the participating artists' self-view as well as in the perspective of a distinct historical sensibility) as the "avant-garde". (See my further elaboration of this idea in *The Myth of the Artist as Rebel and Hero* elsewhere in this issue).

The confrontation of these two themes reveals a common ground of synthesis in the fundamental of consciousness of the central European tradition in art. I would assume that Brett has no problem in accepting the absolute Eurocentricity of the mainstream of our tradition of visual culture from, say, the period of the International Gothic up till the middle of the 19th Century.

The importation of extra-European visual material such as certain Islamic motifs in the *trecento* or the orientalising chinoiserie of the late 17th and the 18th Centuries are clearly conditioned by a highly formalised (and transformed) co-option of *style* that is completely isolated and abstracted from its indigenous cultural context. In these cases, we can surely observe cultural appropriation operating in one of its purest forms.

It is only after the advent of the industrial-capitalist form of colonialism defined by the economic and technological development of the 19th Century that we are able to observe any coherent awareness of the cultural integrity of non-European societies. Brett's citation of Durer's response to Aztec art would seem at first glance to have been an isolated reaction that stands out from his contemporary world-view.

Nevertheless, he has here raised an important point which had not been adequately dealt with in my text, although I have tried to tackle this problem elsewhere:[1] the contribution of an individual to a cultural ideology and the contradictions that develop between progressive insights and the consensus structure that comprises a cultural ideology.

Durer's response was perhaps not so much uncharacteristic of his own immediate cultural climate, as it was the result of the brief and fragile ascendance of the notion of subjective individualism typical of the High Renaissance. The artistic self-view of the artist as an autonomous sensibility, visionary and reflexive, already waning in Durer's lifetime, was set back by the forces of the Counter-Reformation and only re-surfaced with the full ascendance of the bourgeoisie at the completion of the Industrial Revolution.

The expedition to the Nile and the subsequent Napoleonic appropriation of Egyptian and Arabic motifs into an imperial *style* initiated a process that culminated in the 1851 exhibition of "art and industry". The new technology of cast iron and steam power was celebrated through the development of a visual ideology that leant heavily on the *decorative* use of visual material expropriated from the far corners of the Empire.

There would seem to be no question that there is a clear relationship between the political ideology of imperialism and the visual ideology of the Victorian bourgeois style. Brett accurately cites Poynter as an embodiment of bourgeois culture in this regard. And he opposes to this the example of Gauguin and maintains quite accurately that there is "a world of difference and a difference of world-view".

Unquestionably, Gauguin's world-view was politically and socially, as well as aesthetically, progressive in opposition to the reactionary and static character of Poynter's academicism. Of course Gauguin was personally involved in a relationship of sympathy, even in an inarticulated relationship of "solidarity", with a colonially-oppressed minority, and, at that, quite consciously it was the result of a form of individualised revolt against the merchantile and pragmatic value-system of bourgeois society.

Brett's comparison, however, is one that is *direct*. He observes, as it were, the two artists within a mutual and enclosed continuum. The extreme contrast between Poynter's reactionary stance and Gauguin's progressive one is presented as if they were, respectively, points along a spectrum of virtue and value in terms of socio-political (and, concomitantly, aesthetic) value. By implication, a line is postulated on this spectrum from which it ought to be possible to define left and right, progressive and reactionary.

However, is it really possible to define such a value demarcation between, for instance, the Victorian "imperial" applied-art style, the middle-class romanticism of Pugin's reactionary gothic, the high-art exoticism of Pre-Raphaelite and Ruskinian medievalism, the dandified artificiality of Whistlerian orientalism, the various *voyages imaginaires* of Rimbaud, through Huysmans to Roussel and the post-impressionist use of the conventions of japoniserie and oriental orthogonal perspective?

At one extreme of our spectrum, we *know* that the relevant cultural attitudes and artefacts are reactionary, contributions to a static and extra-historical (extra-geographical, for that matter) world-view that justifies and reinforces a repressive and imperialist society. At the other extreme of our spectrum we equally *know* that the relevant cultural attitudes and artefacts embody a progressive and liberating world-view as a result of the fact that the individual artist is engaged through the intervention of a constantly mutating aesthetic sensibility in the process of inventing itself and humanising the world. The two poles would seem to be self-evident in regard to a socio-political orientation.

Yet, traditional art-critical method is clearly not capable of locating a distinct and implicit point where one set of assumptions melds and mutates into the other. Indeed, the standard analysis constitutes, in effect, the abandonment of analysis; and contradiction is skirted via an abrupt transition from one set of assumptions to another one. A discontinuity is evident between the acceptance of an integral *bourgeois* culture (which is amenable to a socio-political understanding since it constitutes an adopted value system) and the assertion of an opposing structure comprising a network of autonomous individuals.

Academic visual culture is commonly regarded as a closed structure while the *beaux-arts* tradition of modernism is considered both to be an open continuum and an axiomatic antithesis of institutional form. This discontinuity is presented in the paradoxical manner of contraposing the essential *ideological* character of "middle-class' visual culture (Poynter, etc.,) with the free-floating autonomy of individual creative genius (Gauguin etc.).

As long as the spectrum is regarded as being integral this contradiction cannot be resolved. It may be, and usually is, obscured, however, by the assumption that there exists a certain type of rupture that is dependent upon the notion of a personal intervention operating absolutely independently of ideological factors.

What is surely here necessary to understand is that the *avant-garde* itself proposes a distinct ideology that stands in contradistinction to that of absolute bourgeois culture. Actually, it would be more strictly accurate to say "proposed up until the recent past . . .", since it now seems clear that this opposition no longer holds. The recent development of the progressive institutionalisation of culture has resulted in an interlocked mutuality developing between the "academic" and the *avant-garde* positions. At the time of abstract expressionism, for instance, the world-view of the self-defined *avant-garde* and that of, say, a painter like Andrew Wyeth were in clear ideological confrontation. Today, however, we tend to regard these previously separate traditions as being coexistant in a homogenous body of visual culture.

Putting to one side the whole question of the "demise" of the *avant-garde*, the insistence upon the free-floating autonomy of the individual artist only becomes possible with the postulation of a rupture. But this rupture is evidently not one that is conceived as being located somewhere on the spectrum between left and right, between progressive and reactionary. Rather, it is implied that this is one that somehow isolates and insulates the individual artist.

In this regard, art criticism, though perhaps not consciously, adopts a paradigm model analogous to the one proposed by Kuhn: the individual artist, through the forces of his genius, is seen as personally deflecting the course of history. Stated thus baldly (and bearing in mind alternative forms of *coupure*, that of Bachelard's epistemological break, for instance), the ideological basis of the avant-garde may be observed to be ultimately conditioned by a bourgeois concept of competitive individualism.

It may well be possible here to apply Hadjinicolaou's[2] analysis of art history to the field of criticism since the conventional view of the *avant-garde* (adopted also by Guy Brett) would seem to depend on a view of art history as the sequential history of individual artists rather than that of the production of cultural artefacts. The fetishisation of the artist as the autonomous instigator of innovation is, of course, at its most blatant extreme, evidence of a simplistic coffee-table-book understanding of artistic reality. I wish in no way to imply that Brett's sensibility demonstrates a tendency to such vulgarity; however, it does seem reasonable to assert that our collective unreconstructed thinking is obscured (even polluted) by elements of such fetishisation.

We are clearly trapped in the contradictions that result from the discrepancy between our notion of the artist as individualist innovator (including, of course, the artist's own self-view concerning his role and function) and the awareness that visual culture contributes to the concretisation of an ideology that is either bourgeois or counter-bourgeois in nature.

And it must be here remarked that the "counter bourgeois" may only in comparatively rare instances be equated with a socialist consciousness. The progressivity of individual artists is frequently that of a radical-liberal cast of mind. But even when a stance is self-defined as "socialist" or "marxist", all too often it discovers itself to be vulnerable to co-option and appropriation by establishment culture as the result of an insufficiently rigorous analysis, of a dichotomy between the intent of a passionate social anger and a diffused understanding of the socio-political dynamics of culture.

Brett cites Aime Cesaire, quoting the writer's enthusiasm for his discovery of the liberating aspects of Surrealism, and maintains here a distinction between the negativity of European imperialism and the progressivity of European modernist culture. The paradox is that Cesaire was so steeped in European culture that his allegiance ultimately extended beyond a simple commitment to the progressive, humanist and vitalising traditions of modernism. In 1958, the militant anti-colonialist succumbed to the subtle mystification of Eurocentric bourgeois culture: as mayor of Fort-de-France he ritually received and embraced Malraux, the neo-colonialist emissary of De Gaulle charged with "securing the umbilical cord which tied the Antilles and Guiana to France",[3] with the words "I salute in your person the great French nation to which we are so passionately attached".

The correlation between bourgeois values and European colonialism seems to be inescapable. It also seems luminously evident that an understanding of this correlation will enable us to comprehend (and thus, despite Brett's structures to "provide weapons" for the struggle) the mechanism by which the elements of *progressive* visual culture are constantly eroded and absorbed by the ideology of the capitalist visual culture of absolute property and institutional prestige.

Kenneth Coutts-Smith
Toronto, 24 January 1979

Footnotes

1. *Ten Theses on the Failure of Communication in the Plastic Arts*, Praxis 3, Goleta, California 1976.
2. Nicos Hadjinicolaou, *Art History and Class Struggle*, Pluto Press, London 1978.
3. David Caute (who narrates the incident), *Fanon*, Fontana-Collins, London 1970.

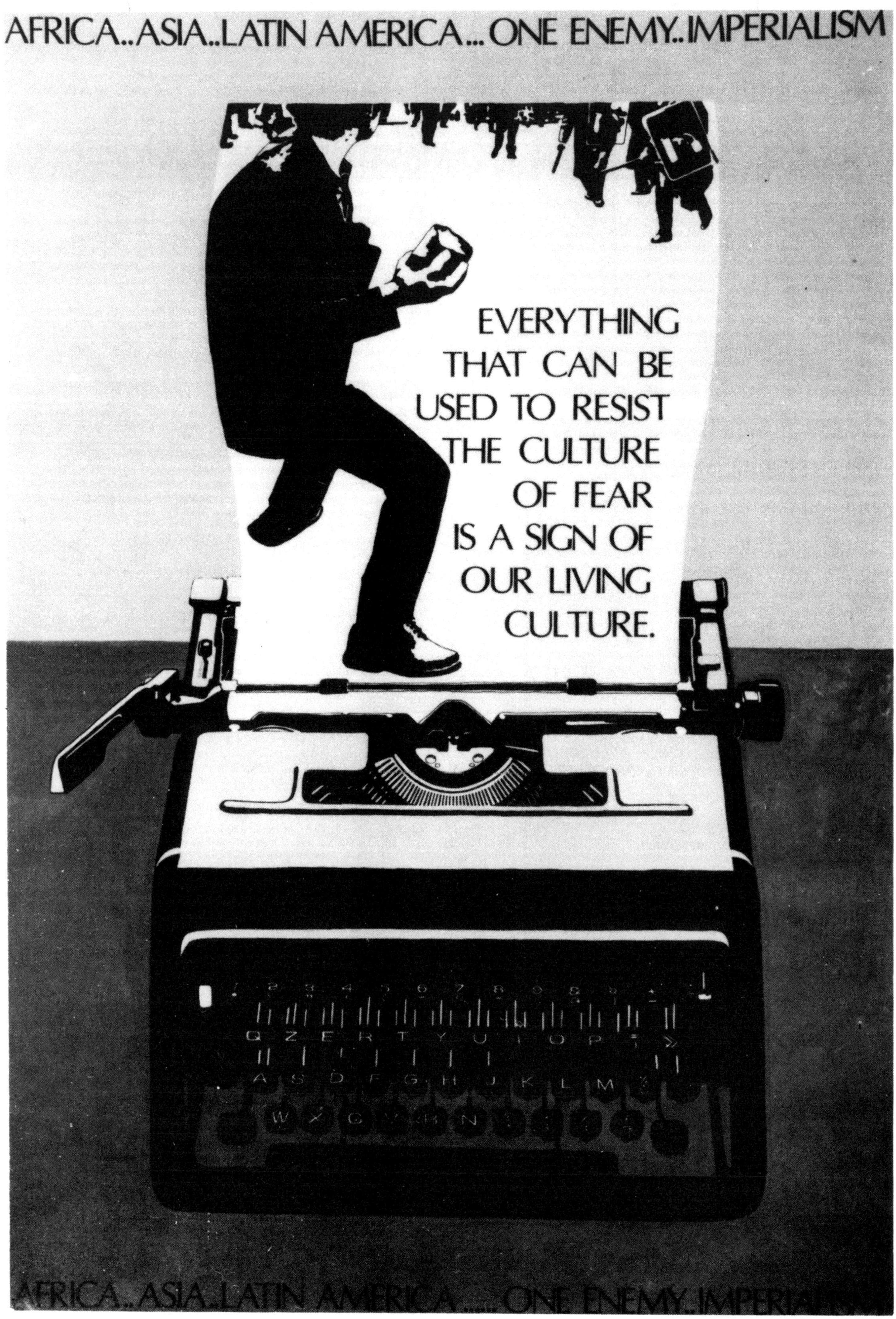
AFRICA..ASIA..LATIN AMERICA.... ONE ENEMY..IMPERIALISM
EVERYTHING
THAT CAN BE
USED TO RESIST
THE CULTURE
OF FEAR
IS A SIGN OF
OUR LIVING
CULTURE.
AFRICA..ASIA..LATIN AMERICA..... ONE ENEMY..IMPERIALISM

ISBN: 978-1-7365346-7-0

Black Phoenix: Journal of Contemporary Art and Culture from the Third World (re-subtitled *Third World Perspective on Contemporary Art and Culture* for its second and third issues) was published in three issues from 1978 to 1979 and edited by Rasheed Araeen and Mahmood Jamal. This volume collects all three issues in their entirety.

Editors: Rasheed Araeen and Mahmood Jamal
Managing Editor (2022): Rachel Valinsky
Managing Designer (2022): Dan Bourke

Primary Information
232 3rd St, #A113
The Old American Can Factory
Brooklyn, NY 11215
www.primaryinformation.org

Printed by Versa Press

Primary Information would like to thank Renée Bosman, Lucas Darden, Josh Hockensmith, and Alice Whiteside of University of North Carolina at Chapel Hill Libraries; Alejandra Altamirano Brett; Emmy Catedral; Joseph Henry; Maria Victoria T. Herrera; the Ayyub Malik Trust; Rick Myers; Adam Nankervis; Nathaniel Otting; Javier Anguera Phipps; Lori Salmon and Phoebe Walker of New York University Libraries; Angel Shaw; and Hamza Walker.

Primary Information is a 501(c)(3) non-profit organization that receives generous support through grants from the Michael Asher Foundation, Empty Gallery, the Graham Foundation for Advanced Studies in the Fine Arts, the Greenwich Collection Ltd, the John W. and Clara C. Higgins Foundation, the Willem de Kooning Foundation, the Henry Luce Foundation, Metabolic Studio, the National Endowment for the Arts, the New York City Department of Cultural Affairs in partnership with the City Council, the New York State Council on the Arts with the support of Governor Andrew Cuomo and the New York State Legislature, the Orbit Fund, the Stichting Egress Foundation, Teiger Foundation, The VIA Art Fund, The Jacques Louis Vidal Charitable Fund, The Andy Warhol Foundation for the Visual Arts, the Wilhelm Family Foundation, and individuals worldwide.